THE CRISIS OF THE
FRICAN-AMERICAN ARCHITECT

To Richard Tager
Our Old and Dear Friend!

Nov. 2006

THE CRISIS OF THE AFRICAN-AMERICAN ARCHITECT

CONFLICTING CULTURES OF ARCHITECTURE AND (BLACK) POWER

REVISED 2ND EDITION WITH A NEW PREFACE BY THE AUTHOR

MELVIN L. MITCHELL, FAIA

Writers Advantage
New York Lincoln Shanghai

The Crisis of the
African-American Architect
Conflicting Cultures of Architecture and (Black) Power

Writers Advantage
an imprint of iUniverse, Inc.

For information address:
iUniverse
2021 Pine Lake Road, Suite 100
Lincoln, NE 68512
www.iuniverse.com

ISBN: 0-595-24326-6

Printed in the United States of America

Dedication

To my late Howard University architecture school professors, classmates, faculty colleagues, and fellow practitioners

Teachers
Leon Brown, FAIA
Louis Edwin Fry, Sr. FAIA
Granville Hurley, FAIA
Howard Hamilton Mackey, FAIA
Leroy John Henry Brown
Hyman Cunin
Morton Hoppenfeld
Kermit Keith
Alexander Richter
Frank G. West Jr.

Classmates & Fellow Practitioners
Robert Bryant, FAIA
Walter Blackburn, FAIA
Robert J. Nash, FAIA
Michael Brooke Amos
Andrew Daniel Bryant
Donald Bruner
Leroy Campbell
Theodore Capers Jr.
Robert Ballard Gordon
Stewart Daniel Hoban, Sr.
Lawrence Casey Mann, II
Mwata Mitchell
Robert Moore
Robert "Skip" Perkins
Bernard Quarterman
Carl Robinson
Harry Simmons Jr.
Benjamin Skyle, Jr.
Lorenzo Wray

Contents

New Preface

After a great deal of personal soul-searching during the final stages of preparing this book for its initial 2001 release, I decided to stay with my earlier decision to eschew the use of any kind of architectural drawings, graphics, photographs of buildings or architects, or other visual aids. Since the actual Fall 2001 availability of this book and after a subsequent series of cross-country lectures that I delivered to usually small audiences of architecture students, faculty, professionals and reasonably informed lay persons, a single question has been asked repeatedly by the broad cross-section of people; **what does** *Black Architecture* **look like?** A fair enough question; architecture is ultimately visual. But the question addresses only one of the universally agreed upon triptych of terms that define architecture—*delight* (the two unaddressed terms are *firmness* and *commodity*). In my first several lectures, I attempted to answer that question by posing a counter question: **what does** *Black Music* **sound like?**

One very astute senior African-American professor (whom I have great respect for) was troubled by my references to black master jazz musicians as models for thinking about another paradigm in architecture. He reminded me that the jazz masters were successful because they ignored white and European rules, authorities and canons while en route to inventing their own new modern music. *How*—he asked— *is that possible in architecture today?*

I reminded my astute friend that the currently incubating generation of African-American architects can do precisely the same thing that the early twentieth-century black musicians did. Today's black architects do not require the approval or permission of the architectural establishment,

developers, construction managers or other so-called "risk-taking" intermediaries in order to start directly meeting the basic shelter and community development needs of the expanding lower-middle, middle, and
nascent upper classes of Black America. Still, the question persists:
"What does Black Architecture look like?"

Since this revised second edition of my book is still sans pictures, in
attempting to answer that question I concluded that I have no choice
but to give concrete examples while naming names (that I thought I
had done sufficiently in the first edition).

We must be reminded that early twentieth-century black musicians
invented the base of the new modern American music, but they were
not the only Americans who could play this music (remember Paul
Whiteman, et al?). But given the economic base of the new modern
music-making, the black originators—from Buddy Bolden, Scott
Joplin and Louis Armstrong to Ellington, Basie, Miles, Coltrane and
the young Wynton Marsalis—were able to maintain their positions of
dominance and authority.

The force and energy source driving the new black-led music was the
same force and energy source driving new paradigms in modern art.
That force was the holistic art and music-making cultures of the people
of West Africa who were transplanted to America. In the new world of
the transplanted Africans, making art was separated from making music.
It fell to the young Spaniard Pablo Picasso to "discover" the forsaken
African art tucked away in a Paris museum in 1907. Picasso's adaptive
re-use of African art and sculptural masks—to become a movement
known as Cubism—quickly evolved as a new aesthetic system. By 1920
that aesthetic had morphed into the new modern architecture of the
young, Swiss-French architect Eduoard Charles Jennerette (universally
known as Le Corbusier). But manifestations of the new art in the new
architecture actually preceded the European-based Corbusian architecture in the first decade of the twentieth-century in the United States.
Frank Lloyd Wright conflated the African-derived aesthetic with Asian
and Native American influences in his design of a series of breathtaking

homes in the suburbs of Chicago. Wright would self-label his work as "organic architecture."

So there it is! My bodacious contention is that the two icon architects of modernist architecture were the first practitioners of the all-important visual (or "delight") component of *Black Architecture.* I am saying simply that what *Black Architecture* looks like is the architecture that Wright and Corbusier were making between 1905 and 1960 in Europe and America. Unlike in the case of the new modern music of that period, African-Americans could not make architecture that looked like Wright and Corbusier's architecture; music, dance, and other non-capital intensive endeavors were the only outlets for creative artistic expression.

At the beginning of the twentieth-century, Wright and Le Corbusier were honing their craft on homes for white bourgeoisie classes of artists, intellectuals and industrialists at a time when no such comparably substantive class of African-Americans really existed. And in those rare instances when black men did attempt to make such architecture for an actually paying client, they certainly dared not attempt to call it *Black (or Negro) Architecture.* Wright and Corbusier were simply doing in architecture what Paul Whiteman et al were doing in music. But unlike Whiteman, Wright and Corbusier had the new modernist architecture all to themselves. Need I hasten to add that this new *Black Architecture* was the true *American* architecture in an America that simply had no room at that time for African-Americans to operate as high-cultural authorities in a "White Gentlemen's Profession?"

What does Black Architecture look like? Traveling through an early 1900s Picasso-Cubism phase of straight lines, flat planes and rectilinear cubes, by 1952 architecture had evolved to its logical aesthetic conclusion in Le Corbusier's voluptuously curvilineal Chapel of Notre-Dame-du-Haut, Ronchamp—known simply as Ronchamp. For Wright, architecture came to its logical conclusion in the spiraled curves of his 1959 Guggenheim Museum in Manhattan. This *Black Architecture* (and the true *American* architecture), for obvious reasons of racial, class, power, and wealth realities in America, could not abide participation by African-Americans or acknowledgment of its black sources.

The sensuous non-European, Dionysian *Black Architecture* represented in these two structures had to be rescued and returned to a more pristine Apollonarian base of rigid conventional geometry. Wright's Guggenheim and Corbusier's Ronchamp sensuousness was also threatening to become conflated with the urban socio-political and cultural upheavals of the 1960s. Things had to be put back on track; high-culture authority in architecture had to be re-asserted. Wright and Corbusier had to be returned to their upper-class Euro-American roots of cool intellectual rationality.

Enter five young New York architects in the mid-1960s, sanctioned by an academic establishment fronted by Cornell-based architecture professor Colin Rowe and valorized by the powerful image-shaping New York Museum of Modern Art (MOMA). Independently wealthy, young, architect-propagandist Peter Eisenman and his four architect cohorts, John Hejduk, Michael Graves, Charles Gwarthmy and Richard Meier produced a book of their design drawings and theories. The book was titled *Five Architects*. This bright and ambitious young Jewish-WASP coalition would become known simply as "The New York Five." They and their crafty sponsors proceeded to displace Wright and Le Corbusier's *Black Architecture* (and *American* architecture), while also forestalling the intrusion of the dark forces of the exploding 1960s urban ghettos into *Architecture*.

But again, **What does it (Black Architecture) look like?** And again, my answer is *"everything that Frank Lloyd Wright and Le Corbusier designed—from Wright's suburban Chicago Prairie Houses of 1907 to his Manhattan Guggenheim Museum, and from Le Corbusier's seminal Parisian Villa Savoye of 1920s to his Chapel at Ronchamp in 1952."*

Added to my answer would be *"a) the obvious architectonic music and style of everything composed or played by Bolden, Joplin, Armstrong, Ellington, Miles, and Coltrane; b) the visual style of all of the movies made by Spike Lee and John Singletary et al; and c) many of the street-based videos made by the two African-American socio-economic class extremes of Howard*

University business major Sean "P Diddy" Combs and New Orleans public housing project spawned Master P (Percy Miller). There is now an undisputable bourgeoisie class of African-American artists, intellectuals and industrials (including athletes, entertainers, communications moguls, etc.) who can afford or support *Black Architecture.* New York architect Jack Travis has demonstrated that members of this group of African-American may be highly desirous of a *Black Architecture.* The burning question is whether there will be black architects participating in doing this architecture. For a host of reasons today, Black America's bourgeoisie does not for the most part retain African-American architects to design or build their homes. *I believe that they are most susceptible to doing so* if approached in the right way and the right context. Designing and building the shelter and homes for this class will lead inexorably to providing much of the class's other architectural needs.

If the virtually lilly-white architectural academy has a problem with me "sullying" the sacred 1907–1960 canonical modernist architecture of Frank Lloyd Wright and Le Corbusier by claiming it as *Black Architecture,* I have a proposition (let us readily concede that the academy does not openly or consciously think of or refer to Wright and Corbu's work as *White Architecture); let the academy start immediately to seriously, openly, and enthusiastically acknowledge the black roots of Wright and Corbusier's architecture in the same way that the black roots of American music (interchangeably known as "black music" and "American music") are openly acknowledged by America and the rest of the world.*

For my primarily intended audience, I have concretely answered the question *"what does Black Architecture look like?"* while also naming names. So much for the "delight" part of the three-word definition of architecture. "Firmness" is obviously the easiest of the three words to be dealt with. The "commodity" word is also relatively straight forward; it is simply *any architecture undertaken for the purpose of the individual and/or group empowerment of African-Americans (ownership and control are litmus tests).* But an even bigger question remains; *"are future African-American architects (and others) prepared to follow the example of black New York architect Jack Travis in openly acknowledging, while actually doing, Black Architecture (the true American architecture)?"*

Melvin L. Mitchell
Washington, DC
August 2002

Original Preface

When African-American architects and architecture students get together to talk about architecture—or on rare occasions *write* about architecture—we quickly fall into our own inverted version of the *"Look! The monkey speaks"* syndrome. Translated: *"we black architects do architecture as well as white architects."* But I suspect that this is not a very interesting issue for most reasonably informed persons. Most such persons take for granted that black architects are as capable as architects of any other race. What possible basis could there be for assuming otherwise?

An affirmative assumption that black architects are as capable as white architects will be made by thoughtful persons despite that no such evidence of that reality can be gleaned from mainstream architecture textbooks and periodicals (the architects shown in such material are virtually always white males). But thoughtful people also know that as recently as forty years ago there was no visible mainstream evidence that anyone other than white males did big-time college and professional basketball and football.

Architecture—in ways quite different from math and the hard sciences—is about *culture*. It is about the confluence of culture and power and capital and politics and land and war and so on. So the really important issue of "have (or why haven't) black architects created a *Black Architecture*" is rarely discussed. *"Black Architecture!"* Young architects—of all races and gender—immediately raise their eyes in eager anticipation at the sound of this phrase. Older African-American architects lower their eyes and either deny its existence, or simply change the subject.

Yet as a black architect, I can count on being asked the following multifaceted question sooner or later by otherwise reasonably informed African-Americans that I come in contact with:

> *Is there a "Black Architecture?"...An architecture that reflects the spiritualism, dynamism, improvisational complexity, rich uses of color, strong sensuous rhythms, and the West African roots of African-American culture—in the same vein as black music and other black literary and artistic achievements? And if not, then why not, since there is a palpable "black culture?" And finally, is there any need for a "Black Architecture?"...Could it make a positive difference in the group struggle of African-Americans for economic parity and added cultural affirmation in the United States?*

Like most of my fellow African-American architect colleagues trained in the early 1960s era when the "International Style" Modern Architecture idiom was at its apex in the United States, I have usually equivocated in my own response to such queries. This book is an aggressively revisionist attempt to address my equivocation as well as what I believe to be the underlying cultural implications of those provocative and multi-dimensional queries.

In previous attempts to address the *"Look! The monkey speaks"* issue in hard print, only two books—both essentially of the "coffee table" genre—have been available thus far to provide visual evidence to a general audience. With the 1991 release of his book, *African-American Architects in Current Practice,* New York architect Jack Travis provided black and white photographs of selected built projects, along with head busts and short biographical sketches of thirty-five of the most prominent African-Americans practicing at that time. The Travis book was an important effort even though the guest essays were much too short, while leaving many critical questions unexplored. The frame of reference of the essays was primarily centered on the ability of black architects to persevere despite racist resistance from white American institutions and society.

With the 1993 release of her book, *Paul R. Williams, Architect: A Legacy of Style*, Karen Hudson offers a richly illustrated and loving portrait of her grandfather who was ultimately a first rate American architect by any fair measurement. In both books, the written essays were ambivalent or resistant on the issue of a *"Black (or African-American) Architecture."*

I have been heavily influenced by my long-standing admiration of Harold Cruse's seminal 1966-released book, *The Crisis of the Negro Intellectual: A Historical Analysis of the Failure of Black Leadership*. My book addresses that above stated *"is there a Black Architecture?"* question that I believe is on the minds of most people, in the spirit, if not the letter, of Cruse's vastly more comprehensive treatise on the struggles of the black political and cultural intellectual of the twentieth century. My responses and tendencies about the parallel struggles of the black architect occur within an *a priori* framework. I have posited the following three part *alternative* (to current spoken and unspoken orthodoxy) point of view that is derived from my personal experiences and critical re-reading of twentieth-century American cultural and economic history:

- *Twentieth-century modernist American architecture has its roots and aesthetics as much in West African and African-American culture as in European culture—just as does American music;;*
- *A modernist architecture with a consciously black culture style, a black music based aesthetic, and a "black economy" oriented modus operandi should have evolved out of the 1920s Harlem Renaissance era and re-energized itself during the "Post-Modernist" Black Power 1960s;*
- *Taking a leadership role in the drive to center hegemony of a significant portion of the design and production of the housing needs of Black America **within** black institutions and enterprises is the missing key to an effective "New (Black) Urbanism" strategy for the African-American architect and an African-American architecture in the twenty-first century.*

My interests are the issues surrounding African-American architects and the reasons behind the absence of their meaningful presence
in the shaping of the cultural (and intertwined economic) life of Black
America. I contend that this has been the reality for African-American
architects since the end of the 1890–1915 Booker T. Washington—
Tuskegee Institute genesis of African-American architects, and the
1919 start of architectural education at the W.E.B. Du Bois-modeled
Howard University in Washington, DC. The start of the Howard
University era of architectural education also coincided with the onset
of the Harlem Renaissance 1920s decade. I maintain that the Tuskegee
to Howard transition is the fundamental starting point of a larger crisis of marginality enveloping the African-American architect today
(along with all other architects). This crisis will only deepen if not
addressed on the most fundamental *cultural* plane. My intent is that
this book will provoke long overdue debate and ongoing discourse
throughout the black world about the past, present, and future role of
architecture in African-American culture within the context of
American culture.

As I slip quietly past my sixty-second birthday as a Washington-
Baltimore area architect, housing developer and university professor, I
constantly encounter an earnest curiosity from African-Americans—
lay persons as well as young architects-in-training. They all want to
know more about the relationship of architects and architecture to
African-American culture. They accurately sense that architecture
must share common roots with art and music as the expressions of the
culture of nation-states or ethnic groups. They suspect that this must
apply especially to a distinctive people who have experienced extraordinary challenges to their existence as full-fledged members of the
human family. [1]

The rational part of the minds of most African-Americans gravitates
naturally to certain *logical ideas* on culture-related issues. One such idea is
that a people capable of producing one of America's truly original art
forms—the blues and jazz music—would also have played a major role
in creatively adapting the new turn-of-the twentieth-century Modern

Architecture. The rational mind expects that such an African-American influenced architecture would be on an original plane, complete with an unmistakable "black aesthetic."[2]

Yet, they notice the conspicuous absence of printed or verbal allusion to a "Black (or African-American) Architecture" in mainstream black cultural discourse. Similarly, people note the equally conspicuous total absence of the African-American architect on the stage of twentieth-century American architecture. That architecture is depicted in countless mainstream textbooks and regularly published professional and academic journals on architects and architecture.[3]

The prevailing view of twentieth-century architectural historians and theorists is that the sole black contribution to twentieth-century American architecture is the Louisiana "shotgun house."[4] The unspoken corollary is that modernist architecture is a combined invention of early twentieth-century Western European avant-garde architects, and the American architect Frank Lloyd Wright. This view goes on to concede the influence of a late nineteenth-century "Chicago (Skyscraper) School" led by Wright's mentor, Louis Sullivan. The logical extension of this view of history is that a black mirror image replication of American architectural culture and practices was (and remains) the only feasible option for African-American architects.

Most published written commentary or analysis on black architects by other black architect practitioners or educators share the same worldview. Such commentary is invariably aimed at the issue of the historic racially motivated exclusion of black architects from an equitable share of design commissions in the larger *white world*.[5] This line of thinking is also unconsciously concerned with the resultant *invisibility* of the black architect in White America more so than in Black America.

Though written in the spirit of Harold Cruse's seminal *Crisis of the Negro Intellectual*, this book is without Cruse's personal hostilities.[6] Despite my having spent nearly the last half of the twentieth-century intensely steeped in the broad cultural and professional milieu of architecture, my political worldview remains substantially shaped by my late 1960s reading of Cruse.

That book, despite its flaws, and several later books by Cruse, is still a favorite personal refuge that I re-read from time to time for bearing and sanity. Unlike Cruse, I have no scores to settle with the current small national leadership fraternity of African-American architects and educators. I know most of the members personally. I share deep and warm fraternal bonds with them. Those bonds were forged over the last thirty years of joint struggle to be recognized by our own communities as well as the larger community.

I also have no desire or need to replicate the density of historical detail found in Cruse's *Crisis*. I shall leave that to the work already accomplished or underway by a handful of mostly (though rightfully, not exclusively) African-American scholars who are sure to eventually publish their completed or in-progress doctoral dissertations as books. I am especially looking forward to the published work of young African-American architect-scholars such as Craig Wilkins—now in a doctoral program at the University of Minnesota—and others who will eventually follow Wilkens in publishing their research.[7]

My *Crusian* worldview is tempered only slightly by my careful reading of the optimistic *technical* accuracies of Abigail Thernstrom's opus magnum *America in Black and White: One Nation, Indivisible—Race in Modern America.*[8] I agree with much of Thernstrom's central thesis that African-Americans have made great strides in achieving gainful employment in the professions. I am also in agreement about the significant gains in basic civil rights over the last half of the twentieth-century. But the Abigail Thernstroms of the world are either deliberately ignoring— or are in sharp disagreement with—the real need as well as growing perceptual obsession of most thoughtful African-Americans in the post-Civil Rights Era. That need and obsession is focused on capturing an equitable or proportionate share of America's appreciating assets, risk capital and strategic business sectors; in short, that group power issue— in contrast to *individual* constitutional rights—that was so compellingly addressed nearly forty-years ago by Harold Cruse. Acquiring all of the accompanying levers of *effective group power* in America has only just begun by Black America.

I have taken the liberty to extrapolate Cruse's healthy skepticism of the relevance of orthodox Marxism in twentieth-century America to mean that today there are no more "workers" who can be organized and brought to a "higher state of consciousness." There will be no "smashing of global capitalism" and replacing it with black, gay or feminist led "socialism." Protest marches and other similar 1960s forms of "resistance"—as many of my hardcore progressive friends still advocate—must be waged on much more technologically and culturally sophisticated grounds.

The world we have inherited is about *literacy (especially math), (capital producing) information, and knowledge* within differing cultural overlays (and as so compellingly argued by former Student Nonviolent Coordinating Committee civil rights activist and now middle-school algebra teacher Robert Moses).[9] That world is divided up between groups of people who have access to those three commodities and groups of people who don't. The former group "runs" things. Many of them are white but an increasing number of them are African-American or black. The latter group is trapped in the web of an ever-tightening spiral of economic obsolescence. Far too many of them are African-Americans. The task at hand for those in the former group is to expand access to those three commodities to those in the latter group. But within that latter group *it is the young children of the black so-called working class and underclass that must be the former group's first priority!*

Conversely, too many of my conservative friends are still trapped in their own enduring myths. Their myths are anchored in the fantasy of a stand-alone, profit-motivated "private sector" that is not wholly dependent upon a "big government" public treasury and public policies for seed capital and profitability. Conservative myths also favor the preposterous notion that thirty years of "affirmative action" in elite graduate and professional schools have compensated for the prior one-hundred years of government-sanctioned "whites only" policies in such arenas. Too many conservatives believe that a "correct culture" is all that is required to trump the obscene imbalance in risk capital and appreciating assets that exists between Black America and White America.[10] Sooner rather than later people in this camp will have to come to terms with the full implications of 1880s Reconstruction Era betrayals of Black America.[11] *At that point myths and fantasies will have to be dispensed with for once and for all.*

Melvin L. Mitchell
Washington, DC
August 2001

Acknowledgments

I have used few primary sources in support of my speculations about the early twentieth-century aspects of the evolution of African-American architects. I have instead relied on three currently obscure and unpublished doctoral dissertations. Essentially, this book is an attempted, combined, cultural critique of those dissertations. Opinions, theoretical positions, and observations are mostly my own, though sometimes influenced by the three dissertation authors.

Every member of today's American architectural community is greatly indebted to former Morgan State University history of architecture professor Richard Kevin Dozier. Now a professor in the School of Architecture at Florida A & M University in Tallahassee, Dr. Dozier's professional life-long odyssey of doggedly persistent scholarly research has unearthed countless precious details about the origination of today's African-American architects and predecessor black building craftsmen dating back to the 1600s.

Dozier's 1990 dissertation is on the role of Booker T. Washington and Tuskegee Institute in the development of black architects at the turn of the twentieth-century between 1881 and 1915. The second dissertation, completed in 1979 by the late white Washington, DC, historian Harrison Etheridge, delves into the follow-up role of Howard University in architectural education from the early 1920s to the beginning of the 1970s. Dr. Etheridge gave me a copy of his dissertation in early draft form for my comment back in 1973. At that time I was a young faculty member in the School of Architecture at Howard University and much too self-absorbed to be able to offer a useful perspective on his work.

The third dissertation, completed in 1992 by Texas A & M University architecture professor Wesley Henderson, is on the life and times of Los Angeles-based architects Paul R. Williams, the most celebrated African-American architect in the twentieth-century , and James Garrott, an as yet obscure but pivotal black avant garde modernist of the 1940s era. Having grown up in Los Angeles between 1945 and 1960, I have a particular appreciation for the breath, depth, and richness of Dr. Henderson's research. This is a landmark effort of scholarship that extends far beyond the lives of the two magnificent African-American architects who are the focus of that dissertation.

I am particularly grateful to Dr. Henderson for the fascinating details about Williams, Garrott, and other Los Angeles African-American architects that I previously had only superficial knowledge about prior to leaving the city for a new life in Washington, DC.

Taken together as a whole, the three dissertations strongly suggest that Tuskegee, Alabama (along with several adjacent southern states), Washington, DC, and—to a meaningful extent—the city of Los Angeles, formed a single triangular shaped national tapestry in the early twentieth-century making of the African-American architect.

I am indebted to Washington, DC, landscape architect Dreck Wilson for his many helpful observations. His long-standing interests and research on African-American architects made him an ideal person to read and comment at length on an early draft of my work. Similarly, Dr. Sidhartha Sen, an architect, urban designer, city planner and also coordinator of the graduate city & regional planning program at Morgan State University, read my manuscript and provided numerous helpful and timely comments. I thank Ana Srygley for her critical comments and early editorial assistance. I also thank Dr. Claudia Phillips, coordinator of the landscape architecture program at Morgan, for her editorial assistance. I especially thank Salimah Hashim for her many helpful suggestions and untiring efforts in typing all of my many early draft manuscripts. However, none of the above persons bear any responsibility for this final document. *Any errors or inaccuracies are mine alone.*

I am also indebted to the students that I had the opportunity to teach or mentor over the course of my five years at Morgan between July of 1997 and June of 2002. Morgan students were constantly seeking out a "cultural context" study guide and bibliography that would shed more light on the relationship of African-Americans to architecture in the twentieth-century. Those students were my biggest motivation for completing this book. Many of these young people will be part of the next generation of African-American, Hispanic-American, Asian-American and White American design and planning professionals. Hopefully, they will practice those professions in ways that acknowledge and celebrate African-American culture and its actual contributions to American architecture, landscape architecture, and city planning.

PART I

ARCHITECTURE AND BLACK AMERICA AT THREE CRITICAL TWENTIETH CENTURY JUNCTURES

CHAPTER 1

Personal Genesis—1939–1962, and the Structure of This Book

Even at my current age of sixty-one, my memories are still vivid about being dragged away kicking and screaming in the dead of night in 1945 from an idyllic childhood by my beautiful and distant young mother. I was enjoying life in what has, for me, since become the "old country" of Louisiana. My mother announced to all in earshot that night that she was taking me to California to live.

At that time of my life, I was spending wondrous, lazy summers in the "country" with my mother's mother "Mama Maude" in Bayou Goula, a little rural sugar cane plantation village just outside of Baton Rouge. I spent the rest of the year living the life of a pampered little prince in the home of my father's mother "Mama Mary" in the "Gert Town" section of New Orleans, ninety miles south of Baton Rouge. "Mama Mary's" house was a short walk from the campus of historically black Xavier University. I had been born seven years earlier in the New Orleans Charity Hospital just a few blocks beyond the French Quarter to my smart, high-spirited, tart-tongued, "red-bone" mother when she was about eighteen years old and still single. Her name was Viola Derizan and her biological father was a black Creole from New Roads City in Pointe Coupee Parish—about one-hundred miles north of Baton Rouge—where my mother was born. I had never met "Papa" but was raised on many tall tales about him.

3

While my mother was still pregnant with me, my father joined the army and left town. He eventually ended up in France to fight in World War II. The two of them would somehow rendezvous nearly three-thousand miles away from New Orleans in South Central Los Angeles eight years after my conception and end up getting married there. My mother came back to New Orleans to retrieve me (and a younger sister who came along in my father's absence). I would lay eyes on my father for the very first time on my arrival in Los Angeles shortly after my seventh birthday. He was a barely literate common laborer who was prone to bouts of drinking that sometimes unleashed a violently abusive side of his normally bland personality.

I would grow up in the Jordan Downs public housing project in the Watts section of South Central Los Angeles. The four of us—my father treated my sister as though she was his own flesh and blood—always had enough to eat at home. My daily 5 AM morning *Los Angeles Times* paper route kept me in pocket money for movies, hamburgers, and 78 rpm "rhythm and blues" records (*anything* by Louis Jordan and his Tympany Five, or "doo-wop" singing groups). Just as important, we—along with much of the rest of the section of the "projects" where I lived—transported, practically intact to Watts, many of the food preferences and religious rituals of our richly textured black New Orleans culture.

At least three times each year there would be a steaming pot of "file` gumbo," filled with shrimp, crab, oysters, chicken, smoked sausage, and beef stew meat. There were also red kidney beans (with cut-up smoked sausages when times were good) over white rice several times a week. Our little church services had some of the same mysterious Haitian "voodoo" overtones overlapping the fire and brimstone Baptist jam sessions that I remembered from Louisiana.

By my early junior high school years, I had developed a serious reading habit, centered on novels like the terrifying and occasionally erotic *Dracula* classic by Bram Stoker. My reading "habit" was carefully hidden from some—*but by no means all*—of my housing project peers. The "projects" of 50 years ago were very different from those of the last quarter of the twentieth-century. In *my* housing project none of my friends ever got shot, the occasional pregnancy of an unwed neighborhood girl usually resulted in a hasty "shotgun" wedding (or a "fixin"), and nearly everyone had a daddy at home.

I can recall no childhood dreams about wanting to "build things." There were no blinding light epiphanies about becoming an architect. I indirectly drifted toward architecture through the simple matter of having to decide between two vocational tracks upon entering senior high school in 1954. I had to pick between "wood-shop" and "mechanical drafting." The latter choice aligned squarely with my well-developed aversion to working at what I disdainfully viewed as manual labor. The third choice of pursuing a college prep track, which could have logically led to enrollment at the University of Southern California or Cal-Berkeley, was simply not a part of my social reality at that time and place in my life.

My high school drafting teacher was a gentle and elderly white man—he seemed elderly to me at that time—that I knew only as "Mr. Welty." He always treated me as his most prized protégée. I was the first one of his students to capture one of the three cash prizes in a prestigious annual citywide mechanical drawing contest for Los Angeles high school students. All of my high school friends and teachers at David Starr Jordan High School knew that in the Los Angeles of the 1950s, the mechanical drawing skills that I had become most known for could lead to a decent paying job right out of high school.

Upon graduation in 1957, I did indeed land a job as an entry-level draftsman. I actually spent the next two years in a downtown Los Angeles county government office working alongside of white boys with architecture, civil engineering, and city planning degrees from the University of Southern California, Cal Poly, or Cal-Berkeley

During my first year out of high school and on my new downtown office job—ten miles away from my isolated Watts neighborhood in South Central Los Angeles—I overheard some of the architecture school graduates raving about a juicy novel that was supposedly a fictionalized account of the early life of Frank Lloyd Wright, the great architect.[1] I went out, found this big formidable paperback, and could not put it down until I had finished it. By then, I was convinced that I did not want to spend the rest of my life as a civil service draftsman. But the possibility of actually becoming a licensed, practicing architect still had not occurred to me before a return visit to my high school a year after my 1957 graduation.

My graduating high school classmates were landing jobs mostly as machinists or general laborers at nearby industrial plants, or as clerks and janitors for the same Los Angeles County government that employed me as a white-collar, sub-professional. I still lived in Watts and was a minor celebrity of sorts because of landing a job as a local government draftsman with permanent civil service status. I was set for life in a way that exceeded the hopes of my parents as well as some of my teachers.

A year after I graduated, Mr. Welty invited me back to the campus to introduce me to a well-dressed visitor. This person was an architect on an inspection tour of a gymnasium addition he had designed for the campus. He was very dark-skinned with course hair and broad African facial features. The sight of him holding an open set of drawings and giving orders to a racially mixed crew of construction workers left an indelible impression on me.

During this time I was right at the doorstep of matrimony with my senior year high school sweetheart—a stunningly pretty, almond-eyed girl with a deep ebony complexion and who still haunts my memories to this day. We were both convinced that my Los Angeles County draftsman job was paying me enough money to support a family. I was as madly in love as nineteen-year-olds are capable of but the growing notion of becoming an architect was starting to overpower the essentially passion-driven need to get married. I became consumed by my struggle to prepare myself for admission to a reputable university architecture school. I had accumulated mostly mechanical drawing courses on my high school transcript and I had not saved very much money. While I did manage to earn a varsity letter in a tough inner city high school football league, I was not even remotely in the zone of consideration for an athletic scholarship to a decent college.

During my second year of working downtown and going to night school at East Los Angeles Community College (we called it "junior college" back then), *Ebony Magazine* did a splashy photo-feature article titled "Successful Young Architects."[2] That article—in conjunction with my earlier meeting with a black architect, and having finished reading Ayn Rand's *The Fountainhead*—was indeed that blinding light epiphany. I had no clue that Rand's book was just a right-wing political tract. But judging by the ages of many of my African-American architect peers around the country today, I wasn't the only one affected by that electrifying *Ebony* article or Rand's impressionable book.

The article estimated the existence of just over 100 licensed black architects around the country out of a national total of 20,000 licensed American architects. The *Ebony* article was actually my first exposure to a growing contingent of black Los Angeles architects other than the already legendary Paul Williams. Clyde Grimes, a young practitioner who was building a reputation around Los Angeles, immediately impressed me.[3] I was also taken with the brooding image of established practitioner Carey Jenkins and the exhilarating drawings of his churches and residential projects.[4]

I was even more enthralled by young New Yorker and Columbia University graduate Daniel Watts.[5] I began to entertain fantasies of immediately packing up and heading for New York with the hope of meeting Watts and getting his help in enrolling in Columbia's evening program. Instead, I started making regular visits to the University of Southern California campus in mid-South Central Los Angeles. On those visits I would stroll through the architecture school and reaffirm to myself how I was going to save the tuition money I needed to enroll there. I spent the next two years completing the requisite college prep courses during the evenings at several of the city's junior colleges.

My resolve to become a full-time architecture student was heightened even further. After two years of working for the Los Angeles County Government, I went to work for a nearby private sector architectural firm. Kistner Wright & Wright hired me on the basis of my drawings in an architectural drafting course I had completed at East Los Angeles City College. My instructor, a stern Egyptian architect that I knew as Mr. Hasuna, was determined to get me in the School of Architecture at the University of Southern California where he had connections. After six months at the Kistner firm, I ventured further west to the Beverly Hills area to work for the small, Jewish-owned architectural firm of Palmer & Krisel for another six months. But three years after high school graduation I still had not accumulated anywhere near enough tuition money to play the "Joe College" full-time architecture student role.

The solution to my dilemma came in the form of a flyer from the US Army recruitment office. I found out that rather than waiting around another two years for that inevitable "Greetings" letter from Uncle Sam, I could volunteer to be drafted immediately at age twenty-one. I was inducted into the army in the late winter of 1960. After several months of basic training at Fort Ord, California (and several glorious weekends in nearby Monterey and Saturday nights at the Black Hawk Jazz Club in San Francisco), I was posted as a construction draftsman to the Fort Belvoir Army Engineering Center right outside of Washington, DC. There were more glorious weekend nights in DC spent in the "9th and U Streets" area darting back and forth between the old Bohemian Caverns nightclub, Abart's Lounge, and The Hollywood nightclub. I once actually caught Miles Davis *and* John Coltrane in the same month. I also caught the act of an unknown young comedian named Bill Cosby during that period. In the fall of 1962, I completed active duty and at the ripe old age of twenty-three, I enrolled as a first-year student in the five-year Bachelor's of Architecture program at Howard University.

With that brief personal introduction out of the way, let me inform the reader that I have endeavored to structure this book as a three-part series of independent essays. The three parts do not have to be read in sequence. It is feasible to go directly to any one of the three parts of the book that are of most immediate interest to the particular reader. I believe that the other two remaining parts will be equally informative and easily comprehensible to most readers having an interest in the overall subject.

In *Part I* of the book, I look at what I consider to be three critical junctures between architecture and Black America over the full span of the twentieth-century. The first juncture is on the campus of Tuskegee Institute around the turn of the last century that I consider being the start and base of a nascent *Black Architecture*. This was the architecture that Booker T. Washington commissioned in the creation of the over fifty substantial structures on the 2,000-acre main campus that grew out of the original 100-acre farm Washington bought in Tuskegee, Alabama, in 1881. Washington's architects were also responsible for producing the surrounding model residential community just outside of the Tuskegee campus gates. All of this work was built between 1881 and Washington's death in 1915.

I contend that the "blackness" of the Tuskegee architecture was to be found in the uses, as well as the spirit, intent, and organizational processes employed in achieving the built works so meticulously documented by Dozier.[6] There was a clearly evolving parallel black aesthetic in larger black life and culture at that point in the start of the twentieth-century in urban America. The black aesthetic and culture would soon become the driving force of the *American* national aesthetic and culture. I speculate—hopefully in an informed manner— that the black aesthetic could have inevitably manifested itself during and beyond the 1920s through a continuation of the Tuskegee modus operandi of making architecture.

I explore an idea that the nascent *Black Architecture* foundation established at Tuskegee Institute was unwittingly sacrificed and abandoned in the pursuit of an elitist WASP idea known as "professionalism." For architecture that term was actually a euphemism for the drawing of a sharp class-based distinction between the genteel architect and the more folk and craft-based building contractor. The "abandonment" occurred when architectural training for African-Americans shifted north from Tuskegee to Howard University in Washington, DC, several years after Booker T. Washington's death in 1915. This shift was all but completed by the pivotal World War II years in Washington, DC.

In what I consider to be the second critical juncture, I move laterally from Howard University in Washington, DC, back to the Harlem Renaissance period in New York City in the 1920s. Principal leadership of the Harlem Renaissance is overwhelmingly credited to Alain Locke who was literally shuttling back and forth between the Howard campus and Harlem during that time. There is evidence of at least a mild ideological connection between the black architect and the Harlem Renaissance. This was mainly through the unrelenting social housing commitments of young Washingtonian Hilyard Robinson. He was hired by Howard University to teach and chair a fledgling architecture program after receiving his B.S. in Architecture from Columbia in New York City in 1924. He would retain this position at Howard intermittently up until 1933. During that time, Robinson was very much aware of Harlem Renaissance happenings and was in tune with Howard University professor Alain Locke's concept of *The New Negro*. Robinson actually came to think of himself as a *New Negro*.[7]

Robinson's activities as an effective community public housing activist throughout the 1930s are exemplified by his cutting edge, modernist design of the large Langston Terrace public housing complex in Washington, DC. The near hegemony that Robinson and the other Howard University faculty architects held briefly in the housing of the black working classes in Washington, DC, must be reinterpreted in today's terms by black architects.[8] Housing in black urban and suburban communities, I contend, is the vital heart of the matter for the next generation of African-American architects.

In this part of the book, I also exhort African-Americans, Americans, and the next generation of African-American architects to give greater importance to the roles and contributions to Modern Architecture of people who were not formally trained as architects, and to events or projects that were not literally architectural. The most obvious group in this category was the natural scientists, engineers, and technologists of nineteenth-century Europe and the projects they precipitated.

Equally important were the people of West Africa whose culture had an approach to arts and crafts that are at the root of aesthetics and ways of seeing in the modern western world. This West African foundation of modern art and architecture aesthetic systems formally began with Picasso's 1907 days as a young Paris artist. This West African influence is well documented and openly acknowledged by many serious art and architectural thinkers and scholars.[9]

I speculate about the truly tantalizing prospect of early modernist architecture in the hands of 1920s Harlem Renaissance artist Aaron Douglas, "the father" of African-American modernist art.[10] That could have had a profound impact on the idea of a black culture-based modernist architecture. Douglas was uncompromising in his commitment to West African and African-American cultural roots as the basis of his art. Douglas was also acutely aware of the connections between the new western European cubist art that he favored and its West Africa roots. The great African-American artist Romare Bearden was just a child at that time but would flower during the second black renaissance of the 1960s. Much of my speculation about Douglas applies equally to speculation as to what Bearden might have accomplished as a modernist architect during the post-modernist Black Power 1960s.

For the third juncture, I look at the period between the 1960s Black Power Movement era at Howard and Washington, DC, and the *post*-post-modern period of today at the dawn of the twenty-first century. The numbers of licensed African-American architects grew explosively between 1958 and the early 1990s. In 1996, a University of Cincinnati study documented the existence of nearly 1,100 licensed African-American architects and roughly 200 professional practices by the early 1990s (out of a national total of just over 100,000 licensed American architects and between 15,000 and 20,000 independent professional practices).[11]

The growth curve for African-American architects has flattened out considerably since then. That Cincinnati study also documented that the small band of Historically Black College-University (HBCU) based architecture programs (see *Part III—Chapter 9* of this book) continues to enroll and graduate nearly half of all black architecture students. Accordingly, those HBCU-based programs must be understood as scarce national resources that cannot afford to simply function as smaller "blackface" versions of their white across-town architecture school counterparts. Most if not all of those white counterpart schools are uncompromisingly committed to the replication of trend-setting Harvard Graduate School of Design pedagogy of a "studio culture" of "form making" and "cultural preferences" (aka "design excellence") arbitration. While there clearly are a number of traditionally white counterpart schools with the context, mission, and financial resources to replicate the Harvard pedagogy, this is decidely not the case in any of the HBCU-based programs.

American architecture is a cultural-technical enterprise with a historically ultra-elitist image, a carefully constructed shroud of mystery, and orthodox racial views that remained steadfast throughout the first three-fourths of the twentieth-century. In spite of this, many scholars, including those I cited earlier, have given substance to the probability that there has been over 1,600 certified professional architects over the past one-hundred years in the United States who have all acknowledged their African ancestry by referring to themselves as "colored," "Negro," "black," or "African-American."

That is a substantially larger number of African-American architects than is generally assumed to exist in the collective perceptions of African-Americans.[12] Most African-Americans perceive that over the last one-hundred years there have been only one or two black architects to have lived and possibly have built substantial or important structures in America. Accordingly, black aspirations toward architecture careers and practices continue to be abysmally small in comparison to the need and opportunities for black architectural leadership in the twentieth and twenty-first centuries.

I continue on with the idea that a "black aesthetic" resides at the very heart of much of today's seemingly all-white American modernist architecture that is an integral part of larger American culture.[13] The design output and written theories of Swiss-French icon status architect Charles Edouard Jenneret—known universally as simply "Le Corbusier"—and the quintessentially American genius architect Frank Lloyd Wright both remain as the presumed aesthetic and cultural fountainheads of American modernist architecture.[14]

This is despite the now growing recognition that the city planning, urban design, and sociological theories that Le Corbusier espoused were tragically naive and destructive. Much the same can be said for Wright's equally disastrous "Broad Acres" notions that telegraphed today's ubiquitous suburban sprawl.[15] But for the architecturally designed building output of the two men, I look at the heavily documented West African art and sculpture sources of their work and the accompanying analytical discourse including the famous 1936 Alfred N. Barr Jr. graphic diagram depiction of the modern art-architecture movement *and draw what I believe to be logical conclusions* (Barr places "Negro Sculpture"—actually West African masks and sculptures—at the pivotal centroid of this 1890–1935 period.[16]

While having arrived at some of the above conclusions on my own, I owe much to the writings of American cultural critic and philosopher Cornel West. The written body of work by West played a major part in helping me think through my architecture culture hypothesis. West is the most notable black public intellectual to speak at length on the subject of architecture. I find West to be by far and away the most lucid and insightful thinker about architecture on the scene today, black or white. West expounds at some length in a chapter titled *"Race and Architecture"* in his most recent book *The Cornel West Reader*.[17] According to West, the article is a piece that he worked on over the last five years.

In *Part II* of this book I return to the Howard campus during the 1940s era completion of the transition period where the architectural education paradigm shifted to a Du Bois worldview. All traces of the philosophical paradigm of the Tuskegee architect-professors who followed Booker T. Washington's personal secretary Emmett Scott to DC were eradicated. I work my way through the architectural highlights of several seminal black Ivy League trained architect-professors who developed the school at Howard. These men embraced the WASP "professionalism" that comported with the conventional larger white worldview of the gentleman architect's role.

Having actually personally connected with several of these Du Bois-minded first generation architect-professors while studying at Howard, I segue into the period overlapping my youthful architectural awakening after high school in Los Angeles. This was followed by my arrival on Howard's campus in 1962 after nearly two years on active army duty just across the Potomac River at Fort Belvior, Virginia. This period flows into the explosive late 1960s period of my finishing up at Howard and entering the master's program at the Harvard Graduate School of Design in Cambridge. Along the way I look at the relationship between the African-American architect and Jewish architects and Jewish public officials, who were African-American architect's biggest allies outside of Black America. This relationship has tracked remarkably well with the larger twentieth-century relationship between the African-American and Jewish communities.

I then returned to Washington, DC, to teach at Howard while building an alternative-style affordable housing development-oriented practice. I spend a considerable amount of time attempting to establish the atmosphere for what it was like to be an aggressive, politically observant African-American architect during the reign of an uncompromising pro-black Mayor Marion Barry. This period was in Washington, DC, during the Reagan-era 1980s. During that time, there were positive as well as negative gains for black architects within an architecture profession that was subject to the same economic vicissitudes, globalization forces, and political ideology shifts affecting other important American institutions.

The past one-hundred years of interaction between African-American architects and the African-American community of Washington, DC, holds critical object lessons. These lessons must be understood and extrapolated globally into the twenty-first century.

Even today—in the face of such emerging modern black capitals as Accra, Ghana, and Lagos and Abuja in Nigeria—Washington, DC, would still meet any object criteria as being the most important center of black political influence on the planet. Washington, DC, also represents the greatest indirect economic muscle in the African Diaspora world. There was a literal changing of the guard in African-American architectural leadership in DC over the period beginning with Barry's 1979 inauguration and his final exit from politics in 1998. The city went from total dominance of the local black marketplace by Howard University trained architects to that of leadership by a new crop of African-American architects that had no prior affiliation with Howard.

And in *Part III* I attempt to provide straight talk to the next generation of African-American architects, landscape architects and city planners (as well as those *other* than African-Americans, who are disposed to seeking out new paradigms in urban practices). Many of them are now in grade school, secondary school, and university architecture school. Of the African-American architecture students, nearly half of them are also to be found in the country's eleven Historically Black College-University (HBCU) based architecture schools and programs including the one I recently headed. I use my Howard University, University of the District of Columbia, and Morgan State University experiences gained over the past thirty years as the basis for making observations, assessments, and to suggest generalized reorganization imperatives about all of the HBCU-based architecture schools and closely related programs.

I also pose questions about the meaning of the rapidly growing and ideologically influential "New Urbanism" movement in America. My questions go to the fate and future of African-Americans, as well as African-American architects in the context of "New Urbanism." I set forth a proposition that *a basic focus on community development and the housing of urban African-Americans is a must for the next generation of African-American architects.* I return once again to the themes of comprehensive black business enterprises and today's growing black

film/music/communications industrial-cultural complex. That pha-
lanx holds important lessons for the survival and flourishing of the
African-American architect in the information age of instant capital
and information movement.

I speculate about a spiritually rewarding future for the next generation of African-American architects. Such a future is premised on the
likely prospects of completing the reforms that have barely begun
inside several of those HBCU-based architecture schools. In addition
to the retention and strengthening of all of the existing HBCU-based
schools, there should be at least an equal number of more new architecture programs initiated at other historically black universities over
the next several years. Architectural education, much like legal or
engineering education, has the potential of being an excellent holistic
experience that results in the ability to "do good" while also (contrary
to prevailing orthodoxy) "doing *very well*."

I reflect upon my recent stay in Ghana, the first independent nation
in Black Africa. That was a personal religious experience. I received
reinforcement in my long-held belief that Du Bois was right about the
potential of Ghana as "Zion" for African-Americans. There should be
no *"either a democratic non-racist America or a separatist back to Africa"*
dichotomy for black Americans for the same reasons that no such
dichotomy exists for Jewish-Americans. Ghana (rather than Liberia)
continues to hold the same importance for the psyche of African-
Americans that Israel has had for the psyche of the JewishJewish-
American community. I therefore address the West African architect
scene that I observed in Ghana. I believe that it may hold a key for the
next generation of African-American architects. That key is primarily
spiritual and cultural, and perhaps only incidentally economic.

The Ghanaian architects were quick to openly acknowledge the
existence and the nature of their own state of crisis. Similar acknowledgment of a profound state of crisis by young professional and academic African-American architect leadership is the first necessary step
toward a positive resolution of the crisis afflicting the Black Diaspora
architect.

CHAPTER 2

Context of the Crisis

African-American architects—comprising 1.3 percent of all American architects—are in crisis because the other 98.7 percent of *American* architects are in crisis. African-American architects occupy the role of *the canary in the mineshaft*. The crisis in architecture has been most recently articulated by a rash of trenchant books that include University of Minnesota architecture dean Tom Fisher's *In the Scheme of Things*, Martin Pawley's *Terminal Architecture* and *Theory of Design in the Second Machine Age*, and Nan Ellin's *Postmodern Urbanism*.[1]

However, the crisis is not evident in places like the Harvard Graduate School of Design, currently the top-rated design school in the country according to a (hotly resented within the rest of the academy) *US News & World Report* survey. If you read Harvard's marketing literature, *there is definitely no crisis there*. Many of the Harvard design school faculty and students are an integral part of the high culture and financial power elites of America. Those elites ultimately control the larger building culture that produces the *signature* buildings that are considered "architecture" by that high culture. Harvard is an aberration *and* a paradigm in American architectural education.

On the professional front, erstwhile *New York Times* architecture critic Herbert Muschamp reminded us in one of his patented extended "Arts & Leisure" section feature articles in 1996 that most of the architects performing at the front of the stage of American and western world architecture are Jewish. That is in sharp contrast to the other stages full of players performing the uniquely American cultural art forms of music, dance, and increasingly, film. Here African-American musicians and entertainers, film actors and, filmmakers, are at the forefront of the stage. Despite Muschamp's stage full of high-profile Jewish architects, the *average* African-American architect shares with his fellow *average* white architect the burden of *a growing marginality*. That marginality is driven by the larger culture of building, capital, and real estate development that produces architecture in America.[2]

Muschamp's "star" architects are the ones who design America's museums, large public and civic facilities, and other cultural institutions and upscale commercial complexes. In some important ways, these men (substantively, there are still few women) are an accurate reflection of the distribution of money and power throughout American society in fundamental White versus Black terms. The design and construction of those museums and commercial complexes are accomplished through *risk (or excess) capital*. That is a commodity that White America spent considerable deliberate effort at limiting Black America's capacity to accumulate between the end of slavery and the 1970s. Black risk capital is still in short supply in the music and film sectors but the need is dwarfed by the capital requirements of buildings.

The virtually all-white world of the "high culture" modernist-post-modernist architectural *academy* dominates all aspects of architectural socialization including what goes on inside of the handful of black architectural schools.[3] As a general proposition the academy is either ignorant of or uninterested in the extent that modernist architectural aesthetics are beholden to African-American culture.[4] The academy has also been deeply instrumental in imbuing the African-American architect with a modus operandi and ideology that is ill-suited to the realities, imperatives, responsibilities, and opportunities in the worlds of the Black Diaspora

Today some observant African-American practitioners watch events in Black America with mixed feelings of dismay. Some black practitioners believe that there are no viable long-term clients in black communities. The thinking, to paraphrase one of the country's top black practitioners, is that "black communities, unlike an IBM or a government agency, don't have *repeat* business to offer." Yet, one after another of the traditional as well as newer and wealthier entities inside of Black America continuously enter into lucrative business partnership relationships with non-black-owned, *finance-develop-design-build-manage* enterprises. These comprehensive operations provide everything inside Black America from personal customized shelter for the affluent to the housing needs of low, moderate, and middle-income masses. These partnerships increasingly include even (or perhaps especially) the soaring religious edifices that Black America loves to build. But these substantively all-white enterprises increasingly come with a non-African-American architect as an integral part of the arrangement.

There is an urgent need to grasp the full implications of an economically awakening Black America that now has personal financial resources far beyond those available in the 1920s Harlem Renaissance era or the succeeding 1970s Black Power period. In addition to the black church and the historically black college, there are also now high elected offices in key urban municipalities. There are also large numbers of professional athletes and entertainers *(whose risk capital base is growing but under whose control and for what purposes?)*. Black America also now has a growing collection of highly sophisticated business enterprises and entrepreneurs of every type.

But alas, the African-American architect does not now register on the most important and authoritative gauges of economic development that are watched regularly by African-Americans.[5] Conversely, and most tellingly, the image of the black architect on the African-American *cultural* front is now confirmed as, *at best*, nonexistent. The initial 1999 released *Africana Encyclopedia* compiled by Harvard-based Henry Louis Gates and Ghanaian philosopher-scholar, Kwame Appiah, is now the definitive catalogue of the culture of the African and African-American Diaspora.[6] There are over 2,000 pages packed with nearly as many profiles of black achievers from the worlds of music, the arts, and general or popular culture. While the name of architect Albert Cassell is mentioned in an incidental way, *not a single African-American architect is indexed or profiled.*

Gates' and Appiah's *Encyclopedia* makes no mention of Robert Robinson Taylor who was the very first black graduate in 1892 of America's first recognized architecture school at the Massachusetts Institute of Technology (MIT).[7] Taylor went on to become the turn of the century "fountainhead" of African-American architects. He coordinated the design and building of the Tuskegee Institute campus and the surrounding model black community for his patron Booker T. Washington. Nor did Gates and Appiah include any substantive information on Cornell-educated Albert. Cassell, who performed a similar feat for the modern-era Howard University's first black president Mordecai Johnson between 1926 and 1939.[8] The prolific Los Angeles icon and "architect to the stars" Paul R. Williams was also not included.[9]

Missing was contemporary New York City architect Max Bond Jr., the designer of the Martin Luther King Jr. complex in Atlanta. Bond's design is probably the most recognized building in Black America by other black Americans (and most of informed White America). Missing also was Charles MacAfee, a visionary Kansas City architect and national leader of a cutting-edge, urban modular housing movement. Bond and MacAfee are arguably at the top of the list of the several most important African-American architects still working and practicing today. Thus we can only conclude that Gates and Appiah simply do not regard African-American architects as *culturally* relevant in the black world.

However, it must be said that Gates and Appiah would have every right to place the blame for their glaring snub of African-American architects on precisely that group of architects. The conspicuous absence of the written words of African-American architects in forums of serious and sustained black cultural discourse has not helped their cause. As a class, today's African-American architects have also largely failed to advocate or provide working support to cultural issues of importance to a significant spectrum of the black world. Further compounding matters for the African-American architect, I am mindful of MIT architecture dean William Mitchell's warning. During a lecture several years ago, Mitchell cautioned that soon a $29.95 hand-held computer would render all of the architect's traditional technical skills economically worthless. Malcolm McCullough, a close collaborator of Mitchell, reinforces the idea of a very different reality for the world of architects.[10] In the Information Age, none of the skills that have distinguished architects through the ages and up to the recent past hold any utilitarian or commercial value.

Mitchell's ground-breaking books, including *The Reconfigured Eye: Visual Truth in the Post-Photographic Era* on the mind-blowing impact of digital photography, and *e-topia: "Urban Life Jim—But Not As We Know It"* substantiates his clarion calls for new paradigms of architectural thought.[11] However, Ray Kurzweil's eye-opening book, *The Age of Spiritual Machines: When Computers Exceed Human Intelligence*, goes even more to the point. Kurzweil expounds on the larger subject of the inexorable direction of the Information Technology revolution. He reveals the extent to which Mitchell was actually pulling his punches with the already shell-shocked sensibilities of a largely architectural audience. Kurzweil substantiates the imminent certainty of Mitchell's seemingly tongue-in-cheek allusion to coming affordable hand-held computing power that will certainly exceed the capacity of the human brain.[12]

While a student at Howard University during the turbulent 1960s period of the Black Power Movement, I wanted desperately to be seriously involved. I wanted to be a useful participant in that movement. Being in architecture school made that a dubious proposition. The movement was about politics and above all *culture*. The watchword of the day was "power" as in *Black Power*. Every culture-related, academic discipline on campus was proudly adopting the "black" prefix. There was *black* art, *black* theater, *black* music, *black* literature, *black* film, *black* dance, and *black* social sciences—all integral parts of a universally acknowledged *black* culture. But architecture fiercely resisted the idea of any type of association or conflation with the word *black*.

Architecture is now under immense pressures attributable to the iron-gloved fist of the post-modern condition.[13] Profound cultural issues are being intersected and compromised by equally profound wealth creation and economic development imperatives. The intersection of culture and economic development seems to be precisely where the larger 135-year-old black post-emancipation struggle is now either hopelessly stalled or precariously poised for a major breakthrough. The choice depends on one's frame of reference and worldview.

Harold Cruse, in his entire body of late-1960s work, never to my recollection made a single reference to a "Negro architect." Cruse never raised the issue of "architecture" within the context of his exhaustive writings on the cultural and economic struggles of the Harlem Renaissance. Nor did he do so in his writings on the period up through the late 1960s. But Cruse continuously makes reference to the issues of land ownership and the dominance of absentee-owned housing and cultural facilities throughout Harlem since the 1920s Renaissance days. On larger black cultural and economic development issues throughout the twentieth-century, his thoughts hold important implications for architects. Like Cruse, I see an urgent need to sound a sharp warning alarm to the current young generation of African-American architectural practitioners and academics. Nearly all of them profess commitments to wanting to provide leadership in the solution of major socio-economic problems confronting urban Black America. Some even profess that those commitments vastly outweigh their desires for recognition and participation in mainstream American architecture.

On balance, the modes and methods of the young practitioners do not always appear to be informed by twentieth-century African-American architectural history in proper cultural context. The extent of the rapidly accelerating marginality of the overwhelming majority of orthodox architectural practices may be still unappreciated. The full implications of twenty-first century information age realities for effective architectural practices are also not sufficiently appreciated by many young academics and practitioners. It may be the tantalizing possibility of a breakthrough and crossover recognition from his (or the occasional her) still largely "White Gentleman's Profession" and peers that inhibit many young black architects from consciously focusing on building serious and effective black culture-rooted practices. Such practices must speak directly to the economic development and cultural affirmation needs of an enlarging black lower-middle and middle-class American *customer* base. I deliberately use the term "customer" rather than "client" or "patron." I expand on this critical distinction further on in *Part III* of this book.

CHAPTER 3

The B.T. Washington-W.E.B. Du Bois Debate in "Bricks and Mortar"

"I must study politics and war that my sons may have the liberty to study mathematics and philosophy. My sons ought to study mathematics and philosophy and geography, natural history, and naval architecture, navigation, commerce, and agriculture in order to give their children the right to study painting, poetry, music, and architecture..."
John Adams, circa 1700

A consensus exists throughout the white mainstream academic and professional wings of the world of American architecture that Thomas Jefferson (1743–1826) is the ultimate father figure for the nation's architects.[1] At the end of the 18th century Jefferson was at a transitional point in his life as a political theorist, gentleman architect, and owner of nearly 200 slaves.[2]

Jefferson spent his post-William & Mary college life pursuing his architectural ambitions and education through reading and practicing the drawing rules of the Ecole des Beaux-Arts, the Paris-based authority on all matters of architecture in the western world at that time. His 1780s stay in Paris heightened his architectural aspirations. From his political writings and recorded utterances, we know a great deal about his innermost thoughts. Jefferson had grave misgivings about the intellectual capacities of African slaves surrounding him in his home state of Virginia.[3]

We now know authoritatively that Jefferson's slave and mistress Sally Hemings bore sons for Jefferson and that at least one of the sons was trained on the plantation as a carpenter.[4] We know that Jefferson would have found the idea of a full-blooded African (someone of no known or obvious evidence of white parentage) capable of being educated and socialized as an architect—as Jefferson understood that term—to be highly improbable. We can only speculate on how Jefferson felt about the prospects of a mulatto, quadroon, and even an octoroon slave becoming an architect.

Virtually any slave—undiluted blood lines or otherwise—that Thomas Jefferson would have chosen to mentor and publicly acknowledge as his architectural protégée would have very likely gone down in history as one of America's most revered architects with "fountainhead" status. Had Jefferson, for instance, chosen to send his carpenter son (or nephew) to the Ecole des Beaux Arts with full acknowledgment, such an act would have had a profound impact on the historical image of the African-American architect throughout the nineteenth and twentieth centuries.[5]

At mid-nineteenth-century, white American architects were emulating Thomas Jefferson's earlier actions of traveling to Paris. Richard Morris Hunt was the first American architect who would go on to achieve icon status as a result of making the trek to Paris. Hunt studied at the Ecole des Beaux Arts in 1855 before returning to America to train others in his ateliers.[6] Richard Dozier and Sharon Patton are two African-American scholars who position an American man of color in Paris receiving architectural training and returning home to build in the nineteenth-century. Both report the presence of Louis Metoyer at the Ecole in 1875. Metoyer's father was French and his mother was a black slave in Louisiana.[7]

I have found no such scholarly mention of a black person being trained in the American atelier of a white Paris trained architect in the middle of the nineteenth-century. Formal American training or professional education for a black person in architecture would have to wait a few more decades.

Besides Hunt, other white American architects who dominated the period between the mid-nineteenth-century and the beginning of the twentieth-century included Henry Hobson Richardson (1838–1888) and his Boston-based New England practice of massive, Romanesque-inspired architecture. Another seminal figure was Daniel Burnham (1846–1912) and his robust Chicago-based practice of Beaux Arts architecture. There was also Charles McKim (1847–1909) and Stanford White (1835–1906) of the New York City-based firm of McKim, Meade, and White.[8]

Frank Lloyd Wright, who would become the leading icon in the American architecture world, was born in 1865. In that same year, a nine-year-old Booker T. Washington was emancipated from slavery and was within sixteen years of founding Tuskegee Institute in 1881. Washington graduated from the industrial education program at Hampton Institute several years earlier. Meanwhile the white American architect icon figures were servicing clients who were the titans of this country's mushrooming industries. Those architects were designing factories, office buildings, and grand estates to show off the great personal fortunes of the new industrialists.

William Ware, one of William Morris Hunt's students, would set up the very first American school of architecture at MIT in 1865. The curriculum was patterned after the Ecole des Beaux Arts. However, Black America would have to wait nearly twenty-five years before seeing a black person accepted into the MIT program.

By the last decades of the nineteenth-century, the closest comparable African-American equal of Thomas Jefferson's earlier late eighteenth-century role and impact on the development of white America's architectural world was Booker T. Washington.[9] Today's black architects and their practices are direct spiritual descendants of the architects that were deliberately created just over one-hundred years ago by the much-maligned Washington.[10]

Washington, unlike Jefferson, did not actually study architecture, or fancy himself as an architect. However, Washington was resolute in his belief in the need of the professional architect's skills in order to carry out his vision for Tuskegee and newly freed slaves. Like most vision-aries, Washington appreciated the end product of architecture. He was in awe of what he regarded as a profound cognitive developmental conceptualization process of making the drawings necessary to pro-duce architecture.[11]

Washington exhausted all of his resources in the development of the first rudimentary campus structures in the first nine years after found-ing Tuskegee in 1881. He passionately believed that it was essential that he first create full-fledged architects—as opposed to merely car-penters and bricklayers. Washington viewed the actual design and the construction management of his *"Black City"* in the heart of the Alabama black belt as something too important to be "contracted out" to white architects and builders.[12] Richard Dozier places Washington's role in proper context:

> *Tuskegee Institute shares the educational concept of Thomas Jefferson's design for the University of Virginia. Jefferson had designed the Virginia campus as an environment that would teach, inspire, and provide a physical experience for students...(The) use of buildings to educate and proclaim the program's achievements were perhaps Booker T. Washington's most significant addition to Jefferson's work of architecture.[13]*

In Washington's mind, the black architect-practitioners he caused to be created at Tuskegee one-hundred years ago were the synthesis of what would eventually become known as the Washington-Du Bois debate dialectic. Tragically, standing squarely in the way of Washington's ambitious plans was a venal white power ethic that was aptly characterized by Supreme Court Justice Roger B. Taney's infa-mous Dred Scott dictum that *"the Negro has no rights that a white man is bound to honor."*

Mr. Washington believed that the principal role of the black archi-tect would be that of change agent and catalytic instrument of black community economic development on a land base. Conversely, we have to surmise that Du Bois' turn-of-the-twentieth-century thinking about the necessity of a black land base and a "black economy" was conflicted. Du Bois was rightly convinced that without the vote, civil rights, and social equality, black land holdings and black economies were hopelessly vulnerable to white caprice.

Clearly, both men were right. In retrospect, it is hard to conceive that there was no silently understood middle ground strategy between the two of them. Each man operated from two completely differing geographic and political arenas. One harbored a specific goal-oriented agenda of constructing a physically rooted institution. The other was about a grand idea of political consciousness, struggle, and resistance. Future history may prove that there was indeed a joint understanding and coordinated strategy. Conservative African-American intellectual Glenn Loury provides us with a counterpoint to progressive left intellectual thinkers in summing up the assessment of the *"epic battle between Washington and Du Bois"* this way:

> It cannot be said that history has proven Washington right and Du Bois wrong in their debate about what blacks should have done a century ago. Yet given the way the history of black people has evolved it can now be said that the animating spirit of Washington's philosophy offers a sounder guide to the future of blacks than that reflected in the worldview of his critics.[14]

Thanks to Dozier's research we know much about the first architects Mr. Washington recruited in the early 1900s. These men bore little resemblance to intellectually limited, vocationally trained carpenters and bricklayers. Many people to this day assume that such "mechanics" were the only logical products that could have resulted from the Booker T. Washington educational, social and economic philosophy at Tuskegee. Mr. Washington's original architects differed from America's turn-of-the-century white architects and the architecture created for the white American leisure and industrialist classes.[15]

The early twentieth-century South had no black leisure class. The several extant black industrialists and real estate developers were far too few and isolated to be in the business of building on a scale anywhere nearing that of Mr. Washington's Tuskegee campus.[16] Mr. Washington's architect-builder teachers and those they trained went forth throughout the Deep South to build black churches, Jewish philanthropy-funded schools, and the occasional business place or private residence. Washington was not inclined to mince words:

> *In America the Negro race for the first time, is face to face with the problem of learning to till the land intelligently; of planning and building permanent and beautiful homes; of erecting school houses and extending the school term; of experimenting with methods of instruction and adapting them to the needs of the Negro people; of organizing churches, building houses of worship; and preparing ministers. In short, the Negro in America today is face to face with the fundamental problem of modern civilization; and for each of these problems he has, to some extent, to find a solution of his own.*[17]

Mr. Washington's architects mastered the same architectural design rules, principles, canons, vocabularies, and technology used by the nation's white architects.[18] But they were building structures on the Tuskegee campus and throughout the Deep South. The buildings were for the use of powerless, illiterate, and landless ex-slaves seeking to transform themselves into a modern people. All of this was taking place under now unfathomable conditions of the most degrading form of racial apartheid.

In 1892 Robert Taylor, the son of a successful North Carolina builder, would be the first black person to graduate from the architecture school at MIT. Taylor was the valedictorian of his class and none of this was going un-noticed by Booker T. Washington and his wide-ranging circle of confidants. Taylor, under Washington's sponsorship, would prove to be the black equivalent to Richard Morris Hunt, the "fountainhead" figure in the white world of architecture. It had to have been in one of Mr. Washington's early 1890s visits to Boston and eventually the MIT campus through the suggestions of others, that Washington may have met Taylor.[19]

Whether Taylor had to be coaxed back to the Deep South and Tuskegee or whether Taylor saw this prospect as the opportunity of a lifetime is conjectural. What is certain is that Washington felt that Taylor was the perfect blend of the Du Boisian and Washingtonian agendas. Taylor possessed formal exposure to classic aspects of western civilization. But he also possessed the practical hands-on skill and knowledge to actually design and manage the construction of a building of any size or function.

The simplicity of conventional thinking about Washington is highlighted through careful re-reading of August Meier's *Negro Thought in America*.[20] There are also Washington's own words at the Atlanta Cotton States Exhibition in 1895, and Mr. Du Bois' critique of Washington in that familiar chapter, "On Mr. Washington and Others" in the seminal book, *The Souls of Black Folk*.

Mr. Taylor, along with the faculty he recruited, and his most talented students, was focused on those design and building opportunities available inside of black communities scattered about the Deep South and the eastern seacoast. Booker T. Washington's dreams of economically self-controlled black communities could only be partially and sporadically achieved. Yet, in spite of the rigidly imposed caste and racial system of his time and space, Mr. Washington's early architects in black communities were often at the center of such successes.

A consensus exists between reputable architectural scholars and historians that 1890–1920 was the crucible period of the formation of a uniquely American architecture.[21] This is the time when American architectural icon Frank Lloyd Wright and his principal mentor and former employee Louis Sullivan rose to the fore. Many scholars credit these two men with giving physical expression to an American version of what would come to be known later as *International Style* modern architecture.

That 1890–1920 period is best symbolized by a combination of seminal architectural events that would also help to define American architectural culture. The 1893 Chicago World's Fair of monumental European Beaux Arts architecture that so captivated the country's ruling elites was one such event. Better known as the Columbian Exposition, this fair was the physical centerpiece of the observance of the 400th anniversary of the landing of Christopher Columbus in the new world in 1492. The event was also intended to showcase the US as a world power. Frederick Law Olmstead, designer of Central Park in New York City and the father of American landscape architecture, was tasked with laying out the fairgrounds.

Daniel Burnham, the influential Chicago architect, was the executive designer with the responsibility for selecting the various architects for the World's Fair buildings. The opening words of Burnham's famous and often quoted dictum, *"Make no little plans, for they fail to stir the hearts of men..."* captures the spirit of the start of the twentieth-century. Burnham symbolized the Midwestern architects who would be the chosen instruments of American captains of industry and commerce. Another less often quoted statement by Burnham even better sums up the dreams of America's architectural leadership class. His desire was to serve the personal wealth and burgeoning corporate and industrial ambitions of the virtually all-white world of American business. Burnham can be paraphrased this way: *"I want to build a big organization that can do big things for big businesses."*

In that same era only Booker T. Washington was about a big physical idea that would afford black architects the opportunity to pursue Burnham-type architectural dreams. For African-American architects, *"The White City,"* as the fair became known, referred to more than just Burnham's choice of the color of most of the Fair's more prominent buildings.[22]

By 1900, the 100-acre farm and scattered chicken shacks that Washington acquired from the Alabama Legislature in 1881 had grown considerably. By then, there was a 2,000-acre campus with many substantial buildings and over 1,200 students.[23] Washington never posited the original Tuskegee as being a college. He saw it as a vocational school that would prepare some people to go on to prestigious colleges for final training and return to Tuskegee and other industrial schools. Washington was apparently willing to serve as a useful straw man to the very necessary urges of W.E.B. Du Bois for classical university level education for a "Talented Tenth" of Black America.

At the start of the 1900s, Tuskegee's Taylor and his students achieved levels of self-sufficiency in the design and construction of the Tuskegee campus that are breathtaking in retrospect. They constructed a brick-making plant that provided all of their bricks. They developed and built all of their own hoisting and heavy materials moving mechanisms.[24] Here was comprehensive, fully integrated, environmentally balanced land development, design-build construction management, and critical materials manufacturing. The scope and magnitude mirrored the best large-scale commercial and industrial efforts occurring then in White America.

I argue that a vital connection existed between black culture and architecture for a brief moment in history from 1881 and 1915 at Tuskegee. It may also have been extended briefly to a few other southern locations including the state of Oklahoma and points west. In Dozier's words:

> The years 1881 and 1929 frame perhaps the greatest Afro-American building period in America's history. As early as 1879, former slaves such as Henry Adams, Benjamin "Pop" Singleton and Edward McCabe led freedmen west to Kansas and the Oklahoma Territory in search of freedom, land and opportunity. Nicodemus in Kansas, Boley, Langston and 25 other towns in Oklahoma were among the "Black Towns" founded by these men. By 1916, 59 of these towns and five settlements existed throughout the U.S. Located mostly in the south, these towns were founded, developed and built, for the most part by Afro-Americans...Architecture became the symbol of racial progress and pride...In keeping with the 'race pride' concept, the majority of these buildings were designed and built by Afro-American architects and contractors and in some cases financed by Afro-Americans.[25]

Washington evolved a clear modus operandi in developing his scores of campus buildings, farm structures, and an adjacent residential community of homes for Tuskegee faculty and administrators. His endeavor, driven by his architect-faculty and students, entailed acquiring hundreds of acres of virgin farmland in the midst of a hostile and violent Alabama. A University of Michigan landscape architecture professor has written what will prove to be an important paper for today's black planners, designers, and artists of all stripes. In that paper, Professor Kendrick Ian Grandison has posed at least an inference of a potentially revolutionary environment. Grandison sketches out the relationships that were briefly forged in the development of Tuskegee during this period of American development. Professor Gradison opines openly that orthodox thinking about Booker T. Washington's political ideology is simplistic and often dreadfully misinformed:

> *The development of Tuskegee's campus is an inspiring story of the creativity and perseverance of blacks as they struggled against and triumphed over formidable obstacles…Difficulty, however, when it does not exceed human will and capacity to survive, necessarily results in compromise and innovation as people adapt to their circumstances…The shortage of funds in the early days motivated a self-help approach toward accomplishing the school's goals of black education, campus development, and* **community building** *(bold italics mine)…A campus had to be built and classes taught in the midst of (this) reign of terror. The process of development differed fundamentally from conventional implementation of design in landscape architecture in that it was not an abstract linear mechanism bringing together discrete client, planner, and contractor entities to build the campus. Instead, it was a cyclical process that dissolved the boundaries between the three in the interest of integrating development with community uplift…*[26]

Architectural historian-critic Robert Twombley characterizes twentieth-century architecture as three types of building structures: *signature, generic, and vernacular.*[27] All but the signature building type were academically invisible along with the architects. Twombley provides us with a useful perspective. By Twombley's definition, all buildings designed by black architects would have been classified by mainstream architectural historians as generic or vernacular, even though considered signature buildings by African-Americans.

There were "signature" buildings designed at Tuskegee and throughout southern black communities by Mr. Washington's early twentieth-century architects. These buildings represented a classic example of architecture and architects that have remained invisible. This work is completely unheralded to this day on the larger American stage of twentieth-century architectural evolution. This beginning of the practice of architecture by blacks in rural Alabama over one-hundred years ago is viewed with ambivalence by Black America. Mixed feelings throughout Black America about Mr. Washington range from loathing to indifference. Succeeding generations of black architects have yet to establish architecture as a vital and relevant component of black cultural life in the mind of most African-Americans.

Harold Cruse has reminded us that Du Bois actually came around to a Washingtonian point of view much earlier than his 1958 self-imposed exile to Ghana, the first independent state in modern-day Black Africa. Du Bois lived out the rest of his life in West Africa and was buried there upon his death in 1963. By the late 1930s, a disillusioned Du Bois was advocating an ideological program that was strikingly similar to Booker T. Washington's 1900s Tuskegee-based program. Here are the words of Du Bois—less than forty years after Washington's 1895 Atlanta Compromise Speech:

> We must organize our strengths as consumers; learn to cooperate and use machines and power as producers; train ourselves in methods of democratic control within our own group. Run and support our own institutions...We have already got a partially segregated Negro economy in the United States...We not only build and finance Negro churches, but we furnish a considerable part of our own professional services in medicine, pharmacy, dentistry and law...We furnish some part of our food and clothes, our home building and repairing and many retail services. We furnish books and newspapers; we furnish endless personal services...It may be said

*that this inner economy of the Negro serves but a small proportion
of its total needs; but it is growing and expanding in various ways;
and what I propose is to so plan and guide it as to take advantage of
certain obvious facts...It is of course impossible that a segregated
economy for Negroes in the United States should be complete. It is
quite possible that it could never cover more than the smaller part of
the economic activities of Negroes. Nevertheless, it is also possible
that this smaller part could be so important and wield so much
power that its influence upon the total economy of Negroes and the
total industrial organization of the United States would be decisive
for the great ends towards which the Negro moves.*[28]

Thirty years ago, I possessed typically orthodox political views
about Mr. Washington versus my more positive views about Du Bois. I
have since undergone an epiphany-like revelation that Mr.
Washington's primary motivation and instincts were more closely
related to that of a visionary real estate developer. Washington *was not*
a social theorist or deeply philosophical thinker attempting to compete with or counter the thrusts of Du Bois. In overall comparison to
Du Bois, Washington comes off poorly. But when narrowly seen as the
visionary community builder and consummate deal maker that he
clearly was, the predicament of Black America today strongly indicates that he needs to be viewed differently.[29] The Tuskegee campus
and surrounding community subdivisions are still today, 123 years
after its inception, the largest private real estate assemblage and new
development deal ever put together inside of Black America. This
accomplishment was by an all-black cast of characters that was dominated by trained black architects and builders. Even Howard
University in Washington, DC, is not as large or important a physical
accomplishment. Howard's white religious and federal origins
resulted in the domination of its early architectural development by
white federal government selected architects and builders.

The irony is that Mr. Washington, from his base at Tuskegee in the
first decade of the twentieth-century, was also instrumental in aiding
and abetting another large-scale, black-conceived and executed real

estate deal. Mr. Washington was instrumental in the creation of the cultural capital of Black America that we know today as Harlem, New York.[30] Ample documentation exists to show Washington's indirect financial, political, and ideological sponsorship of men like Phillip Payton of the Afro-American Realty Company. Trusted Washington agent and personal secretary Emmett Scott was a member of Payton's board of trustees.[31] I join Dozier and others who have intimated or openly speculated about Washington's grand, if flawed, vision of an openly structural connection between Tuskegee and Harlem as a prototypical northern urban enclave. Washington saw the Harlem, USAs as places that could actually be physically redeveloped using Tuskegee trained talent.

Thus, we have in bold relief the two simultaneously occurring seminal architectural events in Black America and White America in the final decade of the nineteenth-century. For White America, it was the 633-acre, multi-million dollar world exposure extravaganza along the downtown Chicago lakeshore. For Black America, it was a 100-acre farm being transformed into a 2,000-acre, multi-building institutional campus in the middle of the violently racist Alabama black belt. Only the former event is unfailingly featured in standard architecture textbooks as a serious architectural accomplishment. The latter event is, predictably, of no interest or relevance to mainstream architectural media. What was not so predictable is that the latter event would be treated so lightly throughout Black America including the black architectural community.

CHAPTER 4

Tuskegee-Howard Pedagogies Collide, 1919–1945

In 1902, John Lankford, the first Tuskegee-trained architect to arrive in Washington, DC, proceeded to establish a busy office practice in the physical heart of Black Washington. Lankford made himself a vital business and economic development entity immediately upon his arrival. Rigidly segregated Washington, DC, and its white architectural community's quest to develop Washington, DC, as a world-class city, had no role or room for the likes of a John Lankford. There is little probability that Lankford, steeped in the black nationalist tinged self-help ideology of Booker T. Washington, harbored ambitions to be a part of the white architectural world during those early years of his arrival.

Aside from his immediate task of designing the True Reformers Building on U Street (still standing today), Lankford went on to establish a local branch of Booker T. Washington's National Negro Business League. Lankford most probably saw the NBL as the appropriate counterpart to the American Institute of Architects (AIA) which he had no hopes of joining. Today's black architects would be wise to seriously ponder the following quotation from Lankford's promotional description of himself and the services he offered to his black clientele:

> *Expert builder, examiner and instructor. Plans gotten at short notice from rough sketches, pencil drawings or from written or ver-*

bal desk creations and mailed to any section of the country. In the past thirty-two months we have designed, overhauled, repaired and built over $500,000 [$25 million in today's dollars] worth of work in Washington, DC...We make a specialty of church and hall designs and arranging loans (bold italics mine).[1]

In a major speech delivered before Booker T. Washington and the Negro Business League in 1906 in New York City, which Lankford titled *"The Negro as Architect and Builder,"* we are provided with insight to the worldview of this Tuskegee-trained architect. His nearly 100-year-old words represent much of today's imperatives for the twenty-first century black architect:

Historians have recorded enough facts to give the world sufficient reason to believe that the black man, the Negro, in his native country among his own people, with his own black hands, over one thousand years before the Christian era laid the foundations and erected some of the greatest monuments, buildings, and cities that have ever been designed or built by man. In America for over two hundred years the Negroes in the South were the principal designers and builders; they cut the stone, sawed the timber, burnt the bricks and manufactured most of the tools and machinery in the machine and blacksmith shop, to carry out their idea of construction they designed and built...In the past three years, I have designed for Washington and fifteen states of the Union nearly six million dollars worth of buildings. I have designed, overhauled and built in Washington and vicinity over seven hundred thousand dollars worth of property during the same time. The harvest is now great, and the mechanics are comparatively few. As an architect and builder and president of the Washington Negro Business League, I would advise any skilled Negro workman with pluck and push, coupled with some finance, to make a venture along this line; if possible in the community in which you live, if not come to Washington and we will assist you.[2]

We can gather several things from Lankford's words. Booker T. Washington considered Lankford to be one of his finest Tuskegee alumni. We can conclude that the many parts of the speech that were in the black nationalist and Afrocentrist mindset were things that Mr. Washington was substantially in agreement with. Yet, Washington would not be caught publicly uttering such views that actually pre-dated Marcus Garvey by fifteen years.

We cannot fail to note Lankford's reference to himself as an architect *and* builder. Lest we think that this was without literal significance—as was often the case when white architects sometimes rhetorically referred to themselves as builders—Lankford sets the record straight. He has articulated the structure of his multifaceted office operations. He also makes it clear that he views himself and others like him as front line business leaders in their respective communities. We need hardly stretch our imaginations to grasp the scope of a contemporary black equivalency of Lankford's 1903 *"finance-acquire-develop-design-build-manage"* machine. *And Langford's machine was all standard modus operandi for the original Tuskegee-trained architect-builders.*

Richard Dozier's research places William Sidney Pittman among the initial 1895 graduating architectural diploma class taught by Taylor at Tuskegee. Pittman would go on to Philadelphia and complete the architecture program at Drexel Institute. According to Harrison Etheridge's research, Pittman joined John Lankford in Washington in 1905 and left after a year to pursue his own practice. Pittman also married Portia Washington, Booker T Washington's daughter, in 1907 and designed and built their home just across the District line in Fairmount Heights, Maryland.

Dozier, Etheridge, and Henderson are all in agreement that Pittman's greatest legacy in Washington, DC, is the imposing YMCA Building on 12th Street near U Street. The Rockefeller family put up half of the funds to build the structure, but the DC black community quickly met Rockefeller's challenge by raising the other half of the necessary funds:

> *One of Pittman's most interesting local architectural endeavors was his association with the Lincoln Memorial Building Company, which attempted between 1910 and 1912 to raise funds to erect on*

> U *Street a handsome eight story commercial and office building. A theater to seat 2,500 would also be among the building's features. Pittman was president of the company, serving with a group of eleven officers and directors and an initial issue of $100,000 of stock. Pittman presumably designed the building.*[3]

The above project never got off the ground. It was actually tainted with charges of financial impropriety. But it is still a useful example of the entrepreneurial mindset that the Tuskegee transplants brought to Washington at the turn of the twentieth-century. Pittman's most famous and influential project was his 1907 design of the Negro Building at the Jamestown, Virginia, Tercentennial. The same black contractor that built John Lankford's True Reformer's Building in Washington, DC, in 1903 also built this massive structure.[4]

Starting in 1919 and lasting over the following fifty years, the center of architectural preparation for blacks shifted from the Tuskegee campus to the Howard University campus. Over that period, a fundamentally different paradigm emerged for the relationship of architecture and building. The old paradigm used in the building of the Tuskegee campus had prevailed over the preceding thirty years.[5]

William Augustus Hazel was already a highly experienced architectural designer by the time he arrived at Tuskegee in 1909 to join Taylor as an instructor.[6] His previous employment included a seven-year period as a draftsman in a prestigious Boston architectural office. He had previously spent fifteen years in St. Paul, Minnesota, as the representative of a prominent New York architectural firm. His specialty was stained glass design. Hazel is reported to have remained on the faculty at Tuskegee for a period of ten years. From Tuskegee, he went to Howard University in 1919. Hazel's granddaughter, Louise Daniel Hutchinson, historian Franklin Dorman, and Richard Dozier all credit Hazel with organizing an architecture program and teaching the first courses in architecture at Howard University that year.

Washington's private secretary, Emmett Scott, left Tuskegee after Washington's death in 1915. Scott took a prominent position in the federal government in Washington, DC. While there, Scott was also affiliated with Howard University. He may have been an influence in the start of the Washington, DC, careers of Hazel and several other Tuskegee transplants to the area.

The new Washington, DC-Howard University architectural education paradigm encompassed two sub-themes. The first was the conflict between the Du Boisian social vision of classical education permeating Howard and the vocational dimensions of the Tuskegee-influenced architecture pedagogy.[7] The second theme was the series of events occurring right outside the Howard campus gates in the white architectural community. A major preoccupation of this group of white architects was "professionalism." Essentially this required establishing acute formal and ethical distinctions between the genteel (and increasingly university educated) architect, and the builder.

Objective conditions and the spirit of the times may well have made resistance to following the same path that the white architects were pursuing difficult. But in Washington, DC, there were several instances of continuation of the Tuskegee modus operandi. Nonetheless, the doctrine of "professionalism" in architectural education at Howard in the early 1920s was far more compatible with Du Boisian classicism. The vocational Booker T. Washington inspired pedagogy was clearly suspect. Land ownership and development, training of construction and building mechanics, spin-off community businesses, and critical aspects of black common culture characterized the Tuskegee model. Those issues were of less interest to Howard's incoming East Coast trained black architect-professors.[8]

Between 1900 and 1960, the overwhelming majority of African-American architects received their formal education at a small number of historically black universities offering some type of architectural training. Tuskegee in Alabama was the dominant institution offering formal architectural training from 1900 to 1920. By 1923, Howard University was moving onto the scene with what would become the dominant black university-based program after the ending of World War II in the 1940s. Hampton in Virginia and Southern University in Louisiana also started architecture programs during this period.

The Washington, DC-Howard University years are best understood when placed in the proper context. By 1900, there would be eleven American architecture schools, all patterned after the Paris Ecole and its American model at MIT.[9] But the Tuskegee-based architecture program (along with several other programs at industrially oriented black colleges) was preparing students for a role of *master builder*.[10] The white schools were intent on distancing the role of the architect from that of the builder to the maximum extent possible.

This was the path laid out in architectural education for the socialization of the American architect and how he would best function in the building of the dynamic, new American industrial giant. On the basis of American social structure and strivings, the bifurcation of the old master builder and the gentleman architect made sense. This was consistent with an upper class self-image of being people of high culture, refined taste, and irreproachable ethics. The gentlemanly architect was socialized to view himself as above the lowly world of construction rowdies and ruffians.

This view of how the world of building should work made perfect sense at the time for a white world. That world had a parallel universe of builders, developers, financiers, suppliers, manufacturers, and craftsmen who could "make" things with their hands. This white parallel universe also had an abundance of wealthy capitalist-industrialist patrons and clients.

Cornell-trained, African-American architect Albert Cassell was influenced by Hazel to come to the Howard campus to teach in 1924. The two men had worked together professionally in Tuskegee. Cassell would eventually design several major buildings in his hometown of Towson, Maryland, just north of Baltimore. Similar to DC, Baltimore had a growing black population that was a direct and indirect source of work for black architects. Cassell designed five buildings on the campus of historically black Morgan State College. He also prepared the plans for the alterations to the old Providence Hospital and several downtown buildings in Baltimore.

Cassell spent his first two years at Howard as head of the academic program. Mordecai Johnson, Howard University's first black president, then appointed him campus architect in 1926. Johnson could have easily passed for white. He instead committed himself to live out his life in accordance with the prevailing precepts of the *"one drop of Negro blood"* rule. Up to Johnson's appointment, white architects selected by the federal government, which was the major contributor to Howard's budget, had designed all of the buildings at Howard. Cassell's new assignment included the 1929 and 1932 master plans of the Howard campus. He collaborated with Cornell-trained black landscape architect David Williston who had also been the chief landscape architect at Tuskegee in 1910.[11]

Cassell operated out of a campus office. He was charged by the university with designing and overseeing construction of a number of strategically important campus structures. Cassell first used young architecture program instructor Hilyard Robinson as a chief designer. Cassell had hired Robinson to teach in 1924. Cassell would later use young Louis Fry, Sr. as his chief designer and project manager. Cassell was responsible for the design of Founders Library and Frederick Douglass Hall. He also built major dormitory complexes and other important campus structures.[12]

In 1938, Cassell and the University parted company after an acrimonious legal fight with President Mordecai Johnson. The utilization of black architects at Howard continued but with a differing and more orthodox arrangement. University commissions began to go to the recently established off-campus joint-venture practice of Hilyard Robinson and Paul Williams of Los Angeles.[13]

Three other black architect-educators arrived in Washington, DC, in the early 1920s along with Cassell. Each one differed from the preceding Tuskegeans, Lankford, Pittman and Hazel, in educational backgrounds. But despite an Ivy League education, Cassell was solidly in line with the Tuskegean's Booker T. Washington inspired nationalist ideology.

Howard Mackey and Hilyard Robinson received their architectural training at eastern Ivy League universities. Louis Fry, Sr., the other instrumental man in the development of the School of Architecture, was on campus in the 1930s in a non-teaching role. Fry was working in the on-campus Cassell office (he would later return to Howard in 1947 as a professor). Fry received his undergraduate education at Prairie View (a Texas HBCU), and a graduate architecture degree from Kansas State. Fry received another master's from the Harvard Graduate School of Design in 1946.

Over the period from 1926 to 1970, Mackey, Robinson, and Fry prepared people who would more resemble the white world's version of the evolving genteel architect. The architectural education philosophy and professional practice modus operandi of the three Howard educators was "professionalism." This was identical to the path the larger white architectural establishment was pursuing.

Howard would graduate scores of architects who returned to various parts of the US, the Caribbean Isles, Haiti, Puerto Rico, and the West African nations of Liberia, Ghana, Nigeria, and several other countries including India, Iran, and Israel. Differing from Tuskegee, the Howard faculty felt bound by the constraints of their commitment to secure national accreditation for the school. They sought the imprimatur of the still rigidly segregated and racist-minded white architectural profession and educational establishment.

CHAPTER 5

Williams, Robinson, Fry At Howard University, 1935–1955

In 1931, Howard Mackey organized an exhibition of the work of the handful of black architects practicing around the country. By 1934, Mackey would eventually succeed Hilyard Robinson as chairman of the architecture program. Mackey's pivotal Howard University Art Gallery exhibit included the work of Robert Taylor of Tuskegee, Paul Williams of Los Angeles, Calvin McKissack of Nashville, Tennessee, and practices in Chicago and Honolulu. The work of Mackey, Robinson, and Cassell was also showcased.

The presence of the work of Williams in this exhibit may have been a contributing cause of the eventual linking up of Robinson's office with Williams. This duo would join forces within several years of this exhibit, probably at Robinson's urgings. Their initial Washington, DC, commissions were for the design of large federally funded public housing projects. They would also receive commissions to design dormitories on the Howard campus.

Parallel to the Tuskegee and Howard University activities during the 1920s, Paul Williams began his career in Los Angeles as an architect. Williams began by registering with the state of California as a building designer in 1915. He would eventually achieve registration as an architect in 1923. In that same year Williams started what would soon mushroom into a notable professional practice.[1]

45

Williams was born in Los Angeles in 1884 and died there in 1979.[2] In his own words in an autobiographical article, Williams reports a chance exposure to William Pittman. Williams saw photographs, written words, and drawings of Pittman's 1907 competition winning Negro Building in Richmond, Virginia. Williams alludes to this encounter as a factor in his arriving at a position as a young man that it was possible to aspire to a career in architecture.

Several sources including Williams himself in the same autobiographical article have him being rebuffed in high school about his openly expressed desire to become an architect. The teacher attempting to counsel Williams about the folly of his desire is supposed to have made comments that still hold relevance to this day. Those comments highlight the disconnection between African-Americans and architecture. To paraphrase Williams, the teacher summed things up succinctly:

> ...*no white client would engage a black person in such a capacity and your own people don't have any use for architects...*

Of course the teacher was wrong on both counts even then in 1910. But that comment was certainly an accurate representation of near universal white and black perception at that time. In far too much of the black world, that perception has not changed significantly ninety years later. Williams would go on to pave the way for a significant Los Angeles wing of twentieth-century African-American architects. Many of them followed Williams in receiving academic training at the University of Southern California. The most notable ones were John D. Williams, James Garrott, Edward Barker, Carey Jenkins, Cleveland Wing, Robert Kennard, and Arthur Silvers.[3]

Paul Williams had much in common with Hilyard Robinson. Williams did some of his best design work in the new modernist idiom. He also designed in the Beaux Arts Georgian and Federal styles. But it was Robinson who made an exclusive commitment to avant-garde International Style modernism. While Williams was devoted to the idea of the modern house (he published a book on the subject), Robinson was devoted to the idea of "modern housing as social reform." He patterned himself after the Congress Internationale Architects Moderne. This association of socially progressive European architects and planners was known simply as CIAM. Robinson, through his European travels in the 1930s, actually spent time personally touring the modernist Gropius-Mies organized housing exhibitions in Germany. Robinson also toured modernist social housing projects in Amsterdam and Rotterdam.

Robinson's contract to design the 274 unit Langston Terrace public housing project in 1934 was his first big breakthrough. Robinson had completely reinvented himself since his undergraduate days at Columbia in the 1920s. Along the way he received strategic help from white progressive minded government officials. He became the country's foremost black modernist public housing design authority. His 1937-completed Langston Terrace project would win positive reviews from the widely read planner-sociologist and critic Lewis Mumford.

In order to acquire this career-establishing design commission, Robinson demonstrated great entrepreneurial skill and political acumen. With his own still small practice at the core, Robinson structured a "salt and pepper" architectural team. He joined with Williams and a respected and politically connected local white architect Irving Porter. Williams had built an impressive residential practice in Los Angeles. This shrewd relationship with Williams would lead to Robinson receiving Howard University commissions that would have been politically difficult for the University to justify. Federal overseers still retained control of critical aspects of campus development.

In 1941, Robinson sought out and received a major War Department commission. This required his joining forces with the McKissack family firm of Nashville, Tennessee.[4] Robinson was selected by progressive minded white officials at the Pentagon to design an air base at Tuskegee, Alabama. The base was to be used to train the nation's first black combat pilots. This was to the consternation of powerful white politicians and War Department civilians and military officers who were deeply vested in the idea that the term "black combat pilot" was an inherent contradiction. The McKissack firm, then headed by brothers Moses and Calvin, was certified as an architectural, engineering, and general building contracting firm in several deep south states. For this project, the War Department accepted a proposition of Robinson serving as design and production architect with the McKissacks acting as the general contractors.

From 1933 to 1947, Hilyard Robinson was running a very influential "teaching office" within walking distance of the Howard campus. While Robinson designed a number of important buildings on the campus, the most significant commission—in the evolution of black architects and engineers—was the late 1940s contract to design the 100,000 square foot School of Engineering and Architecture (the E&A) Building. This project was a joint venture with Paul Williams. Mackey, Cassell and Robinson all benefitted greatly from the tendency of progressively minded public officials—often Jewish. These officials included black architects on the design teams of large wartime-era public housing projects for blacks in Washington, DC.

In the 1940s and 400 miles to the north of DC, former Bauhaus director Walter Gropius had since left Nazi Germany. Gropius was settling in at Harvard as chair of the architecture department. Louis Fry, Sr. was the first African-American architect to graduate from the program under Gropius. Fry had been in DC from 1930 to 1935 when he was Cassell's chief of design. He eventually left Cassell's office and the campus in 1935 for a job at Tuskegee as a drawing instructor and campus architect. While at Tuskegee, Fry completed several major building projects for the campus of what is now Alabama State College.

In his autobiography, Fry states that he started an architecture department at Tuskegee in 1935.[5] We can only surmise that Robert R. Taylor's original 1892 architectural diploma program had atrophied by the time Fry arrived at Tuskegee. Fry left Tuskegee in 1940 for a similar position at Lincoln University in Missouri. He returned to Lincoln in 1946 right after receiving his master's degree from Harvard. By 1947, Fry was recruited away from Lincoln by Howard University. He came back to Washington, DC, as a practitioner and to Howard as a full professor of architecture. He returned to Howard with impeccable Gropius-Harvard inspired modernist architecture credentials and orientation.

Fry's return was in time to help prepare the first crop of second-generation Washington, DC, architects who were returning from World War II. His partner, Howard University professor John Welch, would eventually leave Howard for a deanship at Tuskegee. Welsh would open a Fry & Welch branch office. The Tuskegee office of Fry & Welch was another instance of the historically circular relationship of the Tuskegee and Howard architecture programs. While the architecture program was dormant at Tuskegee in the 1940s and 1950s, the Howard program was in full official ascendancy. Through Louis Fry, Sr.'s presence, the Howard program received full national accreditation in 1950.

The Howard program assumed a major role in the education of black architects in early 1950s upon gaining formal recognition from the American Collegiate Schools of Architecture (this body was the national accrediting agency for architectural education at that time). By the early 1970s, there was militant agitation by a small group of Washington, DC-based activist black architects and Howard professors (myself included) on behalf of the other HBCU-based programs. This group was instrumental in successfully highlighting the need for the accreditation of those programs.[6]

I arrived at the Robinson-Williams designed E&A Building in the fall of 1962. This was exactly ten years after the initial grand opening of the building for instruction. I was an experienced draftsman looking for a job in an architectural office. I quickly became aware of the existence of each of the black architectural practices in Washington, DC. Several of the principals were also teaching full-time or part-time in the Howard architecture program. These men were still at the top of their energy level. They had an unswerving dual commitment to full-time teaching loads and the development of their struggling off-campus practices.

Most of these practices were small enough to be conducted out of a decent sized single living room. That was not unlike the majority of white Washington, DC, practices. Among the black-owned practices, only Hilyard Robinson's practice could be considered significant in size. Robinson was able to offer employment opportunities to a number of graduate architects including several white architects with no previous affiliation with Howard. The University was far and away still the most important client for black architects. The University was the mainstay of Robinson's busy practice through the end of the 1970s.

There were no sizable black contractors, and only a single fledgling black developer in the DC of the early 1960s. However, there was a small but growing black middle class of civil servants, teachers, and Howard University professors. Some of them were in the position to afford a modest architect designed home. These private residential commissions, the black church, and miscellaneous additions and renovations work constituted the extent of non-government design contracts available to black architects. Several black churches were shrewd enough to build apartments for their congregations. This was another source of private work for black firms.

In retrospect, we can see three distinctive variations of professional practice agendas in the early to middle twentieth-century origins of black architects in America. There is the Taylor—Tuskegee branch of architecture as black social and economic development. There was the Hilyard Robinson-Howard University branch of elite "professionalism." There was also the Paul Williams branch that combines the Robinson-Howard style of practice with a race pride and "vindication of the race" angle.[7] All three of these tendencies are still intact today within the national black architect-practitioner community.

These architects rarely wrote or published other than occasionally on the narrowest technical level. In retrospect, we know how vitally important writing has been in establishing reputations. These architects were also without the benefit of architectural historians or wealthy private sector patrons. They were also without the benefit of the academics and critics who would have proselytized on behalf of the unsung black architects. Such people have been essential to the careers of now icon status white architects.[8]

CHAPTER 6

The 1920s Harlem Renaissance—Key Missed Connections

Indeed there are many attested influences of African art in French and German modernist art...the constructive lessons of African art are among the soundest, and most needed art creeds today...They emphasize intellectually significant form, abstractly balanced design, formal simplicity, restrained and emotional appeal...Surely the liberating example of such art will be as marked an influence in the contemporary work of Negro artists as it has been on leading modernists; Picasso, Modigliani, Matisse and others too numerous to mention."
Alain Locke, 1925

We must be ever mindful that in the first quarter of the twentieth-century there were essentially two American architectures. There was the near universal nationally adopted architecture of the classic Greco-Roman civilizations of western European antiquity. That is the architecture that the young white post-bellum American Republic was enthralled with. In the years leading up to the start of the Harlem Renaissance in 1920, the School of Architecture at Columbia was a dominant authority on architectural styles and tastes.[1] Such styles and tastes were exemplified by the classical Beaux Arts architecture of Daniel Burnham's 1893 Chicago World's Fair.

The new modernist architecture was a social, cultural, and ideological movement that was rampant throughout Western Europe. This architecture was just barely raising its head in urban America through

51

events like the Chicago Tribune Tower Competition of 1922. The competition was ultimately won with a Beaux Arts tower that showed unmistakable traces of being influenced by the new architecture. The modernist die was cast through non-winning schemes submitted by the young hard-core European modernists. The Tribune Towers winner, New Yorker Raymond Hood, would go on to design the Rockefeller Center complex. At that same time, Howard University philosophy professor Alain Locke was declaring a "Harlem Renaissance" and publishing his seminal book, *The New Negro* in 1925.

In the 1920s Harlem Renaissance decade, the American architect Frank Lloyd Wright was in a state of repose. Wright had designed a series of brilliant homes in suburban Chicago that came to be immortalized as the "Prairie Houses." Wright published books on his work that were intellectually and artistically devoured by the European architectural avant-garde. The Europeans were still grappling with how to turn Picasso's West African masks and sculpture derived cubist paintings into sticks, stones, bricks, and concrete.

Wright's designs were a unique blend of German Kindergarten pedagogy, Asian orient influences, and a homegrown Americana which he labeled as "organic." Wright would combine all of these facets a decade later in the mid-1930s. He did so in the masterful Falling Water at Bear Run Creek in Pennsylvania. Wright's client-patron was the progressively minded industrialist Edgar Kaufman. Elements of multi-cultural aesthetic influences (including black "jazz-age" cultural influences) were there in Wright's masterpiece for anyone willing to look critically.[2]

The new avant-garde European imported architecture, as well as Wright's quintessential American Prairie Houses, held a place in the dominant conservative American elite's consciousness. That place was similar to the role that Negro jazz occupied in the first quarter of the twentieth-century. That perspective held that jazz and Modern Architecture were only for the extremes of either the lowest classes and racial castes, or the amoral socialistic cultural avant-garde.

A number of credible scholars acknowledge the derivative relationship of turn of the twentieth-century architecture to the Cubist art movement lead by Picasso, Braque, and Gris.[3] This all ties into the grand icon of Modern Architecture, Charles Edouard Jenneret, or "Le Corbusier" as he is universally known. This seminal twentieth-century architect was a painter who was captivated by Picasso's cubist approach to art. That cubist fascination quickly became the defining characteristic of his architecture. Art historian Robert Hughes places things in perspective for us:

Attached to the idea that modern art was foreign was the notion that it was influenced by blacks and thus uncivilized. Cortissoz related it to "a world full of jazz"...sexual, convulsive, primitive. Since "primitivism" had been and still was a great issue in the European avant garde, through early Cubism and Expressionism, Cortissoz's observation was not altogether wrong; only his hostility was. Whereas most white Americans around 1910–20 thought of cakewalk, ragtime, and jazz as mere jungle music, French composers since the 1890s had taken it with the utmost seriousness, recognizing it for what it was: the great indigenous American musical form.[4]

The reasons that black culture and Modern Architecture failed to connect in the 1920s during the Harlem Renaissance are varied and often complex. Cruse's *Crisis of the Negro Intellectual* reminds us of the reality of the American social, economic, and cultural construct. America is a *nation of groups* despite the focus of the US Constitution on the *individual*:

The economic philosophy of the black bourgeoisie, whether radical or reform, reflects a kind of social opportunism that has been forced on this class by the American system. The black bourgeoisie is self-seeking but in a shortsighted, unsophisticated, apolitical and cowardly fashion. It is one of the rare bourgeoisie classes of color that will sell itself out to white power without a principled struggle for its economic rights.[5]

Cruse's words might also shed some light on today's African-American architects. There is a magnificent world acclaimed black cultural scene raging around them to no apparent visible effect in their work. Again I look to Cruse, this time by repeating words he reminds us that Richard Wright uttered. Wright was struggling to come to grips with the reality of a Black Nationalist culture:

> *No attempt is being made here to propagate a specious and blatant nationalism. Yet the national character of the Negro people is unmistakable. Psychologically this nationalism is reflected in the whole of Negro culture, and especially folklore. Let those who shy at the nationalist implications of Negro life look at the body of folklore, living and powerful, which rose out of a unified sense of common life and common fate.*[6]

Richard Wright's seventy-year-old words remind us that *African-American architects must understand themselves to be* **cultural** *agents* rather than merely technically oriented business persons. However, matters are further clarified by Cruse as he illuminates the soul-searching twists and turns of Malcolm X and Du Bois on the questions of nationalism versus integration, and the Du Boisian "double-consciousness" theory:

> *American Negro history is basically a history of the conflict between integrationist forces and nationalist forces in politics, economics* **and culture***, no matter what leaders are involved and what slogans are used (bold italics mine).*

So much else was occurring in the world swirling around Harlem. Not the least activity was the Marcus Garvey movement that was vying for the attention of Harlem residents. Cruse puts his finger on what was probably the most far reaching development:

> *During the 1920s, the development in America of mass cultural communications media—radio, films, [the] recording industry, and ultimately television—drastically altered the classic character of capitalism as described by Karl Marx.*[7]

We also are indebted to Cruse for placing the Harlem Renaissance inside of an extremely important larger American context of time and cultural development:

> *The 1920s renaissance was actually a culminating phase of a previous renaissance that had emerged with the initial growth of black Harlem around 1910. James Weldon Johnson refers to it as the 'third theatrical period.' The second or middle period had begun in 1890. It can be said that the modern Negro artistic movement that produced the music, dance, and theatrical innovations that left their ineradicable mark on America, began with the second period in 1890.*[8]

Like Cruse above, Alain Locke comments below on the scope and depth of the Harlem Renaissance when he observed that:

> *This movement would, we think, be well under way in more avenues of advance at present but for the timid conventionalism which racial disparagement has forced upon the Negro mind in America.*

I take the liberty to speculate that Locke would have included architecture under *"more avenues,"* but there were other major limiting factors. No matter the optimistic gloss, Harlem was still an occupied quarter that was owned mostly by white absentee landlords and shopkeepers.

Alain Locke joined the Howard faculty in 1912 as a professor of English after a series of distinguished academic achievements including having been a Rhodes Scholar. Before joining Howard, he made a stop in Tuskegee where he seriously considered an offer from Booker T. Washington. By 1917, Locke was a professor of philosophy on the Howard campus. He was vigorously championing the cause of a "school of Negro art."[9] By then, he was a major figure in the Harlem Renaissance. He was on the Howard University campus exhorting the fine arts faculty and students to use their art to express the black experience and aesthetic.[10] A number of artists that Locke came in contact with on and off campus proceeded to do this brilliantly.

Lois Mailou Jones was on the Howard campus by 1930 and was a prime example of the fruits of Locke's exhortation to the black artists.[11] Jones, in a small way, was eventually responsible for bridging the fine arts program's art department and the architecture department through a course in water color painting that she taught every spring. She would be later be joined by renowned artist James Wells who offered a course in freehand drawing that was also a freshman architecture course requirement.

Locke was in contact with all of the seminal black art figures based in New York. Locke was an admirer of Aaron Douglas, who was producing brilliant cubist-inspired art work in the 1920s. Locke considered Douglas to be the leader of the small group of black visual arts modernists. He chose Douglas hands down to be the illustrator of the book, *The New Negro.* There is a reasonable certainty that these artists were deeply conscious of the black jazz and blues musical geniuses of their day, including Duke Ellington.[12]

Parallel to the beginning of the Harlem Renaissance in 1920, young German aristocrat and architect Walter Gropius was setting up the Bauhaus in Dessau. Gropius would gather around him a collection of architects and artists who would advance the new modernist architecture throughout Europe. These men would eventually arrive in America to posts in elite design schools. Modernism and its relationship to community development and social housing was also a raging issue amongst this growing avant-garde movement. The Europeans pursued architecture in conjunction with painting and sculpture.

The relationship between African art and western modernism was at the very heart of the concerns of Locke and other key theoreticians and activists of the Harlem Renaissance.[13] Yet despite young Howard architecture department chair Hilyard Robinson's interest in modernism and social housing, there is little tangible evidence of a functional connection between him and Locke. No evidence has surfaced to indicate that the black architects on the New York scene during the Harlem Renaissance decade of the 1920s were forcefully pressing a cultural point of view. Yet the notion that architecture was a critical cultural art form was *precisely* the position of the proselytizing European modernist architects.

The white intellectuals who frequented Harlem and befriended the black writers, poets, and artists were of no help to the promulgation of a black modernist architect movement. At the turn of the twentieth-century, the act of a white person listening to music in a club, buying recordings, viewing paintings in a gallery, or buying paintings by black people was not dependent on the establishment of intimate personal relationships between equals. A white person (or institution) hiring a black architect to design a residence, industrial facility, school, eating establishment, social club, or bank would be similar to entering a marriage—complete with real sex. The white-black relationships of the 1920s Harlem Renaissance did involve sex. But that was not the kind of relationship of true social equals that had to exist between an architect and his patron-client.[14]

In parallel to the 1920s Harlem Renaissance movement, Los Angeles architect Paul Williams saw no prospects of building a practice that would be dependent on the black community. Williams saw his opportunities with a small elite group of wealthy white people of liberal to progressive-radical political leanings. Those personalities saw a personal glorification in having a "Negro architect" design their home.

Wesley Henderson, in his doctoral dissertation, places Williams in New York in the mid-1930s in the probable acquaintance of Carl Van Vechten, a white intellectual and professional photographer. Cruse placed Van Vechten at the center of the prior Harlem Renaissance decade. A July 1937 issue of the widely subscribed *American Magazine* contained a lengthy article by Williams titled "I Am a Negro."[15]

The social and political views Williams expressed in that article infuriated or dismayed many influential black people and black organizations. Black New York City-based Pittsburgh Courier columnist George S. Schuyler, a bitter skeptic of the previous decade's Harlem Renaissance movement, lashed out at Williams. Schuyler's vitriolic denunciation served to reinforce the image of the black architect as a culturally sterile and politically amoral elitist technocrat. That was most likely already the image of the black architect held by most progressive cultural intellectuals of that era.

Geographically closer to Harlem was Washington, DC, and Howard University. Locke was on a campus that had a fine arts school, as well as a fledgling architecture school. Unfortunately these two schools were not on the same page relative to the issues and ideological notions of black culture and a black aesthetic. Kelly Miller, a major dean at Howard, has a lengthy article in Locke's book *The New Negro*. Miller merely notes in passing that the University awarded a single B.S. in Architecture degree that year. Howard graduated no more than eight architects over that 1920s, decade-long Harlem Renaissance period.[16]

In fairness, certainly the leadership of the architecture program at Howard saw a role in and responsibility to the economically and socially depressed condition of the black race:

> *Our teaching must reflect the fact that the young Negro trained as an architect and handling problems originating essentially among the Negro masses, urban and rural, still has the work of a pioneer to do.*

These were the words of the architect Hilyard Robinson, chairman of the architecture department in 1933, according to late historian Harrison Etheridge. We can reasonably infer that those words were reflective of Robinson's thinking throughout the preceding 1920s of the Harlem Renaissance. Robinson was most likely the most progressively minded practicing black architect in America during the 1920s. His avant-garde leanings were squarely in line with the social housing and town planning movements of Europe and America.

But in sharp contrast to visual artists such as Aaron Douglas, Robinson—*like most other African-American architects*—had been socialized to see architecture only in White Anglo-Saxon Protestant cultural terms. In the early 1920s, Robinson was commuting to the University of Pennsylvania in Philadelphia to study in a Beaux Arts program. He was spending summers in New York working for Vertner Tandy, a Robert Taylor-Tuskegee trained architect. Tandy became the first black registered architect in New York in 1912 after graduating from Cornell in 1908. Robinson transferred to Columbia and was there in the latter part of the 1920s Harlem Renaissance decade completing work on his master's degree.

Robinson would shortly become fully enmeshed in the Modern Architecture movement through his European travels after graduating from the still Beaux Arts dominated Columbia University. Robinson's nearest black counterparts on the New York City scene were architects such as John Lewis Wilson and Robinson's former summer employer Vertner Tandy. Between 1923 and 1928, Wilson was also completing the Beaux Arts curriculum at Columbia. By the early 1930s and the start of Depression Era New Deal public works programs, Wilson would benefit from Harlem community agitation.

Wilson would be included as one of seven architects hired by the New Deal Work Progress Administration—known as the WPA. The charge of this architectural consortium was to design the sprawling 600-unit Harlem River Houses public housing complex. The project opened for occupancy in 1937. During the Harlem Renaissance period, Wilson most likely held progressive social views about the emerging Modern Architecture movement and social housing.

No evidence indicates that Wilson or Tandy were advocating a black architectural component to the Negro intellectuals' and artists' movement of the 1920s Harlem Renaissance period. Tandy was an otherwise important figure in turn of the century Harlem. Tandy designed homes in Harlem as well as upstate New York for black hair-care industrialist Madam C.J. Walker between 1912 and 1917.[17] In the book, *On Her Own Ground*, Walker's great-great-granddaughter A'Lelia Bundles has provided extensive detail about the fruitful business relationship between Walker and Tandy. In his designs for Madam Walker's homes, Tandy showed no apparent interest in either a Picasso-Cubist inspired modernism or an Afrocentrist vernacular.

We are left to speculate, hopefully usefully, about the course of African-American architectural history had a Madam Walker type patron commissioned an Aaron Douglas minded black architect to design a house or apartment building. Such an act might have been on par with Le Corbusier's stream of villa commissions by Parisian artists, intellectuals, and industrialists of the 1920s.[18] The teaming of Douglas with a technically competent black architect such as a Vertner Tandy to address functional and constructability issues could have easily rendered this to be a plausible scenario. The clues to a probable outcome are readily available in the world-renowned murals Douglas executed for the Countee Cullen Branch of the New York Public Library. The very words used by Douglas to describe his intent in those panels provide ample fuel for this line of speculation:

> The first of four murals…indicates the African cultural background of American Negroes. Dominant in it are the strongly rhythmic arts of music, the dance, and sculpture—and so the drummers, the dancers, and the carved fetish represent the exhilaration and rhythmic pulsation of Africa.[19]

Douglas describes panel four of the quartet of murals in a way that hits home in the most gut-wrenching fashion:

> A great migration, away from the clutching hands of serfdom in the South to the urban and industrial life in America, began during the First World War. And with it there was born a new will to creative self-expression which quickly grew in the New Negro Movement of the 'twenties…

Tragically absent from this period of the Harlem Renaissance was a black architect counterpart of Aaron Douglas, whose demonstrably cubist-inspired design ideology, skill, and passion was clearly equal to the skills and passion of avant garde European and American architects of that period. That absence has had a lasting deleterious effect on the position of the black architect in black and larger American culture.[20] Contrary to Douglas and his art, the handful of blacks attracted to architecture *were socialized away from seeing architecture as an appropriate media for expressing black culture and struggle.*

Rather, the black architect came to believe that architecture was a medium best used to demonstrate the parity of black technical competency with white architects. In architecture, black architects believed that their primary role was to demonstrate mastery in the use of the dominant style of the conservative white elites. Black intellectuals were not entirely innocent in propagating the view that architecture was too concrete to express universal black cultural ideas. Yet the European and American avant-garde architect was encouraged to view architecture as *precisely* the right medium for expressing (white) culture. In discussing the work of Douglas, the late Columbia University scholar Nathan Huggins had this to say:

> *...The objects that he worked with could only suggest. They could not be something that was palpable. The more recognizable a thing was—the more particular—the less essential and universal. His work was, thus necessarily abstract: mere design through which he wanted one to see a soul-self which united one with race, race with humanity, and man with God...*[21]

We are left to wishfully speculate about the tantalizing results that would have arisen if Douglas, like Frank Lloyd Wright or Le Corbusier, had turned to architecture as his primary medium of cultural expression. Wright's Prairie Houses of the first decade of the twentieth-century, along with his churches and other culture related structures, were an attempt to express the essence of (white) American culture, spirit, and oneness with nature. Le Corbusier's early architectural intentions were meant to express the essence of French and European culture in the emerging *Machine Age* era.

Since the Harlem Renaissance, black music, black literature and critical components of black performing and plastic arts have been acclaimed the world over. So also are the black men and women who have made, and continue to make, that music, literature, and performing arts. The then still new American nation's musical, artistic, and architectural expressions cannot be neatly categorized or compartmentalized from each other. There is a consensus that the 300-year African-American slavery experience resulted in one of America's original art forms of the blues and jazz music. The same impact of that black experience would also have to apply in large measure to the new turn of the twentieth-century modern art and architectural design aesthetic of the young American nation.

CHAPTER 7

Engineering, Kindergarten, West Africa, and Cubism

As background to today's modern art and architecture, a brief summary tour of the past several thousand years of how western architectural development is universally taught will be useful for the otherwise reasonably informed lay reader. From the perspective of most architectural historians, history usually starts in earnest with the fifth-century BC "golden age" of Periclean Greece. Things move rapidly from that point to Imperial Rome of 2000 years ago and the dominating architect, Vitruvius.[1]

The immortal three-word dictum *"firmness, commodity, and delight"* is the Vitruvian definition of architecture that has endured through the past 500 years since the Italian Renaissance as the consensus standard definition of architecture in the western world. Today's architectural history books usually move perfunctorily through the period between the dawn of the Imperial Roman Empire in 400 AD and the onset of the thirteenth and fourteenth century periods of European gothic architecture.

The period in between the fall of Rome and the start of gothic architecture is generally referred to as the "middle ages" or "dark ages." In the thirteenth and fourteenth centuries, great emphasis is placed on having architecture students learn to identify pictures of the plans and photographed perspective views of the magnificent soaring gothic cathedral structures by name. The cathedrals are conceded to be the works of obscure "master builders" rather than architects.

When the architectural historian fast-forwards to the revered fifteenth-century Italian Renaissance several names of architects are literally engraved in stone. We absolutely *must* know Brunnelleschi, Alberti and Michelangelo. And then there is the near sainted Andrea Palladio.[2] Each one worked in the service of historically significant popes and merchant princes. Each one was as much artist and master builder as architect. These architects form a sacred part of the architecture catechism.

Historians spend some time on the period between the end of the Italian Renaissance and the onset of the nineteenth-century precursors to the modern period. But it is manifestly clear that the main event is the onset of "modernism" toward the end of the nineteenth-century. The mainstream historians are in consensus that this new modernist period holds up throughout the 1960s. By then, the period between the onset of the 15th century Italian renaissance and the mid-nineteenth-century was brought back on stage as a legitimate source of exterior applications of design devices and features. In architecture this line of thinking became popularly known as "post-modernism."

There is a plethora of names of late nineteenth-century and early twentieth-century architects that the architectural world shares consensus on as the heroes and high priests of Modern Architecture. These men are grouped in two tiers: the first constitutes the original "form givers." The trinity of men best represented by this group is the American Frank Lloyd Wright, the Swiss-Frenchman Le Corbusier, and the German Mies van der Rohe.[3]

There is also a strictly American trinity of architectural form givers. This is again Wright, joined by his mentor and Chicago skyscraper icon Louis Sullivan, and the rotundas Paris trained Romanesque architect Henry Hobson Richardson.[4] A collection of early twentieth-century Europeans has been accorded second-tier status to the form giving trinity of Wright, Le Corbusier, and Mies. Several of these men actually preceded the sainted trinity. This second group would include the German

Walter Gropius, Dutchman J.J.P. Oud, Scandinavian Alvar Aalto, Frenchman August Perret, Austrian Adolf Loos, and Scotsman Charles Rennie Mackintosh.

The problem, as I am constantly reminding students and young faculty, is that this unconditional hero worship of early twentieth-century modern architects is misplaced. The real heroes were the nineteenth-century scientists, engineers, and miscellaneous technologists. The real accomplishments are the marvelous practical applications of science these men brought to bear in the solution of mid-nineteenth-century Industrial Revolution induced building problems.[5]

Architectural historians tend to obscure the projects and people who provided us with, for instance, the solutions to the materials and technical connections problem of the skeletal frame that made high-rise buildings possible. Without such engineer and technologist inspired framing materials and techniques, there could be no high-rise structures for architects to wrap seductive cultural message bearing curtain wall-type skins around.

No such high-rise skeletal framed building is of the slightest practical value without the key features of the Eiffel Tower of the Paris World Exhibition of 1867. Here engineers brought together and solved the problem of the need for high-speed elevators, high-strength steel, and sophisticated wind resistant structural connections. High-strength, reinforced concrete is another engineering breakthrough that allowed our early twentieth-century modernist heroes to turn Picasso's West African aesthetic-based Cubist art into architecture.

Bridge building engineers solved real needs for incredibly large spans by their creative use of steel or concrete. This also provided the tools and techniques that would allow architects to build with artistry that extended beyond purely practical considerations. Much too little attention is directed to, for instance, the Great Exhibition of 1851 (better known as the Crystal Palace of London). This one million square foot structure of steel framed glass enclosed exhibition space rivals the magnificent soaring railroad stations of Europe. Horticulturist Joseph Paxton, who created the Crystal Palace, along with the designers of most of the grand railroad terminals of Western Europe, was not an architect.[6] Historian Ian Sutton gives us another way to think about the engineer in comparison to the lionized architect during the nineteenth-century:

> *Engineering—in the sense of the science and technique of construction—has always been part of architecture, but in the nineteenth-century with the development of new materials it became a subject for specialists. The two professions drew apart and for reasons of cultural snobbery, critics were reluctant to give them equal esteem. Architecture, after all, was an art; engineering required only technical expertise. But at a certain point it was realized (sooner by some than by others) that while the art of architecture was apparently headed for a cul-de-sac, the science of engineering was only discovering its potential. Now, in retrospect, it seemed to many that it was engineers who had been the real pioneers and that the way forward was through new technical processes, new materials and a new aesthetic of functionalism. The search for style was over.*[7]

Translation: it would be impossible to imagine the modern world, as we know it without engineers and scientists. Conversely, a plausible case can be made that "beauty"—the commodity that architects contend is their real expertise and contribution to society—would be ever present in an all engineer-scientist world. People who made no clear distinctions between themselves as builders, engineers, or architects have handed down the notion of beauty through the ages.

The history that will be written in the twenty-first century may show that the modern European architect icons of the early twentieth-century were more propagandists than critical innovators. The new history may show that engineers and scientist were the real heroes we should be enshrining.[8] For the next generation of African-American architects, a much deeper review of the true contributions of nineteenth and early twentieth-century engineers and scientists is a first order of business. The next order is for deeper reviews of the influence of Cubist art and jazz and blues music on Modern Architecture. The need for a complete integration of all black art forms with architecture must take place. This will only happen through new realizations throughout Black America that presumptively "white" Modern Architecture can be no whiter than today's American music and other cultural art forms.

Architect-author Norman Brosterman's research reinforces his contention about German kindergarten founder Friedrich Froebal's (1782–1852) educational philosophy. Brosterman has shown how that philosophy has influenced the course of western art history over the last 150 years.[9] It turns out that a number of the most towering figures of the turn of the twentieth-century modern art and architecture movement studied under strong variants of the Froebal system in their kindergarten years.

Most people in or near twentieth-century architectural lore are familiar with the story of American architectural genius Frank Lloyd Wright's mother. She used a set of educational toys to shape the mind of the young Wright during his early formative years of life.[10] I have for a long time been intrigued by the thought of what might have been the impact of the wholesale access and use of Froebal's revolutionary educational pedagogy on the black toddlers of newly freed African slaves in 1865:

> *In effect the early kindergartners created an enormous international program designed specifically to alter the mental habits of the general populace, and in their capable hands nineteenth-century children from Austria to Australia learned a new visual language. While focusing on kindergarten's many educational and social benefits, these pioneers overlooked a potentially radical outcome of their efforts that is obvious in retrospect: kindergarten taught abstraction (bold italics mine)...By explicitly equating ideas, symbols, and things, it encouraged abstract thinking, and in its repetitive use of geometric forms as the building blocks of design, it taught children a new and highly disciplined way of making art...By emphasizing abstraction, kindergarten encouraged the value of unconventional reasoning...If one intended to shake up Victorian society and affect broad change in the areas of philosophy, music, science, and art, exposing nineteenth-century preschoolers to the influence of a regime like the Froebelian kindergarten would be a good place to*

begin...We are justified, then, in asking whether the great change that occurred after 1900 in visual design and the plastic arts, the cultural domain with which kindergarten's language of form was most closely allied, was related in any way to the spread of kindergarten.[11]

Keep in mind that Brosterman is describing an educational movement that was sweeping through the European population that would eventually arrive on American soil. The movement would arrive at a time in history when it was illegal to teach the still enslaved black population to read. Blacks were to be taught only to accept their fate as an innately inferior people whose lot in life was to hew wood and carry water for the white populace. Brosterman hammers home the profoundly influencing impact of German kindergarten on Modern Architecture. He has neatly tied kindergarten together with Cubism and with the twentieth-century's two modern architect-fountainheads:

The triumph of Cubism and geometric abstraction came just as architects were searching for new modes of expression. Their simultaneous adoption by architecture, which was recently untethered from classical models and possessed a grab bag of nifty technologies, was assured....Architecture was not, generally speaking, an **influence on art, but Cubism, Futurism, and Neo-Plasticism found their way into architecture, and brought kindergarten along for the ride** *(bold italics mine)....Even more direct connections can be drawn, however, between kindergarten and the profound shift in architectural expression that occurred in the early twentieth-century. If, as a kind of case study, we look at the work and writings of the two architects conventionally thought to be the century's greatest, Frank Lloyd Wright and Le Corbusier, we can find suggestive evidence pointing to a fact that has been confirmed by their biographies; both were children of the original kindergarten.*[12]

As further reinforcement of the role of West African art-based cubism, we need to inject the words of British architect-professor Tom Porter as he reminds us that:

*Linear perspective was completely abandoned in the early twentieth century by the cubist painters who, influenced by Cezanne's perceptual rationale of form, Kepler's cine-camera and **primitive African abstractions of space**, experimented with the portrayal of the whole structure of any given object and its position in space...(bold italics mine)*[13]

The primary source that Picasso attributes his invention of the cubist style of painting is West African artwork and mask making. The African artwork awoke within Picasso a whole new way of seeing and thinking about representation. Le Corbusier quickly adopted this new phenomenology as he moved between his painting and his architecture. The other European masters picked up on the cubist architecture and the rest is twentieth-century architectural history. The new West African derived way of seeing, thinking, and drawing by the European art and architecture masters was based on an animating West African spirit and genius. That is the same spirit that spawned the black musical genius that invented the indigenous American art form of the blues and jazz music.

CHAPTER 8

The "Music-Art-Architecture" Triptych

In the chapter "From Duke Ellington to Wynton Marsalis" in Dick Russell's book *Black Genius*, Russell quotes Marsalis:

> *The musicians who are the most successful are the ones who cause the most eras to resonate....In democracy, as in jazz, you have freedom with restraint. It's not absolute freedom, it's freedom within a structure...Played properly, jazz shows you how the individual can negotiate the greatest amount of personal freedom and put it humbly at the service of a group conception...*[1]

Most architects that were trained in the modernist idiom will vouch for the interchangeability of those words and thoughts with the best and most enduring aims of Modern Architecture. On the Modern Architecture scene today in America *New York Times* architecture critic Herbert Muschamp forcefully reminds us of the "unchallengeable" supremacy that Jewish architects occupy today in the world of architecture. *That appears to be precisely equivalent to the supremacy that African-Americans hold in the twentieth-century world of modern music generally, and America's "classical" music, the blues and jazz specifically.*

From time to time a major black intellectual will draw a metaphoric allusion to the relationship of music and architecture with telling insight. I read profound significance in the way master black cultural intellectual Albert Murray and his apt pupil, the iconoclastic Stanley Crouch, contrasted music and architecture. In commenting on the seminal twentieth-century American musical genius Duke Ellington and that seminal twentieth-century American architectural genius Frank Lloyd Wright, they remarked:

> ...As the master bluesologist Albert Murray has observed, he (Ellington) is tuned into Frank Lloyd Wright through his successful invention of a musical architecture that blends so perfectly with the shifting inner and outer landscapes of American life.[2]

As seemingly insignificant and casual as is the Murray and Crouch allusion to architecture, it is highly useful. But Murray and Crouch had it only half right. A "musical architecture" and its flipside "architectural music" are fitting metaphors for Wright and Ellington. Both men were raised by bright and ambitious mothers. Along the way, both mothers convinced their precocious sons that they were very special persons who had been put on earth to do important things. Wright's intense interest in music is well documented in the many biographies about the man.

Ellington's interest in and knowledge of architecture was clearly evident in his sartorial splendor and sophisticated style. Ellington's vast range of interest included a pronounced appreciation of art and architecture. In Ellington's autobiography, *Music is My Mistress*, he reminds us of his more than casual interest and skills in art and drawing as a child. Ellington actually received an art scholarship to Pratt Institute in Brooklyn. In his autobiography, there is a page where Ellington blows a "riff" that he simply titles "Walls." There he reveals an understanding of architecture that exceeds that of some of the world's most acclaimed twentieth-century architects. When Ellington passed through Hong Kong in 1972, he labeled that city's "...soaring skyscrapers" as "...man's phallic symbols." Ellington was quite insistent about the interchangeability of music and design.[3]

While a great deal has been made of Wright's fondness for European classical music, Wright most certainly was in tune on some level of consciousness to Ellington's (and his predecessors Louis Armstrong and Scott Joplin) creation of brilliantly architectonic music.

Wright may never have admitted to such awareness of America's black musical geniuses but that does not affect the inevitability of the impact of those men on Wright's architectonic evolution.

One is usually left with having to speculate about what thoughts today's young black intellectuals may harbor about architecture. In New York University professor Robin Kelley's *Yo' Mama's Disfunktional: Fighting the Culture Wars in Urban America*, the word *architecture* is rarely explicitly used. However, this powerful and compact feat of wide-ranging scholarship and often-brilliant insight makes it clear that Kelly will have much to contribute on the subject of architecture if he takes an inclination to do so.[4] The same can be said for most of the intellectuals who contributed articles to the book *The House That Race Built*. Particular attention should be paid to the chapters written by Evelyn Higginbotham and David Lionel Smith where each of those intellectuals explore the subject of *black culture.*

Forty years ago in architecture school some of us would pose the question—*where are our architectural equivalents of Joplin, Armstrong, Ellington, Miles, and Coltrane?* The usual retort of—*where are our client equivalents of Rockefeller, Mellon, Carnegie, and Hearst?*—missed the point. The next generation of African-American architects should no longer have to wonder—as some of us did incessantly back then—as to the whereabouts of the Frank Lloyd Wright class black architectural genius.

Once one is able to grasp the interchangeability of jazz and blues musical creation and performance with modernist architectural creation and performance, such questions answer themselves. *The cultural conditions that produced black musical genius has also already produced black architectural genius. Acquiring the confidence to proclaim that genius through analysis and scholarship is the task at hand today for the next generation of designer-scholars.*

A closer re-reading of Albert Murray serves to reinforce the notion of music, art, and architecture as the inextricably entwined cultural base of any substantial nation, nationality, or ethnic group. In discussing the inter-connectivity of all art forms and culture, Murray puts things into sharp perspective:

The creation of an art style is, as most anthropologists would no doubt agree, a major cultural achievement. In fact it is the highest as well as the most comprehensive fulfillment of culture; for an art style reflects nothing so much as the ultimate synthesis and refinement of a life style. Art is by definition a process of stylization; and what it objectifies, embodies, abstracts, expresses, and symbolizes is a sense of life....Accordingly, what is represented in **music, dance, painting, sculpture, literature, and architecture** *of a given group of people in a particular time, place, and circumstance is a conception of the essential nature and purpose of human existence itself (bold italics mine)*[5]

There is certainly no reason for assuming or believing that the culture of the United States is not the sum of all of its art forms including music and architecture. In fact, given the uniqueness and relatively newness of the just over 200-year-old American nation and her "gumbo stew" of racial strains and cultures, the case for the inseparability of American art, architecture, and music is even stronger.[6] In accepting the proposition that:

...All the arts are really just one art differently expressed because their materials are different...[7]

The question is not just *"where is Black Architecture?"* It is also "why has *American* architecture, unlike American music and to some extent American art, been able—with such spectacular success—to avoid appearing to have anything to do with black culture, black experiences, and black aesthetic notions?" Thus, the search over all these years has in actuality been to find answers to what I see as the *ironic disconnection* between black culture and modern American architecture. This disconnection is in the minds of black as well as white people. This disconnection is in sharp contrast to the connection that exists between black culture and American music in the minds of nearly all blacks and most other Americans.

The reality is that twentieth-century modern American architecture is as black as it is white (or Euro-American)—in the same vein as

American music. Stated bluntly, a legitimate question would be "if modern American music is so thoroughly infused with a black aesthetic, how can modern American art and architecture not also reflect a black aesthetic?"

None of this speculation is aimed at taking anything away from anyone. The objective is simply to open a thoughtful dialogue that can lead to the ending of the long and tragic exclusion of Black America from a rightful share in the ownership of the twentieth-century American architectural aesthetic. The same joint custody that is acknowledged toward Black America's relationship and ownership of America's musical heritage should pertain to architecture.

In this vein, the most recent New York City Black Architecture movement led by Jack Travis must not be confused or conflated with the more formalist notions of a timeless Afrocentric architecture.[8] That particular revivalist school of thought was usually meant to imply an as yet unresolved theory of atavistic cultural remnants from Pharonic Egypt. The thinking was that there might still be aesthetic representations of ancient Egypt present in today's architecture throughout the African Diaspora physical world.[9]

The Pharonic Egypt school of thought holds that a black race of people built those 4,000-year-old pyramids and other stone monuments.[10] This idea holds plausibility only in the sense that in another 1,000 years the North American continent may be considered as having been inhabited by a "black" race. There will certainly be enough cultural evidence to support such a proposition. But as to the philosophically static and caste based slave civilization of Pharonic Egypt, this idea of a "black" race of Egyptians is also a potential albatross around today's collective black neck.

This position appears to prematurely place a lesser value on non-stone cultures of black western and central sub-Saharan African societies. The position panders to the perception as well as the reality that white western civilization has higher respect for monumental stone architecture than it does for the less monumental adobe (or mud) architecture of western Africa (Wilson Jeremiah Moses brings great clarity and depth to this in his engrossing book *Afrotopia: The Roots of African American Popular History*).[11] However, the Pharonic Afrocentrist can take heart that there was indeed a formidable black stone building culture within the last 500 years in the south central African region of modern day Zimbabwe.

On the possibility of a historical African architectural influence in America, I am much more susceptible to the proposition of architectural heritage being found 2,500 miles west of the Nile Valley in the 1,000 to 1,500 AD Mali, Songhay, and Ghana empires. I would also include the slightly earlier Nigerian Nok culture of ceramic arts, and iron ore smelting technology in that same region of western Africa. It might also be of some interest to note the similar relationship in time of those West African periods to the fifteenth-century Italian Renaissance.

Architecturally, the Italian Renaissance is about the rebirth of Imperial Rome of 2,000 years ago. An interesting question might be *"what were the parallel West African empires and cultures a rebirth of?"* There is a strong likelihood that the answer will be found a lot closer geographically to the western coast of 1,000–1,500 AD Africa than the lower Nile River and Mediterranean Sea of 4,000 years ago. In short, West African influence on American architecture is far more profound than the currently popular one and only purported African influence of the Louisiana "shotgun" house.[12]

The late 1960s saw the apparent collapse of the authority of orthodox International Style architecture. The new order saw the resort to renaissance classical devices or allusions as a legitimate design ideology. Concurrent to this "new" architecture, African-American artists were in sync with the thrusting of the civil rights movement into an irrepressible quest for black power, black dignity, and a black aesthetic. A variation of the 1920s Harlem Renaissance era was back with a vengeance in the 1960s Black Power-Black Arts Movement.

Painters, sculptors, and other artists on Howard's campus during the 1960s were uncompromising in proclaiming their work and aims as black art. An influential group of New York artists lead by Romare Bearden (who was an artistically awakening teenager during the 1930s in Harlem) was a prominent example. We own much to art scholar Sharon Patton for reminding us of Bearden's motivation:

> *Bearden's modernist aesthetic is based upon black cultural sources: African art, African-American quilts, and jazz. The cuttings of paper, the reassembling of segments of photographic reproductions (water, grass, metal, wood, leaves, cloth, art—often African art) create fractured forms, simple shapes and an elaborate abstract design from which figures, landscapes, and the architecture of the street emerge...Bearden realized Alain Locke's goals for the "New Negro" artist: African art as the formal foundation for his collages, and African-American folk culture—strip quilt and jazz—as the subject-matter and basis for his compositional design.*[13]

Today in the year 2001, a New York City movement, centered on architect Jack Travis, is amassing an impressive body of important work for a range of sophisticated high profile African-Americans. These affluent clients are interested in what Travis terms "culture specific" work. To the extent that today's Jack Travis-led New York architects are focused on the combination of African-American and West African culture, they are on solid ground. That interconnected continuum of the last 500 years as the primary sources of their work holds immense and exciting possibilities for "Black Architecture."[14]

There was clearly a nascent "Black Architecture" from the 1890s Tuskegee era that was not sustained beyond that period. For that failure, black architects are now paying a painful price. That failure has now metastasized into major consequences for the psyche, image, cultural relevance, and economic effectiveness of today's black architect. A continuation of that turn of the twentieth-century "Black Architecture" could have been holistically rooted firmly in the cultural values and the rudimentary economics of Black America. There could have been a physical manifestation for an unbroken continuity between the tactically accommodationist policies first articulated in the 1895 Atlanta Compromise speech by Booker T. Washington, and the nearly identical position espoused by a disillusioned W.E.B. Du Bois forty years later.

CHAPTER 9

Blacks and Jews as America's Twin Cultural Engines

"Colleagues are few, exemplars and mentors fewer. Business contacts are made in social settings to which one is not always invited. Lacking experience in big projects, one is rarely entrusted with such jobs—and therefore never gets the needed experience. All told, it is difficult to be a black architect, even in the best of times."
David Dunlap, 1994

"A generation ago, Jews were American architecture's most enlightened patrons. Now they are its most gifted practitioners too."
Herbert Muschamp, 1996

Charles Murray, author of the provocative book *The Bell Curve*, thinks architecture is a high IQ profession.[1] Murray may possibly be influenced by the current apparent dominance of the field by Jewish architects heralded by influential *New York Times* architectural critic Herbert Muschamp. I say *apparent* dominance because one should be wary of assuming that specialized media dominance, based on the design of high-profile cultural complexes is *actual* dominance—but that is another story.

On "Affirmative Action," there are two clear polarized positions in Black America and conservative (and much of liberal) White America. The consensus black position is that *test scores be damned; only one percent of the seats at elite university professional schools are*

77

simply unacceptable. The white and Jewish position is that *in the deter-mination of who gets seated in those schools, either you tested on the right side of the Bell Curve or you didn't—case closed.*[2]

For the record, I see no earthly reason that thinking African-Americans should feel self-consciousness about "goals and quotas" in elite schools. Immeasurable financial rewards and political connections result from attending such schools. This is the reality despite conservative black intellectual Shelby Steele's principled and passionate argument to the contrary.[3] Black America would be foolish to abandon affirmative action without a concrete financial concession on its replacement. Moreover, that replacement can only be made available within the boundaries of a financial settlement on the damages that have accrued from Reconstruction Era betrayals up to this day.

In the interim, I believe that there must be massive infusions of corporate and foundation money into strategic black urban universities. There are only about fifty such institutions fitting this description. A two billion dollar endowment of high growth stocks and valuable real estate to each of the urban-based HBCUs would only be a pittance out of white corporate American wealth. That would be my own version of an immediate good faith deposit on the *Reparations Settlement* that is inevitable.[4] This deposit would be payment against compensatory damages for what I believe will prove to be the easily documented destructive impact of failed Reconstruction Era commitments by the federal government.

Black America should not have to wait for white American corporate business elites to arrive at a comfort level or positive consensus. The emotionally compelling but constitutionally difficult concept of compensating individual African-Americans for slave labor is not the immediate issue.[5] Today's white American corporate elites give life to a pithy suspicion that Balzac is purported to have attributed to the 19th-century writer class; *"...behind every great fortune lies a crime."*

Some people believe that African-Americans should feel stigmatized by "quotas" and massive injections of capital to HBCUs and other strategic black institutions. Those same people must believe that black people are completely ignorant about the federal government's role in the economic development of certain groups in America. That role has been central to the advancement of this country's White Anglo-Saxon Protestant *group* interest since the end of slavery in 1865.[6] The problem may be that those people who are so adamantly against race based compensatory actions may simply have willfully induced themselves into a state of blissful ignorance about earlier actions of the federal government.

Today there is a significant percentage of the American population that is consciously or unconsciously comfortable with certain notions. One such notion is that black representation of less than two percent in professions other than sports and music is a *natural state of affairs*. Our *Bell Curve* authors believe, for instance, that a black presence exceeding two percent in "high IQ occupations" would be un-natural, misguided, grossly unfair to more deserving whites with higher IQ scores, and a threat to national safety, health, and general welfare. *The Bell Curve* authors lists architects in their group of eight "high IQ occupations." Their following assertion about lawyers and other "high IQ occupations" is quite to the point:

> To be a first-rate lawyer, you had better come from the upper end of the cognitive ability distribution. The same may be said of a handful of other occupations, such as accountants, engineers, **and architects**...the mean IQ of people entering those fields is in the neighborhood of 120...

Former Secretary of Labor and now Harvard professor Robert Reich describes Murray's high IQ group as "symbolic analysts." Those are people who make their living by analyzing and manipulating language, numbers, abstract symbols, and other forms of critical information.[7]

A most telling paragraph can be found in Murray and Herrnstein's 600 pages of speculative narratives, statistics, graphs, and charts (and shameful homage to the theories and propaganda of hardcore white supremacists Arthur Jensen, Phillip Ruston, et al.). They inform us of what they believe to be the bottom line meaning of all of their numbing statistical documentation and research. They talk candidly about that infamous and tenaciously clung to *15-point gap* between black and white IQs. It is a major wonder to me that the gap is *that small*. Tremendous vested psychological capital and brute physical effort was expended to assure a gap that was at least three times as large.

Our two *Bell Curve* scholars remind us with a seeming vengeance that based on the IQ score gap between blacks and whites, Du Bois' "Talented Tenth" would today more accurately be described as the "Talented One-Hundredth." They conveniently fail to discuss just how diligently all institutional levels of American society worked to achieve that end. Over the period between the end of slavery in 1865 and the 1960s, the destruction of serious black intellectual capacity was still a national obsession.

For all of the obvious reasons, Black America has produced only a single twentieth-century "marquee" architect. Only Paul R. Williams of Los Angeles managed to make a small imprint on national black (and to a degree, white) consciousness. Williams, though of another era from today's Jewish mega-stars, is the closest thing there is to a "star" twentieth-century African-American architect.[8] Williams, in his most productive period of the "heroic modernism" era of architecture in the 1950s, did not operate within a framework of uncompromising devotion to the avant-garde modernism of American Frank Lloyd Wright or the reigning European trinity of Le Corbusier, Mies van der Rohe, or Harvard-based Walter Gropius. Accordingly, despite all of Williams' relative commercial success, he was in no position to have played the role of mid-wife to a next higher level of black architect careers and reputations. We have Cornel West to remind us of a profound American cultural reality that has bearing on architectural cultural reality:

> *And what Blacks and Jews have done with their intelligence, imagination, and ingenuity is astounding. Twentieth-century America—a century that begins only a generation after emancipation of penniless, illiterate, enslaved Africans and the massive influx of*

poor Eastern European Jewish immigrants—is unimaginable without the creative breakthroughs and monumental contributions of Blacks and Jews. At the highest level of achievement, we have Louis Armstrong and Aaron Copeland, Duke Ellington and Leonard Bernstein, John Coltrane and George Gershwin, Sarah Vaughn and Irving Berlin, Tony Morrison and Saul Bellow, W.E.B. Du Bois and Hannah Arendt, Romare Bearden and Jackson Pollock, August Wilson and Arthur Miller, Paul Robeson and Pete Seeger, Ralph Ellison and Irving Howe, Kathleen Battle and Beverly Sills, Richard Pryor and Lenny Bruce...Willie Mays and Sandy Koufax, Andre Watts and Itzhak Perlman, Jacob Lawrence and Mark Rothko, Babyface (Kenneth Edmonds) and Carol King, Thurgood Marshall and Louis Brandeis, Marvin Gaye and Bob Dylan, James Baldwin and Norman Mailer, Lorraine Hansberry and Neil Simon, Aretha Franklin and Barbra Streisand, Billy Strayhorn and Stephen Sondheim. This short and incomplete list of towering black and Jewish figures is neither an act of providence nor a mere accident. Rather it is the result of tremendous talent, discipline, and energy of two ostracized groups who disproportionately shape the cultural life of this country.[9]

That list could go on for several more days. It is doubtful that there could be an equitable and non-patronizing pairing of a series of African-American architects and Jewish architects where the black half of the equation would be as readily recognizable by black and Jewish architects alike. This brings us to the critical role of money, mentors, and relationships.[10] Also looming large in this equation is the role of the formal architectural historian establishment and the entire literature genre under their effective control.[11] This includes the entire mainstream architectural press as a determining factor in the making of the reputation of American architects.

Even though black architects never openly debated the matter, I was unable to suppress troubling mixed emotions at the audacious but technically accurate *New York Times* architecture critic Herbert Muschamp's 1996 article. Muschamp brazenly extolled the hegemonic influence of Jewish architects on both the American and international scene today.[12] This influence is palpable throughout the intertwined academy of elite eastern architecture schools, the mainstream architectural press, and the small but vastly influential patron driven segment of private practice.

Muschamp dangles before us images of the near cult-like figure of the late Lou Kahn; the omni-present Frank Gehry of Bilbao, Spain Guggenheim Museum fame; Moshe Safdie and his list of many museums; and James Ingo Freed and his Washington, DC, Holocaust Museum. Muschamp reminds us of the now immortalized "New York Five" of Richard Meier (the Getty Museum); Peter Eisenman, inventor of the influential "deconstructivism" movement; and others.[13]

Left unsaid by Muschamp is the reality that virtually every one of today's Jewish artist-architect stars is the end-game result of a combination of an informal mentoring system. Also a key factor is the economic achievements of previous Jewish middle and upper classes. Those groups made it possible for their architect grandsons and sons (daughters are another story) to become serious architects through uncompromising commitments to a personal artistic and high culture architectural vision:

> The twentieth-century has been nothing less than a golden age of Jewish achievement…in architecture, the point is beyond argument. This art has produced an unprecedented flowering of Jewish talent in recent years…Today Jewish architects lead the field…Is this worth comment? There is a minefield of reasons not to. To talk about Jews in the arts—or, for that matter, in the media, finance, psychiatry and many other fields—is to risk echoing anti-Semitic ravings about Zionist conspiracies.

I am in agreement with Muschamp's speculation. Authorship of a similar article by an African-American architect or architecture critic on the spectacular success of Jewish architects would have indeed carried the very serious risk of being labeled as anti-Semitic diatribe.

Just two years earlier New York Times reporter David Dunlap wrote a lengthy article about the plight of black architects.[14] He also had some pithy observations. All of the black architect's desperation from seemingly permanent quarters in the basement of the big time world of New York architecture was instantly confirmed boldly in the *Times*.

Muschamp's *Times* article extolling the unmistakable dominance of Jewish architects in the academy and the world of high culture design made the contrast even more striking. In one swoop, the obscurity, poverty, and utter lack of influence of black architects—and their stark invisibility—was now exposed for the entire world to see when holding these two articles up to the light together. Yet, the plight of black architects in the cultural capital of the world could not be otherwise, given the assumptions, paths, strategies, and modus operandi chosen or accepted by all too many black architects. The first quarter twenty-first century black practitioners will continue to suffer as long as they continue playing the game of architecture on someone else's terms. Continuing to do so can only guarantee black marginality.

Ultimately both Jewish and WASP high culture academy and design architects are chasing rainbows and illusions in their quest for real power and influence in the larger world of the built environment.[15] But Jewish and WASP high profile media architects at least have large enough patron bases. Corporate, institutional, public sector, and most importantly, the media-image making worlds portray these architects as people who are doing incredibly well financially while also doing much social and cultural good for all.

The practicing black architect who could even remotely be placed inside of the same conversation with the contemporary members of Muschamp's star Jewish architect camp is Max Bond Jr. of New York City. Bond has the pedigreed academic training as well as teaching credentials in elite eastern architecture schools that is common to many star architects. However, Bond, while on his own, did not find the type of high culture patron client base that is also typical of Muschamp's star Jewish architects.[16]

Bond's nearest brush with national stardom is a result of his selection by the Martin Luther King Jr., family to design the King Memorial Center in Atlanta—now probably the most recognizable piece of contemporary architecture throughout Black America. Bond had no influential New York based "critic" praising his talent, as is often the case with Muschamp's "stars."

Black architects instinctively know the importance of early commissions from "mother" as the starting point for establishing "design" personas and getting noticed.[17] So they are inclined to suspect that white or Jewish architects have an infinitely better chance at starting out with "mother" type commissions. Such projects can lead to other quality patron-clients and even sometimes-academic appointments. Black architects spawned from the still evolving and financially marginal black lower-to-middle and middle classes rarely have such "mothers." Black "mothers" are rarely capable of commissioning retreat houses on budgets that allow for publishable quality "delight" architecture.

Bond solved this problem neatly during the early years of his working career after acquiring undergraduate and graduate degrees from Harvard in the late 1950s. Bond had the foresight and wherewithal to use the Nkrumah government of the newly independent African nation of Ghana as his "mother." Bond designed and built several houses and schools in Ghana that demonstrated his talents as a designer in possession of a firm grasp of the best in the Euro-modern idiom.

CHAPTER 10

Black Patron, New Monuments, and the "Black 35"

Instances of private (or nonpolitical based) black patronage in architecture are still rare at this juncture. The most outstanding recent example was the large financial gift to Spelman College by Bill and Camille Cosby in 1990. Spelman is a small liberal arts college in Atlanta with a constituency of bright, aggressive, and mostly black females.

Mrs. Cosby's objective was to fund the construction of a new multipurpose academic and cultural center in the middle of the bucolic Georgian architecture structures dotting the Spelman campus. This would be accomplished with the aid of an unprecedented 20 million dollar cash gift from the Clara E. Jackson Foundation—funded by Cosby money. Mrs. Cosby is reported to have felt strongly that somewhere in America there ought to be a practicing woman architect who could project an image of the very essence of an architect.

The architectural fee on a project of this magnitude attracts a great deal of attention not only locally but also nationally from white and black firms of every size and shape. Mrs. Cosby undoubtedly had people around her, both white and black, advocating that she pursue a course of one of several standard variations. At bottom was the orthodox course of selecting a "star" architect from the list of "usual suspects." A "star" would garner instant and generous mainstream architectural media publicity for the project.

The architect selection approach would certainly have been the "invited competition." Here, a dozen of the most media prominent architect-artist stars submit credentials and portfolios, and are interviewed by a group of their "star" architect peers. A favorite further twist on this approach, when ethnic or gender sensitivities must be acknowledged, is to suggest that the invited signature architects bring along a black or female architect as the "associated architect." *This is usually a truly ugly and demeaning state of affairs for most black architects.* The stated rationale that such exposure will lead to similar opportunities for black architects as primes is rarely the reality.

With only 108 licensed black female architects (out of over 100,000 licensed American architects—1,100 of whom are black) in 1990, this made the odds of Mrs. Cosby finding what she undoubtedly really wanted, practically nil. There were any number of licensed black female architects who were *technically* qualified in the narrowest sense to design Mrs. Cosby's project. Practically speaking, this commission needed to be entrusted to the hands of a woman functioning as an owner-principal in an established practice with a track record of built works. That record should include work approaching or exceeding the scope and anticipated 15 million hard "bricks and mortar" cost of the Spelman project.

Using whatever calculus or criteria she finally chose, Mrs. Cosby narrowed her search down to several architectural firms in 1991. The most prominent finalist was a team headed by Norma Sklarek, a seasoned African-American and a member of the prestigious College of Fellows within the American Institute of Architects. Sklarek was also the former director of production management at different points in a long career with big, white, West Coast giants, Victor Gruen, DMJM, and most recently, the flamboyant urban shopping mall specialist, Jon Jerde.

Sklarek, a 1950s Columbia graduate, had sterling credentials. For good measure, she brought along a white partner Kate Diamond, also a seasoned West Coast woman architect with outstanding design credits. Mrs. Cosby's "short list" also contained Roberta Washington, a solid New York based practitioner and also a former student at Howard while I was on the faculty in the 1970s. There was also Donna deJongh, with her partner-husband Robert deJongh, who were both classmates of mine at Howard in the mid 1960s. Mrs. deJongh had been quietly distinguishing herself for the past fifteen years as equal partner to her husband in one of the leading architecture firms in the Caribbean Islands.

At this point, Mrs. Cosby could rest assured that she had three teams that could all deliver a competent product. As is so often the case, it was down to the all-important matter of "chemistry." Who does the client want to spend the next three-to-five-years working with? Who does the client feel best represents the ideal image of architecture to the world of Atlanta, Spelman, and several thousand bright and articulate young African-American women?

Donna deJongh was finally selected hands down by Mrs. Cosby. Mrs. deJongh spent the next three years working closely with all of the vested stakeholders in the project. She delivered a well-crafted building that was just right for the Spelman campus and constituency. *The Atlanta Business Journal,* the influential weekly newspaper, was quick to notice deJongh's work. The paper applauded the elegantly proportioned brick exteriors and the sumptuous interiors that were all adding value to the campus and the city that extended well beyond the actual cost of the building.

The completed building was never featured—or for that matter even published—in any of the mainstream architectural magazines that specialize in elaborate spreads on patron-sponsored projects. Had Mrs. Cosby followed conventional norms in selecting an architect, she could have had her building featured in all of the mainstream design journals. In instances where one is desirous of erecting a prominent edifice, selecting a "signature" architect who can get the project featured in the media journals is good strategy. This is a proven technique where money for the project might still have to be raised for debt retirement after actual opening day ribbon-cutting festivities are over.

But Mrs. Cosby is that rare African-American capable of writing a check for the twenty million dollars needed to cover hard and soft costs as well as fixtures and furnishings. She apparently decided that the symbolism of having just the right woman architect outweighed any Cosby family need to see the building lionized by the lilly-white high-culture media world of architecture. The Cosby-Spelman project relates well to my central thesis that there is a persistent residual predilection throughout Black America to want to support the use of African-American architects on high profile, community-based projects. This sentiment exists at the highest as well as economically lowest levels throughout Black America. I strongly advocate that black architects eschew the need for generous patrons as the basis of their practices. But black patronage has a vital role to play in the rejuvenation of a black culture-based architecture.

The real fault line in a potential nasty public fight between black architects and white American architects, Jewish or otherwise, looms ominously. Black America is now at the point of wanting to construct significant commemorative and cultural edifices. Some of these will be major sized prestigious commissions that will attract the attention of the "high culture" designers. Influential New York Times architecture critic Herbert Muschamp has already declared the unquestionable hegemony of Jewish architects in this building genre.

So what will happen, for instance, when the Black "Middle Passage" Museum—counterpoint to the Jewish Holocaust Museum that Black America badly wants—finally reaches the point of architect selection? In replicating the now established modus operandi of community architect selection boards used during the late 1960s Black Power Movement in Washington, DC, (and undoubtedly throughout the rest of urban America), a question arises. What if a panel of distinguished black citizens selects a distinguished national panel of primarily African-American architects to organize an invitational competition to design the ultimate black museum? How would the signature museum architects and the Jewish community react if the invitees turn out to be mostly black, with none of Herbert Muschamp's reigning Jewish media stars on the list?

I don't claim to know the inside details of how James Ingo Freed, a high profile Jewish architect and partner in the firm of I.M. Pei & Partners, was selected to design the Holocaust Museum. But I am reasonably certain that Max Bond, Charles McAfee, and Don Stull—arguable the three most distinguished living and still practicing "design-oriented" architects produced by Black America (and of roughly the same age and similar academic backgrounds as Freed)—*were not* on the invited "short list" of designers for the Holocaust Museum. Will Jewish architects feel that Black America is engaging in an insidious form of "affirmative action?"

My guess is that the first reaction of Jewish architects and the Jewish community will be one of indifference. Another reaction could be that if Black America finances its own Holocaust museum (as the Jewish community did), architect selection will be nobody else's business. But if Black America will need public funds (they will) or privately donated funds (they will—all of those black NBA/NFL millionaires and their mostly white agents will be strangely missing in action; this is another story for another day), then the competition had better be "open." *This will be an interesting discussion.*

We have to remind ourselves that none of the media star Jewish architects profiled in Muschamps's December 1996 *New York Times* piece built their reputations on work that is of significance to or located in the black community. The Jewish architect clients and patrons are overwhelmingly private high culture (and now rarely Jewish) institutions. Their client list includes a handful of world traveling real east estate developers who hire hot media star architect-artists. Those architects must assure that their client's mega-ego building statements will end up on the cover of the mainstream architectural magazines.[1]

Young black New York City architect Jack Travis caused a mild stir inside the small national black architect community with the 1991 release of his maiden book, *African-American Architects in*

Practice. Travis provided a random black and white photo sampling of the work of 35 of the nation's most prominent and busy black architects. Of the group, all but two were operating practitioners. The actual accomplishments of these 33 practices ranged from significant to marginal.

The Travis selection of these firms as representative examples of black architects in private practice was actually accurate within a certain context. There were two non-practitioners (both licensed and members of the College of Fellows within the American Institute of Architects). Harry Robinson, then dean of architecture at Howard in Washington, DC, and Sharon Sutton, a prolific scholar and also holder of a doctorate in environmental psychology, were the two academicians. Of the remaining 33 firms included Lou Switzer of New York City, which is actually an interior design practice, but the only one in the group with a largely private corporate clientele.

Among the group was the unusual practice headed by three generations—the father, son, and grandson members of a family firm of Louis Fry, Sr. (now deceased), Louis Fry, Jr. and Louis Fry III of Washington, DC. Fry, Sr. and Fry, Jr. hold a highly unusual father-son combination membership in the AIA College of Fellows. The list of practitioners included Harry Simmons Jr. of Brooklyn, New York (now deceased). Two others, listed separately, Charles McAfee and Cheryl McAfee, are a Kansas City father-daughter combination. Shown together is another father-daughter team, Wendell Campbell and Susan Campbell of Chicago.

The lone husband-wife team was William J. Stanley and Ivenue Love-Stanley of Atlanta.[2] There were two sets of partners, each shown as an entity—Paul Devroaux and Marshall Purnell of Washington, DC, and Howard Simms and Harold Varner of Detroit.[3] And there is a big sister, Joyce Whitley of Cleveland, a professional city planner, and her younger twin brother architects James and John Whitley.

I have a familiarity with much of the work showcased by most of these firms through my travels around the country over the years. This work appears to be an accurate representation of the overall scope and quality of the output of the country's several hundred currently independently practicing African-American architects. The work Travis profiles is best approached by first setting aside the glossy magazines that publish the work of the country's all-white media stars and thrusting young would-be stars. To directly compare one of the few known examples of published works of black architects with the work routinely showcased in the all-white publications would be misleading at this point in time. Such an act of direct comparison would simply reinforce the opinion of the architectural literati that the design capabilities of black architects are, on balance, of a mediocre quality. Those quarters feel that the black architect's work ranges from shallow sophomoric banality to occasional flashes of brilliant intellectual insight executed with consummate technical skill.

The "mediocrity" involved is driven by a usually nearly bankrupt, overly cautious, and unimaginative municipal government "public works department" type clientele. That is the clientele that African-American architects have been mostly stuck with. This is a proverbial "monkey" on the back of too many black architects. These architects are going to have to help in the struggle to wean the next generation of black architects off of dependence on this clientele.

In retrospect, the issue to be confronted regarding the Travis book and the thirty-three relatively small and mostly orthodox practitioners is this; *what is the appropriate strategic model to be utilized in addressing the physical environment needs of 35 million African-Americans in an advanced capitalist information age economy?* The overwhelming majority of these citizens will still live mostly together in urban and nearby suburban communities. If this African-American community were an independent nation, it would have the tenth largest gross national income in the world. A "market needs assessment in a competitive environment" is how the entrepreneurial sector of black businesses attempting to serve that market would conceptualize its opportunities.

Unfortunately, the architectural mindset and paradigm does not lead to such straightforward conceptualization of marketplace opportunities. In her book, *Architecture: The Story of Practice,* Dana Cuff, a

West Coast architect-historian, provides us with an easily readable broad insight into the culture of today's architect class including its schools, its practices, and the cultural belief system that bridges both.[4] Predictably, but not irrevocably, today's African-American architect owner-practitioners are totally in line with those cultural belief systems. Since the 1920s start of "professionalism" at Howard University, this "blackface" version of the "white gentleman's profession" has been the dominant model.

A key starting point of the current modern era of black architects was the period of the 1970s Richard Nixon-era Black Capitalism. This time also saw the start-up of the multi-billion dollar national urban mass transit program including the Northeast Corridor high-speed train line modernization. Participation in that multi-billion dollar project was also a high water mark for the public facilities oriented black engineering practitioner. Interestingly enough, because these federal spending programs were so large, black design participation had the appearance of being much larger than it was in actuality.

Black professionals started out from a previous 1940s and 1950s base of statistically zero participation in federal government programs. Those programs were limited to isolated examples of public and deep subsidy housing. The 1970s goals of up to a five percent share of defense and transportation contracts were literally enough to inundate the handful of black firms likely to be selected to partake of the feast. Predictably, the driving force behind the actual enforcement of those higher mandates for black participation were strategically situated black cabinet level officials. A typical but major example was Philadelphia lawyer William Coleman, who served as Richard Nixon's Secretary of Transportation.

By the late 1970s, black architects and engineers were literally running into each other in airports as they criss-crossed the country on the way to interviews for new design commissions. Cities were eager to hire design consortiums to draw plans to spend massive federal dollars building mass transit systems. In those days, every black design firm with an actual commercial practice (as distinguished from "kitchen table" operations) had a Department of Transportation funded contract.[5]

More often than not, these contracts were actually five to ten percent subcontracts from large white engineering firms that were the prime design contractor. As still relatively fledgling businesses, black firms usually lacked the track record, capitalization, credit access, or manpower to be the "prime." Late in this game—near the end period of free flowing federal funds—there would be an occasional black firm (usually engineering based) capable of functioning as the prime designer.

During those days, I was serving as a director of marketing for Jenkins-Fleming, a black-owned architectural firm with offices in Los Angeles and St. Louis. We were right in the thick of this transportation design contract chase. I made an observation and recommendation to this firm just before leaving to establish my own new urban housing development practice in 1978. I opined that true growth opportunity and viability for orthodox black architectural firms required the offering of full comprehensive services. This had to include engineering infrastructure design and construction management. I further stated that the future was bleak for conventional black architectural firms, despite the free flowing public sector contracts at that time.

It was clear to me back then that the coming 1980s and 1990s would see the emergence of several substantial sized full services and well-capitalized Information Technology based black engineering firms. I predicted that such firms would eventually establish in-house architectural divisions that would exceed the size and competitive capacities of most existing conventionally configured black architectural firms. Today, I see no fundamental reason to doubt that the ultimate accuracy of my prediction will become manifest within the first several decades of the twenty-first century.

At the start of Year 2000 there were a number of prominent black-owned architectural firms around the country. While these are also the largest of the black-owned firms, they are predictably small by national standards. The most highly accomplished of these firms are **Stull & Lee** of Boston; **Devrouax & Purnell, Turner Associates (Al Edgecombe), Fry & Welch,** and **Bryant & Bryant** of Washington, DC; **Turner Associates (Oscar Harris)** and **William Stanley & Ivenue Love-Stanley** of Atlanta; **John Chase** of Houston; **Wendell Campbell, William Brazely,** and **Andrew Heard** of Chicago; **Gale Jenkins Martinez,** and **Kennard Associates** of Los Angeles; **Madison International** of Cleveland; **Sims-Varner** of Detroit; **Bills-Manning** of New Orleans; **Moody/Nolan** of Columbus and Nashville; the nearly one-hundred-year-old **McKissack** family firm of Nashville, Tennessee; **Emanuel Kelly** of Philadelphia; **Robert Trayhan Coles** of Buffalo; **Leon Bridges** of Baltimore; **Ronald Frazier** of Miami, **Harry Overstreet,** and **Michael Willis** of San Francisco; **Fleming Corporation (Charles Fleming, Jr.)** of St. Louis, **Charles MacAfee** of Kansas City and Atlanta, **Robert & Donna deJongh** of the Virgin Islands, and **Phil Freelon** of Raliegh-Durhan.

The Moody/Nolan firm has been showing up over the past several years on the tail-end of the annual list of the *Engineering News Record Magazine's* "Top 500" architectural firms in the country as measured by gross annual fee revenues. A review of this firm's brochure is revealing. They are structured nearly exactly as I had predicted twenty-years earlier as a necessary condition for success in the larger marketplace. Their services and expertise encompass architecture, civil infrastructure engineering, transportation planning, and construction management.

Similar to Moody/Nolan, the McKissack firm has always consisted of architects, engineers, and construction managers. The firm is now under the control of the widow of the late DeBerry McKissack. Leatrice McKissack had no formal architectural or engineering training or experience when she took over the leadership of the company a few years ago upon her husband's death. She runs the company with her two daughters, both Howard University civil engineering graduates. McKissack is one of the strongest and most enduring black firms in the country. The firm is openly discussing their intent to focus on the bedrock business operating strategy of the founding patriarch of nearly one-hundred years ago. They are adapting that strategy to the cyber age of virtual reality based develop-design-build services.[6]

The McKissack daughters are mindful of the fact that their grandfather Moses McKissack and his brother Calvin were licensed architects, engineers, and general contractors. Those men designed big important projects on black southern college campuses, developed family owned projects, and constructed buildings for important black and white clients. The following words make clear how the current matriarch and CEO Leatrice McKissack views things:

> *"We need long-term investments and development that, five or six years down the line, really are an annuity...And that's what Moses and Calvin did. There's nothing new to it. They developed the projects and that was the annuity they had down the road."*[7]

One must also notice that, with few exceptions, the practices that I have cited are in cities that are now or were recently headed by strong-willed black mayors. These mayors provide black architects with mostly public agency clients who use scarce public dollars that leave little room for the "spectacular gesture." It is just such "gestures" that are usually found in the corporate, institutional, or commercial projects featured in mainstream architectural magazines. But these black-owned firms all manage to produce work that is, on balance, technically competent by any measure.

Robert Trayham Coles is a productive upstate New York architect who is one of only three black architects out of a total of 800 architects listed in Roxanne Kuter Williams' book *Architects and the Mechanics of Fame.*[8] Coles first posed in writing in the late 1980s his thoughtful but misdirected observation that black American architects were an "endangered species." Coles would have been on firmer ground had he explicitly targeted African-American owned and operated architectural firms. In either case, Coles' paper was poorly received in some black architectural circles.[9] The reception was reminiscent of the open hostility that black social activists and intellectuals greeted Daniel Patrick Moynihan's report in the 1960s.

Moynihan ultimately proved to have been on technically accurate, though culturally flawed, ground. His unwelcome alarm bells about the growing threat to black family stability posed by skyrocketing illegitimacy could not then be heeded. Serious problems for black-owned architectural practices will prove to be inevitable unless appropriate corrective course altering steps are undertaken in earnest. Most of the current principals of these firms have proven to be wily visionaries who have survived thus far as still viable business enterprises.

The need to pursue structural reorganizations, mergers and expansions into full service firms is a twenty-first century reality for these businesses. Another excellent source of verification of the reality of the total dominance of the design and construction of the built environment by full service firms is the latest *American Institute of Architects Practice Handbook*.[10] This four-volume document contains a series of highly revealing graphics depicting what type of firms design and build our world.

The stakes are very high in this all or nothing game. Just as I predicted twenty-years ago, there are now a handful of black engineer headed comprehensive service firms with in-house architecture staffs. Such firms, typified by the Washington, DC, based national firm of Delon Hampton Associates, are models of a viable design services organization. In short, there are very limited prospects for the successful start-up of the conventional single dimensional architectural firm. That was relatively easy to do in your basement or on your kitchen table yesterday.

That is not to say that one cannot start a new firm today. The critical issue is that such a start-up must be a "virtual corporation." The entity must be composed of not just architecture school classmates but also, engineering school classmates along with classmates from law school. Most critically there must be classmates from the finance and management department of the business school. This upstart group had better be able to advise prospective clients (who could just as well include black architects themselves) *on where to find all of the money needed for any contemplated project.*

PART II

BLACK POWER, URBAN REBELLION, BLACK MAYOR, BLACK ARCHITECTS IN WASHINGTON, DC

CHAPTER 1

A Gentleman's Profession(alism) at Howard, 1945 and Beyond

Back during my Los Angeles County government draftsman days in 1959, I developed an acquaintance with James Silcott, a young black staff architect who worked in my building. He was a graduate of something only vaguely familiar to me at that time. Silcott's Howard University alma mater in Washington, DC. was a possibility that had never before occurred to me. Just before I left L.A. for active duty in the Bay Area, Silcott, gave me his old Howard architecture school catalogue. I was immediately intrigued. Having the army send me to Washington, DC, after basic army training at Fort Ord was a stroke of fortune apparently written in the stars.

Before leaving Los Angeles to head east for the start of army duty in 1960 and eventually enrollment at Howard in 1962, I had an apartment on the west side of town. I lived two blocks from the prominent corner of Western and Adams. The impressive Golden State Mutual Life Insurance Company headquarters building was also located at that corner. By that time I was completely conscious of Paul Williams and that he was the architect for the project. Golden State Mutual Insurance Company was by far the largest black-owned business in Los Angeles.

The company had enjoyed a reputation as an important black institution since pre-World War II days. In his dissertation on Williams,

99

Wesley Henderson reminds us of the extent that the company made special efforts to hire Williams to design their headquarters building in the late 1940s as a deliberate marketing strategy.[1] This was the icon building of black Los Angeles and I never tired of passing and entering the lobby every chance I got.

While I never enrolled at the University of Southern California— simply known as "SC"—my earlier visits to the School of Architecture proved to be immediately fruitful. There were several African-Americans studying architecture there at that time. Each one of them quickly assumed the role of a mentor to me upon sensing my seriousness. Each one of them also went on to fulfilling careers as practicing architects with significant built-work accomplishments. Two of these men in particular, Eugene Brooks and Lafayette Beamon, literally adopted me back in their SC student days. My successful transition through two years of active army duty and an architectural life after that on the East Coast was greatly influenced by the earlier mentorship of Beamon and Brooks.[2]

Within days after landing in Washington, DC, from the West Coast in the dead of the winter of early 1961, I managed to find Howard's campus. When I finally located the School of Architecture, I thought I had died and gone to heaven. While completing my Northern Virginia based Fort Belvior army tour of duty over the next eighteen months, I was a regular campus visitor. Here on Howard's campus I was bumping into not just architects, but *black* architects; *black* licensed architects with not just bachelor's degrees but master's degrees from Ivy League schools. Not in my wildest imagination had I encountered anything like the Howard campus. Howard's predominately black faculty of architects, engineers, Ph.D.s, medical doctors, lawyers, scientists and obviously very bright students was all a pleasant cultural shock.

During my freshman year, my already oversized "architect's ego" caused me to blow an opportunity for a job in the office of Hilyard Robinson, the great man himself. While in Los Angeles, I had vaguely heard of Robinson. I had posed the question about whether Paul Williams had a black counterpart of similar status elsewhere around the country and Robinson's name came up. My hard-won interview with Robinson was an unfortunate hour of fierce confrontational interchanges. An exasperated Robinson abruptly ended the interview by telling me that my arrogant attitude was not one he wished to have to deal with.

I continue to this day forty years later to console myself with the belief that Robinson and I had merely engaged in a salary negotiation session that didn't go well. I was unreasonably unyielding in my position. I had prior Los Angeles office experience. I had also been an army construction draftsman. And I held fast to the view (most un-welcomed by Robinson) that there were "deficiencies" in the work of Howard student graduates. I felt that I should be paid the same hourly rate that Robinson was offering those recent Howard graduates.

The black Washington architectural world I entered in 1962 was one of optimism and sincerity.[3] We were confident about our ability to transcend the blatantly racist patterns dominating much of the local architecture profession. All private commercial commissions and virtually all institutional work went to white firms. Public sector commissions of any substance or prestige were firmly in the hands of white firms. Up through the 1960s, white Washington, DC, architects were the beneficiaries of the "mother" of all "affirmation action" "set-aside" programs.

Little did I realize at the time that I would become part of a first wave of Howard graduates being hired by white downtown Connecticut Avenue firms. Up to several years before I arrived, the established norm for Howard architecture graduates was jobs in the black uptown Georgia Avenue offices of earlier Howard graduates. The other option was the west of Rock Creek Park offices of a small group of Jewish architects. The Howard architecture faculty was quite proud of the growing downtown employed students and graduates that were bringing added affirmation to the program.

There had been only a short forty years between the 1923 arrival of Howard Mackey at Howard University in Washington, DC, from Philadelphia, and the 1960s black rebellions and Black Power

Movement on the campus. Jewish architects were a key part of the teaching faculty spanning over the last half of that period. By the 1950s, Howard's architecture department bridged the separate worlds of Washington's white architects and black architects. When I arrived to begin my studies in 1962, the faculty contained six black and three white full-time professors. The white professors were all Jewish. Leon Brown was one of the Jewish practitioners who integrated his office by hiring Howard graduates back as early as 1947. Dean Mackey then strategically recruited Brown to the faculty. Brown, a decent and principled man, proved to be the department's ambassador to the white world of Washington architecture. Being white, this Brown was naturally given the nickname of "Vanilla" Brown in counterpart to our other beloved black (and crypto-Garveyite) Leroy John Henry Brown who was affectionately known to everyone as "Chocolate" Brown.

I distinctly remember Leon Brown's courses in architectural interiors, theory of architecture and his tutelage as a design studio critic. While many Howard architecture students of that period were from black middle and even upperclass backgrounds, the world that they were knowledgeable about was still eons away from the needs, styles, tastes and perceptions of white upper-class Washington. This group was our presumed ultimate clientele. Leon Brown managed to at least shed some light on these strange elite WASP customs for most of us. This was especially the case for me, coming as I did from the projects of South Central Los Angeles.

The Jewish faculty commitment to heroic Modern Architecture was typical of new converts. They were uncompromising in their quest to assure that the nearly all black graduates of the program would be capable of earning a living wage. I enjoyed a special relationship with Leon Brown. His Atlanta, Georgia, family name was actually Braunstein (I never pressed him on this matter). He was the most cosmopolitan of the three original Jewish faculty members brought in by Dean Mackey.

Other Jewish architects joined the older Jewish faculty core at Howard in later years. Before I would graduate in 1967, the most notable catch was Mort Hoppenfeld who was a special coup for Mackey. Hoppenfeld had been hired earlier by the now legendary late James Rouse, founder of the new town of Columbia, Maryland, located midway between DC and Baltimore.[4] All of the other men maintained small practices along with teaching schedules at Howard and, needless to say, were often the first sources of employment for Howard graduates. In the 1950s and 1960s, the other graduates could at least look forward to going to work for other Howard graduates who became licensed and opened small offices.

I cannot recall having a serious discussion or lecture session with any of my Jewish instructors about the real business and economics of architecture as a real estate based enterprise. However, I sincerely doubt that any of them other than Hoppenfeld actually knew anything about the subject or even cared about the subject. Hoppenfeld's world-view as a planner was actually more socialist bureaucrat than capital-ist entrepreneur. The stereotypical assumption by some of my classmates that our Jewish faculty was holding out on us was probably false.

There was indeed a main source of friction and disagreement that would inevitably develop between the 1960s Black Power wing of the architecture student body and our Jewish faculty (and several of our integrationist minded African-American faculty). All of a sudden we wanted to do and talk about things and issues in design studio and history classes that had been heretofore glossed over. On the even more fundamental issue of design contracts for rebellion inspired work in the black community, conflicts with Jewish firms were there, however well managed through civility and professional courtesies.

There were Jewish firms in DC who had established records of accomplishment and linkages within the still largely WASP domi-nated old boy network of un-elected officials controlling architect selections in DC. There is no question that the Black Power Movement caused a number of major design contracts to be diverted to black firms. Several of these projects were ones that the white as well as Jewish firms had every expectation of getting as they had in the past.

Clearly, Jewish architects have been no different than the larger Jewish community in their historic role of championing the cause of justice for African-Americans. Therefore, I know how deeply and justifiably wounded many of my Jewish friends were at the sickening spectacle on the Howard University campus in the spring of 1994. An over exuberant young Nation of Islam lawyer instigated that now infamous call and gleeful audience response sing-along of *"...who was it that did blacks badly, etc., etc.? The Jews, etc., etc.!"*

In stark contrast, many black architects of my generation and the ones before could also do a peer call and response piece about Jewish architects. Only, ours would have to go something like this:

Which architects gave us our first jobs when no one else would, behind thinly disguised—or sometime not so thinly disguised—racist reasons?....Jewish architects!

Which architectural firms actually shared design projects (joint ventured) with us because it was the right thing to do?"...Jewish firms!

Which significant firms actually took some of us in as full name and financially participating partners at times when such an act would have been unthinkable by others?...Jewish firms!

Which politicians and public officials actually awarded black firms commissions to design significant housing and community facilities at a time when the black community had not achieved the political clout to insure such acts?...Jewish politicians and officials!

Nonetheless, a part of the problem is the danger that young black architects, largely through slavish uncritical adherence to the culture of today's architectural academy based high profile architects—Jewish or otherwise—will continue lusting after a mirage. This is in large measure because design schools effectively socialize the young architecture student for either media stardom or professional marginality and poverty, with no in-between positions.

One should not be surprised to know that I was in another kind of total shock, dismay and disbelief at TV news on the eruptions in Watts in 1965. I was in my third year of the five-year Bachelor of Architecture program at Howard. I had not yet become fully radicalized by the creeping Black Power Movement of strident campus militancy. I could not conceive of a personal confrontation with the Los Angeles police. I thought that Watts, with its wide palm tree lined streets and neat suburban rambler style stucco houses, had been a great place to live.

But things can quickly change. In the coming year, I would go on to lead a group of radicals who raised serious questions about the "brain drain" from the now awakening Black Washington, DC, community. This was all much to the dismay of that same conservative, integrationist-minded faculty that was so pleased with our own downtown white office breakthroughs. By the start of my fourth year in 1966, the Black Power Movement was firmly entrenched up on the main campus. My little radical wing inside of the school was doing all we could to connect architecture up with the Movement.

My recollection of the curriculum course content and design studios at Howard during those pre-Black Power era sixties is still clear. We held unquestioning acceptance of the assumptions, premises and hero cult figures of the International Style Modern Movement. This was of course no different from any other American architecture school.

The seminal 1960s architectural school "design theory" books were of some curiosity to a group of us who were interested in ideas.[5] We had no critique or dissatisfaction with heroic orthodox modernist architectural dogma. And again like many architecture students of that era, a few of us actually thought that Ayn Rand's *The Fountainhead* hero architect Howard Roark was actually the story of young Frank Lloyd Wright's life and times.

For me and several of my most talented classmates, the hero and the source of our design ideas and drawing styles was Yale architecture school head Paul Rudolph.[6] The most serious intellectual demands on us by most of the faculty were the constant admonitions to "draw." Stepped up demands on us to read voraciously, write constantly, and think critically would start around 1965. That new demand would come mostly from several earlier Howard graduates who would lead us to the next stage of consciousness.

Different things radicalize different people in unpredictable ways. For me it was a series of things. The defining event was a 1966 project to design a residence for the Vice President of the United States at the Naval Observatory site on Wisconsin Avenue. I was convinced that my class should have been working on low-income community housing. I also thought that we should be combating downtown urban renewal plans. It was already clear to our newly radicalized eyes that "Urban Renewal" actually meant "Negro Removal."

Faculty expectations in the mid 1960s still persisted that in spite of obvious remaining rampant racism we were no longer being prepared for jobs in small black architectural offices. Even small uptown Jewish offices weren't all that attractive as an option. We were now made to believe that it was okay to prepare for jobs in prestigious white downtown architectural firms or for graduate work at prestigious eastern universities. A job in a Connecticut Avenue office was the new prestige objective. Howard was equipping us with skills that were highly marketable in still southern Washington, DC, of the mid-1960s.

Howard classmate Bill De Eiel (known then as Bill Levy) was working at a downtown Connecticut Avenue office during our freshman year that straddled 1962 and 1963 (after our graduation in 1967 he would eventually ascend to a partnership in the spectacularly successful West Coast shopping mall design firm of John Jerde Architects). At the time—having failed in my quest for a job with Hilyard Robinson—I took a temp job as a dishwasher in a fancy downtown restaurant. One day in design studio I mentioned to De Eiel that I was working downtown in a building located at 1120 Connecticut Avenue. He responded by informing me that he also worked in that same building.

I spent all of my time in the kitchen washing dishes with the other blacks and Hispanics. Because De Eiel was a Caucasian Iraqi and fairly new in the country, I assumed that he probably worked as a waiter in the same restaurant. Eventually, De Eiel made me understand that he was actually working up on the fourth floor of the building in an architectural firm. He felt certain that I could also be hired and he arranged for an interview. The firm's managing architect-partner was a taciturn southern white boy named John Heath Hunton. This Virginia Tech graduate took one look at my old drawings and made me an acceptable offer of $2.25 an hour on the spot. As it turned out, that amount matched De Eiel's hourly rate.

Within two weeks time, it was obvious that I had more hands-on experience and local technical knowledge than De Eiel. So the owner of the firm called De Eiel in and made him an offer. He was told that he had to take a *50 cents an hour reduction in salary.* He reluctantly accepted this "Godfatherly" offer. I thought that the logical thing would have been to call me in and offer to raise *my* rate by fifty cents an hour. I let that thought pass. I reminded myself that I was still on Connecticut Avenue and my stock was up quite high with my fellow students and many of the faculty.

This firm was small by Washington standards but was growing rapidly. They asked me if I knew of any other student talent at Howard. I brought my friend Harry Simmons Jr. in for an interview and it was love at first sight.[7] Simmons was four years younger than me but a year in front of me in architectural school. He was an incredibly gifted draftsman with an encyclopedic knowledge about construction. A part of this came from his having grown up in a family of brick masons and carpenters in his native northern Florida. I was starting to look over my shoulder for that same "Godfatherly" reduction in pay offer made earlier to De Eiel. Thankfully, that didn't happen.

At the urges of owning partner Tony Musolino, Simmons and I carefully hand-picked several other of our Howard classmates for drafting jobs in the office. Musolino, a graduate of cross-town rival Catholic University's architecture school, was a classically dark-complexion Sicilian Italian-American. I could not imagine him being served a meal in a public place in a Deep South state back in those turbulent 1960s. He grew up in Washington, DC, seeing the very best of Black Washington alongside of the most unassimilated black southern transplants. He appeared to me to be somewhat conflicted in his views about race and the Civil Rights Movement. Before long Musolino was making it quite clear to the rest of the office that his Howard crew was a serious profit center. Hunton, Musolino's junior partner and manager who had hired me and Simmons, was a study-in-contrast to Musolino. Hunton was classical Nordic in physical appearance. He once confided to me that he had held relatively recent virulently racist views. Hunton was a very clever architect who also proved to be an excellent example of how racists' views can be virtually reversed through exposure and intense interaction.

Simmons and I eventually left Musolino's office in the summer of 1966 for greener pastures. I got a job as a draftsman on the new Watergate complex and Simmons found work with another prestigious downtown firm. Within another year, I joined the first Connecticut Avenue firm started up by a Howard graduate. With vision and courage, Charles Bryant—along with his late younger brother, Robert—quickly developed the most substantial black-owned practice in the country. I was recruited to Bryant's new shop by his first draftsman, Colin "Topper" Carew, who was also in the class a year ahead of me. Carew left Howard and took a master's at Yale during the Charles Moore era. Carew would go on to achieve great success as a West Coast television producer of black sit-coms.

By this time, I'm entering my fifth and final year at Howard and becoming increasingly radicalized by civil rights upheavals in the south. Topper Carew was disappearing to join SNNC campaigns in southern sit-ins with increasing frequency. Things come to a boil for me in the spring of 1967. I enrolled in an elective course I needed in order to graduate. Nathan Hare, now a prominent black West Coast radical, taught the course. Hare had recently released the pithy little book *Black Anglo-Saxons*.[8] He had sorely irritated some of Howard's old-line black faculty and administrators. By then we had Watts, Detroit, Vietnam and growing tensions in Washington about black unrest and police-community relationships. Black Power was the new battle cry. Hare's course and tutelage was the next step for me in my conversion from a "reasonable militant" to strident Black Power radical.

CHAPTER 2

The Black Power Architect-Planner 1960s

So why no *Black Architecture*? Why were black people, myself included, so tenaciously ambivalent on even the *idea* of a *"Black Architecture"*? In point of fact, *Black Architecture* was flirted with ever so briefly in those late 1960s on the Howard campus. Architecture as an important *cultural* expression had not been seriously examined at Howard during the Harlem Renaissance decade of forty years earlier. *Black Architecture* at the academic capstone of black culture in America was just as effectively stillborn at the heights of the second coming of black consciousness and cultural awakening of the 1960s.

The notion of a *Black Architecture* as a conceptual and theoretical construct was not well received. The socioeconomic, cultural, and political sense that was actually meant by those of us who were pushing the issue was lost. *Black Architecture* was received by the faculty and professional practice leadership as an *obscenity*. The notion was viewed as unprofessional trashing of the glorious, "politically innocent, and culturally neutral" modernist architecture. Architecture, it was felt, was a medium best suited for demonstrating the *parity of black technical competence*. We were socialized to believe that architecture was *not an appropriate* medium for the expression of black culture.

From the inception of architecture courses in 1919 on the Howard campus, the art and music departments were physically located up on the "Hill Top" flanking the main campus quadrangle. The art and music departments of the 1960s, considered to be fine arts with a close relationship to the soft social sciences, proudly took on the prefix of "black" without black people or white people flinching. For these disciplines, the "black" prefix was viewed as simply objective reality.

Conversely, architecture was physically located down in the part of the campus historically known as "Death Valley." This is the collection of buildings devoted to engineering, physics, chemistry, medicine, and the other hard sciences. Architecture, which logically should have been the bridge between those two worlds, made no significant headway beyond financial gains for the proprietors of African-American architectural firms. Affixing the term "black" to architecture received the same negative reaction that would have greeted any attempt to affix "black" to the other "Death Valley" based hard sciences disciplines such as math, physics and chemistry.

Despite this, I thought—along with several of my architecture school classmates—that we needed to create a separate and distinctive "black" architectural aesthetic. We felt that it was important that this aesthetic possess significant visual and functional differences from the cold sterile aesthetic of International Style Modern Architecture. We failed to grasp back then—and no available history or theory course was even vaguely implying this—that a *black aesthetic* was buried under that sterility. *American* architecture was as "black" at its core as was American culture generally and American music specifically.

It did not occur to us back then that there was an unacknowledged black aesthetic base of orthodox modernist architecture. We were unable to grasp that the same socioeconomic and cultural conditions that led to the invention of the blues and jazz by African-Americans during the latter part of the nineteenth-century also applied equally to the arts and architecture.[1] In all of our attempted playing at militancy, we were aware in only an abstract and disconnected way of the rich writings and heritage of our own Howard University professor Alain Locke. We simply failed to study Locke's leadership role of attempting to institutionalize a black aesthetic through a "Negro School of Art" just forty years earlier in the Harlem Renaissance.[2]

White and African-American art and art history scholars, chroni-
clers, and authors of dozens of comprehensive treatises on the black
arts have consistently elected not to examine the black relationship to
American architecture. Those scholars usually stop after mentioning
slave era building trades craftsmanship. They usually limit themselves
to brief recitations of the number of African-American architects.[3]
Only a single (white) scholar, John Michael Vlach, comes close to
actual casual use of the term *"Black Architecture"* in a published work
on the subject of the African-American traditions in the arts.[4]

The social upheavals of the sixties had profound and immediate
impact on the organized architecture profession and academia. The
white boys who would define and control the design agenda of
Washington, DC, in the 1970s and 1980s were invariably away in New
England studying at Yale, Princeton, Harvard, Penn, or similar prestigious schools with stars teachers. I was a growing militant at Howard in
1966 when I first heard that Richard Hatch, a white New Jersey architect,
was taking white Ivy League architecture students into black New York
and New Jersey ghettos to do pro bono design work. This movement
was formalized as the Architects Renewal Committee of Harlem, which
quickly became known as ARCH. The mainstream architectural press
was taking notice of this new "savior" and his students.

The all-white ARCH would also become known as "Advocate
Planners."[5] High on rage and low on imagination, several of my classmates and I countered by calling ourselves *"Black Advocate Planners."*[6]
Our problem with white advocate designers and planners was very
much the same as Student Nonviolent Coordinating Committee head
Stokely Carmichael's problem with white radicals in the southern civil
rights campaign.[7] We were enraged. *These were our people* and we
should be getting the resources and recognition for redesigning our
own communities.

By the time I graduated in 1967, the white advocate designers were in
full swing up and down the East Coast. It was as if the white kids that
Carmichael and his boys were dislodging from leadership positions in
Deep South civil rights organizations were reinventing themselves in a

new northern urban ghetto strategy. We simply felt strongly that black architects and planners should be providing the leadership in redeveloping beleaguered black communities. Black residents, budding politicians and sympathetic black bureaucrats invariably felt the same way. Serious minded white radicals also shared our views about the importance of black leadership.

A major breakthrough exception to the growing trend of white advocate planners in black urban areas was the reinvention of the formerly all-white ARCH. By 1968, leadership of the foundation funded ARCH was passed to Max Bond, a black Harvard trained architect. Today Bond is the black architect who probably commands more respect from the white academic wing of the architectural establishment than any other living black architect. Under Bond's late 1960s leadership of ARCH, aesthetic and formal concerns were immediately displaced in favor of more intensive efforts at initiating programs within Harlem. Bond was no ordinary architect. For openers, his architectural training at Harvard came entirely after he had already earned a Harvard undergraduate liberal arts degree.

During those incendiary Black Power charged times, Bond brought the ultimate jaw-dropping credential into a highly skeptical Harlem community of rampant Black Nationalist sentiments. A few years after graduating from Harvard in 1958, he took his considerable skills to Black Africa's first independent state. Bond designed and built public facilities for Kwame Nkrumah's state design and construction arm. He also helped train young Ghanaians in the fledgling architecture school at the University of Science and Technology, Kumasi.

Other recent black architecture school graduates and young practitioners around the country were thinking similar thoughts about the need to find new roles entirely outside of the architectural box. Listen to the words of Carl Anthony, who was carrying on a West Coast variation of the black-white radical movement of the sixties:

> *I really want to do work for the black community. The minute I realized professional parameters I had learned were not supplying that need I came to a crossroad. I didn't want to do corporate buildings*

so I closed my architectural office. Now I'm in community develop-
ment and that meant that I had to lay down my T-Square and raise
money.[8]

Right after graduating from Howard in 1967, my three radicalized
Howard classmates and I sprung into action to reclaim our inner-city
turf from encroaching white "advocate planners" in Washington, DC.
We were determined to be the architect-planner wing of the Black
Power Movement. Our base of operation was the turbulent Shaw
neighborhood adjacent to Howard. Our hell raising militant position
was that the exploding black urban ghettos of America should be re-
planned and designed by black architects and planners.[9]

We managed to get the attention of the great liberal icon Tom
Wicker, erstwhile columnist of the *New York Times.* Our *"black architects*
for black communities" rhetoric was highly offensive to certain conservative elements of the Black Intelligentsia. One highly respected
Howard academic wrote a blistering condemnation of a complimen-
tary article Wicker wrote in the *New York Times* extolling our little
movement. We proudly took that put-down rebuttal as a version of the
NAACP's venerable Roy Wilkens tirade against our new icon, Stokely
Carmichael, and our new religion of Black Power (Wilkins had earlier
proclaimed that *"Black Power was Black Death"*).

The older established black architects in DC found us fascinating
and useful. Some members of the old crowd were acting out of gen-
uine repressed Black Nationalist sentiments. One member of the old
guard quietly but proudly confided in us that he was once a card-car-
rying affiliate of the remnants of the Harlem-based Marcus Garvey
Movement. Others were simply pragmatic opportunists who understood the business development implications of our movement.

We found it necessary to redefine our base and source of black
architectural and planning manpower to counteract the white threat to
our own agenda of being the exclusive planning and design arm of the
Black Power Movement. We identified any historically black university east of the Mississippi with an architecture or city-planning program as an "environmental planning" program. We were stridently

raising the issue that black architects had a moral and political right as well as economic imperative to refocus their growing integrationist aspirations on the task at hand of rebuilding black communities.

Stokely Carmichael was just back in town from the Mississippi war campaigns (along with future Mayor Marion Barry) and had exposed nerves raw in white and black Washington. He was openly calling for audacious Black Power in local government. And he was also openly espousing the need for black "defense forces" to execute several violent white police officers who seemed to be shooting young black men with seeming immunity from prosecution or punishment by the justice system.

Sometime in 1965 around the end of my third year in architecture at Howard, Jerome Lindsey, a mid-1950s Howard graduate, returned to the campus to teach. Lindsey had spent a few years in the Boston-Cambridge area working in the office of pedigreed modernist architect Jose Luis Sert who had also succeeded Walter Gropius as chair of architecture in the Harvard Graduate School of Design. During all of that time spent in the Boston area, Lindsey also acquired a master's degree in architecture and another master's in city planning from MIT. For a number of us, Lindsey was a lightening rod. Only the recently departed charismatic young assistant professor, Joseph Cabiness (affectionate known as "Joe Cab," he went on an extended leave to teach architecture in one of the new schools in Nigeria), was offering us similar intellectual stimulation prior to Lindsey's arrival. Little did we know at that time that Lindsey was preparing some of us to follow in his footsteps to the Boston-Cambridge area for graduate degrees. Those credentials were instrumental in thrusting some of us into academic and professional leadership positions a decade hence.

Lindsey's MIT-Harvard exposure was our own window into heretofore only *rumored* worlds. Vincent Scully at Yale, Louis Kahn at Penn, Jose Luis Sert at Harvard, Collin Rowe at Cornell, John Hejduk at Cooper Union, and the "methodologists" camp on the Berkeley West Coast were parts of the rumors. All of a sudden we were reading the same design theory books that the white boys at those schools were reading. You could no longer "draw" your way out of design studio. You did research papers and sophisticated "design methods analysis." Some of us would soon start to openly emulate Lindsey by expressing our intent to become "architect-planners."

Lindsey had a keen, though not openly apparent, interest in the Black Power Movement that was unfolding upon his return to Howard. He would not have been caught dead publicly spouting Black Nationalist rhetoric around the school. But the project statements, syllabi, reading lists and course lectures he developed or delivered were premised around black economic development. Lindsey was all about housing schemes for Washington's growing black community.

By the start of my fifth year in the fall of 1966, serious black consciousness was permeating the student body in the architecture school. This was all much to the acute discomfort of much of the faculty, except for Lindsey. He seemed to relish the creative tensions of those days. Some of us maintained relations with Student Non-Violent Coordinating Committee big guns Stokely Carmichael and Courtland Cox who had just graduated a year earlier as liberal arts majors. Lindsey's design studio problems and teachings, though without the buzzwords and cadence of black power rhetoric, aligned squarely with the Black Power Movement.

Seven years after his 1964 arrival back on Howard's campus, Lindsey would succeed Howard Mackey. Lindsey would become the first dean of a new freestanding architecture school at Howard. For the previous forty years, architecture had been the junior partner in the School of Engineering and Architecture. "Dean" Mackey was actually the associate dean to the legendary Dean Louis King Downing, a professional engineer. Mackey also held the official title of chairman of the architecture department.

Several years prior to becoming Howard's first full dean of an independent School of Architecture, Lindsey was the beneficiary of a move by the Harvard Graduate School of Design to integrate its faculty with a black senior professor. Shortly after I graduated from Howard in June of 1967, Lindsey went on a several-year hiatus from his teaching position at Howard to assume a position as associate professor at Harvard. He was encouraged to recruit Howard graduates who he felt could be competitive at Harvard's design school. Within a year after graduating from Howard, I would receive a call from Lindsey in Cambridge. He asked me to put together an application and brochure for the master's program at Harvard.

Several of my classmates would also eventually receive the same call from Lindsey. I applied and was accepted, and I arrived in Cambridge with an all expenses stipend to Harvard in January of 1969. I arrived just in time to witness an unbelievable Cambridge police invasion of the campus. There was a horrible overreaction by the police to a harmless student takeover of the office of an administrative dean that resulted in a tear gas "bust" right in Harvard Yard.

I was fully aware that I was a member of the master's class in architecture at Harvard as a result of a deliberately "affirmative action." I also believed that I fell squarely in the middle of the ability range of my class. But I knew that I would not have been there under the orthodox selection process. I came there with my wife and toddler son Marcus who enjoyed romping through the "yard" and Robinson Hall, then home to the design school. Marcus would return to Harvard fifteen years later after earning an honors diploma from Saint Albans School For Boys, a high-powered prep school in Washington, DC. Marcus also brought along a nearly 1,500 (out of 1,600) SAT score. To me, this was ultimate vindication on that touchy "affirmative action" thing that got me into Harvard years earlier. Interestingly, I know numerous conservative "anti-affirmative action" types who passionately believe otherwise. To their way of thinking, Marcus and I both took seats at Harvard that should have gone to more "qualified" white applicants. Hardcore conservatives, white and black, believe that since Harvard can easily fill an entire freshman class with applicants having SAT scores well above 1,500, then that is precisely what Harvard is "morally" as well as "constitutionally" bound to do.

A number of other Howard graduates would also accept Lindsey's help in getting to Harvard including Harry G. Robinson who would eventually succeed Lindsey as dean of architecture at Howard in 1979. Robinson arrived at Harvard shortly after I graduated in May of 1970. There would be several other Howard architecture graduates arriving in at the Harvard Graduate School of Design over the following years.

Several years before Howard Mackey would retire in 1970, he met a Ford Foundation bigwig for lunch at the snooty Cosmos club in Washington, DC. Mackey was successful in his quest to talk Ford into giving him a large grant. The money was to be used to establish an inner-city "urban problems" oriented graduate city planning program in the architecture department. The grant was for 400 thousand dollars (three times that amount in today's world). Ford attached one large string to their grant. Ford wanted the University to pull the architecture department out of the engineering school and establish an independent and full dean headed School of Architecture (no doubt Ford's "string" had the behind-the-scenes blessings of Mackey).

The Howard University search for a successor to Mackey in 1970 would result in the first full dean and leader of a new era. At that time, Howard had a new dynamic young president, James Cheek. The new president had "short listed" Lindsey along with Louis Fry, Jr., a Howard and Harvard graduate who had by then taken over the reins of the local family firm. The list also included Max Bond Jr., another Harvard graduate who was combining a successful Harlem-based practice with a tenure-track teaching position in the School of Architecture at Columbia University.

I took the liberty of getting a meeting with President Cheek. I spoke on behalf of the Young Turk faction in arguing that Lindsey was the most logical choice to be the dean of architecture at Howard. President Cheek had most likely already arrived at the same conclusion. Lindsey left Harvard to assume the reins at Howard in mid-year of 1971. I had come back to DC after finishing up at Harvard in mid-year of 1970. I took a position on the faculty in the undergraduate community development and planning program at Federal City College (now the University of the District of Columbia). Lindsey called me within weeks after his taking over the dean's office in 1971 and I became a junior faculty member in the School of Architecture at Howard in the fall of that year.

One of the most tangible fruits of the new Lindsey administration was his skill in coaxing President Cheek into giving him the about—to-be-vacated hallowed halls of the historic Howard University School of Law building for the officially new architecture school (now the Howard Hamilton Mackey Building). The law school student body had outgrown the facility and was being relocated to another major university facilities acquisition right off of Connecticut Avenue in upper northwest DC. The new architecture school building had served as the *undisputed intellectual center and source of much of the brain power of the national civil rights revolution.*

Despite the ample new digs in the most historic, strategic and visible location on the Howard campus, the next seven years would prove to be deeply frustrating for Lindsey. He had a political tin ear. He made it clear to the faculty from the outset that he had a vision and it didn't include the old guard. In the final analysis, Lindsey proved to be too far out in front of the old, tired, unproductive, and intractable (but fully tenured) core of the faculty he inherited. Lindsey's battles with the faculty bore out that anonymous quotation hanging on the wall in my barbershop; *"old age and treachery will overcome youth and skill every time."*

As one of Lindsey's several designated Young Turk lieutenants charged with covering his back and helping him to implement his initiatives, I was no match for the crafty old heads who were vested in the status quo. I was hopelessly compromised by my own loyalties that were divided between Lindsey and several of his most intractable old guard antagonists. I had previously studied under these men and had long since emotionally bonded with them.

In addition to my full-time teaching duties, I was also trying to emulate the old guard by trying to run a small undercapitalized general practice. The major job on my boards in those days was drawing plans to rehabilitate a group of old houses not too far from Howard's campus. This design commission was my first plum from the new

Lyndon Johnson appointed "Mayor" Walter Washington. I had already developed serious misgivings about orthodox forms of architectural practice and was experimenting with other forms of small design-build and development projects in affordable housing.

Through George Worthy and John Ross, my former Howard classmates and initial business partners, our firm wrangled an interview with the head of Perpetual Savings and Loan Company. At that time in the early 1970s, Perpetual was riding high as the city's most influential financial institution. Thornton Owens Sr., the venerated old white-haired fox sitting at the head of Perpetual, called us in to discuss a small residentially zoned site he owned. His land was located just outside of the DC central business district. The site was zoned to take eleven new townhouses. We assumed that the old man wanted to hire us as his architects. After listening carefully to his tersely worded proposition, it finally dawned upon us that he wanted to know if we were interested in becoming his *partners*. He wanted us to develop, design, build, and sell the homes that his site would yield.

In DC, "players" do "deals." Owens was a "player" and this was my first "deal." Owens proposed that he would put up the land and have Perpetual provide us with all of the acquisition and construction money. We would do the design, coordination of development, and manage the construction. We would also get the units sold through an agent Owens would recommend. Owens would get his land value price plus interest on his construction money. We would get design and management fees. There was to be a 50-50 split of the remaining profit between the Owens-led savings and loan association and our architectural firm.

The obvious catch here is that *there wouldn't be any profit* left to split after Owens got his (inflated) land price and full "floating" "two over New York prime" interests payments. But this was still a terrific deal for us. The "remaining profit" would eventually materialize down the line on other "deals" after I had gained a lot more experience. The important thing was that *I was in the game that I felt counted the most!*

CHAPTER 3

"The Fire Next Time"—April 4, 1968

On that balmy spring evening of April 4th, 1968, members of a my black nationalist architects group known as 2MJQ and me were sitting around in our DC Shaw Urban Renewal Area community design center. We were busy debating the tactics and grand strategies of the by then searing hot Black Power Movement sweeping America and DC.[1] Suddenly someone poked his head through our front door and yelled *"turn on the radio...they shot Martin Luther King!"*

Barely a year out of Howard's architecture school, my initial gut reaction was about the same as many other very angry people throughout Black America. We all said in near unison that *"this is it....the Man is testing our resolve and fire power...it's time to haul out the guns."* Some people did just that. I, on the other hand (and in typical armchair revolutionary fashion), remembered that I did not own a gun and I had not fired one since my 1960 army basic training days back at Fort Ord, California. *So I went home to my wife and three-month-old son Marcus (as in "Marcus Garvey," to the consternation of his budding young scientist-mother who was much less sanguine about the "revolution").*

By midnight, I was back at our community design center right around the corner from Stokely Carmichael's (then a.k.a. Shaka Zulu, today a.k.a. the late Kwame Toure) headquarters near the corner of 14th and U Streets. Carmichael and Marion Shepoloff Barry were both dressed in the uniform de jour. The big Afro hairdo and colorful African print dashiki over a black knit turtleneck shirt was the uniform of choice for most of the college-educated militants. Barry and Carmichael were trying desperately to channel the raging fury of the angry crowd milling in the streets near the 14th and U Streets intersection. By 3 AM that morning, the whole storefront block of 14th Street from U Street to W Street was in flames.[2]

There was nearly a thirteen-year gap between Marion Barry's later actions as Mayor Barry on his first major capital project and those early morning hours on April 5, 1968, after the assassination of Dr. King. That period saw a study progression of actions around the country that were similar to Barry's actions. The 1968 to 1980 time period was literally a paradigm shift in black and white relations across the country. It was the change from steadily increasing black pressure for basic civil rights up to April 1968, toward uncompromising black demands after April 1968. During this entire decade between 1968 and 1978, Howard students, graduates and faculty were at the center of the fermenting changes in entire belief systems.

Urban Renewal, also known as "Negro Removal," had been the modus operandi of choice by the Feds since inception in the early sixties. Nationally famous urban renewal expert Edward Logue started the ball rolling in New Haven in 1962 and moved his road show to Boston several years later. In the process, Logue trained a cadre of tough hard-nosed white boys who fanned out over the old East Coast cities working this game to perfection.[3] Washington, DC, was not spared. The Redevelopment Land Agency (RLA) was largely unaccountable to local government and the needs and interest of a still unorganized Black Washington.

The RLA made today's congressionally appointed financially controlled board look tame by comparison in matters of riding roughshod over black and local interests. The RLA had its own in-house crew of white architects, urban designers, and other administrative types to carry out the "plan."[4] Millions of dollars in federal grant money was at the disposal of the RLA in order for them to enter into land writedown contracts with big time real estate developers. The RLA also had the authority and the money to hire architects, consultants, lawyers, and accountants to administer the federal funds.

The most talented and sophisticated members of the local white architectural community were well positioned. Many had gone to high-powered eastern US architecture schools. They were able to find common ground with the RLA crowd charged with deciding who would design a renewed Washington, DC. Black DC architects were scratching on the RLA windows, but to little avail. The RLA boys just plain didn't think the black firms were sophisticated or smart enough to play the game at that level. Local and out of town developers buying valuable DC land from RLA at fire sale prices were under no political pressure to deal with architects who didn't run in their social circles.

The most notorious urban renewal-Negro removal project in DC as well as around the country in those days of the 1960s was the Southwest Redevelopment Area. A part of Black Washington had resided on these 550 acres of strategically situated land. By the mid-1960s, most of the African-Americans in Southwest DC were relocated to the areas that would explode in fury and flames on the night of Dr. King's death in 1968. It is just as well that the black architects of DC had nothing to do with this catastrophic citywide dispersal. Large numbers of very vulnerable and needy people's lives were literally destroyed. This was the most blatant example of "Negro Removal" style urban renewal. But some of the complex HUD financing and insured housing project tools used in the new Southwest Urban Renewal Area would eventually be refined. Some of those programs would be made usable to rebuild in the riot corridors of Georgia Avenue, Eight and "H" Streets in Northeast, and the 14th Street Shaw Urban Renewal Area.

These federally-funded "tax shelters for the wealthy" programs would become an enduring source of work in Black Washington architectural circles from the early 1960s through today. Not since Hilyard Robinson's commissions of at least a decade earlier had local black architects experienced new high-rise projects on their drawing boards. Sites cleared by the flames of the riots were now on the drawing boards of many of the second-generation black architects.

The worldviews of the first wave of the second-generation black architect-practitioners ranged from the openly black power converts to those who were mortified by the riots and the aftermath. The more conservative architects were invariably the ones who appeared to be making the most progress in developing their practices under the pre-riot status quo. They were expressing grave concerns that things were getting out of hand. They feared an inevitable "train wreck" with the white DC power structure. That wreck would wipe them out along with everyone else. But the immediate aftermath of the week of rioting, burning, and bloodletting had a radicalizing effect on even the most heretofore cautious black practitioners. Establishment reaction to the angry demands for sweeping structural change played a large part.

Immediately after the smoke had cleared from the riots, the white power civil service clique was still firmly in charge of the DC Redevelopment Land Agency (RLA). The RLA was responsible for hiring outside design consultants to formally assess damages and pose new plans for the burned out riot corridors. RLA went into an instinctive "business as usual" mode. The RLA never even seriously considered the black second-generation architectural firms. The RLA did not see the black firms as technically and intellectually up to a leadership role in the planning and design work needing to be done. The RLA was more comfortable with white firms even for work in riot-torn black neighborhoods.

The work needing to be done was essentially "renovation-rehabilitation" work. This was the very stuff that black firms had a long history of doing inside of the black community. This was the less desirable dirty work that white firms didn't want to be bothered with. But now there was a quarter million dollar contract on the RLA table to be awarded (well over a million dollars today). All of a sudden what had historically been "black work" was now work that needed a more "experienced firm" (this was code wording for "favorite white firm"). This attitude on the part of the white RLA technocrats was a blessing in disguise for the black practitioners.

The attitude of the white technocrats was something that even the most unlettered black person in the streets could understand with great clarity. The universal black street level cry was *"black plans, black planners, black architects, black contractors, black skilled labor jobs for the new workers."* Only the latter two demands for black contractors and black skilled labor would prove to be elusive. Skilled jobs and construction contracts never really materialized on the scale of success achieved by the emerging black architects.

In the weeks right after the King assassination in April 1968, the 12 existing black architectural firms smelled blood. The key players were known to refer to their firms as the "Big Six." They were meeting around the clock. To a man (there were no women practices on the scene), they were enraged at the idea that the white boys still in power throughout the DC government condescendingly thought of the black architects as "small renovation specialists." The white technocrats seemed determined to bypass the black architects on what was now a large and lucrative renovation job right in the heart of black Washington. Robert Nash was probably the most public relations and market savvy of the black practitioners. He was an unabashed Black Power Movement player. He captured the mood that would frame all further dealings between black architects and the white decision-makers over the next ten years. After that period, things would get even tenser. According to Nash:

> *Whites can no longer be the paternalistic stumbling, confused step-parents of blacks. Blacks, in turn, are now at the point where it is necessary for them to take a massive, collective, objective look at themselves with black people doing the defining. It's tough, and what may be tougher is that whites have to understand that any role they play in rebuilding and planning for black ghettos has to be defined by Black people! Whites can participate, but no longer at the leadership or decision-making levels to which they are so accustomed. At this very moment, blacks are establishing their own "design criteria," a good portion of which dictates who is to do what and when. Obviously, these standards will insist on maximum involvement of blacks, from layman through professional. This is*

but one element of the insurance policy against the distrust that has mounted over centuries.[5]

Most blacks and many whites will recognize Nash's words. They are a near exact paraphrase of Student Non-Violent Coordinating Committee chairman Stokely Carmichael 's message to white civil rights workers a few years earlier. Carmichael was then in Mississippi and calling for Black Power.

In April 1968 Hilyard Robinson's office was still serving as a teaching office and incubator for future black architects. Robinson would retire in 1970. With no apparent succession plan for preserving the firm beyond his own working life, Robinson's first generation baton was never formally passed. One of Robinson's most able employees, John Sulton, would go on to establish one of the most prominent and enduring second-generation practices in DC. Sulton was a mid-westerner with a degree from Kansas State University. He teamed up with Leroy Campbell, a talented Howard University graduate to open the firm Sultan Campbell in 1960.

Howard University professor Louis Fry, Sr. had carefully groomed his son Louis Fry, Jr. for increasing responsibility for the day-to-day running of the office. Young Fry's preparation was superb. He had an undergraduate degree in sociology from Howard that was followed by dual degrees in architecture and urban design from Harvard during the late fifties. He was following in the footsteps of "Daddy" Fry who had studied at Harvard under Gropius a decade earlier. Louis Jr. topped off his years at Harvard with a prestigious Fulbright year in Holland studying under European modern master architect, Wilhelm Dudok.

Nash (who would become the first black vice president in the national American Institute of Architects) had begun his practice in 1961. Before that, he worked several years in Nigeria at the head of his own construction company. In 1965, the Bryant brothers would open the doors on the first really significant black-owned practice east of Paul R. Williams' firm in California. By 1968, the most significant client bases for these firms were black colleges, of which Howard University was the most accessible, along with the DC government.

Howard was receiving a large part of its annual revenues from the federal government. The University was under heavy pressure and oversight from the Feds to select proven, established (meaning "white") firms for design commissions exceeding simple renovations to existing buildings. This is a perennial problem that has plagued black college presidents since Booker T. Washington's days at Tuskegee in the late 1890s, when prominent northern philanthropies would routinely attempt to attach their favorite white architects to their capital designated gifts of funds to Tuskegee.

Other black clients of black architects included the occasional private residence for the growing class of black professionals now willing to have their modest homes designed by a black architect. There was also the ever-present black church and the occasional small (by white standards) black community-based business, including funeral homes, medical offices, apartment and homebuilders, or insurance companies.

Significantly, in the Washington, DC, of 1968, President Lyndon Johnson was hand-picking a black mayor and black majority city council. These un-elected leaders were social friends, peers, and admirers of DC's fledgling black architectural firm principals. Some of these ties were formed during earlier student days on the campus and fraternity houses at Howard University.

Julian Dugas was Mayor Washington's right-hand man and de facto deputy mayor for (black) economic development. The acerbic Dugas could have passed for white had he chosen to. He was a proud black Washingtonian to the core of his being. He and Mayor Washington inherited a civil service dominated Department of General Services largely staffed by white technocrats who were most comfortable with other white design professionals. These people controlled all aspects of the built environment of DC including the construction of schools and other public facilities in black neighborhoods. These city government technocrats were also beholden to the US Congress, which was still the de facto city council. Any determined, prominent, politically savvy white architect from any state in the union could call or visit his congressman and express an interest in "getting some work in DC."

He would stand a good chance of getting results. However, the DGS technocrats were politically savvy enough to see the advisability of awarding an occasional modest commission to a black architectural firm from time to time.

During the early 1960s, Mayor Walter Washington had the task of upgrading the public school physical plant. The schools had been left to deteriorate after the 1954 Brown Versus Board of Education Supreme Court school desegregation decision as the city experienced massive white flight to adjoining Prince George and Montgomery counties. Black architectural firms would eventually begin to be the recipients of the lion's share of design contracts on these suddenly all-black schools in quickly blackening neighborhoods. The Dugas grip was tightening on the reins of other parts of the DC government. This included the housing agencies, the recreation department, and other public agencies. Dividends for black DC firms were materializing daily.

At the start of 1968, the political climate in DC was extremely tense. The actual King assassination riots were still to come that spring. The most significant built work by black architectural firms was still the work of first generation architects Mackey, Cassell, Robinson, and Fry. Howard's campus and federally funded public housing complexes were still the largest built work.

Many of the twelve black second generation firms in the city had a number of increasingly visible jobs on their boards. The city government technocrats were starting to award public school additions and renovations to the black firms. But the plum new school design jobs for the white firms were still the norm. The public housing additions and renovations for black firms were getting bigger. But the biggest projects were still just outside of the reach of the black firms. In the final analysis, Dr. King's murder in April of 1968 was the event that opened the floodgates for black design commissions.

In 1968, I was deep in the throes of my militant black power, anti-capitalist phase of life. I was very busy stoking the fires of a *"black architects for black communities"* movement. I was employed as an "advocate planner" in the federally funded Office of Economic

Opportunity (OEO). This was my first job after actually graduating from Howard. I had held a number of jobs in conventional architectural offices while still in architecture school. This new job with the OEO paid twenty percent higher than any offer I had received from any one of the city's 12 black architectural firms.

Charles Bryant had just enticed his older brother Robert from the probable certainty of an eventual full "name" partnership in the Connecticut Avenue office of Jewish architect Edmund Dreyfuss. Robert deJongh, a talented architect who was a year behind me in school at Howard, was now chief designer for the Bryant firm. The Bryants were still bumping along under an impenetrable glass ceiling of modest-sized additions and renovations. Local as well as national white firms were positioned to receive commissions to design several very large public school projects in Black Washington prior to April 4, 1968. After the riots, *everything changed*. This was all much to the obvious dismay of the white firms. Those firms had painstakingly structured the delicate social and political relationships that are necessary to land the "big jobs."

By 1970, the unwritten and unspoken "size of the job" glass ceiling maintained by the Department of General Service technocrats would be shattered. The first generation Washington black architect Albert Cassell's architect-son Charles had completed his training at the highly regarded Rensselear Polytechnic Institute in upstate New York. Young Cassell returned to DC for licensure and a solid career. Unlike the Frys, the Cassells did not connect through the father's firm. Charles Cassell went to work as a designer and hospital program manager for the federal Veterans Administration.

The younger Cassell was a charismatic, natural leader and accomplished public orator with a spellbinding speaking voice and style. He was a determined political activist who was thoroughly in line with the Black Power Movement even though eschewing the dashiki uniform and big Afro hairdo. Young Cassell got himself elected to the DC School Board in 1970. He immediately went for the jugular vein of the DC Department of General Service (DGS). Cassell knew that the new

Home Rule government offered golden opportunities for Black Washington and black architects. Cassell promptly maneuvered himself into a leadership role on the School Board Facilities Committee. Cassell then proceeded to assist other like-minded board activists in the formal instigation of what was at that time a seemingly revolutionary notion. Cassell and his allies reasoned that the tax paying citizens of the neighborhoods and communities slated to receive the new facilities should select architects. In lieu of DGS technocrats, lay citizens should be the ones to interview and select architects for all DC school projects. This was a near revolutionary notion inside the existing scheme of things. Predictably, some members of the local white architectural community reacted badly at first. Ironically, a number of prominent white architects felt that there was justification to bring licensure law charges against black architects for ethical violations. With some irony, a number of the city's white architects were accusing black architects of participating in a "...crass political process" in order to affect "merit based" architect selections.

During Charles Cassell's term on the school board, Bryant & Bryant was selected to design the mammoth and historic Dunbar High School Replacement Project. This was a 20-million-dollar project that was earmarked to go to an influential white Georgetown firm prior to April 4, 1968. The Bryants, also with similar community assistance, landed the lead design role in the nationally coveted Washington Technical Institute on upper Connecticut Avenue (to later become the University of the District of Columbia). Other early 1970s actions were taking place to the advantage of the second generation of DC black architects.

The April 1968 King assassination riots in DC were preceded by numerous other urban outbreaks around the country since the Watts Riots of August 1965. Several big ideas were brewing simultaneously in the policy corridors of federal Washington. Each one would have a profound impact on the rise and visibility of black architectural firms in those other exploding urban centers. However, it was in DC with its 12 fledgling second-generation black architectural firms where these federal initiatives would be most dramatically felt. Sudsidized rental housing was right at the top of the list. Lyndon Johnson was waging his two-front war in the rice paddies of Vietnam and the poverty pockets of black urban ghettos.

As Washington was burning in April 1968, city private commercial investment and development literally ceased. Property values for downtown commercially zoned land in the shadows of the United States Capitol collapsed overnight. Prime land was becoming available for a song and dance. Predictably, it wasn't African-Americans buying up cheap downtown commercial land. That activity was confined to a handful of aggressive young white real estate developers with practically unlimited access to insurance and pension fund capital.

Chiefly among the young lions was Oliver Carr, Jr. Within ten years after the April 1968 riots, Carr would have redeveloped his downtown land holdings as glittering new Class-A high-rise office buildings. Was Carr hyper-smart, or was he the offspring of successful earlier generation WASP homebuilder Oliver Carr Sr.? The answer is yes to both of these questions, but the latter answer holds deep significance for the next generation of black architects.

City real estate fortunes are plotted and made by those who are financially positioned and mentally conditioned to deal in five and ten-year pay-off cycles. During the first five-year period after the April 1968 riots, several prominent white developers acted decisively. Led by Carr, they had access to the resources to buy outright or tie up much of the potentially valuable available downtown land. By 1968, the western "golden triangle" of commercial Washington, DC, was largely built out with office buildings, luxury apartments, and high-end shops. This is the part of downtown bounded by New Hampshire Avenue, Pennsylvania Avenue, and 16th Street.

The city was projecting a need for another twenty million square feet of commercial office space, retail shopping, and hotel rooms over the next twenty years. The old eastern downtown directly surrounded by Black Washington was the only place for the developers to turn. The April 1968 riots adjacent to the old downtown made things that much easier for the white developers to assembly the sites at fire sale prices.

CHAPTER 4

The Marion Barry Era: The Rise (and Fall?) of the African-American Architect in Washington, DC, 1968–1998

On the eve of Dr. Martin Luther King's April 4, 1968 assassination, Washington, DC, had a second generation of twelve black-owned architectural firms made up of mostly Howard graduates. Nearly half of these owners were also on the faculty of the Howard architecture school. The firms consisted of the following partnering relationships:

Leroy J. H. Brown
Andrew Bryant
Charles Bryant and Robert Bryant
Joseph Cabiness
Louis Fry, Sr. and Louis Fry, Jr.
Warren Gray
John "Slim" Gray, Frank West, and Yettikoff Wilson
Stewart Hoban
Herbert McDonald and Harry Williams
Robert Nash
John Dennis Sultan and Leroy Campbell
Henderson Walker

All of the above firms were small but steadily progressing practices that each contained the above licensed working partners with an average of two to four draftsmen and sometimes a secretary. With a few exceptions, this was also the typical size for the approximately 150 white firms in Washington, DC, at that time. Between the nights of the Martin Luther King assassination induced riots on April 4, 1968, and the September 1978 Democratic Party mayoral primary election of Marion Barry, major changes occurred. Those one-dozen firms were joined by another one-dozen similarly sized and structured firms for a total of twenty-four black firms in DC.

This was an unprecedented number of black architectural firms in any single city in the world, including independent black African countries. Howard University and its rich architectural education history has been the factor most responsible for the primacy of Washington, DC, as the architectural practice capital of the black world by the 1970s. Federal government agencies, DC government agencies, and black controlled institutions dominated the list of clients for all of these small fledgling sized firms.

By 1972, I had the occasion to renew my ties with my hometown of Los Angeles just as I was also settling in on the faculty at Howard. I was also the owner of a new small practice in Washington, DC. Though with seemingly firm roots in DC, I was still looking for a way to return to Los Angeles. My agenda was to return to LA as a "name" partner in an established black-owned firm. I still idolized the great black L.A. architect Paul Williams. The "Horatio Alger" character of the life of Williams, as New York City historian Michael Adams so aptly put it, is now in retrospect an understatement. In 1976—by that time Williams had retired—I had become very familiar with the black Los Angeles architect scene. I affiliated my small Washington, DC, practice with the more substantial Los Angeles practice of politically well-connected black architect Carey Jenkins(who had caught my eye back in 1958 before I left LA). Jenkins was then designing and overseeing construction of the massive Martin Luther King Hospital medical complex in the heart of my old Watts neighborhood. Jenkins' black "godfather" was Ted Watkins, a wily old labor union warrior. Watkins

was a West Coast version of the pre-mayoral career of the late
Coleman Young of Detroit.

Watkins and his powerful Watts Community Labor Action
Committee was a well-oiled political machine that had the alle-
giance of powerful Los Angeles County Supervisor Ernest Hahn,
who was the Jewish godfather to black South-Central Los Angeles
business and professional interests. The new one-hundred-million-
dollar Martin Luther King Hospital project was being built on the
site of the old Palm Lanes public housing project near where I grew
up. Jenkins had to begin the first phase, forty-million-dollar intake-
care wing as part of a three-way joint venture with two other large
white architectural firms. In one of the rare instances of things
working as intended, Jenkins (with Watkins' and Hahn's help) completed most of the remaining half-dozen support structures on the
site as the sole architect.

Jenkins's project was literally casting shadows on a house my
mother then lived in and that I had spent some time living in before
moving to the East Coast in 1960. Over the course of a two-year relationship with Jenkins that necessitated regular visits to Los Angeles
during the late-1970s, I was struck by the absence of even a single Paul
Williams-class black-owned practice. That is not to say that there were
no black-owned practices of a size that equaled or even exceeded
Williams' practice during its hey-day several decades earlier.
Apparently Williams was unable to prepare a line of black succession
to his firm. Actually there were several impressive Los Angeles practices after Williams. The most notable black practices were those
headed by Robert Kennard and my new mentor, Jenkins.[1]

The old downtown section of Los Angeles experienced phenomenal
and explosive growth. There was development of private sector commercial downtown office towers, shopping malls, and sports-entertain-
ment complexes. The small collection of African-American owned
practices appears to have been literally inundated with 1965-Watts
Rebellion induced publicly funded housing and social services projects
in the neighborhoods. The big downtown privately financed commercial

projects were in another universe that was far removed from black Los Angeles architects.

The Paul Williams of his prime, with his astute marketing sense, business acumen and entrepreneurial bent would have been in the middle of all of the big 1980s private commercial action. Most of the other black Los Angeles practitioners were of an orthodox mindset in their styles of practice. None of these practices appeared to be capitalizing fully on the opportunities opened up in black or white Los Angeles during that period.

The Williams of his prime would have had the best of both worlds in the Los Angeles of the Ronald Reagan 1980s. Williams would have had white patrons and corporate clients engaging him to design downtown office towers. But his Booker T. Washington entrepreneurial deal making mindset would have had him organizing massive public-private community finance-design-build conglomerates in riot devastated South Central Los Angeles.

In his dissertation, Wesley Henderson reminds us through Williams' own words how much Williams was philosophically as well as stylistically close to Booker T. Washington.[2] With such an outlook on life, the Los Angeles of the middle years of the twentieth-century made the odds of success very high for a smart and quietly determined black person. This was the case even in the elite profession of architecture. Williams' Booker T. Washingtonian worldview may also be the reason that he is so pointedly ignored in the thinking and writings of black intellectuals.[3]

Concurrently back in DC the twelve new third generation black-owned firms that materialized over that ten-year stretch between the April 1968 street uprisings and the 1978 mayoral primary were the following men including myself (there were still no women):

Isham Baker and Philip Cooper
Paul Devroaux and Marshall Purnell
Anthony Johns
Edward M. Johnson

Jerome Lindsey
Melvin Mitchell
Harold Navy, Randall Marshall, and Robert Gordon
Harold Lloyd Sanders
Benjamin Skyles and his son Rhoden Skyles
Austin Spriggs
Marion Thomas
Larry Turner, Albert Edgecombe, and John Carter

With the exception of Anthony Johns—a Howard faculty member with degrees from Hampton and the University of Illinois—and the partners Paul Devroaux and Marshall Purnell, all of the principals of this latest crop of practices were also graduates of Howard University. In time, that 1978 presence of Devroaux and Purnell on this list of new firms would take on great significance.

In January 1979, Marion Barry strolled into the Mayors' Office in the District Building. This is an old ornate Beaux Arts structure on 14th and Pennsylvania Avenue just two miles up the street from the US Capitol and right around the corner from the White House. The twenty-four black-owned second and third generation firms were mostly busy with government design contracts acquired from Barry's predecessor, Walter Washington. Their workloads also included design contract work on new subway stations managed by the independent and mostly federally funded Washington Metropolitan Area Transit Authority (WMATA).

Design contracts on new construction and modernization of public housing projects and subsidized apartment buildings had started to become available to some of these firms under Barry's predecessor Walter Washington. All of the DC government agencies responsible for dispensing contracts of every kind were now under the complete control of the young 1978 Home Rule government headed by Barry and his bright, brash lieutenants. A number of them had served with Barry in the Deep South as members of the Student Non-Violent Coordinating Committee (SNNC).[4]

The early years of the first Barry administration were euphoric times for black professionals of all stripes. The Congress of the United States was still in overall command of Washington, DC, but was eager to delegate much of the authority for letting government contracts of every conceivable type to Barry. Much of this "loosening of the reins" attitude by Congress had begun as early as 1964. President Lyndon B. Johnson replaced the old military engineer officer troika of DC commissioners with an initially appointed mayor-city council version of a Home Rule government structure. Johnson appointed New York City Housing Director and native Washingtonian Walter Washington to the position of "Mayor" in 1967. Washington would be the duly and popularly elected mayor by 1974. Real authority—elected Black Power if you will—would be in full bloom by the time Barry took office four years later.[5]

The Washington, DC, black architectural firms had thoroughly established their technical capabilities by that time. They had proven to be competent professionals fully able to execute moderate to large-scale design commissions. Barry's new young aggressively Black Power Movement oriented agency heads had no trouble carrying out Barry's vision. It had not escaped any of these people that black professionals received no play from the still lily-white private non-governmental sectors of Washington, DC. Private commercial and business life just did not include black architects, engineers, lawyers, real estate brokers, and general contractors.

Several black political journalists, including the influential Jonetta Rose Barras, have already rendered historical judgment that Barry's reaction to all of this was fundamentally flawed. Barras, along with most white journalists including television news personality Tom Sherwood, believe that the hundreds of millions of public dollars Barry used to radically expand the black middle class, the black professional firms, and the black entrepreneurial business ranks, was misguided and mostly wasted. They also believe that Barry's policies were callously injurious to the interests of the Washington, DC, black working classes and the underclass.[6] Though he applied his policies broadly to all sectors of government contracting and hiring, Marion Barry's basic position about black architects can be paraphrased thusly:

> ...*until those white private developers and major corporations (whose campaign money largely funded my election) start hiring local black architectural firms, all of the DC government design contracts will go to the black firms!*

This new Barry escalation of the previously and more cautiously applied Walter Washington-Julian Dugas policy of inclusion of black firms dismayed the local white architectural profession. Many of those white firms had earlier enjoyed access to nearly all of the *desirable, profitable, or prestigious* public works funded commissions in black DC neighborhoods. But these white firms, who viewed themselves as reasonable, fair-minded, even politically and socially liberal, were hardly in a moral position to openly protest. They were all very much aware that they still did not have to compete with black architects for their white private sector and large institutional clients and wealthy patrons. Even so, some white firms protested the new Barry policy though quietly and usually behind the scenes.

In 1979, Barry found himself in control of large blocks of prime downtown real estate. These vacant sites were ripe for development as high-rise commercial office buildings, luxury hotels, and retail malls. Barry had Ivanhoe Donaldson, a former SNNC official during the dangerous Mississippi years, constantly at his side as Deputy Mayor for Economic Development. Donaldson was the Mayor's "deal-maker" and also a certified political strategy genius. He had masterminded Barry's shocking upset victory in the 1978 Democratic primary. Both men knew that black votes were not the only thing that elected Barry in 1978.

They knew that, if this newly acquired Black Power and all of the contractual spoils that went along with it were to be retained, they would have to act immediately and creatively. As Barry and Donaldson saw things, keeping black control of the mayoral and key city council offices over the next generation would require a class of wealthy black merchants. The new group of business owners would have to be capable of financing million-dollar election campaigns.

Barry didn't control all of the old downtown east end commercial land. But the small percentage that he did control was made up of key pieces in the white downtown developer's ambitious plans. Barry felt that the consolidation and perpetuation of long-term black power could be partly found in those downtown real estate parcels now firmly under his control. Other parts of the power equation would derive from the awarding of contracts for everything from the cable franchise, heating oil, and lucrative social service maintenance.

It had also not escaped Barry's notice that mid-twentieth-century downtown commercial Washington, DC, had been built by an easily identifiable eclectic collection of powerful wealthy WASP and Jewish families. These were largely the same families that had earlier built the residential neighborhoods of homes and apartments in the city. They would also build the suburbs that were driven by the mushrooming federal highway program (in addition to eventually public school desegregation) of the post World War II era.[7] The second and third generations of these family real estate dynasties largely financed Barry's general election campaign that resulted in a November 1978 landslide victory. These "families" were now looking to expand their fortunes by completing the commercial development of the old east end downtown DC. Barry had one big policy twist for the white development community that can be paraphrased thusly:

> *"When you come in seeking to acquire development rights to downtown land on favorable terms that will result in tens and hundreds of millions in profits, fees, and long-term cash flow to you and your family businesses, **bring a black partner with you.**"*

Barry reasoned that he could create a whole new class of black millionaires by brokering marriages of established white developers to thrusting, politically savvy but struggling black professionals and business people. These were the same black activists—many who had become lawyers—that Barry had developed ties with over the past fifteen years of the Black Power phase of the Civil Rights Movement.

In 1979, the city's two-dozen black architectural firms were taking note of this potential new source of architectural design work. But the black firms actually had their hands full with DC and federal government schools, housing projects, and subway stations. This new opportunity to be involved in work that had up to now been closed off to black firms was intriguing. But this new work was not yet essential to otherwise busy conventional practices. Certainly the older and more established black architects coveted the opportunity to work for the WASP and Jewish family real estate developers. This would be work on shiny clean new office buildings sprouting up downtown. They knew that unless one of these families built on a parcel that Barry controlled they had no chance of doing this type work.

Over the next three successive Barry terms, the white developers, corporations, and financial institutions would build several hundred structures downtown. There would be office buildings, retail centers, and hotel rooms totaling over 22 million square feet of space. Not a single black architectural firm was hired as a prime or lead architect by a white-owned private sector real estate development entity. Several were hired as "associated architects"—meaning an essentially 15 to 25 percent sub-contractual share of architectural and engineering fees.

CHAPTER 5

Barry, Black Architects, Housing, and Downtown

Mayor Marion Barry was good on his word. There would be near total hegemony in DC public school contracts by black architects. Access to those contracts had already started before the April 1968 King assassination initiated riots. After April 4, 1968, black architects had their way on all housing projects that were directly contracted by the two city housing agencies (one agency focused on fully federal financed public housing and the other focused on subsidized or market rate housing projects as well as commercial developments).

In Barry's early years between 1978–1982, the main source of substantial housing commissions were emanating from the already notoriously mismanaged and corrupt public housing administration. That agency perennially sat on literally tens of millions of unspent modernization funds because of the gross lack of appropriate skills of high-ranking technical managers. Nearly all of the waste and corruption was occurring in the awarding and carrying out of contracts for maintenance, property management and construction. Those were areas that, however potentially profitable, were simply of no interest to the city's busy black architects.

My own personal entrée into the Barry orbit as an architect was one of fortuitous timing. After a brief two-year interlude of my small practice serving as the DC branch office of a substantial black-owned firm back in my old hometown of Los Angeles, I re-opened my office under my own financial control and name. This was just before the all-important September 1978 DC primary election. I charged my new partner and old Howard classmate Harry Quintana (and also the New York Puerto Rican member of my former 2MJQ "black advocate planner" group) with helping to get out the vote for Barry. Quintana knew Barry and Donaldson well from the early 1960s "SNICK" days. Barry's plurality win over incumbent Mayor Walter Washington and City Council Chairman Sterling Tucker was our big break.

I then charged Quintana with getting on the housing policy transition team that would help Barry pick a housing czar. After Barry took office that next January, he promptly lured the charismatic and financially imaginative Robert Moore from Houston to serve as housing and community development director. My specific instructions to Quintana were that he find out what plane Moore would be coming in on and be there to greet him.

Quintana got to know Moore and how he thought. Quintana then arranged for me to meet with Moore. There appeared to be good chemistry between us. Moore's academic background was finance. He was—still is—a highly charismatic personality. He was genuinely fascinated by the *idea* of the black architect. He was proud of the substantial public housing design contracts he had steered into the hands of Houston's small but previously left-out contingent of black Howard University trained architects. He was looking forward to an expanded relationship of support to the black firms of Washington, DC. Moore had checked with the Mayor regarding "favors" to be repaid. Barry assured Moore that he was free to work with whoever he was convinced could get a job done.

Moore had a number of immediate headaches. He inherited several projects that had bogged down in the construction phase. New aggressive "inspecting architect" leadership was needed on these projects. Messy money conflicts had broken out between Moore's housing agencies and several crafty general contractors. I didn't immediately press Moore for new, problem-free design contracts. I offered my services to him on these messy inspection jobs. Moore was quite clear about my real interests. Like any other young architect, I wanted to work on exciting high profile projects that would showcase our talents. My "marketing strategy" with Moore worked. I spent the first year of his tenure down in the trenches for him on dirty unprofitable inspection work. For the next several years after that I had all of the housing design contracts I could handle. So did several other savvy young upstart black firms including the Paul Devroaux and Marshall Purnell partnership.

Moore and his key housing aides had identified my firm and Devroaux's firm as savvy young players who had departed from the "uptown" location in the heart of black DC on Georgia Avenue and long favored by most of the other more established black firms. Devroaux and I joined Charles Bryant on upscale Connecticut Avenue in the "golden triangle" business district in Northwest DC. We quickly established an image with the Barry brain trust as the "slick downtown Connecticut Avenue crew."

Moore immediately tackled a notorious dilapidated drug-infested collection of several city blocks containing hundreds of decrepit row houses that were known simply as "Bates Street." The project was located literally in the shadows of the US Capitol. It was also right around the corner from a large DC government warehouse that Moore renovated for re-use as the new headquarters of his growing housing empire.

Moore made the reclamation of Bates Street for new mixed income black home ownership the centerpiece of Barry's housing and community development policy. The project would eventually become engulfed in scandal and viewed as the symbol of the raw corruption and gross incompetence of the Barry administration. Our firms had only minor roles as design architects with no supervisory inspection or payment certification powers on the Bates Street project. Devroaux and I were both untainted by the shenanigans of the inexperienced black developers Moore had lent millions of interest-free public dollars to for the purpose of totally retrofitting Bates Street homes.

Along with Bates Street, Moore targeted the ten largest (and also the most crime-ridden and drug-infested) public housing projects for comprehensive modernization during Barry's first term. He had available millions in city capital dollars and federal housing grants for design and construction. Black architectural firms including Devroaux and mine got several of the largest of those design contracts. In sharp contrast to the architects, the black contractors of Washington, DC, were simply not up to seriously participating in the Barry-Moore intent to put money into black hands. And as architects, we had no interest in using our management skills as contractors.

Moore set aside two of the ten biggest public housing projects for complete razing and redevelopment as market rate apartments and single-family homes. Moore was effectively predating today's popular "HOPE SIX (and now "New Urbanism")" public housing demolition and redevelopment strategy by well over a decade. In 1982, Moore sent out Request For Proposals (RFPs) on the old Parkside Homes public housing site in far northeast DC. That project had been designed forty years earlier by a "salt and pepper" team that included Howard Mackey, the chairman of Howard's architecture department.

The Bates Street Corporation had not yet been publicly exposed for its corrupt mismanaging of the Bates Street Homeownership Initiative. Moore ranked their Parkside RFP submission as the best among the several submissions. The Bates Street boys retained Devroaux as their architect for the new Parkside redevelopment. Once selected, the Bates Street boys promptly borrowed one million dollars from a neighboring Prince George's County savings and loan association. They used the city owned land under Parkside as collateral for the loan. The primary purpose of the loan was for pre-development expenses but they started spending money on things that were not even remotely germane to Parkside.

At least two of the top principals in the Bates Street Corporation would be convicted on grand theft and tax fraud charges and spent time in minimum-security federal prisons. Upon leaving DC at the end of Barry's first term in 1982, Moore would also eventually become ensnared in the criminal justice system quagmire. He was indicted and convicted while at his next job as housing director in Camden, New Jersey, and eventually served time in a federal facility.

The city would eventually wind up having to repay the Bates Street bank loan in order to entice another developer after the Bates Street boys were carted off to jail. It would be another decade before ground would be broken on the new Parkside project. By then, Marilyn Melkonian, a very creative young white woman lawyer, had been installed as the new developer. She had been an assistant secretary in the Carter administration Department of Housing and Urban Development agency. Her new architect was Suman Sorg, a former Devroaux employee. Sorg, a New Delhi, India, native, is a very talented young woman who graduated from Howard's architecture school in the late 1970s. Sorg's white architect-husband and partner, Scott Sorg, was also a Howard architecture school graduate.

The other public housing site that Moore designated for razing and redevelopment as affordable homeownership was the old World War II era Knox Hill Homes on twenty-six acres just off of Alabama Avenue in Anacostia. I received a contract from Moore's office to do a master plan study for the re-use of the site. That study would be enclosed in an RFP that would "hit the street" nearly a decade later, and I would respond.

In the meantime, the world of the local downtown commercial office developers was practically a complete mystery to the city's black architects. On more than one occasion I overheard the more established black DC architectural firm owners lament that "...*no downtown developer has ever invited us to work on a private commercial office project.*" Established commercial developers did not in those days invite *any* architect to "work on their project." This may have been the idealized academic view of how the game was played. The realities of architect selection bore no resemblance to that perspective.

The downtown urban renewal policies of the incoming 1979 Barry administration would prove to be instrumental to several of us becoming privy to this unfamiliar world of the downtown real estate developer. My young architectural firm—though very busy designing public housing projects—would eventually wind up with a ringside seat. The first test demonstration of the efficacy of Barry's policy of demanding that white developers take on black partners came early. Barry had to first reshape the powerful majority white dominated five seat governing board of the Redevelopment Land Agency (RLA) that came under his control as Mayor. Barry quickly engineered a three-person black majority headed by the late Nira Hardon, a lawyer transplant from Los Angeles. Barry's new board also included Bob Moore, his housing director. The board also had a popular minister with an impressive history of community service throughout black DC.

In 1979, the first significant RFP was issued. Barry's reconstituted RLA board was about to cut its teeth. The RFP was for the redevelopment of a two-acre city block. The site was directly on top of one of the new subway system cross-town transfer stations. The site was zoned to allow more than one million square feet of mixed-use office space, a luxury hotel, retail commercial, and upscale housing. Millions of dollars in professional fees, developer's fees, tax credit syndication fees (thanks to 1964 tax laws that drove the 1980s real estate boom), and long-term cash flow from lucrative leases were at stake.

There were numerous development teams submitting offers to Barry's hand-picked RLA board to purchase the land. The land sale would be at a mere fraction of the site's appraised value of over 20 million dollars. The RLA board focused in on two proposals. Herbert Miller, the young Jewish head of Western Development Corporation, headed up one proposal. Miller was a brash, brilliant, and an already wildly successful shopping center developer (today Georgetown Park and Potomac Mills are among his most notable projects). Miller was a high-ranking fundraiser in the Democratic National Party apparatus who was comfortable with well-educated and politically savvy black people. His carefully chosen black partners were Ruby McZier, Carolyn Jordan, and Larry Williams. All three were lawyers who were also close confidants of Barry. They were also close acquaintances with Barry's board appointees, lawyer Nira Long and the Reverend Ernest Gibson.

The other proposal was from Melvin "Cash Call" Lenkin, an equally brash, brilliant, and also successful (but older and more establish) Jewish family development firm head. His carefully selected black partners were Billy Fitzgerald, Samuel Foggie, Orlando Darden, and Doyle Mitchell Sr. These men were the heads of DC's four black financial institutions. Fitzgerald was particularly close to Barry and would provide Barry with a "below market rate" loan to purchase a family home in Anacostia.

Each proposal had to have fairly definitive architectural designs so the architects were prominently featured. The Barry RLA board knew that this was going to be the only way into downtown commercial development work for black architects. The board encouraged white developers to also prevail upon their white architects—firms that the developers had long-standing prior relations with—to take on black architectural joint venture partners. This was self-servingly interpreted by the white architects to mean that the black architectural counterparts could be "associated architects" rather than fully equal joint venture partners. Barry's people did not see a gain in challenging this issue.

My young, two-year-old firm formed an alliance with the young firm of Devroaux and Purnell. Our two firms were the "associated architects" to Miller's big white regional powerhouse architectural firm, Vosbeck, Vosbeck, Kendrick & Redinger of Alexandria, Virginia. Our inclusion on the team came primarily as a result of the social relationships we had developed with Miller's three black lawyer-partners.

The Lenkin team's black "associated architect," Bryant & Bryant, were peers and colleagues of Lenkin's black banker partners. My three partners, Casey Mann, Robert Jayson, and Harry Quintana, and I had all worked for the Bryants back in 1966 while we were all still in architecture school at Howard. Back then Bryant's new office was the birthplace of 2MJQ (Mann, Mitchell, Jayson, Quintana) "Black Advocate Planners." Now 14 years later, all of the 2MJQ members were partners in my new Connecticut Avenue office. My firm, along with Devroaux's firm, was now in a face-off with the mighty Bryants, who by then had become one of the largest and most successful African-American owned firms in the entire country. The Bryants were shrewd (and cash-flush) enough to have pledged a big part of their anticipated share of the project architectural fees in exchange for an equity owner-ship position alongside the four African-American banker-partners.

After much agonizing, the RLA board selected Lenkin along with the black bankers and the Bryants to develop the project—with Barry's behind the scenes nod. Barry made the only logical call. Devroaux and I were still political novices, and were unable to fathom or accept Barry's call at the time. But Barry also knew that he would be in a posi-tion to hand out consolation prizes to all of the losing black develop-ment partners and associated architects later on—*and he did.*

Barry's objective of creating a new class of millionaire developers out of his old allies and cronies ran into a roadblock on this first big test. Mel Lenkin was having second thoughts about giving up thirty-five percent of his deal to people he felt were bringing nothing of sub-stance to the table beyond their political alliance with Barry. It turned out that not a single one of these heads of DC's four struggling black banks and savings and loan companies had the personal net worth or cash liquidity to be viable partners in a big-league, high-stakes down-town development (and they were forbidden by law from pledging the marginal assets of their financial institutions).

Meanwhile, the local press was having a field day breaking stories on how Barry was "forcing" white developers to take on black part-ners who had no actual cash equity. But all of this was nonsense. The very measure of a successful developer has always been the ability to minimize the use of his own money. But the rules of all lucrative games have a strange way of changing when black people figure out a way to get a seat at the table. The reality is that black people were sim-ply "skunks at the party" in this lily-white high-stakes poker game that had always been an exclusively WASP-Jewish affair.

The modest sum of cash that the black bankers actually did surren-der in "cash calls" was serious money in the black world. But those sums were only petty cash to the white developers. This project never got off the ground due to the arrogance and greed of the white players. They were demanding that the blacks either pony up more cash and pledge larger hard assets *or* agree to reduce their equity share of the deal. Their stated rational was that the (usually one hundred percent) financing that was always available to white developers from cash laden syndicates was no longer attainable. This assertion was, again, patent nonsense though seemingly good hardball politics. The project floundered and never got off of the ground (but since reborn by Herb Miller and John Akridge).

Barry's RLA board had several more opportunities to "get it right." Barry had even more potentially lucrative downtown parcels under his control. The next "deal" on the table was a strategically located five acre parcel of land sitting over the main transfer station at the very center of the new regional mass-transit system known simply as the "Metro." This project was known appropriately as "Metro Center." Exclusive development rights to the project had already been awarded by the previous Walter Washington administration. Walter Washington's bureaucrats, without much fanfare, had selected the Oliver T. Carr Company, the city's premier downtown office building developer and the Clark Construction Company, Carr's mammoth contractor partner.

During that previous administration of the 1974 to 1978 period, Mayor Washington had become increasingly bold in awarding public facilities design contracts to black architects. However, Walter Washington moved with caution in dealing with the downtown urban renewal land barons. In 1980, the contrast between Walter Washington and Barry fell into bold relief. Aspects of the Walter Washington award of exclusive rights to develop the nearly two million square feet Metro Center mixed-use complex to The Oliver Carr Company had yet to be fully consummated.

Mayor Barry's position on going forth to sign-off on Carr's rights to the project land was breathtakingly cheeky. I can hypothesize with reasonable certainty that Barry met with Carr and Clark and promptly posed the question *"where are your black partners?"* I can similarly hypothesize that Carr's response was equally cheeky and to the point while completely avoiding Barry's thrust—*"I have all of the partners I need including all of the financing I need to go forward."*

Barry didn't blink…"*yes but you still need me to sign-off on the land disposition agreements.*"

Barry was determined to be more careful about making sure that he had the right black person with the real estate development smarts and toughness as well as the hard assets, net worth, and cash liquidity to sit at Carr's development poker table. That person could be none other than Theodore "Ted" Hagans, already a legend in black Washington for his real estate business acumen and accomplishments.[1] So Oliver Carr, at the mayors' suggestion, calls Hagans for the purpose of discussing an equity partnership opportunity on the Metro Center project. Carr's builder would put in a call to Roger Blunt, a West Point civil engineering graduate, retired army colonel, and the owner of one of the only two large black-owned construction companies in the metropolitan area at that time.

Hagans came into the game with a solid track record of achievements. Over the previous twenty years, Hagans had acquired, rehabilitated, and managed nearly 1,000 apartment units around the city. More impressive and important, Hagans came to Carr's table as the sole managing general partner of Fort Lincoln New Town, a 330-acre tract of vacant land in Northeast Washington, DC, overlooking the rest of the city with panoramic views. Hagans had already gotten the previous Mayor Walter Washington's administration to put in the massive infrastructure needed at the site. Hagans envisioned building 5,000 units of a variety of apartment complexes and homes. The project would include public schools, and commercial retail facilities. By the time Hagans was contacted by Carr about a partnership at Metro Center, Hagans had already successfully built hundreds of new apartments and new homes for moderate and middle income black Washingtonians at Fort Lincoln.

Hagans originally started out at Fort Lincoln back in the early seventies as the "minority" partner on the team of a national white developer selected by a majority white RLA board to develop the project. That previous white developer had assembled nine all-white architectural firms (out of a total of ten firms) to design the sprawling complex. The white developer eventually tired of the political hassles he was getting from the mostly black middle and lower middle class community immediately adjacent to the Fort Lincoln site. The developer walked away.

Hagans had the skill and personal resources, along with the backing of the surrounding black community and the rest of black political Washington, DC. Hagans became the sole owner of all rights to redevelop Fort Lincoln. Hagans quickly demonstrated his gratitude to the black architectural firms that had lobbied relentlessly on his behalf in the struggle to take the reins at Fort Lincoln. Hagans severed all existing contractual relations with most of the white architectural firms and proceeded to hire a new crop of architects. Under Hagans, seven black firms and one Asian firm was in the new mix of firms. The biggest contract as executive architect went to his old Howard University college classmate, Charles Bryant. Hagans had gotten his degree in civil engineering from Howard in the 1950s while Bryant was pursuing an architecture degree there.

For the Metro Center project, Carr already had an established relationship with the giant Chicago-based Skidmore, Owings, and Merrill architectural firm. Universally known as SOM, the company had come to DC twenty years earlier with the John F. Kennedy administration. Gordon Bunshaft, the imperious SOM partner in charge of all design matters, had been appointed by Kennedy to the powerful and prestigious National Fine Arts Commission. The SOM grand old man, political mastermind, and top gun rainmaker for the DC office was the venerable original founding partner Nathaniel "Nat" Owings. Back in 1962, Owings was selected by the young president to come up with the plans and sketches for Kennedy's grand vision for the revitalization of the seedy and down at the heels mile-long Pennsylvania Avenue stretch connecting the White House and the Capitol.

Owings handed day-to-day charge of the SOM Washington office to carefully groomed protégée David M. Childs, a bright charismatic Yale architecture school graduate. Owings took care to use his considerable political influence to see that young Childs was placed on the powerful National Capital Planning Commission (NCPC). This agency protected the federal government's interests on all matters relating to design and planning throughout the metropolitan region. NCPC also coordinated the massive capital budget for publicly funded projects throughout the region.

Childs and the Washington SOM office were largely responsible for changing the visual and stylistic character of downtown commercial Washington. During the 1960s and 1970s, local white architects serving the downtown developer were, with a few exceptions, stuck in the throes of an increasingly crass and mediocre level of growingly passé' "International Style" modern architectural design. Black architects were not afforded the opportunity of contributing to the mediocrity of the "K Street Corridor" architecture.

Childs, with his fluid style, upper class New England grace, and obvious intelligence, was delivering high caliber classically tinged "post-modern" downtown office building designs for prestigious national SOM clients relocating to DC. Those clients were accustomed to the SOM corporate style of practice that was not available from local architectural firms. Childs' work had no trouble getting through the National Fine Arts Commission, and the National Capital Planning Commission. Most importantly, none of this was going unnoticed by local developers who understood the value of having SOM-Childs as their architect.

Oliver Carr, Jr., the smartest and most ambitious of the local developers, tapped SOM-Childs to design Metropolitan Square. This was to be Carr's "break out" project on the revitalizing Pennsylvania Avenue and across the street from the White House. But Carr was not prepared to jettison a long-standing relationship he had with local architect Vlastimil Koubek. This firm had established a solid performance record with Carr by consistently delivering efficient, functional, though uninspiring, design drawings that Carr's contractor-partner James Clark could build within Carr's budgets and on time. Carr, in "shotgun marriage" fashion, teamed SOM up with Koubek on Metropolitan Square.

Having been earlier retained by Carr during the pre-Barry mayoral days to design the big important Metro Center project, SOM-Childs had already anticipated the new Barry policy of "giving up a piece" to a black counterpart. SOM had black architect Reginald Griffin already lined up as the associated architect. The executive director's position at NCPC was also open. Griffin, who had an undergraduate architecture degree and a master's degree in city planning from MIT, found the NCPC position more appealing. Carr, with Ted Hagans' blessing, gave Childs the job of selecting a replacement for the associated architect spot—subject to final approval by Carr of course. Any one of the old original "Big Six" from the two-dozen black DC architectural firms would have been a logical choice for Childs. Bryant & Bryant; Sultan & Campbell; Fry & Welch; Gray, West & Wilson; McDonald & Williams; and Robert J. Nash Associates would all have gladly accepted a chance to claim—even though indirectly—the Oliver Carr Company as a client. However, none of these firms or their principals were of the slightest interest to Childs.

At about that time my two-year-old firm was actually doing a modest sized subsidized housing project in Anacostia with SOM. The big SOM type commercial firms didn't normally do housing—especially modest housing east of the Anacostia River. In this instance, SOM was merely trying to accommodate an important downtown commercial client. That developer had entered a quid pro agreement with the DC government to build 60 units of housing in Anacostia in exchange for increased floor area allowances on a downtown parcel. An SOM associate partner and old personal friend recommended my firm to SOM. I would be the "associated architect" since the developer's downtown parcel needed favors from Barry in order to be feasible.

SOM-Childs was at that time a part of a massive *design-build-construction-manage* consortium on the Nixon Administration-inspired Northeast Corridor Railways and Train Station Revitalization Project. Local architects were selected by the consortium to develop detailed design packages in accordance with overall SOM master plan and design guidelines. As fate would have it, I was then the partner in charge of the Washington office of a black-owned, West Coast-based architectural firm. I had made a presentation to a Northeast Corridor architect selection panel chaired by Childs. Even though our team wasn't selected, I had apparently left a good impression with Childs.

I ran into Childs in the SOM lobby during one of my meetings at the firm's office on the Anacostia housing project. Seemingly out of the blue after the exchange of pleasantries, Childs asked me to stop by his office after my meeting was over to discuss an opportunity that he thought might be of interest to me. That was the birth of a long-term relationship as associated architect to SOM on the Carr-Hagans Metro Center project.

Barry's RLA board and Robert Moore, his community development director, would go on to execute the land sale agreement with Carr. I then had the ringside seat I had always coveted. The view was fascinating and instructive. It became clear to me that without Barry's aggressive policy stance, black architectural firms would see hell freeze over before *"being called in to work on a downtown project."* That just wasn't how this little insular world of private real estate development worked. The realities of this game were not like anything we had been exposed to in our socialization in architectural school or our later world of friendly black controlled government agencies that we would all structure our practices around. This was all about interlocking political, social, personal, and business relationships *that were deeply culturally based.*

During Barry's second term of 1982–86, there was one bigger parcel of commercial land in the Barry RLA arsenal for bargaining with the voracious developer crowd. Left over from the notorious 1960s Southwest Urban Renewal days was a magnificent 14-acre parcel known as The Portals. The site was right off of 14th Street and a prime gateway into the downtown business district on the banks of the Potomac River and facing Virginia. An active railroad train line also bisected the big square block site. Only the most imaginative and expensive design solution could overcome this inherent defect. But the site location could also justify one and a half million square feet of Class-A commercial office space as well as a five-star hotel and upscale retail shops.

The long-awaited RFP drew responses from several big-time developers. Among the local heavy hitters, the star attraction was The Lerner Corporation, developers of White Flint, Wheaton Plaza, Landover and other big regional malls. Our former unsuccessful clients and owners of Western Development Corporation, Herbert Miller and Richard Kramer, had built the classy Georgetown Park mixed-use mall and the gigantic Potomac Mills mall. After losing out to Mel Lenkin and the four black bankers on the China Town-Gallery Place site several years earlier, Miller was back in the hunt. They had black super-lawyer and Barry confidant David Wilmot as their partner.

To sweeten matters, Georgetown architect Arthur Cotton Moore, a perennial heavy hitter, had provided Miller's team with a brilliant Baroque inspired design concept. Moore's design had already been lauded by influential Washington Post architecture critic Ben Forgey as the best design of the five submissions. As an interesting aside, Moore's black associated architect partner was the St. Louis based Fleming Corporation. This company was the successor to the black-owned Los Angeles and St. Louis based firm that I had been affiliated with prior to re-opening my own practice with my three Howard classmates.

The eye-popping suitor was the Rockefeller Center Development Corporation from New York City. At the center of this family owned empire stood the now immortal Rockefeller Center. The company owned millions of square feet of office space in addition to Rockefeller Center. The driving force behind this Washington, DC, pursuit was Rodman Rockefeller, son of Nelson. Rodman Rockefeller was the aggressive young great-grandson of John D. Rockefeller. The Portals was to be Rodman's version of his great grandfather's Depression Era-constructed Rockefeller Center. In a slick multimedia presentation to the RLA board, the Rockefeller scion brashly asserted his intention to build this 250 million dollar project out of family corporate cash flow. He didn't need an all-important, make-or-break construction loan. This offer was backed up in writing. Its obvious credibility made the Rockefeller team look like a sure bet to be selected by Barry's RLA board.

The local black partners quarterbacking young Rockefeller's run at immortality was the law firm Hudson, Leftwich, and Davenport. This was unarguably the smartest and politically savviest black law firm in town. They could give most of the larger white law firms a few lessons the in art of "wheeling and dealing." Willie Leftwich was a Howard University engineering school graduate before deciding on the law. He was a close confident of Mayor Barry. James Hudson was a Morehouse College graduate before coming to Washington to study law at Howard. Chester Davenport was Hudson's classmate at Morehouse and became the first black graduate of the University of Georgia law school. I thought then that Davenport was the smartest lawyer in all of DC, black or white. His wheeling and dealings these days suggests that I wasn't far off the mark. He is now a communications venture capitalist with a personal net worth well in excess of 100 million dollars. I am one of legions of African-Americans who know Davenport and are convinced that, had he been born white, *his net worth would be at least twenty times larger.*

Consistent with well-established Barry policy, all of the teams pursuing the project had the usual "salt and pepper" complements of development partners, general contractors, architects, co-bond counsels, and leasing agents. From a black perspective, the Portals deal would be even more successful than the Metro Center deal that had paired developers Oliver Carr and Ted Hagans, contractors James Clark and Roger Blunt, and architects SOM and my firm, Melvin Mitchell Architects.

The Rockefeller team looked unbeatable. *And I was one of the associated architects* along with my Howard classmate Edward Johnson. We were teamed up with the big New York City design firm of Brennen Beer Gorman who was a favorite Rockefeller architect. We also had Hartman-Cox, a nationally reputable Georgetown firm. Warren Cox had softened Rockefeller's New York architects scheme with a fetching internal open park-like concept for the mammoth project. My ticket onto the Rockefeller dream team was through a long-standing business relationship I had developed with Hudson, Leftwich, and

Davenport. Leftwich, as a confidant to Barry's predecessor Walter Washington, was instrumental in helping me to get a small design contract out of Walter Washington's housing department. I got to know Davenport when he represented me in a lawsuit I filed against a well-heeled but deadbeat client. *I got my money!*

Davenport had taken a leave of absence from the firm to serve in the 1976–1980 Carter administration as an assistant secretary in the Transportation Department. He and Hudson were instrumental in helping me land a large design contract from that agency. So their call to me to join the local cast they had to assemble for Rockefeller's Portals bid was not unexpected. With a Rockefeller win, Johnson and I were looking to split 25 percent of a seven-million-dollar design fee. Several trips to New York City at Rockefeller expense to coordinate the final presentation to the RLA board gave Johnson and me a taste of what it would be like to have Rockefeller as a client. But there is never a sure thing, no matter how good it looks.

The voting and selections went through several false starts but eventually someone had to blink. In the final analysis, two votes on the five-member RLA board felt that it was now local boys Miller and Kramer's turn. The other two votes were solidly in Rockefeller's corner. The swing vote was Barry's housing director and my good friend Robert Moore. He shocked everyone inside of the packed and electrified Department of Housing auditorium that day. Moore bypassed the Miller and Rockefeller teams in favor of a compromise proposal to go with Lerner. Moore's reasons for this action could not be fathomed. Several years later, aspects of the city's developer selection process would become the subject of a federal corruption probe. Just suffice it to say that I was in the middle of big-league, raw politics that was way over my head. It took me a good while to recover from the shock of losing. Lerner was awarded the project but after a year he threw in the towel due to an inability to attract the level and quality of tenants needed to get a construction loan at reasonable rates. After the RLA had hastily rescinded Lerner's designation, a new round of bids were solicited. By then Rockefeller had lost interest and Miller walked away with the coveted Portals prize.

By the start of the second Barry term in office in 1982, still sky-high interest rates and scarce money was taking a toll on even the biggest and wealthiest real estate developers. This had a very negative impact for black firms that were dependent on city work. City tax receipts from real estate developers were down dramatically. Local and federal government curtailed capital spending and contracts dried up. By the end of the third Barry term in 1990, the DC government was in the throes of a financial meltdown and black architectural firms were in crisis just like every other business.

But by the close of the 1990s, Barry and the old Black Power crowd from the late sixties to early seventies would have lost all control or influence over the financial reigns of DC government. That control and eventually the entire government would pass to the "civic minded—good government" regime of Mayor Anthony Williams. Though an African-American, Williams appeared at first to be indifferent to a Black Power-Black Nationalist zeitgeist that Barry was so committed to. After two years in power, Williams has revealed a positively sophisticated attitude towards black power that was not readily apparent during the early months of his administration. Williams has assembled a cadre of young African-American planning and design professionals in policy and decision-making roles. However, their clearly articulated objectives and commitments to the continued utilization of African-American design firms are proving to be far more difficult to achieve than twenty years ago during the Barry years. With the glaring exceptions of Devroaux and Purnell, Sorg Associates, and my old alumni firm of Bryant and Bryant, there is a conspicuous absence of attractive and high profile black-owned architectural firms to choose from in Washington, DC.

I personally gleaned a great deal from my nearly decade-long association with SOM and the Carr Company. My personal and profession interests were still evolving over the course of that relationship. By 1986 and the start of Barry's third term, I had restructured my professional life around full-time teaching in an undergraduate architecture program at the uptown Connecticut Avenue campus of the University of the District of Columbia.

The flexibility of teaching gave me the opportunity to seriously explore my long-held ambition to pursue real estate development with a focus on affordable housing. By 1990, I had completed the transition of my once orthodox practice. I was no longer an architect-planner, but I had become an architect-developer. I keep my hand in public life by accepting several Barry appointments. The first was to the Board of Registrars and Examiners of Architects (later shortened to the Board of Architecture), and the second was to the powerful but contentious Historic Preservation Review Board.

I put my previous experience and exposure to the world of big league real estate development to good use on my own behalf. I was able to assemble several residential parcels, organize investors, and substantially complete several modest sized housing development deals. By acting aggressively and with a developer's modus operandi, I created significant architectural commissions for myself that would not have been available to me under an orthodox practice structure.

The largest such project was Mount Vernon Plaza, a new 250-unit, high-rise-townhouse apartment complex on the edge of downtown. I started planning and assembling this project in the mid-1970s. I had to find just the right lead developer-equity partner. I turned to a former client, the Bush Corporation, out of Norfolk.Norfolk, Virginia. This was an all-white southern family firm that had become comfortable with black architects as lead firms on fairly large housing complexes the company had previously developed in Washington, DC. The Bush people fully accepted my ambition to completely control all architectural design, construction supervision, engineering consultant selections, and fees. In situations such as this, the wrong *partner* would have immediately brought in their favorite big white firm and relegated me to "associated architect" status despite all of my hard work and political connections. Those type of "money" partners will do so without so much as a backwards glance.

The project had to have the help of several classmates and friends in order to pull off this twenty-million-dollar deal. For openers, Duryea Smith, a housing department official, found a two-million-dollar site acquisition grant from the city for us. The late Debbi Hurd, a dear friend and ally from our Harvard days, quarterbacked a crucial four-million-dollar Urban Development Action Grant application through HUD. Shirley Diamond, also a friend and DC housing official, kept a ten-million-dollar bond deal in place long enough for the other pieces to fall in line.

My most professionally fulfilling accomplishments have taken place in the Anacostia section of the city. My "east of the river" activities began in the middle 1970s before I left the faculty at Howard. I began by re-designing small abandoned rental "walk-up" apartments into "co-ops" and "condos" for modest income people. My next "deal" was a 100-unit apartment building renovation-conversion in the Alabama Avenue corridor. I bought the project (for less than ten thousand dollars and a "take over the payments" arrangement) from an old client, who just wanted out of the headaches of owning "slum" properties (his word). In order to complete the project I needed help from a large tax shelter syndication company to raise the five million dollars needed for construction costs.

I went on to do another deal in Anacostia that was located only a short block away from the completed apartment conversion complex. In 1988, I won exclusive rights to develop this project from the city housing agency. I responded to an RFP for submissions from developer-architect teams. My developer client was to be the daughter of the late Ted Hagans, developer of Fort Lincoln and co-developer (with Oliver Carr) of Metro Center. Michele Hagans elected not to go forward in the deal and I was able to eventually move forward on my own as developer-architect.

Over the next ten years I was able to transform this vacated 26-acre site into a newly planned community subdivision of 120 new single-family homes for moderate-middle income families. I had earlier designed a master plan for the site that also made provisions for a new city police precinct building on seven acres and a 125-unit elderly public housing mid-rise structure on four acres. Earlier city government completion of those two projects, both designed by

Sultan Campbell Architects, made the marketing of the single-family homes easier.

There has been a cumulative expenditure of nearly twenty million dollars over the decade-long duration of the project. The "revolving" nature of residential subdivision development allowed me to limit the combined exposure of myself, the city housing agency, my community development corporation equity investors, and my commercial bank lenders to no more than two million dollars at any one time. As the developer of this project with complete control of all critical financial decisions, I had the ability to establish my compensation for design services. My assessment of the value of my services to this project as an architect was very different from the views of a typical subdivision developer.

Most importantly, I can say with confidence that my initiative in pursuing this project in the multifaceted capacity of developer-architect-builder-seller over a decade ago caused a firestorm of similar near-by developments totaling several thousand new homes and condo apartments that are now under construction by previously wary developers.

CHAPTER 6

The 1990s—A New Black Vanguard in Washington, DC

Clearly the 1970s and 1980s period during the first years of a black mayor heading DC was dominated by Howard graduates Bryant & Bryant. The Bryant brothers were the local leaders of two-dozen black-owned architectural firms comprised of principals who were mostly Howard graduates.

Equally clearly, the 1990s belonged to non-Howard graduates Paul Devroaux and his partner Marshall Purnell (D&P). This was largely the result of their superior ability to penetrate the private sector world of institutions and real estate developers. The defining moment in the evolution of this firm was the 1978 vision of founding partner Devrouax, who was able to entice Purnell to join the fledgling young firm.

Devroaux was a rare black Washington, DC, architectural firm head who was not a Howard graduate. In 1979, he was holding forth in a small Dupont Circle basement office doing mostly housing rehabilitation design work. Purnell, also a non-Howard graduate, had spent the past several years working at the national American Institute of Architect headquarters as a minority affairs specialist. Before that, Purnell, a quick-study type, learned the ropes of Washington, DC, over a several year period as a designer in the Georgia Avenue office of Louis Fry, Jr. and Louis Fry, Sr. From there Purnell would join the staff at the national headquarters of the American Institute of Architects. He would be instrumental in helping a small group of the most successful African-American architects from around the country to found the National Organization of Minority Architects (NOMA). The organization was formally launched in 1972.

Purnell was a University of Michigan architecture school graduate. Devroaux was a graduate of historically black Southern University in Baton Rouge, Louisiana. Theirs was a partnership based on highly complementary strengths. Purnell's sophisticated design sense, solid modern management skills, and public relations savvy worked well with Devroaux's highly polished political and "rain making" skills. Their combined strengths would lead them to a series of breakthrough commissions for black firms.

Their first breakthrough came in the early years of the first Barry administration in 1979. Mayor Walter Washington's Jewish public works director Colonel Sam Starobin and his then mainly white technocrats had previously selected a three firm joint venture headed by the big white firm known as VVKR to design a large new municipal center. The joint venture included the two black firms of Devroaux and Purnell (D&P), and Robert Coles, a highly regarded Buffalo, New York, architect. Coles was a University of Minnesota architecture school classmate of VVKR head, Randy Vosbeck.

Barry's government inherited $25 million from the Walter Washington Administration that was earmarked for this new project. The design work by the Vosbeck-D&P-Coles team was largely completed and paid for by the DC government by the time Mayor Barry inherited the project in 1979. Barry decided to abandon that design and re-commission the same design team to redesign the project. Against the advice of his still largely white city planning staff, Barry ordered that the proposed facility be built on the site of the buildings that were torched at the corner of 14th and U Streets on the night of April 4th 1968. *This is the same site that fourteen years earlier a dashiki clad Marion Barry had unsuccessfully tried to help Stokely Carmichael (the late Kwame Toure) to divert an angry torch-bearing crowd away from.*

During the redesign process, Devroaux's firm assumed a higher profile and bonded with Barry and his key lieutenants. Devroaux was now in charge of all interior design, space planning and furnishing fit-outs including Mayor Barry's command center and satellite offices for all of Barry's cabinet members. Devroaux and Purnell were now playing a role with the Barry government that in a perfect world would have fallen to the Bryants or one of the other "big six" Howard graduate headed DC architectural firms.

In yet another example of Devroaux and Purnell's sophisticated thinking, they fully grasped that the renovation work that black firms had historically survived on was now becoming fashionable and lucrative as a result of the national historic preservation movement. The D&P firm won several modest sized historic preservation awards for design work. Meanwhile the Barry government was determined to use another 24 million dollars to completely retrofit the old Pennsylvania Avenue city hall building that housed the Barry Administration. Barry was equally determined that Devrouax and Purnell had established sufficient credentials as preservation experts to justify being selected as sole architects for this project.

There would come to pass an interesting present day twist on this project. Due to the 1990 National Democratic Party loss of control of the US Congress (which still controlled the DC budget), Devroaux and Purnell's completed retrofit design for the Pennsylvania Avenue city hall project was never started. After Barry's internationally infamous Vista Hotel—Rashida Moore FBI sting operation bust, control of the mayor's office and all of Barry's awesome powers shifted to Sharon Pratt-Kelly in the 1990 local elections. Pratt-Kelly had no interest in remaining in the dilapidated Pennsylvania Avenue facility a day longer than was absolutely necessary. Pratt-Kelly was also hell bent on sweeping away all traces of Barry insiders from business dealings with her administration.

Pratt-Kelly got 300 million dollars in fresh funds from a Republican Party controlled Congress that was deliriously happy to see Barry gone. Pratt-Kelly decided to invest some of those public dollars in fitting out a privately leased office building near Judiciary Square for her new administration. Not surprisingly the polished, state-of-the-art computer automated Devroaux firm quickly won the confidence of the new Pratt-Kelly people. Devroaux would get the lucrative interior design contract for Pratt-Kelly's new Judiciary Plaza city hall "palace."

Pratt-Kelly's 1990–1994 "interlude" term has been characterized by some people as a completely disastrous miniature replica of the earlier one-term Jimmy Carter presidency. History may reveal that neither Carter nor Pratt-Kelly were as incompetent as they might appear to be today. Paradigm shifts and gale wind economic and political forces of globalization were well outside of their purview. Both served what I believe will eventually prove to have been useful transitional roles.

Over the course of Barry's twenty-year tenure, Devroaux and Purnell got stronger and more viable as many of the two dozen black firms that greeted Barry in 1979 got weaker. By the end of Pratt-Kelly's term in 1994, Barry had literally risen from the dead. He completed his six-month prison term, completed drug and alcohol rehabilitation, joined the DC City Council representing Ward Eight located east of Anacostia River, and rebuilt his political machine. Barry would reclaim the mayor's office in the September 1994 primary face-off against the beleaguered Pratt-Kelly and the luckless city council member John Ray. Shortly there after, a badly broken DC government was placed under the bankruptcy style receivership care of a Congressionally appointed financial control board.

Money was no longer available under the new regime to restore the old Pennsylvania Avenue City Hall landmark. Conrad Monts, a very clever and politically well-connected black developer, talked a slim majority of the DC City Council into giving him full financial control of the building. This was done in order for him to arrange to completely retrofit the project on a turnkey finance-design-build basis. The new price tag under this scenario doubled to $52 million. For his services and risks, Monts would receive a developer's fee of 6 million dollars.[1]

In a complete reversal of the actions of Ted Hagans twenty years earlier at Fort Lincoln, Monts elected to bring in a white architectural firm to re-draw D&P's completed plans. Apparently Monts managed to convince himself that Shalom Baranes—a very high profile commercial architect and favorite of influential Washington post architecture critic Ben Forgey—could do more for the project and garner greater favor with lenders, federal government tenant prospects, and the architectural mainstream press than could D&P. Monts relegated this extraordinarily able and proven black firm to the status of "associated architect."

In stark contrast to Marion Barry and Ted Hagans, Monts was obviously smitten by the old twin shibboleths that are rampant throughout the black world. As such thinking goes, white people's *"ice is colder and their sugar is sweeter."* This line of reasoning quickly leads to the adoption of the vacuous and intellectually pre-judgmental, *"I want only the very best, regardless of race"* sloganeering. Such thinking still too often afflicts even the most intelligent black people when handed the opportunity to exercise real power.

Devroaux and Purnell would disregard this callous slight by Monts. They would eventually go on to make trail blazing breakthroughs on the downtown commercial office design front. Over the Barry years several black firms including D&P and my own firm had achieved "associated architect" roles on now completed downtown commercial work. But it was left up to D&P to actually achieve what had not been done in DC by a black firm since the days of master builder-architect John Lankford in 1902; D&P landed a prime architect role on a massive 300,000 square feet commercial office building to be built on one of the Northeast H Street 1968 riot scarred commercial corridors that Barry was committed to revitalizing.

In the early 1980s, Marion Barry's RLA awarded exclusive rights to develop this tract to a large well-connected white developer. This developer was partnered with the powerful and very competent black controlled H-Street Community Development Corporation. Part of the development rights included a lease from Barry for most of the space in the proposed building to be placed on the site. With Barry's blessing this team was able to go forward on the project with D&P as the prime and sole architect of record for this complex. They completed the design and delivered drawings, specs, and building permits in record time. Ground was broken in the mid-1980s.

Going into the 1990s with full design credit as the prime architects for several large privately constructed commercial office buildings under their belt, this firm was armed with the edge needed to earnestly pursue private developers and large institutional clients who build big downtown type projects. The firm got word of another big office complex being planned in the metropolitan area where black professionals were in the midst of the architect selection process. This time the quarry was the massive Federal Home Loan Bank. The Northern Virginia regional office needed to build a large regional headquarters on a five-acre site in Vienna, Virginia—just seven miles across the DC line. Through his powerful black allies inside of top management of that agency, D&P was able to make the "short list" that contained some of the most recognized architectural names in the country. D&P was able to make the case hands down that the firm was equally qualified to do the project as a prime. They were eventually selected for this commission.

The success of the project led to a similar 150,000 square foot corporate headquarters in Richmond, Virginia. This project was for a regional banking powerhouse. Here also, the firm was able to count on the support of powerful black corporate level professionals inside of that organization. Shortly after that triumph, the finely tuned D&P network antennae revealed that the giant Washington, DC, based Potomac Electric Power Company (PEPCO) was going to consolidate its scattered forces. PEPCO wanted a 350,000 square foot headquarters building in downtown DC.

This was not a project that the Barry administration exerted very much leverage on. PEPCO already had the land, the necessary zoning, and all of the money in the world. D&P was on its own. The firm would have to rely on a now solid track record of several major municipal government commissions, a 300,000 sq. ft. downtown DC commercial office building, the 150,000 sq. ft. corporate headquarters in Richmond, an impressive 190,000 square foot office complex in

Northern Virginia for the prestigious Federal Home Loan Bank and several other completed projects.

But D&P was also a savvy realist. The architectural firms that are attracted to throwing their hats in the ring for 350,000 square foot corporate headquarters buildings will usually have at least ten, and often many more, completed projects of a similar or far greater size to flash on the wall in the all important "slide show" interview. And the people within a company who are charged with making a selection decision usually go for the sure thing. That is simply the safe career move for corporate bureaucrats charged with architect selection. If a corporate manager selects a household name that fails to deliver, that manager is not necessarily assumed to have exercised poor judgment in having chosen that firm. However, if the manager selects an unknown "dark horse" that fails to *deliver spectacularly,* he or she may be looking for a new job or career. This part of the story ends happily with PEPCO's selection of D&P as the prime and sole architect for this fifty-million dollar project. The building they designed was completed in mid-2002 and is being well received around town.

By the middle of Barry's last 1994–1998 term in office, Devroaux was no longer just an architect in the market place hunting architectural fee commissions. He had evolved into a consummate "player" and "deal maker." Big white (and black) prospective clients search him out to be a key member of their strategy team that has to structure complex real estate transactions that require a thoroughgoing working knowledge of how business is done in the city.

After nearly twenty years, the Republic Development Corporation—now owned by Herbert Miller's old 1980s partner Richard Kramer—came back to D&P in 1997. The DC government had another big downtown parcel for development as a 400,000 square foot office building. Republic figured that D&P would be the perfect choice of an architectural firm that combined proven competence with big league political instincts and connections. This project is now slated for a late 2001 groundbreaking.

It was practically inevitable that upon the return of architectural patron saint Barry to the mayor's office in January 1995, Devroaux and Purnell would be well positioned to take full advantage of their hard won experiences over the last twenty years of their presence on the DC scene. Barry's first piece of vintage *Barryism* upon his return was to take up an offer from Abe Polin, the professional basketball franchise owner of the Washington Bullets. Polin wanted to bring the Washington Bullets from Polin's aging Capital Arena in suburban Landover, Maryland to a downtown DC location. This would be the culmination of a long-time dream of Polin, who was raised in DC.

Polin made an audacious proposal to Barry and the city council. Polin's view was that if given a piece of prime downtown city land plus other financial incentives, he would build a new basketball arena and relocate his team there. The new Polin arena would also accommodate the city's ice hockey franchise and provide a place for the popular Georgetown Hoyas basketball team. This was the kind of complex deal that could only happen through Barry's concentrated efforts of bringing all of the conflicting interests together while cutting through the city's perennially sluggish regulatory and permit approval bureaucracy.

The piece of land that Polin wanted from Barry was the same vacant two-acre block sitting on top of the subway that Barry's RLA board had awarded development rights to his black banker friends 14 years earlier. This land had sat vacant for all of those years waiting for the banker group and their white partners to wrap up their deal and put financing in place. It was painfully obvious to Barry that this deal was not going anywhere and he had been forced to terminate the banker's development rights during his previous term.

The Polin Arena deal, which Barry was determined to complete as part of his legacy, ran into a temporary setback of a most unexpected and unusual kind. Over the years of his tenure as Mayor and his commitment to black wealth creation, downtown real estate wasn't the only thing Barry was able to steer to his black friends. During Barry's second term he was in the position of awarding the city cable franchise. Robert Johnson, the brilliant black entrepreneur that Barry selected for this award, went on to use that as the base of vast personal and corporate wealth. By the time of Barry's 1995 return to power—with Johnson's considerable financial help—Johnson had amassed a fortune that ranked him as one of the 100 wealthiest people in the Washington metropolitan area.

Johnson's company Black Entertainment Television, now simply known as BET, came from nearly nothing to being one of the top black-owned businesses in America. All of this occurred on Barry's watch and as a result of his "in your face whitey" commitment to create black millionaires. Johnson now had the kind of undreamed of black wealth and power matched only by the late Reginald Lewis of Beatrice Foods fame. Barry had to go through the formalities of awarding development rights to the China Town subway site to Polin through Barry's handpicked RLA board. At this point, *Johnson threw a monkey wrench in the Barry-Polin plan for a quick closing of a deal on the proposed new 20,000 seat arena.*

Johnson's BET empire had expanded from its Barry conferred DC cable franchise base to national status as a publicly traded company. With a personal net worth now approaching a half billion dollars, Johnson felt that he should be in on this arena deal. It just so happens that Polin had not only wanted Barry and the city to give him the land to build the arena. Polin also wanted the city to provide the 200 million dollar construction costs in the form of a tax-free municipal bond.

Bob Johnson's next moves literally changed the course of history. He began by publicly offering to buy Polin's basketball team for 50 million dollars. An NBA franchise was the perfect crown jewel for Johnson's black media empire. *And* Johnson stipulated that he—*Bob Johnson*—would use his own money to build the arena—thus saving the city a considerable sum of money that would be lost to uncollected tax revenues. Polin had to counter if he had any hopes of realizing his long time vision of seeing his beloved Bullets return to his hometown.

Polin publicly announced his response to Johnson's offer to the city; *Polin's basketball team was not for sale to Johnson at any price.* And that he—*Abe Polin*—would use *his* own money to build the arena. All of black and white Washington was watching this power struggle between black personal wealth of the likes never dreamed of before and Jewish wealth, pride, and expectations of city largess in return for many past good deeds.

With obvious conflicted emotions, Barry's black majority RLA board had to award development rights to the man with the one thing that mattered most—*the ownership of an NBA franchise.* So with a 200 million dollar project hanging in the balance, where were DC's black architectural firms in all of this? Again, one would logically think that one or more members of the "Big Six" that had greeted Barry on his ascendancy to the mayor's office nearly 20 years earlier, would have to be a part of the consortium of design firms needed to perform the required services.

Only D&P emerged as part of Abe Polin's design team. That team was comprised of the de rigueur big powerful white out of town architectural firm (the known as Smith Grylls Hinchman of Detroit, now consolidated as the Smith Group). The design team also included the highly respected local white owned design firm of Keyes Condon Florance (since acquired by the Smith Group). The D&P firm played a major role in the locally and nationally lauded final design outcome of what is now known as the MCI Center. Marshall Purnell, along with D&P's top designer, Anthony Brown, were largely responsible for the brilliant exterior façade designs of the huge two square blocks MCI Center.

The old second generation "Big Six" of DC African-American architectural firms—or whatever was left of it by now twenty years after it was self declared—could only look on with amazement at D&P effectiveness. Paul Devroaux and Marshall Purnell were not only the new confirmed deans of DC black architects; they had positioned the firm as one of DC's premier architectural firms, black or white.

Also by now there was still a paucity of serious black construction firms in DC. This was still an area that was of no apparent interest to the city's black architectural firms. Black construction firms from outside of the metropolitan area were drawn to the arena deal. In addition to D&P on the design team, the Smoot Company, a large, mid-west-based black family owned general contractor, was joint venture partner to the giant Clark Construction Company that submitted the most responsive bid to build the arena.

After the ink was dry but before the ground was broken on Barry's downtown arena deal, the mayor had one more giant public works project that he would add to his legacy before leaving office in 1998. Before Barry left office in 1990 for a four-year hiatus that was divided between jail and a brief reign as the city councilman for Anacostia, he had started plans to build a new convention center. The new center was badly needed to replace the aging undersized convention center built by Walter Washington back in the 1970s.

Barry's replacement convention center preliminary plans had been periodically flashing up on the computer screens of the Devroaux and Purnell firm since the last days of the Barry administration in 1989. It was inevitable that Barry would turn his full attention to this matter once he had the Polin Arena project in the ground. Devroaux and Purnell, with Barry's blessing, would eventually pick one of the many competing national heavyweight architectural firms to align themselves with to respond to the RFP for architectural services on the new 450 million dollar convention center project.

D&P elected to join forces with Thompson Ventulett & Stainback, a big white Atlanta firm with a stellar national track record in the successful design of convention centers. A deal of this magnitude absolutely had to have the participation of a local white design firm. The big Atlanta firm and D&P both had strong past working relationships with highly respected local architect, Ted Mariani. The builder would be the same "salt and pepper" joint venture of Clark Construction Company and the Smoot Company that was now busy building the Polin Arena.

Just as earlier on the MCI Center, the D&P firm was not there just as window dressing. D&P and this project's big white lead architectural firm engaged in spirited internal office-to-office design competitions for the establishment of basic convention center design layouts and building exteriors. And again, similar to events that occurred on the MCI Center, the convention center client representatives consistently chose conceptual layouts and exterior elevations that had been generated by Marshall Purnell and chief designer Anthony Brown of D&P.

A century earlier, Daniel Burnham gave downtown Washington a new "living room" at Union Station, modeled after the Roman Baths of Caracalla. Paul Devroaux and Marshall Purnell would share equally in giving Washington its two most important civic commercial edifices of the twenty-first century. D&P were brilliantly retracing black architect Hilyard Robinson's footsteps of sixty years earlier. In the early 1930s, in order to land the sprawling 274 unit Langston Terrace social housing commission, Robinson put together a team consisting of his own firm, the firm of Paul Williams of Los Angeles, and the local white firm of Irving Porter Associates.

Along the way of racking up equal marquee billing, design responsibilities, and architectural fee sharing in these two giant downtown public works projects for Marion Barry, Devroaux and Purnell are going into the year 2001 well positioned. There is a near certainty that either they can approach—or be approached by—a major equity financial partner with the simple elegant proposition to "...*assemble and acquire a downtown site, program and design a high quality income producing facility, get the facility built, and either sell it for a 100 percent return on our investment or prepare to manage it as a long term asset for our portfolio...*"

However, despite their success in rising to the top of the heap of African-American owned firms in Washington, more questions are raised than answered about the fate and future of the firm. The biggest question has to do with the capacity of the firm to grow in time and scope beyond the founding principals, Paul Devroaux and Marshall Purnell. Devroaux, like myself, grew up in South Central Los Angeles during the 1950s. While we didn't know each other—he was three years behind me and attending cross-town rival Manual Arts High School—Devroaux actually met the legendary black architect Paul Williams back then. In some respects, Devroaux has already matched Williams' incomparable successes even though Devroaux is just turning sixty years old as of this writing. Paul William's firm died along with Williams' death in 1979. Devroaux's ability to build a next generation line of succession may be his greatest challenge.

At the close of the twentieth-century D&P ascendancy must be set in context. Over the course of D&P's twenty-five-years of evolvement from one of the mostly small black firms that greeted Marion Barry's taking over as mayor, Howard architecture school graduates founded no more than five additional firms in the DC area. Only two have survived as potentially viable enterprises. Only one of them, Suman Sorg Architects & Engineers, show evidence of reaching D&P levels of achievement.

Several of the original two dozen black architectural firms that greeted Barry in 1978 are now defunct. Out of the remaining firms, including D&P, probably no more than several at most have any remote prospects of rising to similar levels of institutional and commercial accomplishment within an essentially orthodox practice modus operandi.

Meanwhile, over that same 25-year period, the 200 mostly small white architectural firms in the city have also undergone wholesale transformation. The branch offices of large national full service firms now dominate the annual listing of the city's 25 top fee grossing architectural firms. Howard graduate and New Delhi native Suman Sorg's firm was on the 1999 listing of the city's top grossing architectural firms.[2] Sorg appears to have an abundance of public sector work. Whether Sorg, a former D&P employee in the mid-1980s, has assembled the nucleus of a private sector and institutional clientele that her firm can grow with is not yet apparent.

The late Howard University architecture head Howard Hamilton Mackey aspired to the notion that the best of us at Howard would go on to develop big and important practices or achieve high visibility partnerships in front-line practices on the local scene. And a few actually did so. The most notables were Charles Bryant and his late younger brother Robert; the late Leroy Campbell, the late Robert Nash, Louis Fry, Jr., Harold Navy and Randall Marshall, the late Frank

West, his surviving partner John "Slim" Gray, and Gary Bowden as a senior vice-president of RTKL in Baltimore.

Away from Washington, DC, there were several conspicuous success stories. The most notable include Harold Morrison of Jamaica (who was also the first husband of famed writer Toni Morrison), Robert and Donna deJongh (and now Robert, Jr., their New York City based architect son) of the Virgin Islands, the late Walter Blackburn in Indianapolis, the late Robert "Skip" Perkins of New Orleans, the late Harry Simmons Jr. of Brooklyn, New York, Ronald Frazier of Miami, Oscar "Spike" Harris of Atlanta, William Bruton of Denver, and Harold Thompson of Memphis, Tennessee.

Whether the school, during the third quarter of the twentieth-century Mackey era, should have produced more people doing big things in Washington, DC, after the first early 1960s rebellions is an important question. It is also a difficult and complex question when considered in the larger context of black cultural consciousness. Washington, DC, is an incredibly difficult place to effectively do anything outside of the proverbial "Three A's" (attorneys, accountants, associations).[3] A retrospective thirty-year review of the "Book of Lists" of various businesses in the Washington, DC, area is eye opening.[4] Only several of the financial institutions that were around thirty years ago are still around today.

It is therefore not surprising that the list of 1978's top 25 fee grossing architectural firms bear almost no resemblance to the list of the top 25 architectural firms at the end of the Marion Barry mayoral years in 1998. With only rare exceptions, the largest and most successful black firms such as Devroaux and Purnell do not show up on any of those types of listings in DC and other heavily black populated big cities around the country.

In 1979, as Marion Barry was taking office, Washington, DC, had a population of 600,000 people, down from 850,000 people just thirty-five-years earlier. The black percentage of the DC population was in the middle seventy percent range. An even more interesting set of numbers is that by then DC had grown from its old original 200 year old, 100 square mile L'Enfant-Ellicott-Banneker Plan boundaries to a sprawling 4,000 square mile National Capital Region of nearly four million people. Nearly one million of those people are African-Americans. Over 400,000 of them are in DC, with about the same amount in adjacent Prince George's County, and the rest spread out among the other counties surrounding the District.

Black architects, much like their white counterparts, were conditioned to operate strictly within the parameters of the "design services contract." For white firms, this meant all private sector work plus the choicest public sector work. For black firms, it meant no private sector work (black people have rarely owned businesses that have felt the need to hire architects) and only *some* of the public sector work—usually the most problematic, the most unprofitable, and the most unglamorous.

As of today none of the second generation Howard University trained architectural firm owners have been able to capitalize on the tidal wave of nearly a million new people and the attendant private and corporately funded commercial, institutional, and residential growth throughout the region over the past thirty years. One can only conclude that the development of a conventionally structured substantial black-owned architectural practice is more of an aberration rather than a normal occurrence within the existing paradigms of professional practices. This condition holds with only minor variations in every other major metropolitan region in the country, regardless of the size of the non-white core central city population.

Washington, DC, at the close of the twentieth-century makes clear a number of things about black architectural practices. There are over one million African-Americans currently in metropolitan Washington and they are projected to grow in numbers by another half million people by the year 2020. Yet clearly the traditional governmental client mainstay of the DC metropolitan regions black architect can no longer provide the basis of healthy growth, stability, or financially and professionally rewarding architectural practices. *A fundamentally new model is essential.*

Over the years between 1920 and today, the presence of the School of Architecture at Howard University in Washington, DC, is largely the cause of the presence of over 120 licensed black architects (out of a total of just over 1,500 licenced DC architects) in the District of Columbia.[5] This eight percent of black architects presence is four times the national percentage. However, this has to be seen in the context of the sixty-five percent black population total within Washington, DC, and twenty-five percent in the capital region. *This is a woeful under-representation of black firms in the National Capital Region at the dawn of the twenty-first century.*

At the same time, Howard University may also no longer be a viable client objective for conventionally structured African-American firms. The era when the top leadership of Howard University held a personal commitment to the welfare and growth of alumni architectural firms has passed into history. Current top leadership has, in their own minds, much bigger fish to fry and has completely delegated the issue of architect selection to several steps removed bureaucrats. Those persons hold no sensitivity to black business and professional development or commitment to the utilization of alumni architects in conventional owner-architect type relationships.

Concurrently, the present leadership of the School of Architecture has yet to articulate a position on the atrophy of Howard University trained architectural practice leadership in the Washington area of today or in the coming future. We are forced to assume that there is no "Howard position" or attitude about such matters.

This state of affairs at Howard was recently dramatized in the form of several recent Request For Proposals (RFP) for Architectural Services for the design of major campus research facilities. In the RFPs, the Howard bureaucrats included revealing language that spoke volumes about their state of mind. The RFP asked in effect that all submitting firms give *assurance that they will make efforts to provide sub-contractual opportunities to minority owned firms.* What was being strongly infered by the university officials responsibilities for design firm selection is that as far as they are concerned, *no African-American* *owned firm or firms exist that are capable of fulfilling the role of prime archi-*tect on these proposed multi-million dollar facilities planned for the Howard campus.

CHAPTER 7

The Tuskegee-Howard Family Tree

1892–1972
WASHINGTON, DC, BLACK ARCHITECTS ENTERING
PRACTICE, 1950–1980

Booker T. Washington
Tuskegee Institute
Founded 1881

Robert Robinson Taylor
B.A. in Architecture, 1892
Massachusetts Institute of Technology
Washington Recruits Taylor to Organize
Department of Mechanical Industries, 1892

Faculty
William Sidney Pittman—Robert R. Taylor—Wallace Rayford

Graduate **John Lankford (1876–1946)**
Establishes Jacksonville, FL Office, 1899
Lankford Arrives in DC 1902
Founds DC Branch of Negro Business League 1903
Designed True Reformers Building, 11th & U Streets, 1903

William Sidney Pittman Arrives in DC, 1905
Works in Lankford's Office
Pittman Wins Design Contract for Negro Building
at Jamestown, VA, 1907

William Augustus "Pop" Hazel, Tuskegee Instructor
Arrives at Howard in 1919
Offers First Courses in Architecture
Recruits Albert I. Cassell in 1923

Cassell Becomes Department Chair 1924
Cassell Hires Hilyard Robinson in 1924
Robinson Becomes Head of Program in 1926
President Mordecai Johnson Appoints Cassell as
University Architect, 1926

Howard Hamilton Mackey Arrives, 1924
Mackey Organizes National Exhibition of
Negro Architects' Work at Howard Fine Arts Gallery, 1931

School of Engineering & Architecture Established, 1934

Mackey Become Permanent Chair in 1934
Recruits the Following Full-Time African-American Faculty
Between 1936–1968

Leroy John Henry Brown
Joseph D. Cabiness
Louis Edwin Fry, Sr. FAIA
Warren Gray
Granville Hurley, FAIA
Anthony N. Johns, FAIA

Jerome Lindsey
Kermit Keith
Robert Madison, FAIA
Frank G. West Jr.

**Mackey Receives Ford Foundation Grant to Establish
Independent School of Architecture & Planning, 1970**

Mackey Retires, 1971

President James Cheek selects Jerome Lindsey as Dean, 1971

**Between 1949 and 1978, the Following Architecture Program
Graduates Become DC Area Practitioners as Principals and Partners**
*Michael B. Amos
Isham Baker, FAIA
Ralph Belton
Gary Bowden, FAIA
*Leroy John Henry Brown
*Donald Bruner
Luther Bruner
Andrew Bryant
Charles Bryant, FAIA
*Robert Bryant, FAIA
Joseph D. Cabiness
*Leroy Campbell
John Carter
Phillip Cooper
Albert Edgecombe
Claude Ford
Steward Hoban
James Huntley
*Robert Ballard Gordon
John Gray

Edward M. Johnson
William Lawson, FAIA
Jerome Lindsey
Jose Mapily
Randall Marshall
Herbert McDonald
Willie McGee
William Middleton
Melvin L. Mitchell, FAIA
*Mwata Mitchell
*Robert Moore
*Robert Nash, FAIA
Harold Navy
Jack Patrick
Ralph Poe
Don Roberts
Harry G. Robinson, III, FAIA
Harold Lloyd Sanders
*Benjiman Skyles
Austin Spriggs
Marion Thomas
Lawrence Turner
Henderson Walker
*Frank G. West, Jr
Harry Williams
Yetticoff Wilson

*Deceased

PART III

MANIFESTOS FOR
THE NEXT GENERATION

CHAPTER 1

Beaux Arts-Bauhaus Myths, Rituals, and Fetishes

At the heart of contemporary design studio pedagogy for many architectural schools is the theory and technique of studio teaching exercises popularized by an "underground" paper written in the early 1950s.[1] That paper, *"Transparency: Literal and Phenomenal,"* was authored by several people. The lead author was the late Colin Rowe, who was an extremely clever and facile British transplant. Rowe has been the most influential and intellectually prolific architectural educator of the last half of the twentieth-century. Rowe and a collection of like-minded young Turks—now immortalized as the *Texas Rangers*—captured the Beaux Arts (with an emerging Frank Lloyd Wright wing) architecture school at the University of Texas at Austin. This group was able to turn the school into a laboratory to develop their pedagogy over the middle years of the 1950s.

Most knowledgeable scholars are in agreement that essentially the Colin Rowe-Texas Ranger pedagogy was a conflation of theories and graphic techniques of turn of the twentieth-century cubist painter Picasso, modernist architects Le Corbusier, Frank Lloyd Wright and Mies van der Rohe, and visual aspects of Gestalt psychology.[2] The Rangers were right about a major assertion that their pedagogy was very teachable and learnable by average people. Over the years in academia, I have found this pedagogy to be a more interesting way of teaching the descriptive geometry that I believe is the sole "drawing" skill that is essential to architects (and just about anyone else purporting to have a liberal arts education).

The effect and impact of Rowe and the rest of the Texas Rangers on American architectural education has been sweeping, even though now largely transparent to many of today's young faculty members. Alexander Caragonne, a former Cornell student of Rowe, has meticulously documented Texas Ranger pedagogic development in a compelling book, *The Texas Rangers: Notes of an Architectural Underground*.[3] Caragonne's book confirms my long-held suspicion that in today's information age, the highly ritualized "design studio culture" pedagogy has never truly been essential to the achievement of *Texas Ranger* objectives. Such objectives could have just as easily been accomplished through the use of a series of highly useful graphics lab textbooks (developed from Ranger pedagogy).[4]

In today's world, the setting for the use of these textbooks could be either "on line," in a computer lab setting, or in a standard classroom. The continuation of the design studio ritual and culture throughout today's American architectural schools promotes other hidden "boot camp" indoctrination and socialization agendas. Those agendas have been explored at length by a number of observant educators. Among others, the most compelling, though hostile, and condescending critique of studio has come from University of Wisconsin anthropology professor Amos Rappaport.[5] More recently, Linda Groat, a University of Michigan architecture professor, and Sherry Ahrenstzen, a University of Wisconsin architecture professor, have weighed in on this subject. Both women are offering more balanced and less shrill critiques about the hegemonic influences of studio culture and ritual.[6]

The problem is that many people conducting these supposedly cultural and sociologically neutral studio "boot camps" rarely have even the foggiest notion about the sources and objectives of the "exercises." Rowe held deep reverence for Le Corbusier and Andrea Palladio, but was ambivalent towards Frank Lloyd Wright. Rowe thought that Wright's design approach was much too idiosyncratic for pedagogic adaptation. Rowe possessed an apparently photographic mind for European architectural history and details. While not interested in building, he was a terrific propagandist in the same mode as early twentieth-century European modernist Le Corbusier. Rowe and his Ranger faculty colleagues and their most capable (all-white) student acolytes at Texas fanned out from Austin and literally reshaped architectural education throughout the U.S.

The "Colin Rowe studio" approach to architectural education holds relevance for the typical HBCU architecture program *only when fully comprehended, and placed in proper historical, social, cultural, and Information Technology based context* by those attempting to apply this methodology. The pedagogy is largely confined to formal and spatial technique while purporting to be non-ideological on critical social, economic, and cultural issues confronting the next generation of African-American architects. Without full and proper context, Rowe's pedagogy will only continue to retard the progress and potential of students seeking roles of *effectiveness* in culture specific community development.

One of Rowe's 1950s faculty colleagues and fellow "Texas Ranger" was the late John Hejduk, former dean of architecture at Cooper Union in New York. Hejduk was the creator of the ubiquitous "nine square exercise" design studio problem. This entails the graphic or paper model development of near infinite variations of three-dimensional "rubric cube" descriptive geometry exercises. In most instances, the exercises are conflated variations of Le Corbusier's canonical Villa Savoye house and Palladio's 15th century Villa Rotunda.[7] These first year studio exercises are all staple fare in most early year American architecture school studios including the historically black schools and programs. This easily teachable approach to architectural design—purportedly facilitating "spatial thinking" ("in the manner of" Le Corbusier) by the novice student—can be more efficiently mastered in a complete digital electronic environment by students who have achieved basic competency in the geometries (plane, descriptive, and analytic).

Current super-star architect Richard Meier, a 1960s Cornell University trained architect, was deeply influenced by Colin Rowe's pedagogy and worldview. Meier is a person of obviously high intelligence, discipline, and focus. His uncompromising commitment to the language and aesthetic of Picasso-Corbusian design theory and methodology as conceptualized by Rowe and the Rangers back in the 1950s is beyond question.[8] Some observant people have gone so far as to accuse Meier of having reinvented himself as Le Corbusier (the 1920s Parisian villa era version).

Meier's design for the billion-dollar Getty Museum complex in Los Angeles is the logical outcome of the pedagogy of the "nine square exercise" design studio problem done on that Silicon Valley class workstation. Pencils, yellow tracing paper, chipboard model-making paper, exacto knives, markers, T-squares, triangles, drafting tables, etc.—the standard tools in today's orthodox architecture school design studio—are nothing more than antiquated and counterproductive cultural baggage.

Again, everything must start with the complete abandoning of dysfunctional myths, rituals, and fetishes that have no demonstrable relevance to the past plight or future needs and opportunities of an economically awakening Black America. Those myths and rituals must be ruthlessly replaced with hard realities. Myths and rituals must also be replaced with goals, objectives and methods that are internally consistent with an irreversible (and geometrically accelerating) Information Age Revolution that we are fortunate enough to be actually living through.

The intentions of studio pedagogy can be seen in its clearest form at the Harvard Graduate School of Design. There, the brightest of bright young students are herded together in a three afternoon per week ritual inside of Gund Hall, a giant sloping glass roof enclosed warehouse of a building at the center of the campus. Each of the three different year levels of students are assigned a drafting table in a cubicle lined up in succession. Imagine something that you have seen in actuality or in a picture; a giant World War II era warehouse full of drafting tables and full of engineering draftsman drawing plans for large airplanes or automobiles (the draftsman are all white males of course).

In Gund Hall, design studios are arrayed to allow each group to visually connect by looking up (or down) at another studio. This basic plan layout—the "parti"—of the Harvard design school was conceived and built in the late 1960s era prior to the introduction of computers into architecture. Desktop and laptop computers are now found randomly resting on drafting tables throughout student cubicles. At Harvard, those computers are mostly used as electronic drafting machines rather than as actual design tools while up the street at MIT, the same computers are routinely used to increasingly full potential as design tools.

At Harvard, these young people all quickly fall in line army bootcamp style by personalizing their cubicles with sketches and miniature cardboard models (of late, wood models to simulate the style popularized 500 years ago during the Italian Renaissance). They all spend endless hours making manual drawings and models "in the manner of" the current "star" architect of their fantasies. All else in studio is unchanged from the last one-hundred years. Students are coached to be little "Palladios" from the Italian Renaissance of 500 years ago. Some of them began to think of themselves as little "Le Corbusiers" incarnate from just eighty years ago. Then there are the little "Frank Gehrys," "Tadeo Andos," and so on.

Unlike at the average architecture school, most world-renowned jet-setting American and European "star" architects are regular visitors to the Harvard design studios. The "stars" are a critical integral part of the socialization process. By serving as "one-on-one" critics (each student can count on getting thirty minutes each week with a "master") the "stars" reveal truths to the student acolytes about the thought processes that can result in world class "signature" buildings (there is little interest in either the "generic" or the "vernacular" building).

The real objective of most of the students is to be invited to work in the office of their "star" masters and mentors upon graduation. Starting salaries offered by the masters is usually in the range of what a starting school teacher, fireman, or policeman will earn. This is considered to be an acceptable trade-off for the privilege of working for a "star." Needless to say, these salaries are from one-half to one-fourth of those paid to new graduates of professional programs of similar duration and difficulties such as law, business, computer sciences, engineering, or the medical sciences.

This entire studio pedagogy and cultural dynamic makes perfectly good sense in a perverse way at Harvard. Most of the students are racially, ethnically, and culturally able to completely identify with the virtually all-white male power elite of architecture. Even more important, there is usually an identity of interest with the larger (also virtually all-white male) culture of institutions and private corporations who hire the "star" architect-masters. In all fairness, "star" architects have no problem with hiring black Harvard graduates who fully absorb the culture of the studio and display the appropriate level of "in the manner of the master" design skills. Thus far, such employment has yet to translate into those black employees becoming "star" architects through patronage and commissions from the same clientele base that the "stars" draw from.[9]

But there will often occur the absurdity of black Harvard graduates being puzzled by their inability to establish orthodox style architectural design hegemony inside of the nearby black communities such as Roxbury. Those are the students who completely misread the dynamics of the design studio at Harvard. Those students have much in common with many of the black students exiting from historically black architecture schools. The HBCU programs are attempting to employ the same design studio pedagogy (and culture) used with apparent success at Harvard and similar Ivy League type institutions in the possession of staggering wealth and resources.

In the space of a recent week, I had occasion to spend time reviewing studio work and talking to students at Harvard's design school, and an upper division group at HBCU Hampton in the Virginia Tidewater area. Harvard's studios are, in their own words, comprised of:

"A stellar faculty, unparallel resources, and a global perspective ...the leading institution dedicated to the education and development of design professionals in architecture, landscape architecture, and urban planning and design. Our extraordinary faculty provides an unparalleled range of design philosophies and visions to our students..."(from a current admissions office bulletin, www.gsd.harvard.edu).

As a graduate of the Harvard program who has had occasion to stay in close touch since leaving in 1970, I can attest first hand to the accuracy of the above self-proclamation. The studio pedagogy offered at Harvard is unfortunately also attempted at HBCU institutions that are not remotely equipped to do so. The HBCUs utilize the same textbooks and pedagogic techniques and philosophies as Harvard does in science and math as well as most of the other social sciences. Empirical evidence strongly indicates that this works reasonably well. However, in the matter of educating architects, this "parallelism" approach by the HBCU fails abjectly.

Fundamentally, the Harvard architecture studio is a "high culture" WASP-Jewish parlor game exercise in socialization. The students recruited by Harvard to participate in this game are a mainly WASP-Jewish mixture with a smattering of *others*: Asians, Hispanics, a handful of African-Americans, and an occassional African. The design studio is the arena that sanctions the status quo of the cultural hegemony, aesthetic tastes, and financial-political power assumptions of the "high culture" values of the elites of western societies. The studio is not the arena that engages students in acquiring the skills and mindset to change the status quo distribution of urban land assets and resources. Only the creative combination of the ideology, tools and techniques of the real estate courses in the business school, cultural analysis in the fine and liberal arts, the hard technology of the engineering school, and alliances with the nearest law school offer the prospects of a change in that status quo.

Probably the most provocative thing one can say to young architects is...*stop drawing*. That is sheer blasphemy in the culture of architecture still dominated by professors of my age (and who still hold sway in the schools). Yet in the name of survival and effectiveness we must direct our students to "stop drawing" and instead go over to our university based fine arts departments and *start painting, making videos, and making music.* Those actions, in tandem with our computer-based study of the business and management issues inherent to the making of the built environment, might place them in a better position to exercise the power to change minds, create value and shape the future. The following is the final paragraph in an informative book on the subject of the history and role of methods of visual communications in architecture through the ages by British architect-professor Tom Porter:

> *In the past every architectural design began its life on a blank piece of paper. It is well known that Joseph Paxton initially visualized his ideas for the Crystal Palace with a prophetic diagram scribbled on a blotting pad; that Oscar Niemeyer drafted the basic geometry of the form of Brasilia on the back of a cigarette packet; and that Charles Moore would doodle designs on a table napkin...The advent of a cybernetic technology, however, reverses the journey of a concept and turns the act of design outside-in. Instead of externalizing ideas to experience them, the designer is dematerialized and transposed to be digitally represented by and within the same information system that represents the design.*[10]

Most of the architectural world is in consensus that architecture began about 10,000 years ago in the Tigris-Euphrates River valley when mankind shifted from a nomadic life to one of agriculture and animal husbandry. This single occurrence resulted in the ability to create a surplus of food and leisure time, and a propensity to build places of worship to commemorate such good fortune. But interestingly enough, Professor Porter then reminds us that "drawing" as we understand that word has been a key tool in making architecture for just a little over one-tenth of that 10,000 year period:

> *Plans, as such, were not used in the design of western European architecture until the rediscovery of Euclidean geometry in 1230*

AD. Without this geometry the forms of the Gothic cathedrals would not have been possible...

From the 15th century Renaissance up to today's accelerating information age revolution, architects have been obsessed with drawing, despite there being no essential relationship of the actual making of architecture and drawing (recent historic examples were the built work of skilled black slave craftsmen of the ante-bellum South. Those slaves made magnificent architecture even though they were illiterate and without drawing skills as we understand the term). Professor Porter continues to hit the mark:

During the 1970s and 1980s architectural drawing went beyond the level of a window on the design process and became elevated to the status of a work of art, exhibited on the international art market.

The question that begs an answer is how and why "drawing" still occupies such a hallowed and all consuming place in the typical architecture school today. A significant portion of the tenured professorate of architecture schools may hold the key to part of the answer. That electronic databases and intelligent systems should be the starting point of attempting to conceptualize or physically express a built-environment proposition may not yet be an acceptable notion in many such venues.

The professorate is joined in resistance to this type of environment and modus operandi by many of the still working senior principals in the multitude of small pre-information age architectural offices right outside of the gates of the academy. This is one of the most vexing problems facing school leadership who have looked down over the cliff and glimpsed the digitized future that actually started taking shape over fifty years ago.

Most reasonably informed people are aware of the fact that the industries America still globally leads are computer chip design and manufacturing, aviation and automobiles. Such persons would also have to be aware that those industries owe much of the competitive leadership to their wholehearted adoption of state-of-the-art

Information Technology—not to be confused with CAD. Design, production and manufacturing, and marketing are a nearly seamless digital electronic enterprise. But architects have this strange fetish about their 1,000-year old commitment to pencils and manual drawing technique. Who but today's architects would demand that the computer simulate their beloved ancient hand lettering styles?

Regarding "drawing," all accredited architecture schools have embraced computer-assisted drawing, now universally referred to as simply CAD. However, CAD must not be mistaken for serious holistic and fully integrated-interactive Information Technology. Most architectural school design studio faculty still favor a manual sketching based pedagogy over the intensely Information Technology alternatives now available on a relatively inexpensive basis. Time and retirements may eventually resolve this. An agnostic stance on Information Technology may be acceptable for upper class young people committed to emulating how they *think* their favorite faculty or media star gurus design buildings. *African-American (and other) students harboring serious interest in redeveloping America's cities must be provided with clear headed guidance about the realities of who makes cities and how, versus present day studio myths about city building.*

Much of the electronic studio work taking place in elite high profile design schools is nothing more than mindless esoteric computer modeling of abstractions with accompanying metaphorical musings. There may still be a place for such activity in an architectural curriculum. But it cannot be mistaken as being the main event. We are justified in speculating about whether Columbia's star history and theory professor Kenneth Frampton may also have had his own school in mind in his observation that in the use of computer-aided design, some European architectural schools are exhibiting:

> [a] tendency of studio teaching to oscillate between the simplistic application of technique and the generation of fashionable images.[11]

The unfortunate thing is that I have so many friends throughout the profession and the academy who are convinced with religious faith that their manual drawing skills—inept as those skills more often than not are—are what distinguish and define them as architects from other more authoritative professions such as law and engineering. That is an inaccurate and potentially fatal misreading of the meaning of being an architect in the twenty-first century.

The drawing fetish has no basis in fact. It is no more than cultural baggage. Architect's pleadings about the essentiality of their drawing prowess *abound!*[12] One cannot fail to notice that these pleadings are intended more to convince themselves and gullible students than others. At some point, architects must ask themselves *"if drawing skills are so important, why is it that the profession is so subservient to politicians and lawyer-real estate developers who have no drawing skills to speak of?"* Architects *visualize* but it is politicians and lawyer-developers who are truly providing society with *visions*. Architects' visualizations that are limited to what they can draw are never the answer to the societal problem at hand to be solved. In his book, *Why Architects Draw*, Edward Robbins offers this telling observation:

> As important as drawing is to contemporary architectural practice, it is not a function of some inevitable process of architectural thought or action. It is the result of choices architects made at a particular time in their history, which were made for a variety of reasons and which have had a number of important implications for both architectural creation and the organization of architectural practice…To assure that drawing remains the crucial and shared medium of architectural discourse, its use is kept at the center of architectural education…This form of education makes the architect somewhat unique in our society. While drawing has been a crucial mode of discourse within architecture and a central part of architectural education for centuries, the same cannot be said of the role of drawing in society in general. This too is the result of a social decision…The use of drawing by architects also presumes relatively pliant client and a public willing to accept the architects' mode of symbolic representation as the primary basis for architectural communications. Ironically, it also puts them in a socially and economically dependent situation. Their expertise and the instruments they

use to realize them come into play only after decisions about what is to be built, where it is to be built, by whom, for what purposes, and at what cost have already for the most part been made.[13]

A part of the confusion is that architects have yet to arrive at a consensus as to what is meant by "to draw." Some are merely talking about routine engineering based systems of graphic representation, which can be readily taught to elementary school children. I would be much more impressed if advocates in this camp exhibited more awareness of the potentially profound impact that Froebal type drawing exercises can have on latent spatial cognitive development.

I do not believe that college age is too late to introduce Froebal type exercises when there is no evidence that students have already been exposed to this pedagogy. But many are usually oblivious to this connection in spite of prior knowledge of the role this pedagogy played in the early years of Frank Lloyd Wright, arguably one of contemporary history's most visionary persons.

There is still another camp that interprets "drawing" to mean the freehand sketching ability of being able to look at a landscape of buildings and surrounding entourage and capture that image on paper with a pencil. Some feel that an inability to do this makes it all but impossible to be able to "design." Yet there is no empirical evidence to support this proposition.

Then there is that third camp that believes that there is something called "design drawing" and that there is a "design process" that can only be successfully undertaken through the medium of "design drawing." The fallacy of "design by drawing" was effectively disposed of in the 1970s by the British inspired "design methods" movement. There are still architects—inside and outside of the academy—who claim to be able to immediately detect spaces built from computer assisted design generated drawings. They claim that such spaces are invariably inferior in quality to spaces built from manually designed methods. This is effectively disposed of for the sheer nonsense that it represents by Malcolm McCoughlin's recent book, *Abstracting Craft*.[14] He posits convincingly that the "craft" issue associated with manual drawing is equally applicable to computer usage.

The "manual design drawing" camp would be first in line to extol the brilliance of the spaces created by today's reigning star artist-architect Frank Gehry and his Guggenheim Museum at Bilbao, Spain. It is common knowledge that Gehry's current designs are totally dependent on a highly sophisticated computer assisted design system to produce technical drawing instructions for the construction of his highly personalized manual doodling. According to Gehry, he uses software that was originally used to design high performance French military aircraft to facilitate his current giant free form sculptural fantasies including Bilbao.[15] Yet, Gehry-like creations attempted by architecture students are often encouraged without in-depth discussions about the implications of such inappropriate activity.

When some reluctant architects say that the computer is "just another tool" in the making of architecture—usually in not so subtle attempts at a put-down of the computer—that is tantamount to the 15th century transcriber monk who probably said that the new Guttenberg printing press was just another form of the crow-quill pen. Let me clarify my own position on the issue and relevancy of "drawing" to the task at hand of leading the charge of conceptualizing, constructing and managing the built environment. All persons of normal intelligence possess latent abilities to draw mechanically as well as artistically through freehand. It doesn't require university courses to unlock these latent abilities. The necessary time is more like hours if under the guidance of competent instruction.

I hold no prejudgment against students who come to me in full possession of artistic drawing skills. I simply caution them repeatedly that those beguiling and seductive artistic skills of two-dimensional doodling are not the critical abilities that will assist them in becoming a well-rounded effective architectural practitioner and leader.[16] In fact, I remind them that such skills can work against them if they are not mindful.

My greatest exasperation comes from architects—those who are inside and outside of the formal architectural academy—who simply cannot distinguish between "design" talent and "delineation" talent. I am most distressed upon encountering bright young curious minded people who say, "I could be interested in pursuing a career in architecture but I can't (or don't like to) draw." I become apoplectic when I overhear colleagues reply, *"you're right—if you don't like to draw, architecture may not be for you."* I contend that it is an effectively, if not knowingly, anti-black (and probably anti-female) position to privilege manual drawing virtuosity (or pleasure) as a prerequisite for entrance to architectural careers.

Architects, as a class, seem to live in mortal fear that any renunciation of "drawing" would be tantamount to suicide. Irrational as this might be, it is the ultimate and bedrock belief that "drawing" is the sine qua non of being an architect that still guides curriculum and the core socialization process. Meanwhile, people with no presumptive skill in drawing continue to be the definers and "envisioners" of the built environment.

It could be that architectural icons like Frank Lloyd Wright appear to the uncritical eye and mind as the epitome of the architect as consummate skilled drawing maker. What might have been a correct observation 100 years ago—or even as little as 50 years ago—is simply not true today. Mr. Wright did indeed "draw like an angel." *But that was his least significant skill and qualification.* Wright's drawing abilities were dwarfed by his skills as a communicator in important arenas where drawing was not the medium of communication. Couple that with his towering, bombastic ego, his mesmerizing charisma, his palpably high intellectual powers of analysis, and his leadership skills—and then you began to see the makings of a master architect-builder of timeless proportions. It is vitally important that the next generation be guided to a better understanding of the truly important qualities possessed by the master architects we routinely socialize them to revere. "Drawing" can no longer continue to rank very high on the list.

Think about this....*every single drawing, video, and photograph of the buildings and other artifacts that make up the man-built environment now in existence on earth can be captured as digitized random access memory (it may have already been done)*. The entire environment can now be captured in video form and accessed as "virtual reality." Therefore, there is no possible basis to expect anyone other than an idiosyncratic art-minded patron to be willing to pay to have something built from a drawing, as we have traditionally understood that term. There are those who contend that it takes someone who can "draw" to use Information Technology properly in the construction and capture of those digitized virtual reality images. There is no empirical evidence to support this preposterous self-serving position.

Here also is Robbins' quote of one of the country's most celebrated "design" architects, Michael Graves, who makes his case for the essentiality of drawing as the essence of the architect's practice. Graves, a Princeton architecture school design studio professor, is highly representative of his profession:

> *One could ask if it is possible to imagine a building without drawing it. Although there are, I presume, other methods of describing one's architectural ideas, there is little doubt in my mind of the capacity of the drawn image to depict the imagined life of a building. If we are ultimately discussing the quality of architecture, which results from a mode of conceptualization, then certainly the level of richness is increased by the component of inquiry derived from the art of drawing itself. Without the discipline of drawing, it would seem difficult, to employ in the architecture the imagined life which has been previously recorded and concurrently understood by virtue of the drawn idea.*[17]

That Graves, and many of his fellow architects, passionately believe this doesn't make it true. For openers, I would refer the Graveses of the world to the body of published work by William Mitchell, dean of architecture at MIT. But for my own frame of reference, Edward Robbins provides the most telling rejoinder:

> *The essentialization of drawing and its appropriation by architects creates the material basis for architecture's own ideological mystification. As an apparently natural instrument of cultural discourse*

the drawing hides its own historical specificity and the social con-
struction of its "essential" nature and place in architectural prac-
tice...Essentialization may be a source of empowerment. It may just
as easily become the basis for paralysis. Insistence on an essential
role for drawing in architecture, and the ways that such a role influ-
ences how architects think and practice, may preclude the architect
of the future from maintaining a pre-eminent position as a cultural
creator...Advances being made in computer technologies and soft-
ware, along with others being made in structural engineering, may
make the drawing and the type of thinking it represents and privi-
*leges obsolete. The cultural capital that the capacity to **represent***
***through drawings** brings the architect may become a liability as*
society makes new social and technological demands on the archi-
tect and on architecture itself (bold italics mine).[18]

While Robbins' words are only a few short years old, his "far in the future" speculations have already been borne out by the current state of Information Technology. The irony is that only the most elite and hyper-wealthy architecture schools can afford to ignore his words (but rest assured that those are precisely the schools that will not ignore Robbins' words). A historically black school that does not overturn every conceivable stone to forge ahead of the curve of Information Technology is courting disaster.

The architectural academy has just completed what I thought would be the architectural equivalent of the nearly 100-year old *Flexner Report* that revolutionized the modern medical profession at the start of the twentieth-century.[19] Abraham Flexner, a medical doctor, recommended closing down half of the existing medical schools and reorganizing the remaining schools around a group of highly sophisticated, knowledge-based and clinic-oriented teaching hospitals. Today, despite of the encroachment of managed care accountants, that system of integrated medical education and practice is the envy of the world for the power, prestige, financial rewards and ability to match supply to demand. The implications for the architecture profession are striking.[20]

Understandably, the Carnegie-Boyer Report (CBR) stops short of straying too far outside of the entrenched paradigm of the 123 member schools that comprise the engine of the architectural academy.[21] The client and commissioners of the CBR are a coalition of what is known as "the five collateral organizations" that in effect represent the entire American architectural establishment. The five organizations consist of the American Institute of Architects (AIA), which speaks for and attempts to service the business interests of the professional practitioner.

There is also the National Council of Architectural Registration Boards (NCARB), which attempts to assist the states in the regulation of the practice of architecture through examinations and licensure; the American Collegiate Schools of Architecture (ACSA), which is the faculty voice of the architectural schools; the National Architectural Accrediting Board (NAAB), which maintains accreditation standards; and finally, the American Institute of Architecture Students (AIAS), which is the voice of the students. These collateral organizations are now embarking upon a more intense public relations campaign of trying to convince an increasingly skeptical paying public of the added "value" of the architect.

The CBR does not fundamentally challenge the academy's most cherished myths, sacred rituals, and bedrock assumptions. The CBR apparently endorses the notion that defining and creating beauty is the principal role of the architect. But, the CBR does not address the issue of just how the architect is to come about the naked political or state police power necessary to enforce his views of beauty on the public.

The Carnegie-Boyer Report poses no such Flexner type threat to today's under-funded architecture school—*at least not yet.* But that danger to some schools still exists and may yet still be precipitated by other pressures on university academic vice-presidents and presidents to prioritize spending, refocus missions, and come to terms with the implications of the information revolution. Had the Carnegie-Boyer Report been an actual Flexner Report, several of the HBCU architecture schools (as well as a number of low-profile traditionally white schools) would have been marked for extinction. *My central premise is that the eleven HBCU architecture schools and programs should have their sizes and capacities doubled and their ranks expanded by the inclusion of new or closely related programs at other urban HBCUs.*

Regarding the small group of relatively financially and Information Technology poor HBCU programs educating nearly half of all African-American architect prospects, the question then becomes *"doubled to do what? To function how? And on what set of operative premises, goals, assumptions, and missions that differ fundamentally from existing programs?* Including the most selective and elite schools (usually offering only graduate level degrees), today's architecture school is still overwhelmingly engaged in an unarticulated socialization process. That process is cultural and psychological in nature and is especially problematic for most prospective African-American students.

In spite of the annual outpouring of fresh labor for the profession, the orthodox educated architect's involvement in the actual making of the built environment continues to shrink. Most people still find this statistical reality unfathomable. Robert Cole's controversial article of several years ago warning of the potential extinction of the black architect would have been accurate had Coles specified that he was talking about black-owned and operated architectural firms. The same sword of Damocles hanging over the heads of white architectural firms will naturally find its mark on black heads earlier in the game.

My hunch is that many of today's white schools will save themselves with corrective measures that may not be adopted by several of the historically black architecture schools until too late. In spite of the demurring of the Carnegie-Boyer Report, many within the architectural academy will take note of certain realities. There are elements at the top of the architectural profession that have taken the steps necessary to transform themselves into competitive enterprises that will be most appropriate for twenty-first century success in a changed marketplace.

These are already global based operations that are entirely consistent with twenty-first century realities of instantaneous capital and information movement. These are enterprises ranging in size from giant hydra-headed multifaceted corporations to one-person centered virtual corporations where a single architect's lead of an entity is more a resemblance of today's motion picture producer than conventional notions of the genius architect-artist.

CHAPTER 2

"New Urbanism" versus "New (Black) Urbanism" and Film

I have argued that today's African-American architect has, as a class, been disconnected from the cultural and economic life of Black America since the start of the third decade of the twentieth-century. This is despite the fact that between the Harlem Renaissance era and today, some eighty years later, design commissions for black architects were inside of, and for the virtually exclusive use of, Black America. Because of the combination of powerlessness and an absence of a cultural framework, those commissions were mainly sporadic publicly financed structures that often made no significant or lasting impact on the economic and cultural life of black communities.

The nearly fatal fissure between Black America and black architects over that period has been in the arena of shelter and housing inside of Black America. Contrary to the wishful thinking of Du Bois in his 1930s turn toward Booker T. Washington's economic nationalism, black people filling the big northeastern and mid-western cities did not build their own houses. Potentially the most technically competent group inside of Black America to have logically led such undertakings—black architects—were as disinterested in the *production* aspects of housing as were the white architects (and their university architecture schools).

Throughout most of the history of Black America, power and culture were rarely in balance. I have also argued that the first most significant incident of architecture in Black America was the development of the Tuskegee, Alabama, campus in the first decade of the twentieth-century. Mr. Washington was able to utilize deception and an "accommodation" strategy to overcome utter powerlessness. But without major clients and patrons inside of Black America like Mr. Washington who were committed to a culture based nationalist program, the post-Tuskegee generation of black architects had only one ideological framework: *white cultural nationalism.*

Power and culture can now be aligned in Black America, thus providing the basis for ending the "estrangement" between the people who train to be professional architects and the enduring culture of Black America. All of this would mean that throughout Black America the role of architects would differ structurally from established academic and professional orthodoxy. The starting point is still the same after eighty years; *the need to establish hegemony inside of Black America over all aspects of the housing needs of Black America.*

The very idea of the architect as a passive creature seeking out isolated contracts to design isolated free standing single purpose buildings has never held much relevance to the most pressing social, economic, and cultural issues inside of post-1930s urban Black America. The various components necessary for that modus operandi to work were never really present. A sufficient critical mass of real estate developers, general contractors, homebuilders, risk capital investors, large businesses, and financial institutions were never really able to materialize. The isolated public agency contracts going to black architects were never more than a distortion and distraction. Thus the need for a differing type of architect-entrepreneurial community developer and housing producer that combines all of the above entities is now clearer.

This new twenty-first century architect has a different role, and therefore, needs a different mindset to accompany additional technical skills in real estate finance and heightened cultural awareness.

Accordingly, the educational socialization of such architects must differ fundamentally from the status quo. The redevelopment of the physical environments throughout Black America must involve intense functional interaction of all of her cultural and socio-economic entities.

Unlike Booker T. Washington's America of 100 years ago, citizens of Black America have the three things that W.E.B. Du Bois was then insistently countering as being absolutely necessary; *the right to vote, full legal standing under law with all due civil rights protections, and full access to higher liberal arts based education.* Du Bois insisted that Mr. Washington's advocacy of economic nationalism was doomed to failure without those elements being in place. Du Bois was largely correct despite his eventual adoption of Mr. Washington's economic program by the 1930s. Today, there are no longer reasons to resist a reinterpreted application of the original Tuskegee model in the rebuilding of an urbanized Black America.

Black America continues to prove to be no different from Jewish America, Cuban America, Latin America, Asian America, or other hyphenated sectors of white America. There is a palpable desire on the part of many elements within the group to do business with other African-American professional and business entities, be they architects or new car dealers. But the caveat is that those entities must be nothing less than *state-of-the-art operations in all normative respects and then some.* That, after all, is what the old black architectural fountainhead firms of 100 years ago represented to Black America.

But as today's black firms fade into oblivion through old age and the death of the founding lions, the question remaining to be answered is *who and what is to take the place of these firms?* This is a serious and long overdue debate in the black world of architecture. Without the benefit of a deliberate, openly self conscious, and well thought out national strategic effort to perpetuate competitive black-owned and controlled built-environment making enterprises, such firms are destined to go the way of Robert Coles' 1989 implications about black architects becoming an "endangered species."

The black preacher, school board facilities management director, state housing finance head, the health care maintenance executive, and a growing number of corporate CEOs are in the position to decide who or what entity will provide them with professional services of all types. All things considered, they are desirous of having a partnering relationship with a competitive African-American led entity. But if next generation black-run entities are attitudinally as well as functionally unable to provide that relationship, the black preacher and CEO will have no choice but to move on.

Today's black architectural enterprises that are fading into the sunset and those that have long since departed were once competitive in the marketplaces of their context. Some have even enjoyed relative prosperity as a result of the loyalty and support of black clients and communities. This was so even though much of that work was tightly funded with limited public money that left no room for the spectacular gesture that is required to produce the "award winning" or "publishable quality" works that regularly appears in the white mainstream architectural media.

In taking an instant to look back at the building of the great gothic cathedrals in the Middle Ages, we see that design and construction were simultaneous activities entrusted to the mind of a single person known as the master builder. It is now commonly understood that the formalization of a separate and distinct pre-construction design phase carried out by a cultivated nobleman and non-builder known as an architect was a 15th century concept that crystallized in Florence, Italy, in what is commonly known as the Renaissance.

One of the permanent side effects of the now fifty-year-old Information Revolution is that this formal 500-year old dichotomy between architect and builder has been rendered obsolete. This is certainly so in the mind and worldview of people who purchase or assemble the constellation of services that culminates in a functional, habitable and profitable structure. Martha O'Mara reinforces this in her book, *Strategy and Place: Managing Corporate Real Estate and Facilities for Competitive Advantage*.[1] In this vein, the following passage by Kenneth Frampton, author of the influential *Modern Architecture; A Critical History,* may have been painful for him to have written. Frampton has devoted a professional lifetime to the passionate advocacy of the central cultural role of the modern architect as an important force in the making of the built environment for human habitation:

> *...The consolidation of the construction industry favors ever-larger units of production, and this plus the increased fluidity of international capital creates a climate that is generally inimical to the critical cultivation of architectural form. This has long since been evident in the practice of the "package deal," where architectural and engineering services are provided within the industry itself. However, it has to be admitted that this integration of design and production has, on occasion, been able to produce work of outstanding quality. This is particularly true in the case of Japan, where large contracting firms have been able to produce works of exceptional refinement.*[2]

The message that I derive from the corporate minded business environment is that businesses are *not rejecting the architect in favor of the builder.* That, however, has been the unfortunate architect culture interpretation of the shifts taking place over the last generation. Rather, facilities procurers are simply saying that they see the two distinct entities of architect and builder as now being permanently fused. Facilities procurers harbor no ideological prejudices in the matter of architect versus builder. They have only their permanent interest in acquiring a facility in the shortest amount of time and at the lowest cost. If they approach one of the two traditionalized entities and fail to receive a satisfactory reception, they simply move on until they get what they are looking for.

It has usually been a builder-led entity that provided the facilities procurer with what they were seeking. This is simply an indication that the architect who hopes to practice in the first quarter of the twenty-first century must adopt a new paradigm and modus operandi for the marketplace. This applies to the entire range of building from the small custom-built private residence to the multi-million square feet corporate or institutional headquarters.

On black businesses, the prospect of black, information age moguls is currently well along in the first quarter of the twenty-first century. Evidence abounds that the black mogul may derive the base—not to be confused with the entirety—of his or her fortune from Black American or black Diaspora markets. Today there are two highly instructive examples of the black business mogul. One is the late Reginald Lewis who made his fortune in the leveraged buy-out world of Wall Street.[3] Black America was not an apparent factor—until we look closer at Lewis' early career of mastering finance in federally sponsored minority business lending programs.

After Lewis achieved stunning success on his own steam, his superior skill, intelligence, and tenacity led to his acquiring one of those famous *"....we are highly confident..."* letters from Michael Milken.[4] Out of thousands of such instant multi-millionaire creating letters from Milken, Lewis is the most visible black person to be the direct principal beneficiary. It is not yet clear just how many more black people beside Lewis were the recipients of a Milken letter. Whether that ratio of black to white recipients of a Milken letter is a true reflection of black to white capacity is a matter that ought to be up for discussion between Black America and her most historically dependable ally, Jewish America.

Robert Johnson is the other African-American mogul nearing billionaire status. In stark contrast to Lewis, Johnson has made his fortune to date through the exclusive catering to the needs, longings, desires, and cultural predilections of Black America.[5] Johnson will achieve full status in the nation's official billionaire club through expanding his black-oriented products and services to the white (or "cross-over") market. But Johnson will no doubt be *respectful of his black base.* He will proceed without sentiment from a platform of an awareness that he must hold his base while moving to the next level simply because that is the nature of how all successful businesses are built; *from a firm base!*

Johnson and his Black Entertainment Network (BET) is built on meeting the needs, one on one and one by one, of millions of black households—black customers if you will. Fortunately for Bob Johnson, he isn't faced with a white America of the same mentality that confronted Booker T. Washington or W.E.B. Du Bois 100 years ago. It is Johnson's instincts that must somehow become imbued in the next generation of African-American as well as African Diaspora architects.

The next generation of African-American architects must—like Johnson and many other radio, film, TV, entertainment and telecommunications entrepreneurs—be made to see the tens of millions of customers in black lower and/or middle-to-middle class America. These customers are eager to spend their dollars with other black people who offer first class services while knowing and respecting them on the most fundamental level of black culture, black aesthetics, and black spirituality.

Black America is now in the early stages of a healthy and momentous debate about Johnson's recent consummation of the sale of BET to the giant multi-media conglomerate known simply as Viacom. Johnson purportedly personally pocketed nearly two billion dollars in cash and Viacom stock. This is wealth that exceeds that of the late Reginald Lewis.

On one side of the debate are those who feel that in selling the flagship black privately owned company in America, Johnson "sold out" Black America. Others feel just as strongly that Johnson did precisely what entrepreneurs do; start companies, increase the value of that company, and—in the words of Cathy Hughes, the prominent African-American owner of Baltimore based Radio One—"wait for an offer they can't refuse." Johnson has exposed the deep schism in modern day Black America about capitalism and capitalists. Some progressives in the staunch anti-capitalist camp want to claim Johnson as a member of the "family" who holds the keys to the interpretation, transformation and perpetuation of black culture to the rest of the world through his

BET empire. People in this camp believe passionately that Johnson has obligations to the rest of the "family."

But they cannot have it both ways. Either Black America needs to nurture more Bob Johnsons or Black America needs to extricate itself from capitalism. Of course, the latter choice is an impossible and preposterous proposition. *No one* can be extricated from capitalism for the simple reason that there is no capitalism as that term is casually used. Government, academia, a growing proportion of the middle class "workers," and the corporate business world are all fused around the common denominator of Wall Street capital formation.

The relevance of the BET-Johnson affair to architecture is quite simple. Despite a tumultuous "love-hate" relationship (because of "programming" choices made by Johnson on his BET network), Johnson and Black America were always *culturally fused*. Johnson shares this fusion with the current crop of brilliant young black filmmakers headed by Spike Lee and John Singletary (and preceded by Oscar Michaux of the 1920s era). These men did not bring or attempt to impose an alien culture of fundamentally differing tastes and styles on Black America. Despite Johnson's Ivy League education in high finance and Lee's New York University education in film making (fortified with an undergraduate degree from HBCU Morehouse in Atlanta), they remained *of* Black America.

While each man is always hopeful that their black culture-based art form might have "cross-over" appeal, they were clear about whom they were primarily aiming their work and messages at. They shared that characteristic with Duke Ellington, perhaps the greatest cultural artist of the twentieth-century. Ellington never lost sight of the fact that he was writing "Negro music."[6] Meanwhile, architecture school orthodoxy socializes people to stalk wealthy patrons outside of a presumptively "poor" and (according to the gospel of the Dinesh DeSousa school of thinking) "culturally deviant" Black America. The objective of this stalking is to "make architecture." All the while, the true culture of Black America continues to create jazz, blues, and hip-hop music, cutting-edge film, dance, theater, literature, and new "language" on a consistently world class plane of excellence.

Meanwhile, Black America is being made an unwitting minor partner in what is arguably the only new architecturally related movement to emerge since the collapse of orthodox International Style modernism. That movement goes under the self-adopted name of "New Urbanism." Regarding this movement, Black America must be ever mindful of basic issues. One issue is that no theory about federally financed highways being the prime culprit of urban sprawl can obscure the specter of race in the personal decision making matrix used by many Americans. Many people move in order to evade living in communities that are perceived to become dominated by African-Americans. That is one of the basic causes of what ultimately drives sprawl. Another is the deeply ingrained rural frontier fantasy mentality underlying the American anti-cities bias. Yet a majority of white Americans publicly espouse strong disapproval of racial discrimination. They profess to believe in integration and are probably sincere. The problem is that the nearly forty million African-Americans and the other nearly 240 million Americans are in direct contradiction about what integration means.

Ask a representative example from each camp to define an ideally integrated community and you get answers that frame the fundamental conflict. The white integration ideal ranges from favoring a one-to-ten-percent black resident presence in a neighborhood, depending on social class. The black ideal is for a fifty percent black presence. Douglas Massey frames the issues succinctly in his 1993 book, *American Apartheid; Segregation and the Making of the Underclass,* with his research survey based findings that:

> *For blacks, integration means racial mixing in the range of 15% to 70% black with 50% the most desirable....whites have little tolerance for racial mixtures beyond 20% black...99% of black people have said they would be willing to live in a neighborhood that is 50-50 black-white...63% say 50-50 is most desirable...*[7]

It would appear that the conflict would end tomorrow if black Americans would agree to be dispersed in accordance with white comfort levels. That just is not going not happen. So practically every community that has African-Americans showing up and tipping the racial ratio above the white comfort level is also a community that is in transition from being integrated to becoming all black. But Massey also remarked in the same place in his book that *"no one would move into a poor black neighborhood except other poor black people."* For some inexplicable reason, Massey neglected to explore a phenomena that he surely must have been familiar with at the time of his book's release in 1993—*gentrification.* Black inner-city neighborhoods have in the past and will continue to undergo this reverse version of *block busting.* Georgetown in Washington, DC, is now one of the most upscale residential communities in the nation. Yet Georgetown once contained large sections that were considered to be black slums. Other similar examples abound around the country.

Miami architect-professor Andres Duany raises the neglected subject of residential architecture and clientele types in the April 1999 issue of *Architectural Record.*[8] That issue of the magazine—one of the top high-gloss trade journals that regularly publishes the work of the patron sponsored design elites of the profession—is annually devoted to architect designed houses. Duany looks at this against the backdrop of his own increasingly national high visibility leadership of the *Congress of New Urbanism(CNU)* movement.[9] Duany's wife, Elizabeth Plater-Zyberk, is dean of architecture at the University of Miami where both also teach. The Duanys have restructured the entire curriculum of the school around their New Urbanism movement.

The CNU movement, as it is now labeled, bears some resemblance to the Congres Internationaux de l'Architecture Moderne—better know as CIAM—that was founded in Lausanne, Switzerland, in 1928 by Europe's leading modern architects. Their objective was to reinforce the relationship between architecture and town planning with an emphasis on "mass" or "social" housing.[10]

The final statement at the founding meeting (at which Gropius and Le Corbusier were among the protagonists) argued that architecture should be put 'back in its true sphere, which is economic, sociological, and altogether at the service of humanity.'[11]

While acknowledging its debt to CIAM, Duany and the rest of the CNU leadership point to more recent inspirations—most notably Jane Jacobs and her seminal critique of Modern Architecture in the early 1960s—as their spiritual parent.[12] Duany has correctly identified today's equivalent of CIAM type mass or social housing as a central issue that has been left on the wayside by today's elite architects. He, in effect, puts out a call to arms to his fellow elite architects to supplant what they, as a class, have been relentlessly socialized to view as tasteless, unprincipled builders and developers who have traditionally controlled the mass housing market.

I have for some time advocated an architect-led coup of sorts in the American housing industry. But my call differs fundamentally from Duany's call. His is nothing short of a call for an upper class coup d'etat (of mostly white men) against the riff-raff residential builder-developer (also mostly white men). Mine is a call for the next generation of African-American architects to take a leadership role in housing and community development in heavily black populated central cities and similarly evolving suburban areas. *That is simply not possible through orthodox architectural academic or practice modus operandi.* Duany reminds us that the vast, far-flung housing marketplace consists of four types of entities—patrons, clients, victims, and customers:

*Patrons are architectural sophisticates. They commission a building as a work of art and are willing to put up with high costs and controversy in support of a designer's concept. As they are often a major force behind most of what is deemed worthy of publishing, patrons permeate architectural periodicals. Although patrons are rare, their numbers appear greater because they are geographically concentrated near the media Meccas…A second type, the **Client**, is not so much sophisticated as savvy…**Victims** are those who, due to limited income or a tight local housing market, have no* *choices…the* **Customer** *is the most common consumer of housing. Customers have no contact with architects. They arrive at a decision to purchase in an uneducated state….Only slightly attuned to the rigors of design, a Customer is lured by stylistic kitsch and gimmickry programs offered by developers….The situation is exacerbated by the fact that most good architects disparage and ignore this market, as architecture school has taught them to do.*[13]

Duany and I are in agreement on the need for architects to focus on the "customer." However, Duany apparently believes that those customers need to be "educated" to the taste and aesthetic biases of elite architects. He is merely acting true to form. Architects, regardless of their own original social and economic class origins, are unfailingly programmed by the total apparatus of the academy and the profession to view themselves as ultimate arbiters of aesthetic tastes.

Duany's shifting positions somehow manages to place him in agreement with arch-elite architect Robert Venturi's ground breaking post-modernist views expressed in the late sixties, and in conflict with the thesis Venturi advances in the early seventies.[14] Duany, in spite of his noble and worthy intentions, confirms the thesis set forth by Australian architecture professor Gary Stevens in his book *The Favored Circle*. Stevens sets out to:

Make a case in this book that one of the prime functions of the system of architectural education is to produce cultivated individuals; that the central function of the discipline of architecture is to produce instruments of taste; that efflorescence of architectural creativity at the highest levels can be most readily explained simply by the existence and particular structure of the master-pupil chains.[15]

Duany wants architects to get into the arena with developers and contractors and battle for a bigger share of the vast housing market while also educating the buyers to *good tastes*. I agree with him but for reasons where we would not be on the same page. I am particularly troubled by the elitist class implications of *"good tastes."* Duany's CNU movement rests on reasonably firm footing in its analysis of the *effects*—which must not to be confused with the *causes*—of suburban sprawl and visual blight. Like every theory or movement in the America that legally enslaved and dehumanized a significant portion of its population right up to only 135 years ago, and brutally enforced a vile system of apartheid up to within the last 35 years, race is the fly in the ointment.

Whites left the cities and the growing numbers of black inhabitants for all-white suburbs. Blacks followed whites and whites moved further out. Cities like Washington, DC, and Baltimore could conceivably lose every black family capable of becoming a homeowner to a newly built single-family subdivision in the surrounding suburbs. The greater likelihood is that over the next twenty-five years in a number of cities, black people will live in nearly all black communities within the city limits and in the inner ring of suburbs. The traditional pattern of building subdivisions was to build for exclusively white populations. Blacks would invariably inherit these formerly all-white city or suburban subdivisions as whites fled further out.

Along the way of early-through-middle-twentieth-century subdivisions built exclusively for whites, there were a few conspicuous examples of subdivisions built for black people. The builders, developers, and architects were virtually all white and had access to capital that was not available to African-American builders. There would be an occasional black developer on smaller subdivisions. Today there are numerous subdivisions built where the white developer knew full well that all of the buyers would be black. Many of these new all black communities contain homes that are 250 to 500 thousand dollar mini-estates. However, most black homes are of the "affordable" housing genre for first-time home buyers (in the 90 to 180 thousand dollar range, depending on location and other amenities). The "affordable" housing developments built inside of the urban-suburban metropolitan areas across America virtually always required generous local-federal subsidies. In reality, those subsidies were no more generous that those going to once all-white so-called "unassisted market-rate" developments.

We are looking at the near certain prospects of tens of thousands of new homes and apartments that will continue to be built for black occupancy in those metropolitan areas. This is billions of dollars of new business. These all black communities will also spawn ancillary public and commercial facilities. This phenomenon is happening in all of the urban centers across the country. Black athlete-developers like Magic Johnson, and their world-class corporate partners, are building mixed-use mall-entertainment complexes for these all black housing markets.[16] The prototype for Johnson's project is the movie theater complex he built in 1994 in the once all white, but now nearly all-black, Baldwin Hills section of Los Angeles. Johnson and others of a similar persuasion are now preparing to actually build the housing for these markets. *Black architects must emulate the Magic Johnsons of the world.*

Again, we must hasten to add a counter to Massey's assertion that no white people will move into a poor black neighborhood. There are growing examples of inner-city neighborhoods were whites are content to have 50 percent or more black neighbors. However, these will rarely be whites with school-aged children to be raised. They will most likely be non-nuclear families that will be unconventional in near infinite permutations.

The task is to inspire the next generation of African-American architects to envision the vast untapped opportunities for financial and professional empowerment and cultural expression awaiting them. Things fall in place once architects began to consciously focus their sights on "customers"—the "folk" if you will—as opposed to "patrons." Through "customers" some black architects must fashion a "New (Black) Urbanism" that "re-integrates" black communities. Such communities will, if done right, evolve the "black economy" that Booker T. Washington and W.E.B. Du Bois were in agreement on.

Spike Lee represents a third distinct ideological and operational paradigm to the historic Booker T. Washington and W.E.B. Dubois paradigms within black architectural development in cultural context. In the unfolding twentieth-century development of black architects, there is a clear and inevitable progression from Booker T. Washington to current Du Bois to a new *Spike Leeism*. I place Lee within the architectural context of the "three revolutions" theory so ably articulated by William Mitchell, dean of architecture at MIT.

Mitchell simply reminds the architectural world of the necessity of having a clear understanding that we have for the last 50 years been living in the third of three fundamental revolutions in human development over the past 10,000 years of recorded history. Ours—and Spike Lee's—is the third revolution now known as the Information Age. Washington and Du Bois can easily be positioned in the second revolution, also known as the British Isles based Industrial Revolution that lasted from 1750 to 1950 (the first revolution—agricultural based human settlement—started 8,000 years before the birth of Christ in the part of the world now known as Iraq).

My own awakening to Lee as a black cultural icon who chose to speak indirectly on the subject of architecture occurred while watching Lee's 1990 film *Jungle Fever*. Lee cast his black protagonist and certified Hollywood star Wesley Snipes as the "design" architect who is frustrated in his attempts to achieve partnership status in a white owned firm. Perhaps unwittingly, Lee's make-believe (yet quite believable) architect was thrown into an unflattering comparison to Lee the black filmmaker as image-maker, cultural definer, and community economic development catalyst (look carefully at the list of credits, e.g., jobs and contracts, at the end of Lee's films).

James Sanders, a New York City architect turned filmmaker, puts matters in perspective in a perceptive paper titled, "Cinemarchitecture," in the Spring 1992 issue of Design Review of Books. In this paper, Sanders remarks:

> *What I'd learned in architecture school was diametrically opposed to my experience as a city kid; architecture was either boring description or deadly jargon. Architects tend to fetishize architecture, giving it an exaggerated role in life. For example, architecture magazines are exclusively about buildings—the complexity of experience that go with buildings are not included; the photographs are*

*always without people. Life is edited out. In films, architecture is used as space that shapes the lives of the characters; in the movies, architecture always takes its proper place. **I find that cinema offers a better platform for talking about cities and the way they work.*** *(bold italics mine).*

Sanders' assessment needs merely to be supplemented by the addition of the powerful role that music plays in the *"...platform for talking about cities and the way they work."* Clearly, film has the capacity to influence attitudes at a level that architecture can only fantasize about. In any discussion about the powerful role of film in image making and culture shaping it is useful to look at the very origins of this medium in urban American at the turn of the twentieth-century. Interestingly enough, in *American Visions; The Epic History of Art in America,* art critic and historian Robert Hughes reminds us that it was on New York's Manhattan Island—rather than the popularly assumed Hollywood, California,—that film was first initiated:

Unquestionably, the invention that did most to alter the way Americans perceived the world and constructed their narratives of it, between 1900 and 1920, was the silent movie. It became the folk art of the urban crowd, disseminated from New York when Hollywood was orange groves and dust roads. It assimilated all the visual subject matter that had previously been marketed only through static chromos and illustrations: the disasters, the Arcadias, the ideal families battling adversity....the silent film began to reflect immigrant hopes, dreams, and fantasies...Its comic and racist stereotypes of the black reminded the immigrant that there is always someone beneath him on the social scale...Because film was entertainment, and went down easily, few Americans saw how it was changing the way large publics would interpret images. Its revolution was so big and far-reaching, and affected so many people so diffusely, like a change in the content of the air they breathed, that no one saw it as anything but benign.[17]

The Information Age Revolution has rendered virtually the entire Lee architect character's technical skills irrelevant or obsolete to the most important cultural and economic issues confronting Black America. The character's extremely narrow and naÙve mindset is counterproductive to the cultural and socio-economic needs of his community. Lee's fictional character is in the image-making and communications business but is totally ignorant of that fact. The Lee fictional architect character is in the jobs and wealth creation business but is oblivious to how those dots connect to his obsession with "design." He apparently has no clue about the relationship between "design talent" and 'rainmaking skills." He is who he is as a result of an academic and professional socialization-indoctrination process.

It is instructive to look at Lee's college and graduate school background. Lee was a late-1970s mass communications major who graduated from Morehouse College, an HBCU in Atlanta. To quote Lee:

> To get into USC and UCLA you needed to get an astronomical score on the Graduate Record Examination and I didn't get it. Luckily, I did not have to take the GRE for admission to the New York University film school. All I had to do was submit a creative portfolio....and I got in.[18]

Unlike NYU, both USC and UCLA have highly regarded graduate architecture schools. Within the existing paradigm of the architectural academy-profession axis, Lee would never, under any conceivable circumstances, have had the impact he has had on American and black culture. It should be noted here that one of Lee's filmmaking contemporaries, Ernest Dickerson, did in fact graduate from the architecture school at Howard University in Washington, DC. Dickerson had to completely abandon architecture in order to achieve his objectives as a cultural shaper and critic. This should not have to be so. *A fusion of architecture and filmmaking as critique and shaper of black culture is long overdue.*

I am intrigued with the prospect of an architecture curriculum that repositions relevant aspects of design studio into the cinematography studio and the music making studio. In my scheme of things all of this would occur in a Geographic Information System (GIS) based technology laboratory-resource center. In such a setting, one is then engaging architecture in a way that plays to the strengths and interest of black youth. But even here, we must caution that the merely technical issues of filmmaking is as large a potential dead end for students as the current static two-dimensional methodologies of the drawing board or CAD computer screen. The important issue is to transfer to architecture the fiercely entrepreneurial mindset and profound commitment to the protection and perpetuation of black culture that is typical of today's cadre of black filmmakers and musical impresarios.

CHAPTER 3

The Crisis in the HBCU Architecture Schools

If the African-American architect-practitioner is in crisis as I contend, it follows that the architecture schools so historically critical to those practitioners—and still enrolling nearly half of all African-American architecture students—may also be a highly problematic proposition. And similar to the plight of the practitioners, the situation in the black schools did not began yesterday.

Attempts to replicate or parallel the Harvard studio pedagogy at the HBCU design school were perhaps understandable and even unavoidable in the pre-Information Technology era of as recently as twenty years ago. Today this is not required. The state of Information Technology that is readily available to the HBCU School frees up students to concentrate on the actual political, financial and cultural dynamics of urban redevelopment. Molding and shaping a faculty that will facilitate this is the challenge confronting HBCU design school leadership.

An underlying subtext of this book is that the university level study of architecture is no more intellectually demanding than engineering or computer science. This can be interpreted to mean that Black America *is entering the twenty-first century with a shortage of at least several thousand black men and women architects.* My interests and motivation are driven by a search to find a useful answer to the question of *what those currently missing thousands of black architects, once put in play, could and must do toward the furtherance of the cultural and socio-economic agenda of today's Black America (and themselves and their own families)?*

The 1996 research study by architect-educators Dennis Mann and Bradford Grant have established that approximately 4.5 percent of students enrolled in accredited first professional degree granting programs throughout the country's 123 accredited programs are African-Americans. The study also shows that forty-five percent of those African-Americans are concentrated at the eleven historically black university based architecture schools and programs.

It is therefore reasonable to proceed on the assumption that the roughly 45–55 percentage ratio of black architecture student distribution between the black schools and the other 123 traditionally white schools will hold over the opening decades of the twenty-first century. But my primary interest is about the fate of those African-American students who will be matriculating and graduating from the currently seven accredited programs at **Howard University** and **Morgan State University** in the combined Washington-Baltimore SMSA (a professional program started in 1988 at the **University of the District of Columbia** is still in candidacy for accreditation); **Hampton University** in the Tidewater Virginia area; **Florida A & M University** in Northern Florida; **Southern University** in Louisiana; **Tuskegee University** in Alabama; and **Prairie View** in the Houston, Texas, area.

As accurately pointed out by Maryland University architecture Roger Lewis in his book, *Architecture? A Candid Guide to the Profession,* black students at the handful of black universities offering architectural education have up to now been relatively reluctant to participate, in comparison to their overwhelming choices of engineering or business as academic majors. The savviest students also instinctively know (and have abundant hard evidence) that anything that is not solidly based inside of *Information Technology* should be avoided as though it was a deadly social disease. *It is futile to attempt to sell architecture to black students through the existing paradigms of orthodox architecture culture.*

A major premise of this book is that those HBCU architecture schools must take an immediate leadership position in the necessary renaissance for some of today's and the next generation of African-American architects. Those schools, I argue, must be at the forefront of establishing the theoretical as well as practical framework of a rapprochement between black architects and the Black America they were spawned from. *Logic impels nothing less.* But that is not even remotely possible without a brutally frank assessment of the reality of the situation in those schools in the context of American architectural education.

At the 1998 annual National Organization of Minority Architects (NOMA) conference in Washington, DC, the heads of each of the eight HBCU schools convened around the same table in a public forum. Such a meeting had not occurred in thirty years. Back then professional programs existed only at Howard, Hampton, Southern, and Tuskegee. Only Howard was then actually accredited. Full accreditation of the other three programs would be achieved in the early 1970s. This 1998 NOMA sponsored event had been listed in the conference schedule for sometime prior to the actual conference. Considerable anticipation surrounded this historic ninety minute panel discussion by the HBCU school heads. The small meeting room at the conference hotel was packed to "standing room only" capacity. Students as well as practitioners of all age levels from all over the country were in attendance.

Unfortunately, there had been no pre-planning for this panel. The discussion quickly degenerated into semi-confrontational exchanges amongst the HBCU heads. There were several main points of contention. One centered on "...my program has more CAD facilities than yours." Another was "...my program is engaging in more community 'design center' type technical assistance outreach than yours..." One could easily sense palpable disappointment on the part of the audience. Expectations were that there would be a much higher plane of exchanges centering on how architectural education at the HBCU based programs should or in fact did differ *pedagogically, culturally and philosophically* from education at the other 115 traditionally white schools. Unfortunately, such a discussion could not take place that day *simply because there was no difference.* Even a serious discussion about *why* there was no difference would have been fruitful but it never was even broached.

I contend that this is precisely the reason that all of the HBCU architecture programs are perennial disaster areas in the larger scheme of architectural education. The HBCU program heads have yet to find the time and collective resources to bring their faculties and student leaders together to assess each school, decide where each one needs to go for viability and growth, and devise strategies and time tables for getting there. All of the HBCU architecture schools are in dire need of several things: *substantially increased enrollments, exponentially increased Information Technology infrastructure (not to be confused with CAD—the two are not the same), and a black culture and black "economy" based raison d'etre at their HBCU campuses.*

The rituals, myths, shibboleths, and fantasies of orthodox culture must give way to the life realities that the HBCU business and engineering schools successfully embrace. Each HBCU school must maximize on its natural or historic strength area as part of a larger group. For instance, the need for the doctorate in architecture (or environmental design and planning) is an overdue reality that cannot be wished away. Several of the HBCU schools are ideally situated to begin credible offerings at that level of study. Several others, by virtue of already being integral parts of highly credible engineering or natural science schools in ideal urban settings, could forge ahead in the environmental sciences. *But all of them must seek out close working relationships with the finance and real estate departments of their campus B-Schools while also doing the same thing with their campus film, music, communication, and art departments.*

In reality, all of these HBCU based architecture programs are on the "chopping blocks" of their harried and resources starved presidents and academic affairs provosts. Not even the continued survival of the Howard program—the most well known and prestigious of the HBCU programs—is a "given" with the top administrators of the university.

A 1990 study undertaken by newly appointed Howard president Franklin Jennifer came perilously close to recommending that Howard's architecture program be discontinued. Declining enrollment, extremely high per-student costs, the non-existence of funded research or contractual pursuits by faculty, absence of published scholarship or built works of note on the part of the tenure-heavy faculty, and the inability to articulate an essential and distinct mission for the program were some of the reasons that "euthanasia" was seriously considered. The Howard School of Architecture managed to survive that scare, but consider what has happened as recently as 1999 at Howard.

H. Patrick Swygert succeeded Jennifer in 1995 and immediately commissioned his own new study of all campus schools and colleges. After having existed for the past thirty years as a fully autonomous, dean-headed School of Architecture, Swygert merged architecture back into its original home in the engineering school. Architecture still retained the authority to call itself the "School of Architecture." The reality is that architecture was downgraded to "department" status. The dean's position was downgraded to that of a "director" who no longer reports directly to the university academic vice-president. The director of the "school" now reports to the dean of engineering. The architecture director's new fig leaf was enlarged somewhat by the added honorific title of "associate dean" of a newly consolidated College of Engineering, Architecture, and Computer Science. Under this new world order, one of the very first initiatives of the dean of engineering was to relocate his drab office in the School of Engineering Building to the more aesthetically pleasing office suite of the defrocked dean of architecture in the old Howard Law School Building (now the Howard Hamilton Mackey Building).

Justification for President Swygert's move on architecture at Howard was largely for the same reasons that architecture had come under the threat of extinction by Swygert's predecessor a few years earlier. The net result of these actions at Howard is that today there is no longer an autonomous dean-headed School of Architecture at the only HBCU Carnegie Research Level I doctoral granting institution in the US (out of a total of only ninety such institutions). Florida A&M, Prairie View, and Southern each have autonomous dean-headed schools but are nowhere near to qualifing for Carnegie Level I status.

In of itself, architecture schools existing as integral parts of larger engineering schools at HBCUs is not necessarily a bad thing. It may well even be positive and logical. For instance, the vital but extremely expensive Information Technology infrastructure existing in HBCU engineering schools is simply not going to be duplicated in stand-alone architecture schools (several HBCU engineering schools possess true "super computing power"). To use a shopping mall analogy, the engineering and computer science programs are the "anchor tenants" responsible for big "traffic flows." A strategic administrative and physical alliance with engineering on an HBCU campus can lead architecture into funded research ands high technology waters that architecture would not normally venture out into.

Then there is the cultural "bridging" role issue. During the Harlem Renaissance days of the 1920s and 1930s, architecture at Howard was buried down in "Death Valley" under engineering and the "hard" sciences. Architecture never fulfilled its potential to be the bridge that linked the "hard" sciences with the "soft" cultural arts and sciences. In today's world this need not happen. At Howard, as well as the other HBCU campuses with both engineering schools and architecture programs, this is an "opportunity" (the other word in addition to the word "danger" that are both symbolized by the single Chinese character that denotes "crisis") to rectify an eighty-year-old misalignment between the cultures of architecture and Black America.

But the situation at Howard today recalls a set of events that occurred at Morgan twenty years ago. Back then things at Morgan degenerated precipitously when Harry Robinson, the literal and figurative "architect" of a comprehensive School of Architecture for Morgan, left the top leadership position there for in order to take the dean's position at Howard. Robinson left Morgan before being able to utilize his consummate communications skills to get that program off of the ground. Today at Howard, Robinson's dynamic and visionary leadership skills are more than ever in need in order to make the most of a strategic new relationship with engineering and computer science (while simultaneously embracing the cultural arts). But Robinson has relinquished the headaches of administrative leadership of architecture at Howard for the more idyllic world of the classroom.

Howard is one the two HBCU architecture program that has the capacity and credibility to initiate doctoral level studies in collaboration with the engineering sciences and the cultural arts wing of the University (Morgan is the other). Whether or not this can happen under the present top leadership of the "school" is a question mark in the eyes of any reasonably informed observer at this point in time. This is especially troubling in that Howard's program is the one that should also logically be providing vision and leadership for *all* of the other HBCU schools and programs.

The Prairie View program just outside of Houston was recently upgraded to dean-headed autonomous school status despite its relatively small enrollment of less than 160 students. The dean is Inklas Sabouni, a Middle East born woman with a doctorate in planning from nearby Rice University. She has successfully transitioned the old undergraduate program into a synergistic array of graduate-undergraduate programs, reaffirmed accreditation, and extracted critical resources from her tight-fisted top administrators including funds to construct a new state-of-the-art building.

The program at Southern University in Baton Rouge has existed in an autonomous dean-headed status for the last twenty years. This is despite its small size of less than 100 students in a sole undergraduate degree program. Several years ago, the top administrative leaders of Southern handed the dean's position to Frank Bosworth, a licenced white architect with a doctorate in environmental design from Virginia Tech. Bosworth brought solid grant-writing skills and appeared to be on the verge of re-energizing the program at Southern. Upon his appointment, he was given added resources by an impressed upper administration. But for reasons yet unclear, Bosworth left Southern for the enticing greener pastures of the School of Architecture at nearby traditionally all-white Louisiana State University (LSU). Bosworth was succeeded at Southern by Adenrele Awatona, a Ghanaian educator with a doctorate from UK-Cambridge.

The School of Architecture at Florida A&M University (FAMU) in Tallahassee was started twenty-five years ago under interesting circumstances and motivations. Architecture was located at FAMU by state legislative fiat. This was a subtext inside the drama of desegregating the historically separate but decidedly unequal dual system of higher education in the state. Architecture was a "white" program located at FAMU to attract whites to a HBCU campus (it is completely unclear as to what were the reciprocating equivalent moves at the state's traditionally white campuses). The first FAMU dean was a white architectural educator from Oregon. At the start of his tenure, he hired a virtually all white faculty. In the beginning the students were also predominately white. Today the student body is majority black but the faculty is still overwhelmingly white. FAMU has a comprehensive array of graduate and undergraduate programs in architecture and landscape architecture. Rodner Wright, a University of Cincinnati and Harvard Graduate School of Design educated architect, is the current FAMU dean. Wright, an African-American, is energetic, perceptive, and well regarded in the white world of architectural educators. He is committed to increasing the number of black faculty at the FAMU program.

The Hampton program—existing administratively (though not physically) inside of the School of Engineering and Technology—is under the leadership of Bradford Grant. William Harvey, Hampton's dynamic and visionary president, was able to wrest Grant away from the security of a tenured faculty position at Cal Poly-San Luis Obispo on the West Coast. Grant brought to the Hampton program the added credibility of his published writings and research on the subject of African-American architects. Grant, a relatively young African-American architect, is also widely known throughout the larger Association of Collegiate Schools of Architecture (ACSA) as a result of his all-around activism (Grant became the first black president of the ninety-year old ACSA in 2001).

The still very young program at the University of the District of Columbia is still struggling just to maintain official status as a "candidate" school (for accreditation). Despite the fact that the UDC program runs an innovative professional practice clinic—the Architectural Research Institute (ARI)—that generates over one million dollars annually in contractual fee income, the top administration has not allocated the academic program funds needed to meet the accreditation threshold. The UDC architecture department established ARI in 1988 while I was there teaching. ARI was initially funded by a 250,000 dollar grant-contract I was able to secure from the District of Columbia housing agency. ARI acts as the "teaching hospital" clinic that utilizes architectural faculty and top performing students as paid interns. The services performed for the housing agency includes computer assisted preparation of plans for the rehabilitation of boarded up housing for new homeownership opportunities. This is a model program idea that has taken hold at several other HBCU architecture programs.

At Tuskegee, the fountainhead of African-American architectural education and architects, the situation today is dire according to former head Raj Segal and several refreshingly candid white faculty members (the majority of the Tuskegee architecture program faculty is white). Nothing short of a major transfusion of resources, energy, a renewed sense of its own history, and "outside of the box" thinking will be required in order for this program to live up to its historic role as the fountainhead of HBCU based architectural education.

In a following essay, I talk at some length about the situation at the Morgan program where I held the top position for five years. Let me telegraph here that I was on the same campus with a strong and growing engineering school. Leadership of Morgan's still young (founded in 1984) engineering school has been nothing short of extraordinary. The program is truly the pride of Maryland's one million African-American citizens.

Each of the accredited HBCU architecture programs are situated on campuses with strong and growing engineering programs. Each of those campuses also possess strong programmatic interests in the cultural arts including mass communications and film. In each case, unorthodox positive thinking—relative to much of the conventional wisdom and culture in the majority academy—can lead to the two things desperately needed by HBCU architecture program heads. One is substantial increases in enrollment by African-American students. The other is for the forging of creative new relationships between engineering and technology, architecture, and the campus cultural arts and sciences.

Within the accredited HBCU programs, three are private institutions. The other four are totally state supported and were once integral parts of a dual southern state system. Neither the public nor the private architecture schools including Howard have identified a solvent constituency that is committed to their survival at present. This is in stark contrast to the engineering schools at those institutions. However, engineering schools are no different from architecture in the type of parsimonious per-student financial allocations from the home university. In both cases the university only provides bare minimum space, core faculties necessary to maintain accreditation, and discretionary budgets for program enrichment that are usually piddling.

However, there are several critical differences between architecture and engineering. Engineering has more students and therefore more money. Each HBCU engineering dean is very good at coaxing additional money and other resources out of the external, high-profile constituencies of the engineering programs. Those constituencies include the large corporations who employ engineers. There are also those government agencies that are heavily vested in scientific research. These include the National Aeronautical Sciences Administration (NASA), the National Science Foundation, the Department of Defense, the Corp of Engineers, and other similar federal agencies. None of those entities are inclined to extend similar support or research funds to architecture programs *as such programs traditionally conceptualize their academic and professional missions.*

It is usually from those outside constituencies that engineering deans and their programs receive virtually all of their funds for travel, development, scholarships, state-of-the-art equipment and computers, and other vital resources. At several traditionally white universities, architecture program heads and faculties have started to seriously engage in convergence with engineering and science. Interesting avenues start to open up for architecture where this takes place. In addition to the MIT architecture school, the school at Rensselear in upstate New York under the visionary leadership of Alan Balfour is a good example. Joint initiatives by the Georgia Tech architecture and engineering schools is another. There are still others amongst the 123 accredited architecture programs and their campus engineering schools. HBCU architecture school leadership has much to learn from their engineering school leadership counterparts.

The key issue is the attitudes the architecture heads bring to the idea of administrative relationships with engineering schools. Orthodox thinking throughout much of the architectural academy still frowns on such relationships. This is due primarily to often deeply internalized inferiority complexes on the part of the architects. At the HBCU campus, it is imperative that still prevailing mainstream orthodoxy is rejected if the architecture programs are to have any chance of expanding black student enrollment and acquiring the enrichment resources so sorely needed.

But if the currently threadbare and demoralized HBCU architecture schools are to play the role I envision in the task of increasing the quantity of effective, culturally re-connected African-American architects, more than just exhortation and manifestos will be required. A permanent constituency of support for architecture programs at HBCUs must be quickly identified. Convergence between engineering schools and architecture programs at HBCUs—on an administrative level or merely through informal alliances—towards areas of common interest is a necessary start point. But this is nowhere near *sufficient.*

The metaphor I like to use is that the engineering schools annually back their "trucks" up to the Pentagon doorsteps, the NASA main gate, the National Science Foundation corridors, and front doors of the biggest private sector companies that hire engineers. Discretionary grant money for travel and other faculty development enrichment, contracts, internships, equipment, research funding, and executive exchange programs are just some of the things that the engineer's "trucks" are loaded up with.

What are the comparable places for HBCU architecture schools to back their "trucks" up to and expect proportionately positive results? For openers, we can quickly eliminate several places that are assumed to be good prospects. The nation has over 15,000 architectural firms. Most of them are small, hand-to-mouth operations. With only a few exceptions at the top—usually full service interdisciplinary operations like an RTKL in Baltimore—architectural firms offer virtually no prospects for financial support beyond minimum wage jobs for graduates. This is especially the case with the 200 African-American owned firms. Also, these HBCU programs have no appreciable wealthy alumni who can be counted on. The engineering school constituencies are not interested in the inbred worldview of the dominating "design orient" wing of architectural academe.

I would submit that the natural constituency for HBCU architecture schools consists of two essential camps. The first camp is the large corporations involved in constructing that over 90 percent of the built-environment that most small architectural firms are not yet interested in. Many of these corporations are already being heavily tapped by the engineers. These corporations also use the special talents of those architectural interns and graduates who have eschewed the "design fetish" in favor of acquiring solid management and communications skills.

The second camp is the public and quasi-public institutions vested in the nation's housing and community development efforts. This constituency ties back neatly to the hopefully redefined mission of the

HBCU architecture programs to focus on preparing architects to start out as housing producers and community developers.

So to continue with the "truck" metaphor, HBCU architecture programs must back theirs up to the doorsteps of the federal Department of Housing and Urban Development (HUD). Some must also go to the front doors of the quasi-government entities known as Fannie Mae and Freddie Mac. Still other must go to the doors of the building materials manufacturers and suppliers.

Unfortunately at this juncture, the problem with the "truck" metaphor is that the HBCU architecture programs *don't have trucks*. The first action is for the HBCU programs to convince elements from within their above identified natural constituencies to donate the "trucks." For these programs, currently enrolling an approximate total of 1,000 African-American students and with an immediate objective of substantially increasing those enrollments, the "trucks" needed are actually a base war chest endowment of 10 million dollars. Such an amount would yield an annual base budget of 500,000 dollars. That in turn would support a full-time fund-raising oriented executive and support staff housed at one of the schools in the greater Washington, DC, area. Information Technology resources required to effectively link the schools to each other as well as to other outstanding programs would also be needed. There should also be a needs-based per-school allocation to support or fund minimal discretionary needs, travel, and enrichment that is just not going to be funded by the home university at any time soon.

A priority agenda item for the full-time leadership for this collective entity is to identify resources to support the publishing of books, papers, small-circulation magazines, and a major monthly house organ. The prospects for establishing effective working relationships with already existing entities such as *blacklines Magazine*, the National Organization of Minority Architects, the Organization of Black Designers, to name several, must be pursued relentlessly.

The HBCU architecture schools have already taken a big first step in the right direction. At an Association of Collegiate Schools of

Architecture regional meeting in Jackson, Mississippi, in late 1999, the Council of Minority Architecture Schools (COMAS) was reborn. This is an offshoot of the old Council of Black Architecture Schools COBAS) that was born back in 1971 at Howard University in Washington, DC.

The goal of many of today's black students is usually to become effective participants in the transformation of what is often still referred to as "the inner-city" or "the ghetto" into viable and vibrant cultural communities while "making some money" along the way. *The Benjamins*—as African-American youth say in their always unique, creative, and global style setting ways—is the heart of the matter. Unless he or she is second or third generation family money, it is not a rational decision for a young African-American to go into a career that states right up front, as architectural recruitment material is highly likely to say, that *"you won't make money in architecture but you will achieve personal self-satisfaction."*

As the children of post 1965 Civil Rights Act baby-boomers, black youth are just not yet at that point of placing "self-satisfaction" above "the Benjamins" in their career decision-making matrix constructs. The nascent black upper class is still more rumor than reality and the black middle-class in comparison with the white middle-class is hanging on by its fingernails through a preponderance of government jobs and personal net worth that border on the negative. African-American youth, as ably put by *BLACK ENTERPRISE* magazine founder Earl Graves, *"must aspire to wealth creation."*[1]

The choice of a career in architecture is no reason to negate the imperatives set forth by Graves. We must refuse to assume that a young black person expressing a desire to make serious money is selfish or misguided and ill-suited to the architecture profession. That person is also talking about the creation of businesses, wealth, value, hard assets, jobs and opportunities for others. Most importantly, in their stress on the importance of "getting paid," such young people are pursuing the only method possible for accumulating the resources necessary to defend, define, and promote black culture and black social and political interests inside of a capital dominated economy.

Other HBCU schools might well be poised to grapple with the cultural dimensions of black and Afrocentric architecture. More importantly, all of these specialties and thrusts would be readily available to each of the current HBCU architecture schools on a real time-shared basis through currently off-the-shelf networking and audio-video conferencing Information Technology. And none of these initiatives would be endangering still necessary accreditation requirements. In fact, accreditation maintenance prospects could well be enhanced.

Curricula should have the objective of providing a solid liberal arts education that grounds the student in cultural narratives that correctly acknowledge black culture's contributions to presumptively "white" American architecture. There should also be a thorough grounding in the comprehensive use of Information Technology as a principal tool of network level basic research and scholarship, along with intensive geometric based graphic analysis of natural phenomena—a crash Froebal Gifts course when necessary.[2]

African-American students must rigorously know and possess competence in selective and appropriate use of the techniques and theories of the European duo of Le Corbusier and Mies, and the quintessential American trio of Wright, Sullivan, and Richardson. But more importantly, there must be clarity that media-lionized second and current third generation American and European architects of today have made no useful contributions to the form or discourse of architecture.[3] Therefore, when attempting to structure curriculum and socialization paradigms, the *economic and cultural interest of the African-American community must be the measure of effectiveness and appropriateness as we move into the twenty-first century.*

Now that it is official that the only route to a professional career in architecture is through graduation from an accredited architecture program, we have to start with Brad Grant's alarming statistic that in 1996 there were 4,786 first professional architecture degree (Bachelor of Architecture or Master of Architecture) graduates in the US and only 181 of those (3.8 percent) were African-Americans. Nearly half of them were graduates of the seven accredited HBCU-based programs (out of a total of 123 accredited programs). Experience and intuition tells me that out of those 181 black graduates no more than a half will go on to receive licenses and maybe one-fourth will eventually join the ranks of independent private practitioners. The corresponding numbers for the 4,600 other graduates is that nearly half will achieve licensure (2,300), and half of those will become practitioners (1,150). So comparatively speaking, the 1,375 licensed black architects that Grant-Mann have identified in the most recent update of their study (out of a total of just over 100,000 licensed American architects as of year 2000 statistics reported by the AIA) indicates a *decreasing* percentage of licensed African-American architects and practitioners in the coming future unless steps are taken to alter the course of things.

In using a licensure qualification as an up-front goal, the intent is to assure that the educational process results in eligibility for starting the licensure examinations simultaneous to receiving a professional degree. Achieving adequate preparation to dispose of the licensure issue cannot continue to be left to chance, as is currently the case.[4] A curriculum must explicitly encompass licensure as an integral part of the educational and matriculation process. Fortunately, this model of an architectural curriculum that is designed to result in licensure already has a proven precedent that exists in the form of two variations of cooperative education in architecture. The best-known cooperative version exists at the University of Cincinnati. Less well known but even more effective is the simultaneous work and study cooperative version at the Boston Architectural Center in Boston, Massachusetts.

The burning issue of competitive compensation for a new professional degree holder must be addressed head-on. The marketability of architecture careers to black architecture students without the prospects of salaries for a new graduate being at least equal to or exceeding that of a new undergraduate civil engineer or computer science graduate is not realistic. Since the typical orthodox architectural practice is not financially structured to pay graduating architects salaries at that level, other alternative forms of after graduation employment must be encouraged.

The salaries that orthodox architectural practices are able to afford are generally adequate for work-performed concurrent to student enrollment in architectural schools. But after graduation many of those same students will elect to seek out opportunities in firms and businesses that build the 90 percent of the physical environment that orthodox architectural practices are apparently not involved in or interested in.

Under the approach of concurrently facilitating office practice internship while still in school, new architecture graduates are free to look at a larger range of possibilities for gainful and competitively compensated employment. Those possibilities would include architectural-engineers, engineer-architects, engineers, building contractors, home builders, real estate developers, and processor plant designers just to name a few. There would also be a need to include the jobs in film, television, entertainment, and computer games. *Still other graduates may be ready to start entrepreneurial style businesses.*

The HBCU architecture program has a particular responsibility to deliberately socialize a majority of the recipients of professional degrees into entrepreneurial business start-ups at the earliest possible time. Many of those graduates range in ages from early twenties to mid-thirties. Research and experience verifies that early to mid-twenties is the ideal age for launching businesses. HBCU programs must come to terms with the proposition that a professional degree in architecture is too valuable a scarce resource to be lost to low-paid employment in an orthodox architectural practice. With that realization, much else becomes clearer regarding method and mission.

In any attempt to shift the paradigm of a curriculum, the most difficult issue is getting an existing faculty to come on board. Faculties are able to co-exist and teach in a program only on the basis of an agreed upon consensus about the less acknowledged socialization process that is at work in any program. Today's tenured and therefore most influential architectural professorate were themselves socialized into a belief system that contributes to the abysmally low numbers of black architects. But ultimately the task of converting an orthodox minded faculty is a job of salesmanship and leadership. An existing vision can only be replaced by a compelling and results-oriented new vision.

What remains to be seen is whether any of the heads of the HBCU-based schools will be able to achieve sharp increases in black student enrollment while simultaneously repositioning curricula to align with today's exponentially expanding information revolution. Perennially low enrollments at black university architecture schools, and the continuing structural reality of a conflated Beaux Arts-Bauhaus curricula core and premise of the architect as *"an artist in search of a wealthy like-minded patron"* are two linked issues that must be confronted and overcome.

With 45 percent of black architecture students in the country today attending HBCU programs, the place to start to radically increase today's much too small black presence in architecture is by significantly increasing enrollment in those schools. This requires a strategy of starting new pre-professional undergraduate design and planning majors and minors at other strategically located urban-based historically black universities. These new programs would serve as feeders to the graduate or professional degree programs at the accredited HBCU architecture schools as well as the traditionally white graduate architecture programs.

However, here I hasten to caution that expansion of the enrollments at existing HBCU architecture schools along with starting new programs at other HBCU schools can never be more than half of any strategy aimed at increasing the numbers of African-American architects. *The other half of the slack must be made up at the most elite American architectural schools* (despite the reality that several of those schools still reek with Foucault-Derrida undertones that the brilliant, and iconoclastic Camille Paglia cavalierly dismisses as "...that French Crap"[5]).

Those venues will continue to propagate and exercise hegemony in the arena of high culture "design excellence" as defined by the mainstream architecture media. Those institutions are usually in the best position to continue to thumb their noses at the external pressures from conservative anti-affirmative action ideologues seeking to dismantle racially influenced admissions policies. These schools simply must continue to refuse to compose incoming classes based solely on the numerical ranking of test scores.[6]

Each one of the HBCU-based architecture programs must chart its own specific curriculum and course of action based on its community context, university mission, and student body career interests. Even without a deliberate strategy of curriculum collaboration the schools will have some things in common by virtue of accreditation guidelines.[7] However, it is imperative that the HBCU architecture schools live up to the responsibility of socializing the next generation of architects to see urban communities in the same way that cultural entertainment and real estate developers see them.[8]

> *At the close of the twentieth-century, in the United States as else where, there are three kinds of buildings;* ***signature, generic, and vernacular***...*The vast majority of construction—by convention called "vernacular," and it is 95% of the nation's total—is not designed by architects at all, but consists of easily replicable structures that developers and contractors assemble for shopping malls, tract housing, and roadside services, for storage and distribution, for franchise, chain, and discount merchandising, and as the rest of that sea of aesthetic minimalism that architect Robert Venturi praised in Learning From Las Vegas(bold italics mine)...*[9]

Virtually all of the generic and vernacular work that Twombley is talking about is accomplished as private sector merchant built work by developer and contractor entrepreneurs. The black community rarely has the level and type of leverage over those developers and contractors supplying basic shelter and ancillary community facilities needs to the American consumer including 37 million African-Americans.

The wonder of all wonders is that of all of the books written about and by architects and architecture, it is Robert Venturi's treatise that went on to become the base design theory text book of today's American architectural schools.[10] It is worth pondering how different the discourse as well as the reality of American architecture would be today had then MIT architecture professor and social activist, Robert

Goodman's book *After the Planners*, instead became the base textbook of the academy.[11] Many of today's 22,000 students enrolled in architectural school are unaware of the rich alternative laid out by Jewish radical Goodman and the other black, Latino, Native American and Jewish architectural community activists who vied with Peter Eisenman (the "Whites" of *New York Five* notoriety), Robert Venturi (the "Grays" of *Complexities and Contradictions* fame), and Gehry (the west coast "Silvers") for the heart and soul of the design profession thirty years ago:

> *But in reality, Venturi seems to have little concern with the experience of life. I searched the entire book for any description of how people use architecture; there was hardly a word about it—instead the same aesthetic jargon...the important thing is simply the appearance of architectural forms.*[12]

A crucial step toward establishing the plausibility of radically increased numbers of African-Americans entering architecture is to more accurately define the current world of American architecture. That world revolves primarily around the architectural academy consisting of the 123 mostly university based architecture schools.[13] There is also a mainstream architectural press and media world of lush magazines and vanity company brochures posing as books. In this world, the realities of day-to-day practices are obscured by the attention lavished on the handful of romantic star architect-artists (and their media soothsayers and camp followers who prefer to be referred to as "critics"). These "stars" are religiously promoted— even if unintentionally—throughout the architectural academy.

MIT professor Mark Jarzombek, in his perceptive critique of the role of the *Sustainability Movement* in the architectural academy, recently put forth a plausible alternative curriculum for a professional architectural program.

> *In recent years there has been a growing interest in the project of Sustainability as a site where ethical commitment, architectural practice, capitalism, and good design could come together. But*

before one can assess the legitimacy of the new relationship of archi-tecture to Sustainability, one must study more critically some of the implications, especially for the architectural academe.[14]

From the above opening of his thoughtful article, Jarzombek goes on to discuss in detail the inherent contradictions between natural science-based *Sustainability* and the current standard Beaux Arts-Bauhaus architectural curriculum. It is the natural environment of air, water, and land that is to be sustained in the face of man-made rapacity. Jarzombek delineates the role of advanced capitalism as the necessary bridge between architecture and *Sustainability*.

Jarzombek posits that in a truly consistent relationship between *Sustainability* and the architecture school curriculum, *the traditional design studio will have to evolve into a hard science based building technology lab.* The history and theory courses will have to give way to the need for mastery of high-end computation; and esoteric avant-garde theorizing will have to be replaced by real research skills and competency in select natural sciences. Professional practice—the natural extension of architectural school—will also undergo radical change in Jarzombek's scheme. The dominant small architectural practice could be replaced by corporate and government funded technology research think tanks or *finance-design-build-manage* private sector variations. Of course, there will continue to be a small group of architectural graduates who will find wealthy patrons who wish to preserve the tradition of the status quo.

The bigger architectural firms as we know them today must inevitably give way to big-business technology arms and corporate architectural arms. Knowingly or not, Jarzombek makes common cause with many theorists and prognosticators currently speculating on the contours of the next stage of architectural education and its extension through professional practice. His projections of Sustainability driven changes are quite credible.

An architectural program today is tethered to a conventional university by a life-giving umbilical cord of financial support. In exchange, the school leadership is charged with the acquisition and maintenance of professional accreditation. The charge of American HBCUs and world African Diaspora architecture schools is to continue to honor that unwritten covenant between a program and its university financial support base. But leadership must also move as expeditiously as possible toward each HBCU's own variations of the inevitable curriculum posed by Jarzombek.

In the interests of being able to attract and successfully matriculate savvy African-American students (as well as white and Asian students who are rightly suspicious of anything that is not "Info Tech" based), the design studio—still the heart of any program that expects to maintain the imprimatur of national accreditation—must move closer to becoming a state-of-the art Information Technology resource, and research laboratory. All continued nostalgic concessions to the craft of manual drawing should be abandoned once and for all in favor of the *craft* of full competency in the use of integrated information systems.[15]

Despite my enthusiastic agreement with Jarzombek, I believe that there are other viable ways besides manual drawing studio culture to preserve the positive cultural dimensions of the architecture profession. The continued fostering of an ideology that a relationship exists between what traditionally goes on in a Beaux Arts-Bauhaus studio versus how cities, regional environments, and urban cultures are shaped constitutes a serious disservice to prospective young architects.

For young African-Americans considering any endeavor, the issue is ultimately about their perception of the prospects of success on a level playing field. The "game" must be oriented to their unique strengths, rhythm, and style. This always brings me back to my National Basketball Association and National Football League analogy. We can never forget that it was less than 40 years ago that the NBA and NFL were virtually all white affairs. There was near unanimous consensus among owners, coaches, players and fans that such whiteness was the *natural order of things.*

The HBCU architecture school should have a tax-exempt nonprofit community development corporation facilitating the work of students, faculty, practitioners and Community Fellows. All of them will need to cut across the discrete disciplines of architecture, landscape architecture, emerging environmental sciences, civil-industrial engineering and construction management, urban planning, transportation planning, design arts related communications, and real estate based finance and legal studies. The role of these entities, similar to Japanese models, would be to incubate, nurture and support the integrated networked businesses needed by Black America and the Diaspora to meet its shelter needs while damming up its built environment cash drain problem. *But all of what I have just described happens to be the capabilities and even operating reality of already transformed (or available parallel alternative) studios at a significant number of traditionally white architecture schools. The graduates of those programs will be the competition that HBCU educated students will have to compete with for the opportunity to redevelop urban communities throughout America.*

Several of today's scholars have convincingly described how industry, commerce, institutions, and individuals will procure space, place, and facilities, e.g., architecture, in the immediate future.[16] For those sectors of the built environment that have been of little interest to academy-trained architects—buildings that are ordinary, repeatable, and academically invisible—much of that is already standard modus operandi in corporate America. That raises many serious questions that need immediate responses from white and black architecture schools. Such questions go to the heart of the matter of shaping curricula and imparting a socialization process aimed at producing real leadership in the built environment making enterprise.

The architectural skill of discreet independent building object making is perhaps still necessarily useful. But of particularly importance is the skill to lead and coordinate a group of building users in the design of places and spaces that may exist over a long period of time. A new urban Diaspora architect must have baseline skills in group conflict management to accompany competence and expertise in third dimension Information Technology data base manipulation and real estate finance. A plausible observation is being made in some quarters that leading elements of today's landscape architecture profession are closer to the reality of Jarzombek's curriculum model than today's conventional architecture curriculum. To paraphrase many of today's landscape architecture professionals, *it is the ensemble that is of more interest than the particular object building.*

CHAPTER 4

The Morgan Architecture Program in Baltimore, 1980–2002

The entire state of Maryland lists only 75 licensed black architects (out of a state total of just under 2,000).[1] While this translates numerically into a four percent black architect total, the reality is that the overwhelming majority of Maryland black architects work and practice in the counties directly adjacent to Washington, DC, and are effectively Washington, DC, architects. At the end of the year 2000, less that twenty of Maryland's licensed black architects work and practice either within the city of Baltimore or the directly adjacent counties.

In assessing the role and status of black architects, Washington, DC, and the state of Maryland cannot be usefully separated. The Washington metropolitan area and its over four million people (one million of them are African-Americans) and the state of Maryland and its five million people (one million African-Americans) actually overlap along the critical Baltimore to Washington, DC, interstate highway.

The governments of the Washington, DC, and Baltimore city metropolitan areas have provided a meaningful way of viewing these two entities. The official standard metropolitan statistical areas (SMSAs) of Washington's four million people and Baltimore's 2.5 million people have officially joined forces to comprise a single supra combined SMSA of 6.5 million people. Over 1.5 million—twenty-five percent—are African-Americans, which would logically constitute the market base for the next generation of black architects who might conceivably establish some forms of professional practices in the region.

A twentieth-century assessment of the development of the Baltimore metropolis would show numerous conceptual similarities and patterns to Washington, DC. The most pertinent similarity for our purpose here would be the stark absence of black architects, developers, contractors, and homebuilders from the development process over the last one hundred years.

There were several largely obscure exceptions to the virtually all white architect milieu of Baltimore and surrounding counties during the period between 1900 and 1965. The most notable was black architect Albert Cassell, who was born just outside of Baltimore in Towson, Maryland. After severing his professional relationship with Howard University in 1938, Cassell continued his private practice throughout the Washington-Baltimore area. He designed a number of structures in and around Baltimore including the old Odd Fellows Temple, an apartment building on Fayette and Eutaw Streets, and Providence Hospital in Baltimore. Cassell also designed four buildings on the campus of Morgan College (now Morgan State University). Also during the 1950s, Hampton (Virginia) University's black architect-professor and practitioner Henry Livas maintained a small satellite office in Baltimore. Livas provided services primarily to black church congregations including the First Baptist Church in East Baltimore.

The state of Maryland and the city of Baltimore did not have a university based professional School of Architecture until the mid-1960s—just over thirty-five-years ago. The flagship university of the state opened the doors of a School of Architecture in 1964. The city of Baltimore was bypassed for the Prince George's County location of the main campus of the University of Maryland that is just twenty minutes from downtown Washington, DC. Up to that time, Baltimore's practitioners had been trained in a combination of places including the region's then all white architecture schools at Catholic University in DC, the University of Virginia, Virginia Tech, and the other schools along the eastern seaboard.

Alexander Cochran, trained under Walter Gropius at Harvard in the late 1930s, is a founder of the venerable Baltimore firm of Cochran, Stevenson, and Donkervoet. Cochran is the acknowledged father of the movement of the city towards International Style Modern Architecture in the mid-forties.[2] Cochran finished the Harvard Graduate School of Design program in 1939 and returned to Baltimore. Up to that point and dating back to the start of the twentieth-century, Baltimore, like many other eastern cities, was dominated by Beaux Arts style architecture.

The other modernist pioneers who have played a large role in establishing the present visual image of the city through its distinctive downtown skyline were Archibald Rogers, Francis Taliaferro, Charles Lamb, and George Kostritsky, founding members of now world class architectural powerhouse long known by the corporate name and logo, RTKL. The firm was founded in 1946 and has been the dominant architectural force in the city under the driving corporate management style leadership of Harold Adams.[3] Howard University architecture graduate Gary Bowden (who also received a graduate degree in urban design from Carnegie-Mellon University in 1964) is an RTKL senior vice-president and large shareholder of company stock.

The initial early 1970s virtually all-white graduates of the new School of Architecture at the University of Maryland related more to the city of Washington, DC, than the city of Baltimore. The school also drew initial faculty members from Washington, DC. Frank Schlessinger and Roger Lewis were among the most notable faculty members drawn from Washington, DC, practices.

The handful of native Baltimore black architecture students who have matriculated at Howard University almost never elected to return to Baltimore to work in established offices as pre-licensure interns and eventually establish independent practices, as was the pattern in Washington, DC. The several black architecture students who would eventually graduate from the new program at the University of Maryland also shunned Baltimore as an alternative. A poor image was among the reasons for bypassing Baltimore by white and black architecture school graduates of Maryland and Howard University. Post-World

War II through late seventies Baltimore was no match for the excitement and opportunities associated with working (and playing) in the national capital.

For the black architecture school graduates during that period, Baltimore had no visible black practitioner model and no evidence that there was sufficient black political power necessary to acquire meaningful design commissions similar to the scale possible in Washington, DC. In some eyes there was also a sizable gap between the relative affluence, and political sophistication of the black middle classes of the two cities. Meanwhile, as of the early 1970s, Washington, DC, had a sizable collection of black architectural graduates coming out of Howard and electing to remain in DC. There was also, in those post-MLK assassination days, the presence of over a dozen black-owned practices serving as role models. These firms were actually growing in numbers and firm sizes as a result of the aggressive use of black professionals by the black Home Rule government in DC.

In the 1970s, Baltimore's African-American community was just beginning to approach the numbers necessary for a serious political presence on the City Council at City Hall. It would be another decade before those numbers would be sufficient to facilitate an actual take-over of the 1975mayor's office. By 1975, at least two Washington, DC, based black-owned firms had ventured to open satellite offices in Baltimore. This was in response to African-American community demands for black participation in city and state government financed Baltimore public works projects.

Louis Fry, Jr. was successful in landing commissions for at least six city elementary schools in Baltimore. Fry was also able to secure design commissions from Coppin State College in West Baltimore and Morgan State University, the city's two HBCUs.[4] In the early 1970s, Washington, DC, firm Sultan Campbell merged with a small firm owned by well-connected local Baltimore black architect Edward Taylor, a 1950 graduate of Hampton. Taylor and Sultan Campbell parted ways in 1976. Shortly thereafter, the DC based firm sent aggressive Columbia University architecture school trained Stanford Britt to run the Baltimore office. The firm has since designed numerous projects around Baltimore including churches, medical clinics, housing projects, and rapid transit station work.

Several other DC based and Howard University trained architects took advantage of being personal residents of the state of Maryland. In 1977, Seattle-based African-American architect Leon Bridges relocated his entire practice and family to Baltimore. Bridges' clients included the federal and local rapid transit authority, Coppin State College, Morgan State, and the city public school system. The Bridges practice remains the senior African-American owned firm in Baltimore today. Howard trained Washington, DC, native Johnie Lee has also functioned as ether a principal or as head of his own small firm since the mid-1980s.

Eugene DeLoatch, Morgan's dean of engineering, was a young electrical engineering instructor at Howard while I was there in architecture school in the early 1960s as a student. He left Howard in the early 1980s to start a new engineering school at Morgan at the behest of then new Morgan president Earl Richardson. At that time there were six other engineering schools in the state—all at traditionally white institutions. Those six institutions were graduating an annual combined total of less than twenty-five African-American engineers. Half of them were coming out of a single school—the US Naval Academy in Annapolis. Maryland's engineering schools were all convinced that SAT scores of less than 1,200 indicated unlikely success as an engineer. Needless to say, black students—especially those from inner-city Baltimore high schools—were being shut-out of the white engineering schools. This was totally unacceptable to the (then approaching) one million black citizens of Maryland.

One remedy proposed by some influential black Marylanders was a new engineering school at Morgan. A Morgan president commissioned feasibility study for a school consisting of four-hundred predominately African-American students with SAT threshold scores of 1,000 was received with belly-laughs by the white education establishment of the state, not to mention those other white engineering schools. In reality, today's Morgan's engineering school enrollment has soared past the 800 student mark and is still climbing. They have long since outgrown the new engineering school facility that the state somewhat reluctantly built (the state people thought that this facility for 400 predominately African-American engineering students would be grossly underutilized). Also needless to say, all of the Morgan-DeLoatch engineering graduates are zapped up by the engineering industry at the same salaries as the graduates of the white schools throughout the state. The evolution of a successful engineering school at Morgan holds important lessons for the still unfolding saga of the evolution of an architecture school at Morgan.

In 1971 Morgan State University initiated actions that would eventually lead to the formal establishment of a professional architecture degree-granting program by 1980. In 1972, Homer Favor, director of the Department of Urban Affairs in the School of Education, hired Howard University and Harvard Graduate School of Design alumni Harry G. Robinson. Favor gave him the green light to expand an existing Master's in Urban Policy program into a full-fledged School of Architecture to include master's degrees in architecture, landscape architecture, and city planning programs. According to Robinson's proposed plan, there would have been an undergraduate feeder degree component in order to make the graduate programs feasible at Morgan.

Robinson's comprehensive proposal was envisioned as the "School of Architecture" that the city of Baltimore never had. Unfortunately, Robinson and Favor were soon to encounter Maryland state higher education politics. This was all taking place in the mid-1970s. The still fledgling University of Maryland architecture school forty five miles away in Prince Georges County was just starting to graduate its first classes of architects. The Maryland program was then configured as a conventional five-year undergraduate professional program.

The state education authorities denied the Morgan-Robinson plan for an undergraduate architecture program. The basis of the denial was that such a plan was a duplication of an existing program offering at the University of Maryland. Yet, it was clear that Morgan and Robinson's prospects of attracting significant numbers of the virtually all-white group of students heading for College Park was extremely unlikely. Robinson's primary objective was to attract African-Americans to the under-represented professions of architecture, landscape architecture, and city planning throughout the state and in the city of Baltimore. This, after all, was the sole justification for a second state supported architecture school in Maryland.

The compromise that Morgan was left with is that only the graduate programs in Robinson's plan were approved for implementation. This was inherently problematic for the university. This was flying in the face of the historic reality of virtually all of the country's black graduate school prospects heading for schools of education, law, business, science and medicine. The strictly graduate model for architecture works reasonably well at Harvard, Yale, Penn, Columbia, Princeton, UCLA, and similarly endowed top-level research universities. An exclusively graduate school approach had never been attempted at an HBCU. If such a model were to have any remote chance at Morgan, it would have required Robinson's energy, drive, charisma, and resourcefulness. Above all else, Robinson's consummate communications skills would have been the key.

As fate would have it, just before the time came to actually implement the new graduate programs, Robinson left Morgan in 1978 to become the dean of architecture at his Howard University alma mater in Washington, DC. Leadership of the program at Morgan was left in the hands of Jack Daft, a white landscape architect who lacked Robinson's academic credentials, his organizational skills, his easy rapport with Baltimore's all white architectural practice establishment, and his commitment to building a predominately black student body. Needless to say, this turn of events did not impress the local Baltimore architectural leadership establishment. Without an architect-academic of Robinson's caliber, the program would be in for a long hard struggle of trying to establish acceptance within the Baltimore professional architecture community. The identity the program craved as being

"Baltimore's School of Architecture" was just not forth coming without Robinson.

Several other African-American architects in succession assumed the leadership of the program after the end of Daft's tenure in 1982. Michael Amos, a Howard University alumnus with a graduate architecture degree from Harvard, led the program for several years. Amos left to form his own practice in Baltimore. Amos (now deceased) was soon joined in his practice by Dan Bailey to form the firm of Amos and Bailey. Even though Bailey, one of the first graduates of the Morgan program in 1984, is white, this practice was effectively only the third locally formed firm in the city headed by an African-American.

In 1986, program leadership fell to Anthony Johns who came to the job as a seasoned practitioner and retired professor in the School of Architecture at Howard University. Over the next decade—up to the summer of 1997—Johns was able to guide the architecture program through several successful accreditation visits from the National Architectural Accrediting Board. Between the initiation of the architecture program at Morgan in 1980 and 1997, the program conferred over 100 master's degrees. No more than twenty of them were to African-Americans. The rest went to a mixture consisting of whites, Asian Indians, and Nigerian nationals. Several of the Nigerians remained in Baltimore and became naturalized citizens as well as licensed architects. As of 1998, several of the Nigerian-American graduates of the program has established a highly regarded housing-focused practices in Baltimore.

City planner Richard Lloyd, who holds a doctorate in architecture from Cal-Berkeley, is my successor at Morgan. Lloyd is in a position to have the best of two worlds. Morgan president Earl Richardson has always been strongly committed to an autonomous School of Architecture. Before I retired in mid-2002, Richardson had given his seal of approval to a new building that architecture (along with landscape architecture, city & regional planning, and possibly a new doctorate in environmental design program) will share with the engineering school's civil engineering and transportation programs.

DeLoatch and I conceived this new facility as a *Center for Built Environment Infrastructure Studies.*

In the fifty-minute commute between my main residence in DC and my apartment in Baltimore (five minutes from my office on the Morgan campus), I never fail to marvel at the Baltimore city commercial downtown skyline. As skylines go, Baltimore's is nothing out of the ordinary. But as an African-American entering or leaving a city of roughly 600,000 people—65 percent of them are also African-Americans—I am constantly trying to decipher the meaning of that gleaming skyline to the city's black population. I am clear that in a literal sense the office towers have historically had little to do with Black Baltimore. The people responsible for these buildings represent that intersection of Baltimorean culture, power, and accumulated risk capital. The architects selected to express the city's and region's (all-white) business and cultural elite's capital and cash in steel, concrete, and glass is drawn from inside of the social orbits of that same elite.

The essence and rhythm of the subculture of the architectural school culture—the "academy" if you will—is structured around a mythology of preparing people to add to the skyline. The mythology insists that there is rationality at play here. The mythology insists that there is a pedagogy or curriculum that logically leads to these American skylines. My old long lost friend and former Harvard classmate, Lars Lerup, (now Dean of Architecture at Rice in Houston) best cuts through the fog with his recent observation that "architecture comes not from design but from capital" or something to that effect (he makes this point in his most recent school bulletin).

Within a year after I arrived in Baltimore in mid-1997 to head the architecture school at Morgan, I landed a seat on the city's architectural review board (official known as the Design Advisory Panel). Once or twice each month I would spend all day with six other architect, landscape architect, and architectural historian colleagues reviewing five to seven architectural projects. Usually by the time these projects reach the DAP, the architect's public or private client is committed to actually building. In nearly three years of over three hundred projects I have gained a good sense of the city's design and development establishment.

I can count on one hand the times the DAP has reviewed the work of an African-American architect or real estate developer. As of 2001, I have been able to identify only three consequential black developers in the city of Baltimore. The most prominent entity is headed by two very interesting men. A & R Development Corporation was founded in 1977 by the principal players, William Adams, chairman of the board, and chief executive officer, Theo Rodgers. Adams is affectionately and universally known throughout Black Baltimore as "Lil' Willie." He is a self-made individual with a reputation for being an extraordinarily shrewd businessman with deep roots throughout Baltimore's black and white political and business establishments. Adams is also known as the person who used the initial fortune he earned in the 1960s—purported as a "numbers boss"—to finance much of today's existing black business community in Baltimore.

Rodgers, his younger partner, has a more conventional background including an undergraduate degree in engineering from a Tennessee HBCU, and an MBA from Harvard. Rodgers cut his Baltimore business teeth through a stint as executive assistant to the venerated Henry Parks of Parks Sausage fame. This once nationally famous (in White as well as Black America) company was also partially financed by venture capital provided by Adams. A & R has a long future ahead under the day-to-day stewardship of a Rodgers. Theo's son Anthony, a 1997 Georgia Tech graduate, appears to be the heir apparent to his father.

A & R is reliably reported to have well over a billion dollars worth of projects in play. Residential developments for Black Baltimore totaling over 4,100 completed housing units appear to be the staple of the company. A & R has completed several major projects for Morgan State University including a dorm complex and a student activity center. The firm is now getting ready to add a major mixed-use office-hotel-retail building to the Baltimore skyline through a partnership with an established white developer.

The second black developer is Otis Warren, also a self-made second generation Baltimorean. Warren has also made his mark through buying or developing HUD financed or insured rental apartment projects for Black Baltimore. Warren can rightfully boast of being the oldest and most experienced of the three black developers. Warren actually already has completed one of the buildings that make up the Baltimore skyline. In the mid-1980s, Warren was award exclusive right to develop a 334,000 square foot eleven-story office building in the heart of the Inner Harbor area. Warren was able to secure conventional financing for the forty million dollar project on the strength of long-term leases from the federal General Services Administration.

The third and most recently established consequential black developer in Baltimore is an interesting operation that holds great relevance to the underlying premise of this book. The four top principals of Metroventures/USA Inc. are Howard University architecture or city planning graduates. The founder, Olusola Seriki, is a Nigerian-American with a degree in architecture. He finished architecture school just over twenty years ago and, after several years in orthodox architectural offices, went to work as a development project manager for the Columbia based James Rouse Company. Seriki's partners each have similar backgrounds in commercial and residential real estate operations. The fourth partner, Suzanne Graham, augmented her Howard undergraduate city planning degree with a master's in real estate development from Columbia University. Seriki left Rouse recently to set up his own company around a six hundred-unit housing rehabilitation contract in the Sandtown area of inner city Baltimore. The contract was actually from the Enterprise Foundation, which is a well-capitalized subsidiary non-profit arm of the Rouse Company.

In all three cases consisting of numerous projects by these three Baltimore African-American developers, there is no pattern of the cultivation or engagement of African-American architects as primes. This includes major projects undertaken for HBCU Morgan State University. A & R did use the African-American owned Washington,

DC, and Baltimore architectural firm Sultan Campbell on a six million dollar HUD financed rental housing project. Stan Britt, the head of Sultan Campbell, once told me that Rodgers politely resists all overtures for an ongoing relationship. For nearly all of A & R's many other substantial projects, Rodgers elected to commission well-known white-owned Baltimore architectural firms.

On Warren's big, highly visible downtown commercial office building, he elected to use an established white Washington, DC, architectural firm. Warren played it absolutely safe in using the very mainstream commercial firm of Wiehe Associates of Washington, DC. On several occasions, Metroventures/USA paired-up their choice of large established white Baltimore architectural firms with a small suburban Baltimore black-owned architectural firm. It is not clear why Metroventures even felt the need to hire an outside architectural firm on the company's residential projects. One of the Metroventures partners is licensed and in possession of extensive prior senior level experience with orthodox design operations.

One possible big reasons that Baltimore's black private real estate developers are thus far showing no inclination towards a serious commitment to sponsoring and patronizing African-American architects may be due to several factors. In the case of Rodgers and Warren, unlike the late Ted Hagans, the premier black developer of Washington, DC, these men had no long-standing fraternal relationship with black architects extending back to college days together (Hagans attended the School of Engineering and Architecture at Howard with most of the city's second generation black architects). Also the Baltimore developers may not have felt as politically or financially secure as Hagans to make independent decisions on the sensitive issue of selecting or cultivating their own architectural protégées.

Developers look to architects to navigate a city's numerous regulatory design boards. Reputations and images matter. There may be even still other reasons that black developers bypass black architects. Some of those reasons are simply are not going to be discussed candidly for the record. But rest assured that when a black developer remarks that he or she is "color-blind" when selecting an architect, you're are not hearing the whole truth.

I have come to know that it is simply not realistic for the current or next generation of African-American architects to look to black developers as potential clients in orthodox owner-architect relationships. As a rule, black architects should only approach black developers (or any other color developer or property owner) on one level; as a potential *investor and financial partner to that prospective developer.* This is best accomplished through the architect's holding some type of effective leverage with the sources of a project's financing. My view is that this reality should be looked at positively rather than negatively. The only realistic basis of black architects having relationships with black developers—Baltimore or most other places—is as business and financial partners. This of course has profound implications for the academic curriculum and socialization process.

Between mid-1997 and mid-2002 I held the administrative and academic leadership reins of the architecture, landscape architecture, and city planning programs at Morgan. During that period, I also taught senior studio as well as the practice management course. In those courses my pointed agenda was to expand the vision of African-Americans and other open-minded young professionals who could be interested in becoming design and planning professionals.

Each year I collected (anonymously) written survey feedback at the beginning of my course on professional practice, management and law. Students overwhelmingly express career goals of becoming owner-principals of urban-based general practices that will have a significant positive impact on the lives and fortunes of other African-Americans. In short, they appear to be deeply interested in the same thing that has been my own personal interest over the past nearly half of the twentieth-century; *African-American community empowerment, effective African-American architects in the Information Age Revolution, and the flowering of black cultural variations of Modern Architecture.*

My senior studio and my professional practice courses are my primary window of opportunity to wrestle my students (a majority

African-American along with a constant solid minority of whites, Asian Indians, and an occasional Hispanic) away from their architecture academy culture imbibed notions about the role of the architect. I take those opportunities to explore basic realities with my students. For openers, I remind them that Morgan State University, as a large prospective institutional client prospect, might be an omen and example of the sheer impossibility of the course that lies ahead for African-Americans and others attempting to establish viable conventional practices in the near future. The university plays a role in the city of Baltimore that bears striking similarities to the role Howard University formerly played in Washington, DC, years back.

Morgan is in the midst of a *half-billion dollar* campus facilities building boom that matches the scope of the Howard campus expansion under presidents Mordecai Johnson and James Cheek from 1935 to 1980. That work on the Howard campus spawned and sustained several generations of African-American architectural practices in Washington, DC, between the start of World War II and the last quarter of the twentieth-century. That does not appear to be repeatable at Morgan today. Whether this is due to the inherently inhibiting structural limitations imposed by Maryland state politics or the equally inhibiting conservative assumptions by Morgan's institutional leadership is a legitimate question.

Meanwhile, the city of Baltimore and its sixty-five percent black majority of citizens find themselves at the end of the twentieth-century with only four black-owned architectural firms—out of a total of 150 architectural firms—in the greater Baltimore metropolitan area. In a casual survey of architectural practices in Baltimore, it is clear that black-owned practices in the twenty-first century cannot be developed utilizing existing assumptions and paradigms of architectural practices. For prospective black firms there are no "patrons" to speak of and virtually all of the conventional "client" relationships worth having are already well established for the next several decades by the current generation of architectural firms. The prospects of public sector local government as a major client is even bleaker than the area's private and institutional sectors, despite increased black political power in the city. The only viable strategy open to the objective of conventional architectural practice is an *acquisition (of established firms and other appreciating assets) strategy*. Anything or any firm that is of truly positive measurable value is also for sale at a price that would allow the "numbers" to work for the buyer. The debt and equity financing for such acquisitions is also available.

The majority of the next generation black architects must become serious about pursuing a model of architectural practice that has been thus far treated in the academy as an aberration. The facts of what Atlanta architect John Portman accomplished thirty years ago are far more pertinent to the lives of the next generation of African-American architects than the globetrotting, museum designing architect-artists that the architectural academy still socializes prospective architects to aspire to emulate.[5]

CHAPTER 5

A New African-American Architect(ure) Canon

I am encouraged about recent explorations in architecture by Cornel West, the highly regarded black Harvard based philosopher. I first read an earlier draft of his thinking in a 1993 issue of APPENDX, a critical journal of architectural theory founded by three black Harvard Graduate School of Design students.[1] At least one of the journal founders flirted with the notion of seriously exploring a "Black Architecture" in later editions of the journal. That particular founder did go on to complete a very densely written and complexly reasoned post-structuralism doctoral dissertation that juxtaposed architecture and blackness in a panoramic historical context.[2]

West demonstrates a shrewd grasp of the seething world of today's architectural academy and its thus far futile attempts to construct a relevant critical theory of architecture. West penetrates the pretensions and inadequacies of the current crop of academic theorists-critics. In the APPENDX article, West gives perspective to the role of the French literary post-structuralism theorists Jacques Derrida and Michel Foucault, who are the patron saints of the befuddled American architectural academy critical theorists, in his observation that:

> The major challenge of a new architectural historiography is that its conception of the "past" and "present" be attuned to the complex role of difference—nature, primitive, ruled, Dionysian, female, black and so on.

261

West is obviously keenly aware of the reality of very different "historiography" concerns held by most serious thinkers about Modern Architecture.[3] In that same article West connects with me in his remarks on Le Corbusier, arguably the ultimate icon of western modernist architecture. I am a passionate subscriber of the opening line of a big important book by architectural historian William Curtis on the life of Le Corbusier:

> *"It is impossible to understand architecture in the twentieth-century without first coming to terms with Le Corbusier."*[4]

However, my own coming to terms with Le Corbusier may not be what Curtis had in mind. In looking at West's remarks about Le Corbusier, it is clear that West has grasped the real meaning of the relationship of this quintessential French Caucasian architect to black Africans. West is no doubt mindful that it has historically been the French who have taken African art and music most seriously. *My sense is that no Frenchman of his era took Africans and blackness, as an artistic and aesthetic wellspring, more seriously than Le Corbusier.* This modernist icon did what no African or African-American of his time in the early twentieth-century could do as a practical matter: *explore the black aesthetic through the use of concrete, steel, brick, and glass.* In this regard, Le Corbusier shared a similarity with the lives and careers of several white western musical geniuses in their relationship to black music. West simply astounds me with observations that demonstrate a profound grasp of ideas that do not appear to have occurred to other great minds inside of the larger world of Modern Architecture. West makes the vital connection between the highest and lowest levels of a rich black culture and the still enduring positive dimensions of Le Corbusier-Wright based modernist American architecture:

> *The case of the great Le Corbusier may serve as an illustration. His serious grappling with the binary oppositions above reaches a saturation point in his critique of the classical theory of architectural design (Vitruvius) in the form of the Modulor. This new form of measure derived not just from the proportions of the human figure*

but, more specifically, from women's bodies—especially fat "primitive," "uncivilized," non-European, Dionysian-driven, black, brown and red women's bodies...It is no secret that Le Corbusier's paintings and pencil sketches in the early 1930s began to focus on the shapes of women's bodies, highlighting the curves of buttocks and shoulder arches. This preoccupation is often viewed as a slow shift from a machine aesthetic to a nature aesthetic. Like Picasso's use of primitive art to revitalize the art of the new epoch, Le Corbusier turns toward female and Third World sources for demystifying—not simply displacing—the myth of the machine he had earlier heralded...Le Corbusier's move towards these sources was not a simple rejection of the myth of the machine. As Charles Jencks notes: "Le Corbusier found in Negro Music, in the hot jazz of Louis Armstrong" implacable exactitude, mathematics, equilibrium on a tightrope and all the masculine virtues of the machine.[5]

The true meaning of the continuum between Le Corbusier's prior body of work, ranging from his brilliant cubist art derived 1920s villas and seminal apartment houses to his even more openly 1950s West African aesthetic based Ronchamp Chapel at Notre Dame, did not escape West. In one swoop, West substantiates my lingering suspicions that, as a person of West African descent, I do indeed have as much claim to ownership in the Picasso-Cubist inspired architecture of Le Corbusier, as does any person of European descent.

For Black America, the very notion of architecture must actually be painstakingly restructured to include a differing set of people than are normally thought about as critical players in the making of the built environment. The black business, real estate, entertainment, and film entrepreneur sectors are essential to comprehensive cultural and economic development. Such discourse and debate by a critical mass within today's black community will result in a significant increase in the numbers of young blacks pursuing architecture as professional careers.

My overarching attitude about the question of "is there a Black Architecture?" is that the answer can not be detached from the larger question of "is there a black culture?" I shall make my views on that question reasonably clear with several qualifications. The foremost qualification is that American culture is as black as it is white. My second qualification is that black culture may be a sub-set of black-white American culture but is still a palpable culture in its own right. The Black Architecture that I believe exists has yet to be fully developed. Yet it can only be developed through a deliberate and conscious effort.

Woefully small effort has been expended in the sustained publication of scholarship, reasoned polemic, and discussion on the subject of architecture throughout Black America. The subject is not treated as a critical-cultural, political, and socio-economic enterprise in the affairs of the African-American community and the African Diaspora in the twentieth-century. A long overdue serious dialogue about architecture must begin within Black America. There must be a very different twentieth-century narrative on architecture, as a critical and essential mode of expression of black culture and American culture, than what has occurred to date.

In retrospect, it is now clearer to me that neither the formalistic or stylistic issues that have defined twentieth-century Modern Architecture were relevant to the collective or individual African-American condition during the 1920s Harlem Renaissance era. Only the framework and continuation of a Black Nationalist political and economic agenda as expounded by Marcus Garvey at the time or Booker T. Washington (who preceded Garvey by several decades) could have made a difference.

The handful of African-American architects in Los Angeles, New York City, Washington, DC, and several southern states would have to have been ideologically (as well as culturally) driven to look past the slogans and platitudes of *any* architectural movement or style. The continuation of a focus on land ownership and acquisition, use of architectural practice as a community business development strategy, and the deliberate development of a building construction and a real estate industrial sector would have made a difference in the black condition in urban America. However, aspects of Modern Architecture ideology would have been a perfect vehicle to support and justify a Black Nationalist ideology.

Architects operating within a black "economy" would have sought to aesthetically reflect the cultural tastes and traits of their black clients and their client's clients. While those tastes were clearly in line with the Beaux Arts and Palladian tastes of America's white elites in the early 1920s, that could have been changed. Without a nationalist or cultural ideology, Modern Architecture was destined to have the debilitating negative impact on black urban America that it has actually had. This negative impact has been centered in the disastrous approaches to urban housing for African-Americans.

An effective nationalist ideology would have advocated buying cheap land in the suburbs while maintaining beachheads in the Harlem, South Central LA, West Baltimore, and Georgetown, Washington DC, USA's. This would have entailed a similar strategy of land acquisition and ownership of buildings. A coalition of white progressive and conservative forces in America were deciding on high density multi-family public housing projects as the preferred strategy for housing the working class poor. At the same time, government sponsored new homes costing less than five thousand dollars were being made available to the white working classes. Black America paid the heaviest social, economic, political, and cultural costs for this duplicity and chicanery.

Recently, I attended a several day conference in Brooklyn, New York, at the Pratt School of Architecture. The conference was organized and sponsored by a group of young black women architects who operate under the organizational byline of Blacklines Inc. These architects brought together a diverse collection of architects from the USA and the other parts of the Black Diaspora. Issues, symposia, and lectures were centered on black identity and impact within a seemingly lily-white academic and professional world of architecture.

In attendance throughout the duration of the conference was Steve Kliments, a very influential doyen of the all-white architectural media centered in New York City. I had heard that Kliments was completing a book soon to be released by a major publisher on the subject of black architects. Knowing how much difficulty a number of black architects and related discipline scholars are having in attracting mainstream publishers for book proposals on the same subject, I asked Kliments what was *his* angle or "take" on the subject. He informed me that his book was focused on the struggles of black architects for acceptance in White America. I informed him that my book was focused on the struggles of black architects to become effective inside of *Black* America. He quickly responded that he thought that this might be an interesting take on the subject. Kliments then went on to reveal to me what was *really* on his mind that day. He asked me "Do you think that there will ever be a *black* version of the *New York Five*?"

I reminded Kliments of the contextual background of the influential book of nearly thirty years with a similar name. The book served as a launching pad for the careers of current architectural superstars Richard Meier, Peter Eisenmam, Michael Graves, Charles Gwarthmey, and the late John Hejduk. As Kliments acknowledged knowing very well, the publication of *Five Architects* had the combined sponsorship of the influential Museum of Modern Art (MOMA), Philip Johnson (the still living dean of American architecture), and the late Colin Rowe, the most influential architectural educator of the second half of the twentieth-century. And of course, all of the key New York critics and the mainstream architecture magazines jumped on board of the *New York Five* train early. I expressed to Kliments my disbelief that those conditions could be replicated today on behalf of five black New York architects.

I did however remark to Kliments on how incomparably important I thought it would be if a group of black New York architects were to began to develop a body of theoretical or actual work that would excite New York City's black cultural leadership, including the artists, musicians, filmmakers, fashion designers, and community development activists. That is precisely what the young women architect activists (and their spiritual godfather Jack Travis) could be on the verge of doing. These young people and their male colleagues have an eye towards redefining the relationship of architecture to the black aesthetic, black music (the lynchpin of black culture) and to black cultural and economic development.

Some of them appear also to be astutely wondering if the assumed "white (or European) aesthetic" base of twentieth-century American architecture is merely another illusion in a long line of similar distortions about the true impact of black culture on American culture. Their movement is a promising turn of events that bodes well for the future of a "normalized" cultural relationship between a significant portion of the next generation of black architects and Black America. *Kliments was overlooking the trees in his search for the forest.*

Scholars such as Australian architecture professor Gary Stevens, in *The Favored Circle,* has very skillfully illuminated the social class foundation issues that impact the choice of careers in architecture. A seemingly perfectly reasonable question today would be "what possible racially motivated obstructions still lay in the path of a young African-American who decides to pursue a career goal of becoming an architect? Or for a young African-American who has managed to obtain a professional degree in architecture (or landscape architecture) and who looks forward to heading his or her own practice in the near future"? In both cases the answer is "assuming ability, drive, and intelligence, there are no obstructions of any significance." That should be the answer for virtually any other endeavor, be that the Foreign Service, astronomy, the space program, or the National Football League. So why is black representation in any one of those endeavors so disproportionate to actual black representation in American society? The just released US Census Report of 2000 reveals the official percentage of the African-American population as being thirteen percent of the total US population—a count of 37 million people.

African-Americans hold eighty percent of the playing positions in the National Football League and ninety percent of those in the National Basketball League. As was stated earlier 1.3 percent of America's 100,000 licensed architects are African-Americans. As recently as fifty years ago, the NFL and the NBA African-American player population and the number of licensed African-American architects were both virtually statistical zeros. Are African-Americans really *that* much more interested in football and basketball than they are in architecture? Not necessarily, but African-Americans certainly perceive that *access* to the former is far greater than to the latter. More importantly, are African-American natural talents and competitive advantages between football-basketball careers and architecture careers that disparate?

Does any of this even matter? Thoughtful conservative scholars such as Thomas Sowell, in *The Economics and Politics of Race: An International Perspective*, and *Race and Culture: A World View,* are quick to remind us that equal representation of ethnic minorities in professions is an unrealistic expectation. It may well be that when it comes to the profession of architecture, and the apparent relatively low level of black interest in that profession, *we may not even be talking about architecture, as we commonly understand the meaning of that word.*

The construction of a very different cultural and historical narrative about architecture is essential to a more normalized level of representation of African-Americans. Were such a new narrative to materialize, proportionate percentages of African-Americans may well prove to be every bit as interested in architecture as they are in engineering, business, law, and medicine. That would result in staggering increases in black enrollment and graduation from architecture schools. What, in the final analysis, is accounting for what is currently only a fraction of the actualization of such interests? Responses about the lack of role models are only superficial reasons.

Recall Robert Twombley's book, *Power and Style: A Critique of Twentieth-Century Architecture in the U.S.,* and his premise that buildings fall into three categories; *signature, generic, and vernacular.* Twombley posits that architect designed buildings covering all three types make up only five percent of the entire built environment. The signature buildings are relentlessly promoted as the only true meaning in architecture. But signature buildings account for only a fraction of one percent of *all* buildings. Except in a few isolated instances of black controlled institutions, there is no visible evidence that black architects design what mainstream architecture culture deems as signature buildings.

So it would appear that architecture is only *signature* buildings, and signature buildings are commissioned by powerful white institutions and individuals, and designed virtually exclusively by white architects. It therefore appears that black students are currently making rational decisions in bypassing architecture as academic majors that might lead to fruitful career options. But there is the matter of the presence of those 1,300 African-American architects today with nearly sixty percent of them in private practice in black-owned firms. What kind of buildings do those men (and a still inexcusably small but steadily growing number of women practitioners) design? As we pointed out earlier, *all kinds*, but mostly publicly financed rental and social housing projects, K-12 public school facilities, and municipal financed community buildings—mostly in situations where African-Americans politically and culturally dominate architect selections.

So I must conclude that when I say that more African-American youth should pursue careers in architecture and that more African-Americans should become more conscious of architecture, *I am really not talking about architecture when I use the word architecture.* Orthodox architecture culture has for all intent defined architecture as only the *signature* building. My interest is in the generic and the vernacular building and how such buildings can be used to make *places*. Therefore I am actually saying something entirely different. I am really saying that more African-American young people should utilize unorthodox architectural practices and modalities to realize their goals of developing the physical and cultural life of black communities while spiritually, culturally, and financially enriching themselves (remember, "personal fulfillment and self-satisfaction" platitudes don't work with the current generation). And I am saying something similar about architecture to the general African-American populace that ranges from everyday people to the most successful and affluent personalities.

That leaves only the historically black architecture schools as the potential sites for a new culture that is about *architecture* but not about architecture. Clearly such an alternative culture—centered on the cultural and economic empowerment of urban Black America—will have appeal to students other than African-Americans. That is as it always has been throughout the twentieth-century history of HBCU institutions. And that is as it must remain.

This alternative architecture culture and socialization process must proceed from the culture, history, and socio-economic agenda of twenty-first century Black America. However, constructing such a culture by utilizing the built accomplishments and operative personalities of twentieth century African American architects will be probablematic though essential. Understanding how and where the post-Tuskegee era twentieth century black architect's deep-seated cultural values are dysfunctional and in conflict with twenty-first century post-civil rights agendas will be a constant though necessary struggle.

We are back to those unfinished Harlem Renaissance 1920s and Black Power-Black Nationalist 1960s agendas. However, reinterpreted in today's global information revolution, those agendas are fundamentally about *culture* with economic and financial ramifications. Those agendas have very little to do with the signature buildings creation that is still the bedrock of orthodox architectural culture. Those alternative agendas have even less to do with orthodox architecture culture's view that architects must have clients and patrons (rather than customers, investors, and lenders as I contend). The agendas have a great deal to do with the creative use of generic and vernacular buildings as *elements* of an overarching neighborhood, community, and regional development imperative. Sophisticated but inexpensive and readily available digitized versions of the built environment are on most shelves waiting to support this approach. This includes the availability of expert systems for pursuing legitimate issues of environmental sustainability and energy conservation throughout communities dominated by African-Americans.

In such a new cultural paradigm, all of the old assumptions that students must be taught the arcane guild-like skills of how to "design" must be abandoned. Students would no longer be socialized to see themselves as arbiters of visual tastes (masquerading as the need to insure visual beauty). Students and prospective community individual users must have equal access to digitized built environment data. In this scenario, buildings are discreet randomly accessible digitized bits of data. After demonstrating mastery of the properties of descriptive geometry, the student is coached on how to access and critically utilize such data. They are coached on how to assemble useful ensembles of community fabric that accords with predetermined written articulations of communal goals and objectives.

I am going to leave it to the younger activist-scholars to define the "theory" parts of an architectural academy and professional practice modality that supports and sustains Black America's twenty-first century post-civil rights cultural and socio-economic agenda. As a former leader of one of the most strategically located black architecture schools, my interests are in the immediate practical day-to-day battles.

The accomplishments and life struggles of today's 500 principals in the over 200 African-American owned architectural practices, the various related discipline African-American owned built environment enterprises, and those of the twentieth-century dating back to pre-Harlem Renaissance Tuskegee must become paramount in the new paradigm narrative. Not only do these men and several women have much that is useful to teach, but also they would provide the inspirational images and messages that are so vital but rarely in evidence throughout the black or white schools.

The life and built achievements of Frank Lloyd Wright is an interesting and indispensable saga in an HBCU architecture school. But equally so is the life and built achievements of architect Robert Robinson Taylor and musician Duke Ellington, both African-American contemporaries of Wright. The life of Frank Gehry of today's Guggenheim Museum in Bilbao, Spain, is certainly interesting in such a setting. But the life of (Tuskegee trained builder-developer entrepreneur) Herman Russell is of equally compelling and immediately useful interest. It falls to the HBCU architecture school to delineate the black influences of the work of arch-modernist icon Le Corbusier alongside of teaching the architectural implications of arch-black culture oriented filmmaker Spike Lee. In short, the HBCU schools must construct an alternative canon and pantheon of heroes of built environment culture.

On an even more basic level, HBCU architecture schools, including mine, must seek to internally create a modified *Habitat For Humanities* home-builder-home ownership model in lieu of the current *Intern Development Program* model for achieving eligibility to take the Architectural Registration Examination (ARE). Radically increasing the level of homeownership is a life and death issue in Black America generally and the Baltimore-Washington megalopolis location of my HBCU architecture school. Increasing black home ownership cuts across and positively impacts so many other issues of vital importance:

> *"The single most important source of funds for new businesses in the United States is a mortgage on the entrepreneur's house."*[6]

The built environment dimensions of the perennial public health crisis in Black America have yet to even be seriously explored at this juncture. A socialization and skills development process inside of an HBCU architecture school that is not specifically geared to impacting the critical socio-economic indices by which Black America measures its position inside of America is of questionable value. Equally important, the visceral cultural issues that drive or modulate the life rhythms of most African-Americans—music, including the blues, jazz, rhythm & blues, and Hip-Hop-rap; the film arts, television, and the Internet; and education, transportation, security, welfare, and public health to single out a few—must centrally inform a new *American* architecture in a historically black architecture school.

Most of today's African-American-owned architectural practices owe their existence to the raw exercise of black political power in urban communities between 1965 and 1980. This was the period of sporadic urban rebellions and ongoing tensions that saw black communities around the country deciding that there could no longer be business as usual. There was an outpouring of pent-up ethnic nationalist solidarity that extended to decisions about who should design some of the government funded structures and housing projects to be built in riot scarred black neighborhoods. Were it not for such nationalist expressions, black-owned architectural firms would be no more than one-tenth the size of their current total of 210 practices.

Today's black architect-owned practices are only a fraction of the need and potential for architecturally related services throughout Black America. In fact, the surface has yet to be scratched when viewing those needs outside of the orthodox paradigms of architectural thought now dominant in the places that educate and socialize architects.

A significant number of the licensed black architects—as much as fifty-five percent (in comparison to thirty percent for white architects)—are functioning as independent practitioners in their own architectural firms. While those firms have designed major projects mainly throughout Black America, a huge amount of community development potential remains untouched. A large part of the problem of producing a sufficient number of viable black-owned practices in the second half of the twentieth-century was best—though not intentionally—articulated over thirty years ago by Harold Cruse. He identified the failure of entire black bourgeoisie classes to resolutely pursue their own cultural and economic interest within the black world. Cruse posited that this was largely because of the ambivalence of black professional classes *about their own interests.*

Cruse laid bare the prioritized longings of black professional groups for acceptance by elite white cultural interests over achieving economic hegemony over their own ethnic markets. Cruse also illuminated the further confusion caused by black professional class inability to differentiate between the various competing white cultural interests they were seeking acceptance and recognition from. Today's cacophony of white cultural and economic interests in the world of architecture presents the black architect with the same problem Cruse identified in other non-architect spheres over thirty years ago.

Architecture, in the form of the most visibly hyped buildings and the people who design them (and the cheerleading squadron of "critics" who lionize both), is a remarkably accurate mirror reflecting power and prestige in any given western modern society. It is also a remarkably accurate reverse mirror image of today's American penal system. As has often been said, if someone from outside of a society wants to determine which race, caste, and class of that society occupies the bottom rung of power and prestige, they need only tour several representative examples of the prisons. The corollary holds up well for the face of the architecture profession as a reflection of the top end of society.

Adulation is heaped upon the usual suspect collection of "star" white American, European (and several Japanese) architects by the New York-centered self-anointed high priests of so-called avant-garde defining critics. However, it seems that a large body of the informed American public is not buying the hype. The writings of Dutch architect, Rem Koolhaas, currently hailed as the top star and deepest thinker about our urban past, present and future can be easily characterized as mostly circular reasoned pleas for the acceptance of the status quo. Only the most gullible students and semi-literate practitioners could be enamored of Koolhaas.[7] Alarm bells should be ringing loudly throughout the black world now that Koolhaas has fixed his gaze on Lagos, Nigeria. Elite white cultural foundation money will pour in to help him "solve" the problems of the Black Diaspora's largest city through the lavish production of exotic looking computer generated drawings.

Koolhaas is now beginning to receive major commissions and win major "competitions" (actually these are mostly incestuous little affairs amongst friends) to turn his "profundities" into bricks and mortar. The drawings produced thus far call for predictably giant sculpture set pieces that snobbish cultural elites, insecure government officials, and self-indulgent billionaire dot-com capitalists are prone to honor themselves with. Koolhaas is battling for the spotlight with that other rock star quality architect, Frank Gehry, of Guggenheim

Museum at Bilbao, Spain, fame. Be assured that any actual people-functioning accommodations that have to go on in these overblown extravaganzas are after-thoughts.

Philip Johnson, the ninety-four year-old dean of the American architectural high-culture designers, was once an openly Nazi sympathizer from the early 1930s through the World War II era.[8] Johnson has spent the last sixty years plowing through his inexhaustible family fortune to define himself and others he anoints as architectural stars. Johnson and his predictably all white architectural establishment were brazenly showcased in a recent issue of *ARCHITECTURE,* the profession's most prestigious monthly "design-oriented" journal. The issue was simply titled "POWER."

Michael Pyatok is a very capable and perceptive architect with offices in the Bay Area and Seattle. Pyatok's practice is centered on designing affordable housing for an impressive roster of inner city nonprofit housing corporations. Here is his highlight comment on that POWER issue:

> *ARCHITECTURE very consistently focuses on self-aggrandizement and uses of the media to worship those in our profession who are uncritically steeped in the culture of conspicuous consumption.*[9]

Payatok continues his insightful critique in an article that should be required reading for all of those charged with teaching the next generation. In short, the world of the "star" architect is one that has nothing to do with any segment of Black America except by negative inference. I hold scarce brief with my few architect colleagues who believe passionately that the real crisis facing the African-American architectural world is how to produce African-American "star" architects. Such an objective of lusting after membership in that fraternity is a futile and valueless quest.

African-American architects may one day count their blessings that they had nothing to do with the overblown personal statements that the "stars" are literally dropping into urban landscapes. The globalization of capital and information as instantaneous real time commodities that can be moved at the speed of light poses danger to *all* such orthodox architectural practices, as we know them today.[10] Orthodox African-American owned architectural practices run the danger of serving in the role of the *"canary in the mineshaft."*

Architects are socialized to resist structuring architectural practices around entrepreneurial visions of direct service to marketplace needs in ways similar to other successful American and black-owned enterprises.[11] Under the right circumstances, black communities and jurisdictions can and will continue to support black architects. Much of the neighborhood development work in such communities is the economic survival lifeline of many black architects of the current as well as the next generation.

But black community support is plausible only when those architects step completely outside of the box of academically promoted orthodoxy of how an architect is supposed to relate to the marketplace. The cues and clues abound in the actions of other black entrepreneurs in the world of music, entertainment, film, and other vital culture sensitive business enterprises.

The crucial responsibility of a black architect to Black America is to envision and conceptualize productive new environments, create value, and deliberately reflect African-American culture where none of those things currently exists. With the exception of a few black elected mayors and occasional black appointed officials, there are virtually no black patrons or clients as those terms are traditionally understood. There is no one available to act as intermediaries in today's Black America.

The marketplace is viewed according to the implicit socialization and indoctrination that is dispensed in the formative years inside of the architectural academy. Within such a thought process, the patron-client is something or someone—usually known as a developer or construction manager—who actually provides services to the marketplace. In such a system, the architect is merely one of a number of subcontractors.

However, consider the possibilities when the person trained as an architect elects to not follow convention and orthodoxy. This maverick architect instead responds directly to the marketplace without the patronage of an intermediary risk-taking client. The most spectacular contemporary example of this was represented by the actions of Atlanta architect John Portman during the 1970s. More historical examples include architect John Nash of London during the 1850s when he developed, designed and built Regency Street.

For African-American examples we need only look at turn of the twentieth-century Washington, DC, and the arrival of Tuskegee trained John Lankford in 1902 and Cornell trained Albert Cassell two decades later. Other obscure but very real examples abound including the actions of numerous contemporary architects in the increasingly popular "design-build" modus operandi.

The African-American architect has to be attitudinally constituted to be his or her own patron or client who goes directly to Black America as 37 million potential customers. Properly conflated with business, finance, and real estate skills and attitudes, such envisioning and risk accepting propensities for creating value throughout urban and suburban America has to become the new primary mission of the next generation of African-American architects.

An architecture which places black economic, social, political and cultural interest ahead of personal quests for white mainstream recognition will have to develop its own standards of excellence, valorize itself, and engage openly in continuous published polemical writing and dialogues as well as scholarly research. *Architecture is virtually the only major socio-economic and cultural activity engaged in by a critical mass of African-American practitioners and academics who have only barely recently begun to do any of those things on a serious, sustained and systemic basis.*[12]

Out of my assessment of today's black-owned architectural firms, I am singling out alternative models that warrant intense study by young prospective next generation black architects. I pose these models as appropriate alternatives not only to the extreme of the "star" media architects but also to the other extreme of the "government contracts-public sector" based practices that currently dominate black-owned practices.

I hope to instigate debate and counter proposals for viable models of twenty-first century practices. I am making my judgment and final selections from a list of approximately 500 practicing African-American principals.[13] My choices represent the outer opposite polarities of scale. One is a small community-based practitioner. The other is a multi-office national-international practice with a corporate structure and virtual reality based Information Technology.

I will start out by radically departing from convention with a first choice that is not even remotely a practicing architect. She is black writer and cultural critic **bell hooks**. I arrived at this leap of faith in my determination to highlight a female model. This is extremely important on several fronts. While there are today only about 120 black licensed women architects in the country (out of roughly 8,000 licensed women architects), the increase in African-American architects could and certainly must come from a dramatic increase in women practitioners. It should be noted that white women are now making up nearly fifty percent of entering classes in graduate architecture programs at elite universities.

Were I to have allowed myself one additional choice of someone who is not an actual practicing or formally trained architect I would have chosen the McKissack matriarch of Nashville, Tennessee. The non-architect CEO leadership of this full service corporate practice is a problematic choice *at this time*. However, it should be stressed that not including this type of leadership is an approach that cannot ultimately prevail in the search for appropriate models.

Architectural and urban design problems that proliferate in architecture school studio remind me of a chapter in the delicious little book *Art On My Mind—Visual Politics* by the iconoclastic Ms. hooks. She reveals to us her initial serious desire to become an architect.[14] In "Black Vernacular—Architecture as Cultural Practice" she demonstrates a firm grasp of the reality that power and culture intersect to produce architecture. No one has articulated this better than Ms.

hooks. With a superb undergraduate liberal arts education (Stanford) and a doctorate in cultural studies from the University of California at Santa Cruz, Ms. hooks is better positioned to effectively function as an architect than she might imagine. Her words are the ultimate starting point for the prospective young African-American architect. In the 1960s, she was given a house design problem in a high school art class in a southern town. The instructor's benign intent was to stimulate artistic imagination through a decidedly apolitical methodology. Ms. hooks immediately understood the critical issues here:

> *This would have been a radically different assignment had we been encouraged to think critically about the actual spaces we inhabited, [and] the neighborhoods and houses that were our world. Had we been given such an assignment, we would have learned to think about space politically, about who controls and shapes our environments. The assignment might have compelled recognition, the way racial apartheid and white supremacy altered individuals' space, over determined locations and the nature of structures, created a sense of entitlement for some and deprivation for others. Doing this assignment, we might have come face to face with the politics of property, not only who owns and controls space but the relationship between power and cultural production.* [15]

She goes on with similarly keen insight about the powerful political-economic dynamics underlying the art of architecture. Sadly, I would have to confess to bell hooks that I, along with virtually all of the other nearly 1,300 licensed African-American architects living today, had experiences nearly identical to hers for our entire time in architecture school. We all each spent five to eight years in university based architecture schools that painstakingly structured the same type of curricula, lectures, and design studios assignments. While there has been much tinkering around the edges over the past few years, there has been no fundamental change to that status quo throughout most of the academy including the HBCU architecture schools:

> *In segregated southern schools, art has traditionally been taught from a perspective informed by the class and racial biases of Eurocentric traditions. This is an accurate description of the way art continues to be taught in many predominately Black schools, including colleges and universities...while individuals from marginal groups—from non-materially privileged backgrounds-often find a way to make art,* **writing about art continues to be the domain of those who have some degree of class privilege...why are there no great Black artist?** *(bold Italics mine)*[16]

Simply substitute the words *architect* and *architecture* in places where bell hooks uses the words *artist* and *art* throughout her book and you have one of the underlying reasons for the crisis of the black architect within the cultural realm. Ms. hooks is that rare example of a high profile black public intellectual uttering thoughts about architects and architecture. My speculation is that had she gone on to become the architect she acknowledges that she once wanted to be, one of two fates awaited her. Either she would have become a design studio professor—most likely at an Ivy League school—or she could conceivably have emerged as a serious patron sponsored architect-artist. It is easy to envision Ms. hooks in an architectural career that might have paralleled Maya Lin of Vietnam War Memorial fame. Ms. Lin is the young Asian-American architect who won the Vietnam War Memorial competition with her striking black granite wall concept.

In either case, assuming that Ms. hooks would have retained her gifts of critical cultural critique, she would have become a major breakthrough of sorts as a high visibility black architect on the cultural front. She could also have just as easily been swept up in the all-white "star" architect system. What is disturbingly less clear to me is whether she would she have managed the *"...control of the means of production"* of the intentions and implications of her probable black culture based work output. Those are issues of major importance.

My next choice stands like a bronze colossus of clarity, logic, and conviction. Harlem-based **Jack Travis** is one of only a small handful of serious and relatively well known African-American practitioners who openly combines or conflates "black," "blackness," and "black culture" with architecture. The range of Travis clients and the scope of his commissions lay to rest the historic dread that "black" architecture would be viewed as a "devalued" architecture. However, I see Travis as a contrast to David Hughes, a Kent State professor and practitioner, who is the most vocal subscriber to an "Afrocentric" architecture.[17]

We have Travis' own words about his conflictions on the relationship of architecture to culture and ultimately to his own blackness. He opens his book, *African-American Architects in Professional Practice* with these biting words

> *The first black American architect I met was a professor at the undergraduate university I attended. I was in my third year. Mr. Fellows was his name. He was a simple man with a small practice and a real sense of social responsibility. I hated him. Not for who he was, but for what he represented. I was devastated at the picture of a 'black architect' that he painted for me. My future as I had envisioned it and the future he'd shown me were so very different. It never really occurred to me that my color might make my dream to practice architecture improbable.*[18]

Travis has demonstrated that he has the talent and intelligence to practice architecture on practically any scale of his choosing. The barrier that he was not aware of at the time of his encounter with Mr. Fellows was the clash of *cultures*—architecture culture and black culture to be specific. The architectural socialization process demanded that the two not be conflated. Somewhere along the way Travis decided that the two issues of architecture and black culture had to be fused.

This epiphany—and the willingness to act upon it—by a seasoned and highly technically skilled black architect may be a late twentieth-century breakthrough. No evidence exists that such an epiphany occurred during the Harlem Renaissance eighty years ago or even the Black Power Movement forty years ago. Travis has the benefit of a twenty-first century America that differs markedly from the one existing in the decades of 1920–1960. But the realization of his quest is still fraught with dangers of failure and the promise of unimagined success. One of the bright young woman architect founders of *blacklines Magazine* places Travis in perspective:

> *Courage is necessary to take the path less traveled. Vision is needed to see and think differently. Typically, design classes teaching the incorporation of black culture in the design process is not taught in schools of architecture, an area with very little, if any dialogue. It is deemed unimportant. Nevertheless, Travis tirelessly advances the notion of what Black Architecture is.*[19]

Travis is operating on terrain that is reminiscent of the 1920s Parisian villas and apartment building phase of the modernist architect-icon, Le Corbusier. Unlike the parallel Harlem Renaissance in New York City eighty years ago, Travis is benefitting from a clientele of financially able African-Americans seeking personal shelter. They come to Travis deliberately seeking out a "cultural specific" (Travis's term) design approach. This has enormous national implications for today's and the next generation of increasingly affluent African-Americans. In a word, Travis has verified the existence of a conscious market for a "black" architecture among successful African-American athletes, entertainers, media personalities, and corporate CEOs. All of these people are in the position to be patrons and pay for their taste preferences.[20] This sector of the African-American population is playing the historical role of legitimizing cultural expressions. The middlelower-middle-to-middle classes will invariably adopt these expressions. This is a two-way street. The black elite readily absorbs the cultural language, music, clothing styles, and cuisine of the black masses.

New York Times columnist David Dunlap authored a depressing 1994 *New York Times* article lamenting the woeful plight of black New York architects. Dunlap's article appeared just two years before the *Times* article by Herbert Muschap extolling the brilliance and hegemony of Jewish architects. Dunlap mentions in passing the late **Harry Simmons Jr.**, the Brooklyn based African-American architect and my former classmate at Howard University. Simmons is my third of the four selected models.

Simmons' life, his work, and his relationship to the Brooklyn and Harlem communities he served are the stuff of legends. Simmons should be the model representative of those who are committed to a personalized style of hands-on, community-based architectural practice. His practice modus operandi was a late twentieth-century reincarnation of early twentieth-century Tuskegeean John Lankford. The socialization of early twenty-first century African-American architects to aspire to function in the mold of Simmons is the vital task ahead for those of us who presume to teach.

Simmons' life was nearly the exact opposite of every negative thing reporter Dunlap had to say about the plight of black architects. Simmons built an important practice in the heart of Brooklyn in a large old brownstone that housed his practice and his family. That brownstone was a veritable "community center" that spoke directly to the housing, community development, spiritual, and cultural needs of his community.

The core of Simmons' practice was federal, state, and locally subsidized housing for low, moderate, and middle income black New York City dwellers. Keep in mind that all housing built in America is government subsidized. Simmons had a long roster of community-based non-profits and for-profits that acted as sponsors of his projects. But he was the expert in all aspects required to deliver apartments and houses to his people.

There were extra-added benefits to Simmons for his housing services. When the time came for the city of New York to award highly coveted commissions to design large publicly funded projects in Brooklyn or parts of Harlem, Simmons could count on those communities. They saw to him having first rights to such commissions hands down. He bested a number of name brand New York architects on several occasions. His designation as sole architect to design the large Medgar Evers College complex in Brooklyn was a prime example. He was able to complete this project before his untimely death in 1993.

My last conversation with Simmons was in 1992 during a ride I gave him to Washington National Airport. He had just taught a housing studio class for honors students at Howard University. We were on the way to the hanger where he kept his prized twin-engine plane when flying himself to DC. The plane was just one of the fruits of his material success. He told me without the slightest hint of boastfulness that he found it nearly impossible to imagine how he could stop making a personal annual income in the range of 400,000 dollars from his community-based practice. He momentarily lamented that his projects were not getting the mainstream design press recognition that he thought was due him. But he went on to say that he could console himself in the knowledge of how much good his lucrative practice was allowing him to accomplish in his Brooklyn community:

> "Mitch, I put a lot of money in a lot of my people's hands...young kids, college students, young aspiring architects, older down on their luck architects, laborers, skilled tradesmen, suppliers, subs, contractors, real estate agents, the arts community, the banks, and on and on...and of course my family is well taken care of."

Simmons offered me his most prescient brotherly advice back during my early 1980s Marion Barry period of near total dependence on government agency contracts; "Mitch, I have serious concerns about all of those DC government contracts your practice seems to be built around." Certainly Simmons' Brooklyn practice was tied into public spending. But there was a world of difference between how he had structured his practice around the diverse housing needs of his community, and my own dependence on direct design contracts from DC government agencies during that phase of my practice.

The appropriate group of architects for the next generations of black architects to emulate are those rarely published black architects such as Simmons. They are focusing on actually building and developing neighborhood and community scale housing and ancillary commercial complexes throughout urban America. Simmons epitomized that group of architects. The task ahead is to construct an architecture school socialization process that makes Simmons a norm rather than an aberration.

Kansas City-based African-American architect **Charles F. McAfee** is the other architect I put forth as a model for the coming generation to emulate.[21] McAfee is nearing seventy and is clearly in the twilight years of his active career. But he would be the first to advise young architects to pursue housing as early as is possible. I arrived at the choice of McAfee as a black role model much like most people who make such choices which are ultimately personal, subjective, and based on the need to make a particular case. In spite of this I believe that my choice of McAfee is wholly defensible on the objective grounds of personal merit and professional achievement

In the case of McAfee, I was struck by the sheer audacity and breath-taking vision of the manner he chose in expanding his orthodox but successful national practice. In 1994, McAfee re-initiated his earlier venture of founding and operating an inner city-based modular housing plant in his hometown of Wichita, Kansas.

McAfee started independent architectural practice in conventional style in Wichita in the mid-1960s after graduation from the architecture school at the University of Nebraska at Omaha. In the largely white business environment of Wichita, he was fortunate enough to find a progressive minded white business owner-patron. After ten years of producing nationally acclaimed award-winning work, McAfee made a breakout move. By the mid-1970s, Atlanta was already a black-mayor controlled city committed to the use of city hall resources to create black economic power.

McAfee landed in the middle of the nationally raging rapid transit subway system boom. He received a commission to design one of the largest and most strategically located stations in Atlanta. Despite enjoying such successes, McAfee was restless. He harbored a passionate belief and vision in the need for architects to take a frontline leadership position in affordable housing for black urban working and middle classes.

The highly sophisticated modular manufacturing plant approach to building affordable housing had caught his imagination twenty years earlier. McAfee saw modular housing as a vehicle for tackling community development problems. During the mid-1970s he put everything on the line financially in support of his vision. He built a housing manufacturing plant in Wichita that also actually employed many community residents. The plant was turning out finished homes that McAfee had designed. Unfortunately, boldness and vision could not overcome the lack of financial support that existed at that time for McAfee's progressive vision.

He also understood that in order to effectively fulfill such a vision it would be necessary for him to "step outside of the box." He had to forgo the "patron" or "client" seeking route that the typical architect is so relentlessly socialized to be dependent upon. He clearly understood that there was a whole world of black (and other) "customers" out there that he needed to be dealing directly with. McAfee's style of practicing by directly developing-building-selling to the marketplace has other benefits. He is able to connect up with black and other finance based entrepreneurs in ways that are not possible under existing practice orthodoxy. McAfee has a product and service that can be collateralized and used to attract large sums of risk capital. McAfee took the bold step of joining forces with several other prominent black businessmen. They raised the substantial venture and mortgage capital necessary to build a production plant and real estate conglomerate. I view McAfee as a highly plausible entrepreneur model. He represents what HBCU architectural schools must socialize the next generation of architects to began doing and thinking about.

While re-establishing his 20 million dollar modular plant in 1994, McAfee continues to maintain a high profile national architectural practice. He is in partnership with one of his two architect daughters. Cheryl McAfee appears more than adequate to the task of carrying her father's vision to fruition in the early twenty-first century. McAfee and his daughter were the only two black architects listed in the author

Dick Russell's 500 page anthology *Black Genius: The American Experience*.

McAfee has taken his urban inner city plant concept nationwide. He is receiving inquiries from South Africa and other countries from around the world. He has ascended to official national leadership of the inner city affordable housing and job creation modular manufacturing plant movement. That movement holds unlimited positive significance for black economic development and the role that black architects can play.

The most politically visible African-American architect over the past decade—and another potential serious role model—is Charlotte, North Carolina, practitioner **Harvey Gantt.** This was the first black student to integrate the architecture school at Clemson in South Carolina during the late 1960s. Gantt actually served on the Charlotte city council for several terms before ascending to the mayor's office during the early 1990s. In recent years, Gantt has twice seriously challenged Jesse Helms for the Senate seat in North Carolina.

Young black architects must seek to emulate long departed twentieth-century giants John Lankford and Albert Cassell of Washington, DC. On the contemporary front and on a community practice scale, they must look to the late Harry Simmons and rising young Jack Travis. Simmons had just reached fifty at his untimely death in 1993 and Travis is still just short of his fiftieth birthday. They must look to Charles MacAfee for a global scale practice model. Travis, Simmons and MacAfee all clearly understood that the home is the base structure of black culture as it is in all other viable cultures. And above all, they must understand and act upon the deeper meaning of what bell hooks is talking about.

All of these people understood that being a consciously "black" architect does not mean that one is limited to designing and building only for other black people. Nor is one limited to geographically identifiable black communities. Rather it means providing first-rate services to black people. This will immeasurably improve the chances for access, penetration, and marketplace victories in larger non-black venues. One goes forth into the larger global context with the full blessing and support of a black base. That base can be fully confident that the fruits of larger marketplace victories will be shared. Opportunities are now opening up in a pluralist, democratic, information-based economy ("capitalist" and "socialist" labels are, for our purposes here, meaningless). All of the old de jure barriers once facing the old black Tuskegee fountainheads and earliest Howard University architect-professors in Washington, DC, are gone.

African-Americans continue to make the case for the survival, perpetuation, and expansion of venerable black institutions. The church, the Historically Black College and University, business enterprise, the music, the cultural arts, and certain historic residential communities such as Harlem are regarded as sacrosanct and perpetual by most of Black America. The case must also include the institutional construct of the African-American architect and an African-American architecture.

For black prospective architects, and young architects searching for insights about architecture, certain books are most likely to be recommended to them by high school and graduate school career counselors. One such book is the now standard "textbook" titled "Architect? A Candid Guide to the Profession," by University of Maryland architecture professor Roger Lewis. The following statement at the end of this 278-page book is the extent of what Professor Lewis has to offer on the past, present and future of blacks in architecture:

> *Blacks in high school and colleges have tended to choose careers other than architecture, perhaps continuing to perceive architecture as a "white male" profession. Statistically there are relatively few black architect mentors or role models. Yet in the United States, black architects have a long and successful history in both private practice and government, and black graduate architects find jobs readily as anyone else. Within black families and communities architecture still seems to be an especially remote and esoteric profession, one rarely considered by students who nevertheless might have the requisite talents and motivation. **Even predominately***

black colleges have to work hard at persuading black students to go into architecture (bold italics mine).[22]

Much of what Professor Lewis says above about why black students seem to avoid architecture as academic majors and career choices is only *technically* accurate. There is a need for deeper and wider examination of the underlying structural causes if this situation is to be significantly changed.

Architectural historian Carter Wiseman's *Shaping a Nation* is a highly representative example of a rash of big illustrated and scholarly appearing books on American architecture. All of these books ignore African-American people and the architects and architecture they have produced in the twentieth-century. Wiseman's book played a key role as a stimulus to my completing this book. For me, it was the proverbial straw that broke the camel's back. Wiseman curiously ends this 400-page book with the following observation:

> *On of the most basic problems with architecture in the twentieth-century America has been that many of its most famous representatives gradually came to believe that their proper role was not to ask questions, but to dictate answers. It should come as no surprise that their audience was gradually reduced to wealthy patrons, educational and cultural institutions craving notoriety, and credulous students.*[23]

One cannot help but wonder how it could be otherwise. Credible mainstream historians like Wiseman devote 400 pages to precisely those architects his parting observation is aimed at. No other choices or references are provided for those credulous students. Much like, I suspect, most of my African-American architect colleagues and peers who may have read Wiseman's book or others of a similar ilk, I found this insightful but, incomplete work, to be singularly depressing. There is an unrelenting absence of even the slightest hint that the African-American community also produced significant architects who made substantial architecture on their behalf during the twentieth-century. These books describe a role for the architect that holds no apparent relevance to the struggle of Black America for cultural affirmation and socio-economic parity.

There must be an aggressive black presence in and full command of the forces necessary to make architecture. Architecture must play its roll in conjunction with the other black arts. A culture specific and economically sophisticated architecture should be providing physical frameworks for the other black arts (and music) to flourish.

The term as well as the substance of *"Black Architecture"* must be rigorously and enthusiastically pursued by a significant sector of the next generation of black architects. This is the only route to being able to effectively interact with black musical, cinematography, and emerging urban communications and real estate entrepreneurs. Such a proper alignment of black architects at leadership levels with black artists, musicians, and filmmakers will be to everyone's mutual benefit. But mostly this will benefit the twenty-first century black architectural community. Such re-alignments will result in black architects becoming more directly involved with the masses of black consumers. Those consumers are quite capable of "commissioning" architecture, though within a differing paradigm.

This brings me to the matter of the growing fascination among some quarters of African-American architecture students with devising an "architectural expression" of black Hip-Hop music and culture. The students are on historically solid ground in their sense of the importance of Hip-Hop culture to black culture as well as American culture.[24] Unfortunately, some students are attempting to fit this musical phenomenon that shares much with ragtime and jazz music of 100 years ago, into a framework that is an inherent straightjacket. Architecture students are invariably led to attempting to make a connection between Hip-Hop music and architecture through the limiting prism of "drawing" (whether with a pencil or a computer puck). But formally trained architects are not the only ones capable of making architecture as art. The "folk" or the "masses" are quite capable of making architecture as art.[25]

The blues, jazz, and Hip-Hop music are the twentieth-century testimony to the ability of black people to make architectural art. The pencil and T-square, and the computer mouse still currently occupy center stage in architectural education. But it simply may not be possible to *express* Hip-Hop music and culture through those inherently one, or at best, two-dimensionally static and soundless methodologies and tools. The Hip-Hop culture that is being created through music and video by non-architecturally trained black people already contains brilliant serious elements of a *Black Architecture!*

Certainly architecture is art. And equally certain, the architect is or should be part artist. The task of those inside of the architectural academy is to marry West African inspired thinking about art and architecture to the true meanings of dynamic creative urban Hip-Hop culture. The natural tendencies of the architectural academy's socialization processes are to look at these issues from an upper class based "missionary" or "tourist" perspective.[26]

There is a *"control of the means of production"* issue that must be confronted head-on. It is necessary for someone—acting in true entrepreneurial fashion—to divine the physical and capital implications of a multi-billion dollar black production system and then proceed to devise ways to address those implications.[27] Whether or not that "confronter" will come from the ranks of the black architectural profession is questionable at this juncture, given the limitations of the architectural education socialization paradigm.

CHAPTER 6

The Diasporic Perspective and an Alternative Future

It is imperative that we comprehend matters in a globalized Diaspora context. However, from what I am about to write in the next several paragraphs, the reader will not need a degree in psychology to grasp the enormity of the psychic damage that I, along with most other African Americans, have suffered in our American socialization about Black Africa. I was all of 58 years old when I made my first trip back to the original "old country" of West Africa. My two-week stay in Ghana was nothing short of a personal religious experience. This was the first black state to achieve independence in 1957 from a modern European colonial power. I went to Ghana with a vague notion that this is the African nation that should have been *Zion* for black Americans (as opposed to Liberia which was established back in 1850 by white southerners seeking a "final solution" to the black problem). I left Ghana two weeks later even more deeply committed to this "Ghana as Zion" notion.

As a personal and admittedly idiosyncratic aside, in traveling to Ghana I wanted to experience what I felt would be delicious irony. I harbor the belief that there is a good chance that at least one of my great-great grandparents came to the new world of the Americas on a slave ship—in the "hole" or on the deck or maybe both places. I was determined to go back to West Africa via Ghana Airways, the national airline. It had crossed my mind that by now the African natives were indeed meaningfully assisting the European ex-colonialists in flying the airplanes in the modern fleet of American-made machines. I still didn't quite know for sure how I would feel upon finally being locked inside of the cabin of a jumbo jet with no evidence of white people in the cockpit.

One of the many little details that I was unaware of was that on a trans-oceanic flight of over six hours, international flight regulations required two cockpit crews, or a total of six pilots with at least two captains, aboard the flight. So on the big day of my arriving at the Ghana Airways terminal at JFK Airport in New York, I went from having never seen a black pilot in the cockpit of a passenger airliner I was about to board, to seeing six Ghanaian pilots roll up to board and take command of the giant refueling Ghana Airways DC-10 aircraft.

That "irony" I was seeking to experience proved to be more than I had actually bargained for. I scanned the white folks in the crowd of JFK ground and terminal workers to gauge their reactions. Obviously, this was a sight that they had grown accustomed to witnessing. I shifted my curiosity to the reactions of the handful of white passengers boarding our plane. Either this (for me) earth-moving event was not registering with the white passengers or they were doing a hell of a good job of faking no concern. Needless to say, the nine-hour flight, most of it spent suspended 35,000 feet above the Atlantic Ocean, was no different technically than the countless five-hour flights I had made back and forth to Los Angeles over the past twenty-years on American Airlines DC-10s' (never once seeing a black captain although there were reported to have been one or two).

On the completion of our return trip to JFK airport, I sought out the younger of the two Ghanaian captains and started to gently grill him about his flight training. I began by presumptuously asking him if he had received his training in the Ghanaian air force (the dashing image of the youngish Ghanaian head of state Jerry Rollins, former Ghana air force fighter pilot, was in my mind). The young ebony-skin captain patiently explained to me in a perfectly clipped British accent that he—and the other five members of the two cockpit crews—had all been trained in the same giant flight training school at Oxford, England, as were all of the rest of the white British Airways and other European airline pilots.

The many sights and scenes around the big city of Accra and the smaller Ashanti capital at Kumasi, as well as around the University of Science and Technology also at Kumasi, and the industrial port twin cities of Secondi-Takaradi were intoxicating. Ghana has amassed a growing collection of native architectural talent trained in the forty-year-old architecture school at Kumasi, and through overseas training in Russia, Great Britain, Canada, and the US.

The Ghanaian architects are un-reconstructed International Style modernists. They are all "little Le Corbusiers." Ghanaian architects don't appear in the least bit interested in post-modern architecture or any other form of European or American historicism or theory—*thank God!* From high-rise buildings in downtown Accra to the new rural village homes of successful sons and daughters, there are poured-in-place concrete structures under construction everywhere.

The Ghanaian architects emulate the Le Corbusier of his initial formative period of the early 1920s when his work was all straight lines and planes. Though Picasso inspired, this work was not yet as openly black African inspired as Le Corbusier's mid-1950s design of the chapel at Ronchamp or the new Indian city of Chandigar. The Ghanaian architect's predilection for Le Corbusier's "villa period" style of poured-in-place concrete architecture is probably driven by technological considerations relating to the forming and pouring of the ubiquitous concrete.

The Ghanaian architectural educators and professionals appear to be operating within the same paradigm as their American counterparts on the subject of the architect's ordained limited role in the larger building culture. The assumption is that the architect is supposed to react to government patrons and wealthy private clients on the issues of what is to be built, why it is to be built, and for whom. Given the rigidly reactionary Eurocentric mindset of these two client prototypes, this line of thinking

has lead to the same crisis as the one now confronting American architects generally and African-American architects acutely.

There is a golden window of opportunity for African-American
architects who are able to free themselves from the bankruptcy of the
dominant American *"star" architect system in search of a patron* syndrome. There is plenty to do in the development of this country of
twenty million clever and creative people whose nation is still W.E.B.
Du Bois' "Israel" for African-Americans. But African-American architects must accept the fact that there are no available "government contracts" to provide orthodox American style services to the government
of Ghana. In my view, that type of work—what little there is—rightly
belongs to native Ghanaian architects.

The Ghanaians welcome and need black American architects. *But
not as "designers!" The Ghanaians need African-American architects as
risk-taking investors with vision, hard cash, and a passion to address basic
marketplace needs in housing, infrastructure and other related economic
development arenas of national priority.* In turn, African-American architects need Ghana as a part of the solution that African-Americans and
Ghanaian architects both must seek out in their attempts to reconstruct
a meaningful African-American and African architecture for the
twenty-first century.

An all day symposium titled as "Defining African Architecture"
occurred on March 3, 2000, in the auditorium of the University of
Maryland School of Architecture at College Park. This symposium
was organized and presided over by African-American architect and
Morgan State professor Paul Taylor.

There were four main presenters: Mr. W. Enninful-Eghan, a senior
lecture in the Department of Architecture at the University of Science
and Technology, Kumasi, Ghana; Ms. Abimbola Asojo, a Nigerian
native who was trained in London and Awolowo at Ile-Ife in Nigeria
and is currently an assistant professor of interior design in the College
of Architecture, University of Oklahoma at Norman; Dr. Nnamdi
Elleh, a Nigerian native and currently a researcher at Northwestern
University at Evanston, Illinois. Elleh is the author of *African*

Architecture; Evolution and Transformation; and Jack Travis, New York City architect, who is the leading practitioner exponent of a Black (or African-American) Architecture.

I end this essay with with the opening lines of Mr. W. Enninful-Eghan's conference opening keynote address: **African Architecture is in crisis. It is in crisis because it is not developing with a definite character that is authentically African.**

The end of the twenty-first century will still find African-Americans living mostly together through out the country including the Washington, DC-Baltimore region. Some will have done so out of necessity. And some will have done so out of choice. They, along with virtually all blacks including those who were in the position to choose to live in racially integrated communities, are intensely interested in black culture—music, art, literature, theater, dance, cuisine, etc. Significant parts of non-black America also share the same fascination with black culture. This is what the new breed of black cable TV, radio, film, and audio-video entertainment entrepreneurs understand. This is what a small movement of New York City black architects centered on *blacklines Magazine* are at least experimenting with, though on an as yet orthodox level.

The common denominator meeting point of much of the telecom-munications driven revolution is where African-Americans live and sleep each night. They sleep in some form of building structure, also known as their house, and rarely thought of as "architecture." How the next generation of black architects is to be socialized in their chosen academic environments to relate to the question of how other blacks will be housed in the twenty-first century is a major issue for both groups in their struggle to exist as viable cultural entities.

The key to a twenty-first century black architectural practice renaissance requires that young black architects position themselves in the middle of an inevitable integration of all of the cultural art forms of Black America. The home or *place of residence* is the physical center-piece and lynchpin of a true *music-art-architecture* triptych that must be fashioned around the integrated economic and cultural needs of the large sectors of Black America that will continue to live together.[1] The next generation of African-American architects must also assume more of the burden of bringing together the economic and business sectors and interests that are the necessary glue to nurture and protect the cultural life of a people.

All twentieth-century cultural arts endeavors including the making or adaptation of architecture by and for black Washington, DC, occurred under the same social conditions that incubated the musical genius of Duke Ellington.[2] While Ellington's music is quintessential *American* music he was always clear that he was also, in his own words, "creating Negro music."[3] Baltimore and Washington, DC, much like several other urban centers in America, offers ready promise of yielding an acknowledgeable and celebrated *"Black Architecture"* early in the twenty-first century.

As we head into the twenty-first century with the Information Revolution in full ascendancy, there are no legal or racial restrictions or government sanctioned socio-economic constraints similar to those that faced the pioneering first-half of the twentieth-century architect-educators at Tuskegee or Howard University. There is the corollary reality that architectural practice as a state sanctioned set of protective measures for the architects' role in the American marketplace, *has—for all practical purposes—been deregulated.* The same social and Information Technology forces that have been unleashed over the past thirty years and given rise to a new class of black entrepreneurs in the music, film, finance, computer, and real estate industries must also give rise to a new set of black architect-entrepreneurs.[4]

In the twentieth-century, the real estate developer, the architect, and the contractor have been the three basic and distinct operators usually brought together for the purpose of causing a private sector building or facility to come into being. To a limited degree the architect had a protected position in this endeavor up through the 1950s. The "state" enlisted the architect to protect the interest of the public on life safety issues, and through aesthetic taste arbitration (sometimes referred to as "insuring beauty").

In exchange, the state provided assurance to the architect that his dignity, integrity, and basic economic value would be protected in the face of the avarice of the developer and aggressiveness of the contractor. This pact has long since collapsed. State protection of the architect's role is now no more than a fig leaf.[5] The information revolution has now rendered the old iron triangle relationship of the architect, developer, and contractor obsolete or redundant. Any one of the three can legally and certainly financially do all of what the three have historically done as separate entities. We return to the question of which of the traditional architect-developer-contractor threesome is now redundant as a result of the full implications of the Information Technology revolution in private sector generic and vernacular work. The answer depends on which camp you belong to.

No sane developer or construction manager would publicly espouse the view that there is no longer a need for professional architects. The *one or two percent of construction costs* fee that a developer or construction manager carries in his *actual* project proforma for architectural fees is not that big of a deal to him to risk alienating what he invariably views as an ineffective but sometimes useful entity.

Architects hold a range of views about developers and builders but the general tone is set by the views of the elite design architect as we have seen through the eyes of arch "New Urbanism" leader Andres Duany. Usually the elite architect's developer clients are a special bred apart—more like a patron than a client. To the elite design-oriented architect, all other developers and contractors are viewed as boorish cheapskates whose interests and tastes are anathema to the making of good architecture.

The idea of *being a developer* is viewed by most elite or elite-aspiring architects as a horrifying and preposterous notion. Developers, we are taught, are the guys wearing the black hats to the architects' white hat. The architecture school socialization process usually has instilled the view that the architect is a more virtuous, deserving, ethical, and above all, a more intelligent and sophisticated judge of beauty. Thus he will find enlightened public sector, institutional, or corporate clients that will actually function as his *patrons*. Princeton sociologist Robert Gutman has observed that architects are the only profession that is still obsessed with this self-induced need to find *patrons rather than customers*.

It is powerfully instilled in school that architects don't have *customers*—only developers and contractors do.[6] However, the Information Age Revolution has rendered the notion of a separate and independent developer, contractor, and architect an obsolete proposition. Fortunately, Information Technology has also left architects in the position to reinvent themselves. But this type of reinvention may be entirely incompatible with orthodox architectural academy culture. In a number of venues throughout the architectural academy this is understandable. Some elite architects and the academic institutions they are aligned with may lust after power but *not* to the extent of being willing to exchange power for a deeply held, though not openly acknowledged, belief system that the architect is a *de-classe* arbiter of aesthetic tastes (but *de-classe from which class?*).

The HBCU architecture school is the one venue within the far-flung academy that cannot ignore the proposition of the need for a new composite entity under the rubric of *architect*. The HBCU school must socialize the next generation of architects to function as an effective composite of the architect, the real estate developer, and the construction manager. The onus is on those charged with preparing and socializing those future practitioners in the formative school years to re-align architects with their constituent natural housing *customer* bases. The search for clients and patrons must be replaced with searches for customers, partners, lenders, and investors that can assist the architect in *the creation of value*.

Our immediate and urgent task is the need to devise a socialization environment that facilitates the conflation of the architect's problem solving and still useful historically based visual conceptualization skills; the developer's daring and creative ways of meeting the needs of a marketplace through sophisticated financing techniques; and the construction manager's technical ingenuity in getting things built in the face of often times unmovable obstacles. This new conflated entity must also be prepared, largely inside of black schools, *to also pass the Architects' Registration Examination.*

The objective is to produce a new generation of effective practitioners. Here we must measure effectiveness by the degree to which this new architect is able to contribute meaningfully to a change in the status quo of economic under-development in black socio-economic indices of home ownership, property ownership, business and commercial ownership, a wide range of job creation, and affirmation of black culture, music and other creative art forms.

Any attempt to move an architecture school program to a focus on producing architects who do what community developers and housing producers typically do might begin with a reminder of the role that housing once played in the lives of important modernist architects. Richard Meier's recently completed billion-dollar Getty Museum is simply a Silicon Graphics computer generated extrapolation of his pristine little Corbusian houses of thirty years ago during his period of *New York Five* fame. Frank Gehry started down the road to his Bilbao, Spain, Guggenheim Museum by remodeling his private residence with common building materials thirty years ago in Los Angeles. At that time, Moshe Safdie was able to sell a skeptical Canadian Government into turning his McGill University architecture school thesis into the now venerated Habitat modular housing complex at the Canadian World's Fair in Montreal.

Arch deconstructivist Peter Eisenman developed the movement in conjunction with a series of theoretical HOUSE X drawing explorations. Michael Graves broke onto the scene doing housing renovations thirty years ago. The list could go on. The first generation European and American form givers of the modern movement from Frank Lloyd Wright to Le Corbusier were passionate designers and advocates of housing and community development as the most important tasks for architects at the turn of the twentieth-century. Somewhere along the way between then and now, housing ceased to be of interest to architects. Prestige, glory, and fame came to reside in other building venues. Even the building types most readily complementary to housing—retail commercial facilities, shopping malls, and hotels—lost architectural media prestige.

So with few exceptions the architectural academy socializes students to lionize an entire Modern Architecture high priesthood that is uninterested in housing. Architecture schools produce people who have no interest and no clue about how to *produce* housing. They may well be able to *draw* a house or housing complex but they are totally dependent on others to actually *produce* that housing and the stable vibrant neighborhoods that the house is based upon.

The good news here for the schools is that the notion of devoting the entire curriculum to the mastery of functional competence in housing production and neighborhood development may well be acceptable to a competent and well-rounded architectural accreditation team.[7] There is still a need within the curriculum for attempting to nurture pure artistic expression. I maintain that this would be best facilitated by having students enroll in the painting, sculpture, basic design and color, freehand drawing, music (blues-jazz-hip hop), filmmaking, and dance courses that are always available in the fine arts department on the HBCU campus.[8]

At the upper division undergraduate or graduate levels of the architecture curriculum, concerted effort must be expended to make synergistic cause with the campus business school—the most sophisticated and important tool for addressing the business and management skills that architects are notoriously inept at. Black students in five-year undergraduate professional degree architecture programs are perceptively pondering the advisability of foregoing second degrees in architecture. Such second degrees only make sense if they are explicitly structured to address the underlying business management and real estate development dimensions of architecture.

Today a student completing a first professional degree in architecture and seeking full time employment with a typical small to medium sized architectural firm will receive an annual salary that is at least 15 thousand dollars (and as much as 35 thousand dollars) less than the salary of the civil engineer or computer science major. The architecture graduate with high-level Information Technology skills *can* actually approach the higher salary of the engineer or computer science major. But only if she is willing to bypass the orthodox architectural firm. She must instead be willing to go to work in a high-tech oriented architectural-engineering, engineering, construction, or real estate development operation.

If she chooses an immediate entrepreneur track, she must figure out the nature and structure of her local or chosen housing market. She has to know who loans money to develop and build housing, and the rules and criteria of why they lend or invest money and on what terms and conditions. And she has to understand her own motivation and long-term vision as an architect. In order to assure a targeted starting annual income, she has to realize that expected income is simply ten percent (or more depending on her own tenacity and cleverness) of the gross value that she must create and close "deals" on.

She must be mindful that she is—or is in route to becoming—an architect in the full professional, legal, ethical, and artistic sense. She is far more than merely an old-fashioned and often narrowly educated homebuilder. She has simply chosen to go directly to the marketplace rather than *through or with* the patronage or permission of the homebuilder or developer as an intermediary. The real objective is to acquire the combination of skills and finance acumen to be able to function as an effective private sector community development architect. Spending a few years designing-developing-constructing houses will also lead inexorably to similar opportunities in healthcare facilities, retail and office commercial, and other ancillary community facilities. She is preparing to meet non-architect entrepreneurial business counterparts as an equal rather than as someone those people may (or may not) call in after the most critical business and financial decisions have been made. Hopefully, it will not have escaped her notice that the gleaming skyline that dots the downtown of her city, and the surrounding edge cities of the region, were created by people who first built the houses of the region.

What has been proposed is the objective of using the restructured architecture curriculum as a fulcrum that ties together architecture, engineering, the cultural arts, and business. This is a strategy of going where black students naturally gravitate, *and then demonstrating to them how architecture is an excellent vehicle for the joint pursuit of comprehensive urban community development and black cultural affirmation.*

George Fraser's book *Race for Success—The Ten Best Business Opportunities for Blacks in America* is likely to be read or consulted by entrepreneurial-minded black students (or their guidance counselors).[9] Yet in Fraser's over 330 pages of useful information, inspiring narrative, and well-chosen anecdotes, I was unable to find the word "architect." Frazier's book contains a warm foreword by Hugh B. Price, the president of the National Urban League. Price and the League are highly influential voices and catalysts in Black America. They are accurately articulating the now inexorable movement of Black America to a steadily evolving strategy and agenda of urban economic development and entrepreneurship. Price is trumpeting what is clearly understood by most clear thinking people as the dawn of a post-civil rights era for Black America.

Fraser's book includes a potent and fact filled chapter entitled "Rebuilding Our Neighborhoods." I thought that surely there would be a stimulating explication of the role of architects and the architecture profession in addressing this massive multi-billion dollar opportunity.[10] Interestingly, Fraser's poster profile lead-in figure for this chapter is Leon Hogg, an African-American developer and manager with an impressive track record of built inner city accomplishments. Hogg's academic background is in economics and political science. Right up front, Hogg has this to offer:

> *[get] a solid educational background in economics, political science, and or law for anyone contemplating a career that requires navigating complex bureaucratic waters....Fortunately I love people and I've developed good writing, oral, and listening skills—tools necessary for anyone entering the world of urban development.*

Hogg's views are typical—and highly justifiably—advice given to young black persons starting to think and make inquiries about possible careers. Fraser gets right down to cases:

> We need to upgrade our housing stock, to develop small businesses, to improve our schools, and to create financial bases within the community...People skilled in crafts, real estate development, finance, and teaching will be critical to effecting these changes. Look to the needs within our inner cities and determine whether the jobs and opportunities available appeal to you. Here it is easy to find a way to do well while doing good....Urban planning knits together sociology, philanthropy, economics, and education. We will need bankers and financiers, the capital manager type with an impressive track record of built inner city accomplishments necessary to build infrastructure, entrepreneurs to establish thriving businesses capable of serving the larger city as well as the local neighborhood, and educators to teach our children the skills to take part in building their own economies. We also need people with the vision and staying power to see the grand plans to completion.[11]

The above words are the nearest Fraser comes to alluding to architecture. Where Fraser gets down to the nitty-gritty of money as income to be made in the "hood," he points out that *experienced construction managers can earn from $35,000 to $123,000, while skilled craft-workers charge upwards of $35 per hour.* Fraser then goes on to quote a friend, Stuart Deicher, a homebuilder in Cleveland who talks about the opportunities in his company:

> [I could] put to work today any person regardless of color, in any one of the skilled crafts, if I could find them. Within 3 to 5 years they could earn $40,000 to $75,000 per year as a journeyman, and start their own business if they wanted to.

Meanwhile, if those young black people and their guidance counselors, after having read Fraser's book, were to consult books on careers in architecture they will encounter bizarre pronouncements that can be paraphrased as follows:

"Architecture is not about money but about personal self-satisfaction...and that one should be prepared, after 5 to 7 years of university training, to receive a starting salary in the mid-twenties, with possibly an advance to the mid thirties after another 3 years of apprenticeship and successful passing of a grueling nine part four day licensure examination."

Given the state of Information Technology, it simply makes no sense for future architects to spend their university training time learning to be reactors to the professionals that George Fraser and Leon Hogg have so accurately and perceptively pointed out as being the prime movers and determiners in the development of neighborhoods and cities.

After reading the "...Neighborhoods" chapter of Fraser's book, you might be hard pressed to image an entire twentieth-century of African-American architect-practitioners. Those men designed a collection of built works that, if aggregated in a single vacant geographic spot, would constitute an impressive sized urban metropolis. That city would be made up of building types ranging from housing subdivisions to large high-rise apartment buildings; commercial offices to hospitals; neighborhood recreational facilities to large stadiums; elementary through college educational facilities; and every conceivable form of municipal government facilities.

Predictably, most of the occupants of that composite black designed city would be African-Americans, thus underscoring the fact that the twentieth-century African-American architect is truly a creature of Black America. But there would be several glaring shortages in this composite black metropolis. Large-scale manufacturing or industrial complexes would be missing. Most significantly, with the exception of some of the higher education structures, very few of the black designed structures would have been developed, financed, or constructed by black controlled institutions.

Remarkably, this basic absence of the economic "control of production" would include the various and sundry forms of practically *all types of residential shelter.* This is an issue that must assume major importance in the socialization of the coming generation of African-American and Diaspora architects who will function in the period between years 2000 and 2020. This issue is the physical embodiment of Black America's extremely negative "trade balance" with the various other cultural, ethnic, and racial groups of the United States.

As a pertinent aside to the issue of the need of radical curriculum restructuring, I have been blessed with a remarkable son and very special daughter, an adopted godson (my son's best friend all through their K-12 years and to the present), and the ultimate son-in-law (my daughter's spouse). None of the four are architects. They are all total products of the Information Technology age. They literally bristle with high-tech Information Technology expertise (and the concomitant high levels of self-confidence) gained from formal education. Between them, their degrees include my son's doctorate in artificial intelligence from Cal Tech, my God-son's MBA in finance from Columbia, and my son-in-law's master's in education. Each of the four hold communications related undergraduate degrees from elite universities. Added to those credentials are countless hours of high-tech work experience as well as numerous completed industry-training courses. I have from time to time engaged them in such a hypothetical as the following:

> *Suppose a corporation or governmental entity offered you a long-term lease or a contract to design a multi-million dollar structure—not an implausibility in this day and age. Do you feel that the state of Information Technology is at a point that would allow you to accept the contract? And if so, do you believe that your need for an architect extends much beyond his or her license stamp for a fee?*

My young thirty-something-year-old, high-tech non-architect group is confident that there is now available to them sufficient intelligence systems, massive Internet accessible data bases of building technology details and specifications, geographic information systems (GIS), and other peripherals that have rendered obsolete, many of the things that would have been traditionally dependent on the skills of a formally trained architect to provide. We of course have to factor in that the group is also confident that *Old Dad*, the grizzled veteran, is available to them for all of the critical questions that must be asked and judgment calls to be made; and if not *Old Dad* then some old architect codger like him—for a fee of course. Needless to say, my true believer evangelist architect friends find my hypothesis preposterous. *But is it really?*

We need to remind ourselves that architects are, in the words of former Secretary of Labor and now Harvard professor Robert Reich, "symbolic analysts"—just like my high-tech quartet. So what then am I proposing that our young architecture graduates do? The legal title of "architect" and the long glorious history associated with the title makes it worth aspiring to and fighting to acquire. Despite how I answer the question—*what should architects be doing?*—I believe that prospective African-American architecture students already in or contemplating architecture have made good career decisions. For me personally, next to being a husband and a father (and recently a grandfather), being an architect, with all of the remaining rights and privileges thereto, has been my most fulfilling and treasured life accomplishment.

In the final word, architectural power flows not from how talented one might be in the subjective arena of "design." Power rests on how well one understands the marketplace at the consumer or "customer" level and how adept one is at attracting the investment capital required to meet customer needs. This may sound like a strange criteria for an architect but be assured that without such capacity, one has nothing of meaningful value to offer the complex thing known as Black America.

CHAPTER 7

The HBCU Architecture Schools Directory, 2002

SCHOOL	DEGREES OFFERED
Florida A & M University	B.S. in Architecture
School of Architecture	Bachelor of Architecture
Tallahassee, FL	Master of Architecture
Rodner Wright, Dean	Master of Landscape Architecture
850.599.3244	
Hampton University	Bachelor of Architecture
Department of Architecture	
Hampton, VA	
Bradford Grant, Chairman	
757.727.5440	
Howard University	Bachelor of Architecture
School of Architecture	Master of Architecture
Washington, DC	
Victor Dzidzienyo, Director	
202.806.7420	

Morgan State University Institute of Architecture & Planning Baltimore, MD *Richard Lloyd, Director* 443.885.4434	B.S. in Architecture & Env. Design Master of Architecture Master of Landscape Architecture Master of City & Regional Planning
Prairie View A & M University School of Architecture Prairie View, TX *Dr. Inklas Sabouni, Dean* 409.857.2014	B.S. in Architecture B.S. in Construction Science Master of Architecture Master of Community Development
Southern University A & M School of Architecture Baton Rouge, LA *Dr. Adenrele Awatona, Dean* 225.771.3015	Bachelor of Architecture
Tuskegee University Department of Architecture Tuskegee, AL *Timothy Barrows, Head* 334.727.8329	Bachelor of Architecture B.S. in Construction Science
University of DC Architecture Department Washington, DC *Clarence Pearson, Chairman* 202.274.5059	Associate in Architectural Technology Bachelor of Architecture

PRE-PROFESSIONAL ARCHITECTURAL (OR ALLIED DISCIPLINE)
PROGRAMS

North Carolina A &T University   B.S./M.S. in Arch. Eng.
Department of Architectural Engineering
Greensboro, NC
Dr. Peter Rojeski, Chairman

Morris Brown University   B.A. in Architecture
Architecture Program
Atlanta, GA
Donald Blair, Coordinator

Norfolk State University   B.S. in Construction Management
Department of Technology
Norfolk, VA
Dr. Carray Banks, Chair

Tennessee State A & T   B.S. in Architectural Engineering
Architectural Engineering Program
Nashville, TN
Walter Vincent, Head

CHAPTER 8

100 Years of Critical Black Milestones 1900–2000 (And Related Concurrent Critical White Milestones)

*This entire time line was constructed from a combination of sources including the doctoral dissertations of Richard Dozier, Harrison Etheridge, and Wesley Henderson (cited earlier); also from the book, *Contemporary Architecture in Washington, DC,* by Claudia and George Kousoulas (New York: John Wiley & Sons Inc., 1995); the publication *A Centennial History of the Washington, DC, Chapter of the American Institute of Architects, 1887–1987* (Washington, DC: The Architectural Foundation Press,1987); and the document by Betty Bird and Nancy Schwartz, *A Thematic Study of Black Architects, Builders, and Developers in Washington, DC—Phase I* (Washington, DC: The United Planning Organization, 1993).

1890–1899

The genesis of the modern professional period of *Black Architecture* in Washington, DC, begins in Alabama in 1892 with Booker T. Washington bringing Robert R. Taylor, that year's Massachusetts Institute of Technology School of Architecture class valedictorian, to Tuskegee to offer the first architecture classes. Taylor was the first known black architecture school graduate. His drawing course offerings at Tuskegee were essentially the same ones being offered at MIT and Cornell at that time.

In 1895, Booker T. Washington delivers his famous *"like the five fingers on one hand..."* address to a mostly white audience at the Cotton

States and International Exposition in Atlanta. Architect Taylor and his Tuskegee students constructed a building at that expo as a demonstration of black progress and capability in design and skilled trades. The building also contained the works of black painter Henry Ossawa Tanner.

Between Taylor's arrival at Tuskegee in 1892 and Washington's death in 1915 the design and construction of the Tuskegee campus was the largest concentrated physical enterprise in Black America built from the ground up by black people for its intended black use and occupancy.

In 1888, 19-year-old Frank Lloyd Wright is leaving the family farm in Wisconsin for Chicago and a six-year apprenticeship under architect Louis Sullivan. French Beaux Arts classic design work of Daniel Burnham and Romanesque design work of H. H. Richardson is the reigning American style of architecture.

In 1893, the Chicago Columbian Exposition is held to commemorate the 500th anniversary of the Christopher Columbus arrival in the Americas. This 650-acre downtown Chicago lakefront site was intended as a design and construction demonstration of American power and know-how. It became know as the "White City." One of the few instance of a positive black presence permitted at the fair was the ragtime piano playing of Scott Joplin and a few other black musicians and artists.

In 1887, Le Corbusier is born in Switzerland and, along with Wright, goes on to become one of the two greatest architects of the twentieth-century.

In 1883, Walter Gropius, founder of the German Bauhaus movement, was born in Berlin. Mies van der Rohe, a Gropius successor at the Bauhaus, is born in the German *Rhineland.*

1900–1910

By 1900, Taylor hires former student William Pittman and Pratt Institute graduate Wallace Rayfield to round out the architecture faculty at Tuskegee. This triad divided labor to allow one to focus on the academic program; one to focus on skilled campus construction labor training, and one to focus on the design of campus buildings.

By 1902, Tuskegee graduate John Lankford moves from Florida to Washington, DC, to begin a profoundly influential practice. He is the first black licensed architect in DC and he established a local branch of the Booker T. Washington instigated National Negro Business League. He was appointed supervising architect for the African Methodist Episcopal Church. This was a national commission for Lankford.

By 1904, Mr. Washington brings David Williston, Cornell graduate in landscape architecture, to Tuskegee to help shape the site development of the campus.

In 1907, William Pittman won a competition for the design and construction of the Negro Building at the Jamestown Tercentennial Expo. *Young Los Angeles teenager Paul Revere Williams saw a Pittsburgh Courier news article with photos of Pittman and his work. This was Williams' initial exposure to a black architect.*

By 1909, Tuskegee and Cornell graduate Vertner Tandy becomes the first black licensed architect in the state of New York. Tandy designed a New York City brownstone home as well as an upstate Palladian styled villa for Madam C. J. Walker, black hair care tycoon.

By 1910, the Tuskegee campus-building program was substantially complete and Tuskegee faculty and graduates are also building black churches and schools throughout the South.

In the first decade of the 1900s, the Carnegie Foundation is providing grants around the country for the construction of community libraries. Booker T. Washington is instrumental in getting former Tuskegee faculty and graduates commissions to build libraries in black sections of cities and black campuses. One of these libraries was built at Fisk in 1908. Calvin McKissack—who went on to build a formidable design-build practice in the South—designed and built this structure.

Frank Lloyd Wright leaves Sullivan to set up his own practice in Oak Park, Illinois. Wright builds a series of home designs that became immortalized as "Prairie Houses"—the most notable being the Robie

House—that to this today, still constitutes a major influence on American residential architecture.

Building on the base of the 1893 Chicago Worlds Fair, Louis Sullivan, Daniel Burnham, McKim Meade & White, Richard Morris Hunt, H.H. Richardson, and Cass Gilbert are the most notable examples of American architects who go on to design the major private and public structures in New York, Chicago, Boston, and Washington, DC, that define turn of the twentieth-century American architecture.

1911–1925

Due in part to the presence of the federal government and Howard University, Washington, DC, is becoming a black Mecca by 1910 but the early elements of the New York Harlem Renaissance are also stirring. No significant black architect involvement has been documented in the Renaissance but the Booker T. Washington backed Afram Realty Company is buying and building apartments in Harlem at that time.

Paul R. Williams becomes a registered building designer in the state of California in 1915, then gains licensure to practice architecture in 1923, and eventually opens a Los Angeles office that same year.

In 1919, Robert Taylor colleague and Tuskegee faculty member William Augustus Hazel leaves Tuskegee for Howard University to offer the first architecture classes.

Between 1921 and 1925, Howard University hires Ivy League trained architects Albert Cassell, Hilyard Robinson, and Howard Mackey to establish an architecture school. Prior to the arrival of these men as well as Mordecai Johnson, the first black president in 1926, all buildings on the Howard campus had been designed by white architects.

In 1926, Cassell was appointed by Johnson to take on the role of official university architect in charge of the design of the master plan and all major campus structures.

John Lankford continues in private practice.

Washington, DC, chapter of the American Institute of Architects establishes a registration law by 1919 and is a dedicated advocate of the 1902 McMillan Plan to beautify DC in accord with the design criteria established by the 1796 L'Enfant Plan. The city beautification movement is in full swing. There were 80 members in the DC AIA chapter by 1925. An Apartheid styled racial segregation is rigidly maintained.

By 1925, the National Capital Planning Commission is established, the Lincoln Memorial is completed, and the city population has grown to 450,000 people, nearly a third of them black.

Plans for the massive Federal Triangle complex were begun as the depression years of 1929–36 would be abated by the "New Deal."

In the late 1930s, Catholic University enlarged the offerings and increased the enrollment at the cross-town all white architecture school in Washington, DC.

1926–1955

In the 1920s, philosopher Alain Locke was on the Howard campus while also deeply involved in the Harlem Renaissance and urging a "New Negro" consciousness for black artists from all walks.

In 1931, Howard Mackey, architecture department acting chairman, organizes an exhibition of the works of a handful of black practitioners from around the country.

The work was displayed in the fine arts gallery and included work of Howard faculty members Mackey, Cassell, and Robinson; Paul Williams of Los Angeles; and several Tuskegee trained architects including architecture program founder Robert Taylor.

In 1933, the board of trustees of Howard proposed the abolition of the architecture program due to Depression Era induced low enrollment. An influential letter protesting that proposal was written by former Tuskegee student and Washington, DC, practitioner John Lankford.

The School of Engineering and Architecture was established in 1935. The effects of President Roosevelt's "New Deal" began to become manifest in DC and on the Howard campus in the late 1930s.

Cassell, through a hybrid on-campus based private practice, designed and supervised the construction of a series of major structures on the campus between 1926 and 1938, culminating in the dedication of the Founders Library in 1939.

In 1937, a joint venture of Hilyard Robinson and Californian Paul Williams receives the commission to design the Cook Hall men's dormitory complex.

This would be the first of eight major buildings on the campus for Robinson, whose practice became the main teaching office for future second generation DC black architects. Robinson was also designing other major off-campus buildings in DC. Robinson was the most openly "International Style" modernist of the black architects.

In 1937, Robinson, Cassell, and Howard Mackey were selected to participate in the design of large federally funded public housing projects.

Robinson designs the 274-unit Langston Terrace project. In 1941, Robinson designs the 300-unit Frederick Douglas Homes. Cassell designs the 200-unit James Creek project. Mackey designs the 373-unit Parkside Homes project.

In 1942, Cassell develops and designs the 600-unit privately financed Mayfair Mansions for a major black church.

In 1946, the historically seminal Robinson-Williams joint venture was commissioned to design the 100,000 square feet Engineering and Architecture Building that opened for instruction in 1952.

In 1950, the Howard program received national accreditation and is at the time the only such program in the country. Over fifty percent of black architecture students in the country were reported to be graduating from this program.

The Tuskegee program, which retained its largely building-oriented curriculum throughout the first half of the twentieth-century, did not receive accreditation as an orthodox architectural school until early 1970.

Private downtown commercial Washington and the public downtown monumental core are built without black architectural participation.

Brown vs. Board of Education in 1954 accelerates the shift in the changing ratio of city population to surrounding suburban population.

1956–1968

The period of 1956 to 1968 would see the establishment of a series of practices by Howard graduates as well as several other black architects.

This second generation of black DC practitioners would include Bryant & Bryant who opened an office in 1965, and by 1975 would be the largest black-owned practice in the country.

The President Kennedy assassination in 1963 would lead to a Lyndon B. Johnson presidency that would began the installation of a predominately black Home Rule government. Key officials were friends and peers of the second generation of black architectural firms.

In 1968, President Johnson appoints Walter Washington as mayor and sets in motion Washington's election as mayor in 1974. Walter Washington embarks on a massive public works and school construction program

The Watts Riots of 1965 accelerated the Black Power Movement throughout DC and Howard University.

Black developer Ted Hagans gains developmental control over the 360-acre Fort Lincoln New Town site that was zoned for a 5,000-unit community. Hagans selects seven black local architectural firms for the ten available design contracts.

On April 4, 1968, Dr. Martin Luther King Jr. is assassinated and Washington, DC, central city black communities explode in violent rage resulting in massive property damage and loss of lives.

From the 1930s through the mid-1960s, segregation and racism still are firmly entrenched in the DC world of architecture.

In 1932, Phillip Johnson and Henry-Russell Hitchcock introduce European Modern Architecture in a show at the New York Museum of Modern Art titled "The International Style."

By the mid-1940s and the end of WW II, the DC chapter of the all white AIA opened up membership to Hilyard Robinson and Howard Mackey.

In the late 1940s, Jewish architects Leon Brown, Julian Berla, Joseph Abell, and Jesse Weinstein would all hire Howard graduates.

Leon Brown joins the Howard faculty in 1947 at the invitation of Howard Mackey and remains until his retirement in 1970.

The Capital Beltway opens in 1964.

The METRO rapid transit system is authorized that same year.

1969–1999

The April 1968 King assassination immediately results in major design contracts from the DC government that were previously earmarked for white firms to instead become work for the young black practices.

In 1969, the Bryant & Bryant firm is selected to design the 20 million dollar Dunbar High School and Sultan & Campbell is selected to design the 13 million dollar Shaw Junior High School. By 1969, black practices began sharing in the design work with large white engineering firms on the METRO rapid transit stations.

In 1969, a Ford Foundation grant facilitates the separation of architecture from engineering and the creation of the new School of Architecture and Planning at Howard University.

In 1971, Mackey retires as dean of the School of Architecture & Planning at Howard and is succeeded by Harvard architecture professor Jerome Lindsey, a 1957 Howard architecture graduate.

In 1973, Howard alumni Frank West, John Gray, and Yetticoff Wilson's firm is selected in a black-white joint venture with West Coast firm Welton Becket to design the new Eisenhower Convention Center.

Through 1978, black design firms receive an increasingly larger share of city public works and public housing design contracts from the Walter Washington administration.

In November 1978, Marion Barry elected mayor with virtually complete control over contracting, leasing, and downtown commercial urban renewal parcels.

Barry gives nearly 100 percent of public works and housing contracts to local black architectural firms, now grown to 24 practices—the largest number in any city in the African Diaspora world of the US, the Caribbean, and Africa. Barry decrees that white developers vying to develop city urban renewal sites must have black equity partners and black architectural participation.

By 1982, Reagan and the Republican Party gain control in Washington. City budget cutbacks began and black firms feel the pinch of "Reaganomics."

By 1990, Barry is out of office in disgrace and black firms are in crisis. By 1994, Barry returns and Devroaux & Purnell has replaced Bryant & Bryant as the dominant black firm in DC.

Barry structures new public-private partnerships to build the MCI basketball arena and a new replacement convention center. D&P is joint venture architect on both projects.

Barry retires from public life in 1998.

D&P are on the highest echelons of the new Mayor Anthony Williams' transition team.

In 1998, the Howard University School of Architecture and Planning is re-merged with the School of Engineering to form the new College of Engineering, Architecture and Computer Science

Devroaux & Purnell is the first black firm to design large scale private commercial structures in downtown DC.

As of 1998, there are now only 12 viable black architectural firms in DC, down from the 24 firms that greeted Barry at his election to mayor twenty years earlier.

Richard Nixon launches "Black Capitalism," 1968.

William Coleman, a black Philadelphia lawyer, was appointed by Nixon as the Secretary of the Department of Transportation. Coleman's mandate of maximum participation of minority architects and engineers created a bonanza of transportation work nationally and locally. This led to the rise of the black engineer eclipsing the black architect as the large design services practice.

Barry and downtown developers build 22 million square feet of new office, retail, and hotel rooms in downtown between 1978 and 1990.

Anthony Williams is elected Mayor in 1998.

Notes

PREFACE

1. See Robert G. O'Meally, (Ed.), *The Jazz Cadence of American Culture* (New York: Columbia University Press, 1998), 82–101, Chapter 4, "Black Music as an Art Form," Olly Wilson. While Wilson's paper is concerned with the art form of music, the implications for the art form of architecture are compelling. See also in its entirety Wilson Jeremiah Moses, *Afrotopia: The Roots of African American Popular Culture* (Cambridge, UK: Cambridge University Press, 1998) for a brilliant articulation of these "challenges."

2. In 1998, I was appointed to an advisory panel that acts as the city-wide architectural design review board for (the majority African-American) city of Baltimore, Maryland. Shortly after my appointment, the preliminary design drawings and model proposal for a multi-million dollar Museum of Maryland African-American History came before the panel for review and comment (the seven member panel included one other African-American architect in addition to myself). The Museum is under the control of a diverse representative group of people drawn from Baltimore's African-American cultural and political leadership. That group was responsible for the solicitation, "shortlisting," and final selection of the architect. The team they selected was a joint-venture of a local white firm and the local African-American owned firm of Amos and Bailey. The black firm was then headed by Michael Amos who was my classmate at Howard and Harvard. The chair of the museum architect selection committee told me that their selection was based

largely on the passionate oral presentation made by Amos. Tragically, Amos became ill and died before he was able to start the actual design of the project. Members of the museum selection panel members were aware of this. Several of them quietly sought me out after the presentation and insistently posed the question *shouldn't the museum be an expression of a "Black Architecture?"* Others expressed skepticism about the relevance of a *"Black Architecture"* to the museum. The seemingly conflicting positions of the predominatelyAfrican- African-American museum board were highly representative of the attitude towards architecture throughout all strata of Black America.

3. Carter Wiseman, *Shaping a Nation: Twentieth-Century American Architecture and Its Makers* (New York: W.W. Norton & Co., 1998) is a representative example of several hundred mainstream American architecture history textbooks that fail to acknowledge a single example of either a black architect or a black architect-designed building in the entirety of the twentieth-century.

4. See Dell Upton (Ed.), *Roots: Ethnic Groups That Built America* (Wash., DC: The Preservation Press, 1986), 42–48, for the chapter "Afro-Americans" by John Michael Vlach. While author Vlach's concern is centered on the pre-twentieth-century activities of America's ethnic groups, his views are readily assumed by most readers to include twentieth-century architectural contributions.

5. For a thoughtful extended essay that is representative of this genre see the chapter in the book by Thomas A. Dutton, and Linda Hurst Mann (Ed.), *Reconstructing Architecture: Critical Discourses and Social Practices* (Minneapolis: University of Minnesota Press, 1996), 202–234, written by Bradford C. Grant, head of the architecture school at HBCU Hampton University, "Accommodation and Resistance: The Built Environment and the African-American Experience."

6. Harold Cruse, *Crisis of the Negro Intellectual: A Historical Analysis of the Failure of Negro Leadership* (New York: Quill, 1967). Cruse's book has received numerous critical reviews; some highly nega-

tive. However, even the harshest critics of certain aspects of the book concede its overall brilliance. A glaring exception is a very bitterly hostile review of Cruse's book by Ernest Kaiser in *Freedom Ways Magazine*, Vol. 9, No. 1, Winter 1969, 24–41. Kaiser takes major umbridge with Cruse's relentless anti-Marxism and tendency to settle old scores for real and perceived slights from black left-wing luminaries.

7. Craig L. Wilkins is an adjunct professor and Ph.D. candidate at the College of Architecture, University of Minnesota. He writes feature pieces for *blacklines*, a New York based journal exploring Black Architecture. Wilkins also has a major article on Hip-Hop culture and architecture in the September 2000 issue of the *Journal of Architectural Education*, "(W)rapped Space: The Architecture of Hip-Hop," 7–19. He argues with passion, persuasion, and scholarship, for the positive architectural implications of Hip-Hop culture. Wilkins has also compiled an as yet unpublished but highly useful paper titled "Architecting: Architecture As A Verb—A Case For An Activist Architecture (Initial Thoughts On A Working Research Project)" that contains an Appendix I, "A Partial List of Trailblazing African-American Architects Of Some Note" and Appendix II, "An Embarassingly Incomplete Listing of Publications by or About African-American Architects."

8. See Stephan Therstrom and Abigail Thernstrom, *America in Black and White: One Nation, Indivisible—Race in Modern America* (New York: Simon & Schuster, 1997) for a representative optimistic white American view on African-American progress in the US over the course of the second half of the twentieth-century.

9. See in its entirety Robert P. Moses and Charles Cobb, Jr., *Radical Equations: Math Literacy and Civil Rights* (New York: Beacon Press, 2002).

10. A "fatally flawed black culture" is the central premise of the harsh tract by conservative India—American ideologue Dinesh D' Souza. In his widely read book, *The End of Racism: Principles for a*

Multiracial Society (New York: Free Press, 1995), D'Souza—either deliberately or out of ignorance—completely misunderstands African-American culture. In order to support his premise D'Souza had to rely on a description of what masquerades as black culture but what is in reality merely the residual effects of 400 years of White Supremacy that continues to bedevil up to one-third of today's African-American population.

11. It is all but unfathomable to me how the Dinesh DeSouzas of the world could read Rayford Logan, *The Betrayal of the Negro: From Rutherford B. Hayes to Woodrow Wilson* (New York: Da Capo Press, 1997), and still be able to write their treatises with a straight face.

PART I—ROOTS OF THE CRISIS; ARCHITECTURE AND BLACK AMERICA AT THREE CRITICAL TWENTIETH CENTURY JUNCTURES

CHAPTER 1—Personal Genesis

1. Ayn Rand, *The Fountainhead* (New York: Signet, 1952). This was my first time encountering a full blown novel devoted entirely to the subject of architecture—or so I thought then. I was totally unaware that this fictional work was simply the vehicle the author used to express her libertarian and laissez faire philosophy on economics, politics, and (WASP) culture.

2. "Successful Young Architects," *Ebony Magazine*, November 1958.

3. Grimes was an early 1950s graduate of the architecture program at the University of California at Berkeley. After several decades as a modestly successful head of his own private practice in Los Angeles, Grimes took a high level management position in the office of the California State Architect.

4. Jenkins was an early 1950s graduate of the University of Southern California. In 1977, I joined forces with him by turning my small Washington, DC, practice into his East Coast branch office.

5. Dan Watts went to work for Skidmore, Owings and Merrill (SOM), the cutting-edge modernist Chicago-New York architectural firm, after graduating from Columbia. In later years, I learned that Watts was reported to have incurred the serious wrath of the New York office where he worked, by his aggressive pose for the *Ebony* article inside of the Idlewild Terminal. By the late 1960s, he had left architecture altogether to focus on editing, publishing, and writing for *Liberator Magazine*, a Harlem-based journal of black radical political and cultural thought.

6. See Richard Kevin Dozier, "Tuskegee: Booker T. Washington's Contribution to the Education of Black Architects" (A Doctoral Dissertation: University of Michigan, 1990).

7. From Robinson's yet uncatalogued personal papers and writings located in the Spingarn Research Collection of the main library at Howard University.

8. See Angel David Nieves, "African-American Architects and 'Race-Uplift' for the Black Community: New Deal Mass Housing and Black Nationalism in the Nation's Capital," *Planning History Studies*, Volume 12, Numbers 1–2, 1998, for an interesting thesis. Neives posits that the 1930s public housing advocacy and design work of Robinson in Washington, DC, was a form of Black Nationalism. While I do not believe that this case was made, Neives highlights a facet of black architectural involvement in Euro-modernist social housing thinking that is useful and worthy of further debate.

9. See Frank Willett, *African Art: An Introduction* (London: Thames and Hudson, 1986), 35–37. See also Herschel B. Chipp, *Theories of Modern Art: A Source Book By Artists and Critics* (Berkeley: University of California Press, 1968), "Cubism: Form as Expression," 193–280.

10. See in its entirety Amy Helene Kirschke, *Aaron Douglas: Art, Race, & The Harlem Renaissance* (Jackson, Miss: University of Mississippi Press, 1995).

11. See Bradford C. Grant, and Dennis Alan Mann (Ed.), *The Professional Status of African-American Architects* (Cincinnati: The Center for the Study of Practice, 1996).
12. See Kwame Anthony Appiah, and Henry Louis Gates Jr., *Africana: The Encyclopedia of the African and African-American Experience* (New York: Basic *Civitas* Books, 1999). In this lengthy and informative inaugural piece of scholarship on the key cultural players throughout the African Diaspora, one will be unable to find any profiles, indexing or other useful information on African-American architect.
13. O'Meally (Ed.), *The Jazz Cadence of American Culture*, "Jazz and American Culture," 431–447 is representative of several chapters on the relationship of jazz and culture. See also Alain Locke (Ed.), *The New Negro: Voices of the Harlem Renaissance* (New York: Touchstone, 1997), "The Legacy of the Ancestral Art," by Alain Locke, 254–267.
14. See Richard A. Etlin, *Frank Lloyd Wright and Le Corbusier: The Romantic Legacy* (Manchester: Manchester University Press, 1994) for an interesting comparative study of these two men. See also William J.R. Curtis, *Le Corbusier; Ideas and Forms.*(London: Phaidon Press Ltd., 1986), for a definitive and richly illustrated study of Le Corbusier.
15. James Scott, "Tyrany in Bricks & Mortar" *The American Enterprise Magazine,* January-February 2000. While noone is going to mistake the magazine or Scott with being politically unbiased, this overstated treatment of Le Corbusier's physical planning theories is illustrative. Interestingly, Scott made no comment on Wright's "Broad Acres" planning philosophy. For insight on Wright's utopian vision see Brendan Gill, *Many Masks: A Life of Frank Lloyd Wright* (New York: Da Capo Press, 1998), 336–338.
16. See Eve Blau and Nancy J. Troy (Ed.), *Architecture and Cubism* (Cambridge: The MIT Press, 1997), in its entirety but also particularly the chart by Alfred Barr on 146. See also in its entirety

Norman Brosterman, *Inventing Kindergarten* (New York: Harry N. Abrams, Inc., 1997).

17. Cornel West, *The Cornel West Reader (New York, Civitas Books, 1999)*, 456–462.

CHAPTER 2—*Context of the Crisis*

1. See Nan Ellin, *Postmodern Urbanism* (New York: Princeton Press, 1999); Martin Pawley, *Terminal Architecture* (London: Reaktion Books, 1998) and *Theory of Design in the Second Machine Age* (Cambridge, UK: Basil Blackwell Ltd., 1990); and Thomas Fisher, *In the Scheme of Things: Alternative Thinking on the Practice of Architecture* (Minneapolis: U. of Minnesota Press, 2000) are four thoughtful examples of this genre of books on the troubles ailing the professional practice and academy based study of architecture in the final quarter of the twentieth-century.

2. For a comprehensive treatment of the idea of a "culture of building" see in its entirety Howard Davis, *The Culture of Building* (New York: Oxford University Press, 2000).

3. My use of the term "academy" is borrowed mainly from the manner in which the term is used in *APPENDX*, the critical journal founded by three black students at the Harvard Graduate School of Design. I am simply referring to the constellation of American architectural schools and the intricately associated organized media that lionizes the high profile, high-culture architects that the schools promote as models to be emulated. The handful of architectural schools at historically black universities are—while indivisible—ideologically and culturally indistinguishable within the academy.

4. See O'Meally, *The Jazz Cadence of American Culture*, in its entirety. See also Blau, *Architecture and Cubism*, in its entirety for a series of scholarly articles all clearly acknowledging the impact of West African sculpture and art on the Cubist fountainheads beginning with Picasso.

5. *Black Enterprise Magazine* and the annual "Black Enterprise 100" issue that lists the leading business enterprises owned by African-Americans.

6. Appiah, *Africana.*

7. Dozier, "Tuskegee: Booker T. Washington."

8. Harrison Mosely Etheridge, "The Black Architects of Washington, DC, 1900-Present" (A Doctoral Dissertation: The Catholic University of America, 1979).

9 Wesley Howard Henderson, "Two Case Studies of Black Architects' Careers In Los Angeles, 1890–1945: Paul R. Williams, FAIA and James Garrott, AIA" (A Doctoral Dissertation: The University of California At Los Angeles, 1992).

10. See Malcomb McCullough, *Abstracting Craft; The Practiced Digital Hand* (Cambridge: The MIT Press, 1996). McCullough is one of Mitchell's frequent collaborators in discussing the far-reaching implications of Information Technology on architecture.

11. See William Mitchell, *The Reconfigured Eye: Visual Truth in the Post-Photographic Era* (Cambridge: The MIT Press, 1993).

12. See Ray Kurzweil, *The Age of Spiritual Machines; When Computers Exceed Human Intelligence* (New York: Viking, 1999).

13. For our purposes see particularly Kwame Anthony Appiah, *In My Father's House; Africa in the Philosophy of Culture* (New York: Oxford University Press, 1992), for a general treatment on African philosophy and culture. While certainly not the intention of author Appiah, this book has much to offer the searching young black person contemplating architecture or already in architecture.

CHAPTER 3—The Washington-Du Bois Debate

1. Mark Gelertner, *A History of American Architecture: Buildings in Their Cultural and Technological Context* (Hanover, NH: University Press of New England, 1999), 107.

2. Joseph J. Ellis, *American Sphinx: The Character of Thomas Jefferson* (New York: Vintage Books, 1998), 139–189.

3. Annette Gordon-Reed, *Thomas Jefferson and Sally Hemings: An American Controversy* (Charlottesville: University Press of Virginia, 1997), 133–141.

4. According to recent highly publicized DNA testing and findings, a Jefferson—either Thomas or his brother—fathered at least one but most likely all of Sally Hemings' offspring.

5. Roxanne Kuter Williams, *American Architects and the Mechanics of Fame* (Austin, TX: The University of Texas Press, 1991).

6. Hunt's role is acknowledged in most texts but see for instance Wayne Andrews, *Architecture, Ambition and Americans: A Social History of American Architecture* (New York: The Free Press, 1964), 176–184.

7. Sharon Patton, *African-American Art* (New York: Oxford University Press, 1998), 34.

8. Wayne Andrews, *Architecture, Ambition and Americans: A Social History of American Architecture* (New York: The Free Press, 1974), 170–174.

9. Booker T. Washington, *Up From Slavery: An Autobiography* (New York: Carol Publishing Group, 1985).

10. For a typically representative example of late twentieth-century black progressive intellectual assessment of the role and impact of Booker T. Washington in establishing industrial (as opposed to liberal arts) education, see Manning Marable, *Black Leadership* (New York: Columbia University Press, 1998), 23–39. For a counterbalancing view of the actual impact of Mr. Washington on black education and black labor, see August Meier, *Negro Thought In America 1880–1915: Racial Ideologies in the Age of Booker T. Washington* (Ann Arbor: The University of Michigan Press, 1988), 85–118.

11. Dozier, *Tuskegee*, is the source for much of the material in this section on Washington.

12. Dozier, *Tuskegee*, 41.

13. Dozier, *Tuskegee*, 84.

[14.] Elizabeth Smith Brownstein, *If This House Could Talk: Historic Homes, Extraordinary Americans* (New York: Simon & Schuster, 1999), 101.

[15.] See Robert A.M. Stern, *Pride of Place: Building the American Dream* (New York; Houghton Mifflin Company, 1986), for an illustrated discussion of this aspect of American architecture.

[16.] See Lerone Bennett Jr., *The Shaping of Black America: The Struggles and Triumphs of Blacks, 1619 to the 1990s* (New York: Penguin Books, 1975), "Money, Merchants and Markets," 285–342, for a concise review of late 19th and early twentieth-century black business development.

[17.] Dozier, *Tuskegee*, 37. Dozier used this highly appropriate quote from Washington, Booker T., *The Story of the Negro; The Rise of the Race From Slavery*, (New York: Outlook Company, 1909), 24.

[18.] See Dell Upton, *Architecture in the United States* (New York: Oxford University Press, 1998), 259, for a rare occurrence of the inclusion of a photograph and brief text acknowledgment of a building designed by early 1900s Tuskegee based black architect Robert R. Taylor, in a mainstream text.

[19.] Clarence G. Williams, "From 'Tech' to Tuskegee: The Life of Robert Robinson Taylor", 1868–1942. A 16 page research paper available from the *Blacks at MIT History Project Archives*, accessible on the Internet.

[20.] See in its entirety Meier, *Negro Thought In America 1880–1915*. See also specifically 85–118.

[21.] Most standard texts are in agreement here but see specifically Robert Twombley, *Power and Style: A Critique of Twentieth-Century Architecture in the United States* (New York: Hill and Wang, 1995). See also James F. O'Gorman, *Three American Architects: Richardson, Sullivan, and Wright, 1865–1915* (Chicago: The University of Chicago Press, 1991).

[22.] See Robert W. Rydell (Ed.), *The Reason Why The Colored American Is Not In The World's Colombian Exposition* (Chicago: University of Illinois Press, 1999), where Ida B. Wells and Frederick Douglass protested the black exclusion to no avail. The whites in charge of the fair were not content to merely exclude black Americans from exhibiting the stunning progress of the race at the fair. They were determined to allow only those exhibits on black life that were slanderous distortions that sought to perpetuate the most vile racist stereotypes. Numerous texts on twentieth-century black music places ragtime composer and piano player Scott Joplin and other black musicians at the fair as ongoing entertainment which the fair organizers thought was "bizarre" enough to uphold their racist intents.

23. Dozier, *Tuskegee*, 107.
24. Dozier, *Tuskegee*, 95–96.
25. Richard Dozier, "Spaces and Places: A Photographic Exhibit Conveying the Contributions, Aspirations and Aesthetic Values of Afro-Americans As Reflected In Architecture," Copyright 1982, Library of Congress Catalogue No. 85–50420.
26. Kendrick Ian Gradison, "From Plantation to Campus: Progress, Community, and the Lay of the Land in Shaping the Early Tuskegee Campus," *Landscape Journal*, Volume 15, No.3, 17–33.
27. See Twombley, *Power and Style*. These are Twombley's opening words in a spellbinding short read about this subject.
28. Bennett, *The Shaping of Black America*, 332.
29. W.E.B. Du Bois, *The Soul of Black Folks* (New York: Signet Classic, 1969), "Of Mr. Booker T. Washington and Others," 79–95. John Hope Franklin and August Meier (Ed.), *Black Leaders of the Twentieth-Century* (Chicago: University of Illinois Press, 1982),1–18, "Booker T. Washington and the Politics of Accommodation," by Louis R. Harlan. See also in its entirety Louis Harlan, *Booker T. Washington in Perspective* (Jackson, MS.: University of Mississippi Press, 1988).
30. Juliet E. K. Walker, *The History of Black Business in America: Capitalism, Race, and Entrepreneurship* (New York: Macmillan Library Reference, 1998), 198–200.

31. Cruse, *Crisis of the Negro Intellectual*, 19–23, reminds us of Booker T. Washington's involvement and guiding spirit, including financial assistance, in the black capture of Harlem. Cruse also explores Marcus Garvey's relationship to Washington.

CHAPTER 4—Tuskegee-Howard Pedagogies Collide, 1919–1945
1. Etheridge, *Black Architects*, 9.
2. Etheridge, *Black Architects*, 12–14.
3. Etheridge, *Black Architects*, 21–33.
4. See Dozier, *Tuskegee*, 207. A *Negro Building*, the first of several such buildings to be built at expositions in the south, was constructed to accompany Booker T. Washington's famous "Five Fingers" speech at the 1895 Cotton States Exposition in Atlanta. This single story 25,000 sq. ft. Beaux Arts Georgian style structure was designed and built by Washington's architect-teachers and their students as a demonstration of the technical capabilities of the race. The structure housed black produced artifacts ranging from utilitarian products to art work by gifted painters and sculpturers.
5. Etheridge, The Black Architects of Washington, DC, expresses this as the "professionalism" of the program. Whether understood by Etheridge or not, this term was actually a euphemism for the transformation of the architecture program from a Tuskegee styled "builder" oriented socialization to the "gentleman-architect" socialization promulgated by the American Institute of Architects.
6. This synopsis on Hazel was drawn from the published research of his granddaughter Louise Daniel Hutchinson, and Franklin A. Dorman, *Twenty Families of Color; 1742–1998*, New England Historic Genealogical Society, 1998.
7. See Jacqueline M. Moore, *Leading the Race: The Transformation of the Black Elite in the Nation's Capital 1880–1920* (Charlottesville: University Press of Virginia, 2000), 111–131, for an informative recitation on the issue of the Howard faculty's resistance to any

form of industrial education associated with Tuskegee. According to Moore, the specter of Booker T. Washington hung ominously over the campus in the form of Washington's appointment as a member of the Howard University board of trustees in 1907. He served on the board up to the time of his death in 1915.

8. Cassell was Ivy League educated but taught and built at Tuskegee prior to coming to Howard in 1924. The major part of his tenure at Howard was spent as University Architect. After leaving Howard in 1938, he developed, as well as designed, the 600-unit Mayfair Mansions apartment complex in Northeast DC. According to a March 2000 conversation with his architect son Charles, it was verified that the elder Cassell purchased enough land to develop an all black new town in Calvert County, MD. Cassell was anticipating assistance from Truman administration official Harold Ickes Sr. for the infrastrasture funds and loan guarantees needed to realize this ambitious vision.

9. See Dana Cuff, *Architecture: The Story of Practice* (Cambridge: The MIT Press, 1996), 24.

10. Several historians including Dozier actually credit Chaflin College in South Carolina as having offered architectural training prior to the establishment of the program at Tuskegee in 1892.

11. Harry G. Robinson III and Edwards, Hazel Ruth, *The Long Walk: The Placemaking Legacy of Howard University* (Washington, DC: Moorland-Spingarn Research Center, 1996), and Gradison, *From Plantation to Campus,* have Williston moving back and forth between Tuskegee and Howard as principal landscape architect on various master plans.

12. Louis Edwin Fry, Sr., "Louis Edwin Fry, Sr.: His Life and His Work," an unpublished autobiography, 97–103.

13. Fry, 104.

CHAPTER 5—Williams, Robinson, Fry at Howard University, 1935–1955

1. Henderson, *Two Case Studies*, 84.
2. In writing this chapter, I have borrowed heavily from Henderson, *Two Case Studies*. I was also guided by my own experiences and recollections as a resident of Los Angeles during periods covered by Henderson.
3. Henderson, *Two Case Studies of African-American Architects*.
4. Max Bond, "Three Architects of Afro-America; Julian Francis Abele, Hilyard Robinson, and Paul R. Williams," *Harvard Design Magazine*, summer 1997, 48–53. Also from a conversation with Washington, DC, landscape architect Dreck Wilson. According to Wilson, Robinson related this information to him during the course of a personal audience prior to Robinson's death in 1986.
5. Fry, "Louis Edwin Fry, Sr." 122.
6. In 1970, the Council of Black Architects (COBAS) was born in Washington, DC, at Howard University. The new Howard dean-designate of architecture Jerome Lindsey—still an associate professor at Harvard—and other young Washington, DC, based militants including myself, were spearheading a move to pressure the US Department of Education and American Institute of Architect affiliates to lend direct financial support to the accreditation efforts at several other unaccredited HBCU-based architecture schools.
7. Henderson, *Two Case Studies*, has a number of illuminating insights on the "race pride" angle throughout his highly informative dissertation, including his concluding chapter, 456–469.
8. For examples of the role of historians, critics, and the media in the establishment of the persona of an architect on the historical stage see Juan Pablo Bonta, *American Architects and Texts: A Computer Aided Analysis of the Literature* (Cambridge: MIT Press, 1996), and Williamson, *American Architects and the Mechanics of Fame*.

Chapter 6—The 1920s Harlem Renaissance—Key Misconnections

1. Oliver, Richard Oliver (Ed.), *The Making of an Architect, 1881–1981: Columbia University in the City of New York* (New York: Rizzoli, 1981), "Modernism Rears Its Head—The Twenties and Thirties," 103–118.

2. I base what many will view as the outrageous assertion of a black aesthetic influence on a canonical modernist work such as Falling Water on my belief that the case for the "jazz" influence on modernism has been convincingly established by O'Meally, *The Jazz Cadence of American Culture*.

3. This is acknowledged in most standard treatments but for a thorough reading on the subject of Cubism see Blau, *Architecture and Cubism*, and in particular the chart by Alfred Barr on 146.

4. Robert Hughes, *American Visions: The Epic History of Art in America* (New York: Alfred A. Knopf, 1999), 359.

5. Cruse, *Crisis of the Negro Intellectual*, 178.

6. Cruse, *Crisis of the Negro Intellectual*, 182.

7. Cruse, *Crisis of the Negro Intellectual*, 64.

8. Cruse, *Crisis of the Negro Intellectual*, 71.

9. Locke, *The New Negro*, 266.

10. Locke, *The New Negro*, also Patton, *African-American Art*, 116–117.

11. See Tritobia Hayes Benjamin, *The Life and Art of Lois Mailou Jones* (San Francisco: Pomegranate Art books, 1994), for the catalogue accompanying an exhibition of Ms. Jones' work at the art gallery of the Camille Cosby Building on the Spelman campus in Atlanta in the spring of 1999. I, along with hundreds of architects who were trained at Howard University between the 1930s and the 1970s, was privileged to take Ms. Jones' elementary painting and water color class in freshman year. In later years well beyond the Harlem Renaissance, other more occasional interactions took place between architecture students and art students.

12. See O'Meally, *The Jazz Cadence of American Culture*, Chapter 12, Richard J. Powell, "Art History and Black Memory: Towards a

Blues Aesthetic," 184–195, for a compelling paper on the larger
subject of a black aesthetic that also contains thoughtful observations on the relationship of the art work of Aaron Douglas and
Romare Beardon, and blues and jazz music.

13. See Leonard Harris (Ed.), *The Critical Pragmatism of Alain Locke; A Reader on Value Theory, Aesthetics, Community, Culture, Race, and Education,* (Lanham, MD: Roman and Littlefield Publishers, Inc.), "African Art and the Harlem Renaissance: Alain Locke, Melville Herskovits, Roger Fry, and Albert Barnes," by Mark Heibling, 53–84, for a discussion of the interrelations between primitive African art, modernism, and African-Americans including comments on dissenting views about the accomplish-ments of the Harlem Renaissance. The article also weaves in 1996 observations on these complex relations by contemporary African-American intellectuals Henry Louis Gates Jr, Cornel West, and Kwame Appiah.

14. This is one of those instances where I take issue with the Cruse assertion that true equality existed between white and black artists and intellectuals during the Harlem Renaissance.

15. Henderson, *Two Case Studies,* 88, 335, 539.

16. Etheridge, *The Black Architects,* 45.

17. For a full exploration of the relationship between this seminal African-American industrialist and (her complete loyalty to) an African-American architect (and her admiration of Booker T. Washington), see in its entirety Bundles, A'Lelia, *On Her Own Ground: The Life and Times of Madam C. J. Walker* (New York: Scribner, 2001). This relation first surfaces on pages 171–174.

18. Curtis, *Le Corbusier,* Chapter 6, "Houses, Studios and Villas," 71–84.

19. Samelia Lewis, *African-American Art and Artists* (Berkeley: University of California Press, 1990), 61–64.

20. See Romare Bearden, and Harry Henderson, *A History of African-American Artists From 1792 to the Present* (New York: Pantheon Books, 1993), 127–135, for a short informative chapter on Douglas.

21. See Nathan Irvin Huggins, *Harlem Renaissance* (New York: Oxford University Press, 1971), Chapter 5, "Art: The Black Identity," 137–189.

Chapter 7—Engineering, Kindergarten, West Africa, and Cubism
1. Vitruvius (Trans. By M.H. Morgan), *The Ten Books of Architecture* (New York: Dover Publications, Inc., 1960).
2. John Habraken, Dutch architect-writer and former chair of the architecture program at MIT, has provided one of the most insightful assessments available on how and why Palladio continues to be so influential in architecture. See "Palladio's Children," a reprint of a lecture Habraken delivered at the Ball State University College of Architecture, Muncie, IN, on April 5, 2000.
3. See Peter Blake, *The Master Builders: Le Corbusier, Mies van der Rohe, Frank Lloyd* (New York: W.W. Norton & Company, 1976), in its entirety.
4. See James F. O'Gorman, *Three American Architect: Richardson, Sullivan, and Wright, 1865–1915* (Chicago: The University of Chicago Press, 1991), in its entirety. See also Robert Wojtowicz, *Lewis Mumford and American Modernism: Eutopian Theories for Architecture and Planning* (Cambridge: Cambridge University Press, 1996), in its entirety.
5. For a useful and illuminating as well as delightfully illustrated Marxian economic analysis of modern architectural history see Bill Risebero, *Modern Architecture and Design: An Alternative History* (Cambridge: MIT Press, 1989).
6. Paxton's Crystal Palace appears briefly and in passing in practically all standard treatments of modern architectural history. In reality this is a signal and epoch making event that should be looked at in much more depth by the young aspirant or the older inquirer. See Cesar Pelli, *Observations: Lessons for Young Architects* (New York: Monacelli Press, 1999) for an exceptionally explicit acknowledgment. Pelli gives the Crystal Palace its just dues as the signal event marking the onset of the modern era in the mid-

nineteenth century with his assertion that this project was the actual "birth of Modern Architecture," 38–43.

[7.] Ian Sutton, *Western Architecture From Ancient Greece to the Present* (London: Thames and Hudson, 1999), 304.

[8.] Elizabeth L. Newhouse (Ed.), *The Builders: Marvels of Engineering* (Washington, DC. The National Geographic Society, 1992).

[9.] Norman Brosterman, *Inventing Kindergarten* (New York: Harry N. Abrams, Inc., 1997).

[10.] Gill, *Many Masks*, 42–46; see also Meryle Secrest, *Frank Lloyd Wright: A Biography* (New York: Harper Perennial, 1993), 58–61.

[11.] Brosterman, *Inventing Kindergarten*, 106.

[12.] Brosterman, *Inventing Kindergarten*, see also Etlin, *Frank Lloyd and Le Corbusier.*

[13.] Tom Porter, *The Architect's Eye: Visualization and Depiction of Space in Architecture* (London: E. & F.N. Spon, 1997), 20.

Chapter 8—The Music-Art-Architecture Triptych

[1.] Dick Russell, *Black Genius and the American Experience* (New York: Caroll & Graf Publishers, Inc.), 67.

[2.] Stanley Crouch, *Always in Pursuit: Fresh American Perspectives* (New York: Vintage Books, 1998), 45.

[3.] See Edward Kennedy Ellington, *Music is My Mistress* (New York: Da Capo Press, 1973), 32, 360–361, 379, 383.

[4.] See Robin D.G. Kelley, *Yo' Mama's Disf.unktional!: Fighting the Culture Wars in Urban America* (Boston: Beacon Press, 1997), in its entirety.

[5.] Albert Murray, *The Omni-Americans* (New York: Da Capo Press, 1978), 55.

[6.] "Gumbo" is the wonderfully appropriate word for a Louisiana seafood, poultry, and meat "soup" served steaming hot over white rice. I first encountered this word as a cultural metaphor in the writings of iconoclastic New York based cultural critic, Stanley Crouch.

7. The interrelationship of all of the art forms is addressed also by Merriam, *The Anthropology of Music*, 272–276 specifically but also generally through the entire book.

8. See for example David Hughes, *Afrocentric Architecture* (Columbus, Ohio: Greyden Press, 1994).

9. See for example Genell Anderson, *The Call of the Ancestors* (Washington, DC: AMAR Publications, 1991). Anderson, a black woman, is a licensed practicing architect in Washington, DC. On the basis of her travel and study in West Africa, she believes that considerable cultural residue of an architectural nature exists in the work of some of today's black practitioners.

10. See Martin Bernal, *Black Athena: The Afroasiatic Roots of Classical Civilization, Vol. I &II.* (New Brunswick: Rutgers University Press, 1987, 1991), on the case *for* ancient pyramid building Egyptians as a black race. See Mary R. Lefkowitz and Guy MacLean Rogers (Ed.), *Black Athena Revisited* (Chapel Hill: The University of North Carolina Press, 1996), for the case *against.* See also Steven Howe, *Afrocentrism: Mythical Pasts and Imagined Homes* (London: VERSO, 1998), for a more nuanced though ultimately anti-Afrocentrist view. For an engrossing, truly enlightening, convincing, and thorough but succinct treatment that challenges all camps on the subject of Afrocentrism see in its entirety Wilson Jeremiah Moses, *Afrotopia: The Roots of African American Popular* (Cambridge, UK: Cambridge University Press, 1998).

11. Black cultural critics Stanley Crouch and Gerald Early have both publicly raised this issue of "stone monument culture" worship by western cultures. See also Moses, *Afrotopia* who sheds considerable light on this issue.

12. See Upton, *America's Architectural Roots*, 42–47.

13. Patton, *African-American Art*, 187.

14. This group released the maiden issue of their promising journal *blacklines* in December 1999, Brooklyn, NY, published by *blacklines of Architecture, Inc.* See also Jack Travis (Ed.), *African-American*

Architects in Practice (New York: Princeton Architectural Press, 1991). New York architect Jack Travis is the spiritual leader of this growing movement of young New York based African-American architects. Travis has amassed an impressive body of work for a range of affluent black clients who are interested in a "culture specific" approach to architecture.

Chapter 9—Blacks and Jews as America's Twin Cultural Engine
1. Richard J. Herrnstein and Charles Murray, *The Bell Curve: Intelligence and Class Structure in American Life* (New York: The Free Press, 1994), 100–101.
2. *Commentary Magazine*, "Is Affirmative Action on the Way Out? Should It Be?—A Symposium (of Jewish and Black Intellectuals)," 18–57, Volume 105, Number 3.
3. Shelby Steele, *The Content of Our Character* (New York: HarperCollins Publishers, 1990).
4. See "Making the Case For Racial Reparations: Does America Owe a Debt to the Descendants of Slaves?," *Harpers Magazine*, November 2000, a panel moderated by Jack Hitt with leading class-action attorneys Willie Gary, Alexander J. Pires, Jr., Richard Scruggs, and Dennis Sweet, III.
5. See Randall Robinson, *The Debt: What America Owes Blacks* (New York: Dutton, 2000) for a persuasive and passionately argued case for reparations to African-Americans for uncompensated labor over the course of 300 years of slavery.
6. Amos N. Wilson, *Blueprint for Black Power: A Moral, Political and Economic Imperative for the Twenty-First Century* (New York: Afrikan World InfoSystems, 1998), "America's Long History of 100 Percent Racial Quotas in Favor of Whites." 35.
7. See Robert Reich, *The Work of Nations Preparing Ourselves for Twenty-First Century Capitalism* (New York: Vintage Books, 1992), for a fuller discussion of the concept of the "symbolic analysts."

8. See Hudson, *Paul R. Williams, Architect,* for a loving and richly photo-documented treatment of her grandfather who is America's most celebrated African-American architect.

9. Michael Lerner and Cornel West, *Jews and Blacks: Let the Healing Began* (New York: G.P. Putnam's Sons, 1995), 7.

10. Williamson, *American Architects and The Mechanics of Fame.*

11. Bonta, *American Architects and Texts.*

12. Herbert Muschamp, "Architecture View: Architecture of Light and Remembrance," *New York Times,* December 15, 1996, Sec. 2, 1.

13. Irreverent author Tom Wolfe caused quite a stir throughout the academy and the affiliated system of "star" architects with a bitingly satiric perspective on the world of Modern Architecture. See Tom Wolfe, *From Our House to Bauhaus* (New York: Vintage Books, 1984).

14. David W. Dunlap, "Black Architects Struggling For Equity", *New York Times,* December 4, 1994, Sec. 9, 1.

15. Sociologist Robert Gutman makes this point with great tactfulness in his observation about the growing number of architects who have embarked upon a deliberate strategy of offering their services to the built-environment marketplace as strictly "designers." See Robert Gutman, *Architectural Practice: A Critical View* (New York.: Princeton Architectural Press, 1988), 102. Gutman slyly implies that there will surely be others who will prove to be more adept than the orthodoxly trained architect at providing such a specialized "design" service.

16. After a relatively successful life of practice in the black-owned firm of Bond Ryder James, Bond has ascended to the position as a full name partner in the venerable and highly respected New York city firm of Davis Brody—now Davis Brody Bond.

17. The term "house for mother" became a tongue in cheek line about the practice of young upper class architects designing homes for relatives as a way of showcasing their talents for prospective commissions or even academic appointments. See Beth Dunlop, *A House for My Mother: Architects Build for Their Families* (New York: Princeton Architectural Press, 1999).

Chapter 10—Black Patron, New Monuments, and the "Black 35"

1. The primary purpose of the mainstream multi-color high gloss architecture magazines is a type of titillation through highly retouched glossy multi-colored visual images of building exteriors photographed at provocative perspective angles. Meanwhile, floor plans, functionality, environmental controls systems, user satisfaction, and finances are usually relegated to back page small type or more often than not, omitted entirely.

2. The Stanleys designed the recently completed mammoth and openly Afrocentric replacement of the old Ebenezer Baptist Church of Martin Luther King Jr. in Atlanta, GA.

3. The Detroit firm of Simms-Varner designed the large domed Detroit Museum of Black History with the stated intent of homage to the West African roots of African-American culture.

4. Dana Cuff, *Architecture: The Story of Practice* (Cambridge, Mass: MIT Press, 1996), "Beliefs and Practices," 17–56.

5. Not every "firm" was actually a firm. A number of firms consisted of sole proprietorships or loose partnerships with a yellow page listing but no actual established clients. Such "firms" operate out of home basements, garages or spare bedrooms but were not the equivalent of today's "virtual corporation" practices whereby a highly organized Information Technology based architect earns a six-figure annual income through servicing highly credible clients from a home-based office practice.

6. June 1999 news article interview of Chief Executive Officer Leatrice McKissack and her daughter Chief Operating Officer Cheryl McKissack in the June 1999 issue of *SMPS Marketer Newsletter* by Denise Graham, director of marketing for Bovis Construction Company, Washington, DC.

7. Taken from the interview of Mrs. McKissack in the same issue of *SMPS Marketer.*

8. In addition to Coles, Williamson's index of 800 architects lists two other black architects, Julian Abele and Louis E. Fry, Sr., Williamson, *Architects and The Mechanics of Fame*, 269–286.

9. See Robert Traynham Coles, "An Endangered Species," *The Journal of Architectural Education,* Fall 1989, 60–62.

10. David Haviland (Ed.), *The Architect's Handbook of Professional Practice* (Washington, DC: AIA Press, 1994), Vol. I-IV.

PART II BLACK POWER, URBAN REBELLION BLACK MAYOR, BLACK ARCHITECTS

Chapter 1. A Gentleman's Profession(alism) at Howard

1. Henderson, *Two Case Studies of African-American Architects.*

2. Beamon and Brooks, while still students at USC, opened a small architectural office in South Central Los Angeles. Beamon had grown up in families of builders. Brooks, the more introspective of the two men, had also acquired considerable construction exposure in his youth. Both men were highly accomplished commercial draftsmen before enrolling at USC. They, along with the third USC student, Arthur Silvers, have remained life-long friends and colleagues. Silvers is a retired architecture professor who had earlier practiced and built extensively in the South Central LA area in partnership with Robert Kenard. Brooks, after a multifaceted career as an architect-entrepreneur, is retired in Pasadena, CA. Beamon, who I have remained especially close to over the years, practices in Atlanta, GA.

3. While not known to me at that time, the 1962–63 official *DC Registry of Licensed Architects* listed 900 architects. Sixty were African-Americans. A marked-up copy of this registry in the uncatalogued personal papers of the late Leroy John Henry Brown indicates that 44 of these 60 architects were Howard University graduates or alumni.

4. For an informative view on Rouse's development of Columbia, see Robert Tennenbaum (Ed.), *Creating a New City: Columbia, Maryland* (Columbia, MD.: Partners in Community Building and Perry Publishing, 1996).

5. Robert Venturi, *Complexity and Contradiction in Architecture* (New York: The Museum of Modern Art, 1966).

6. Futagawa, Yukio, *Paul Rudolf*, (New York: Architectural Book Publishing, Inc., 1972). No student epitomized our Rudolfian infatuation more so than Harry Simmons Jr. a dear friend who went on to achieve great success as a Brooklyn architect before succumbing prematurely in a plane crash in 1993.

7. Simmons finished the program at Howard in 1966 and completed the master's program at Pratt in Brooklyn in 1968.

8. See Nathan Hare, *The Black Anglo Saxons* (New York: MacMillan, 1970), for a more radical, though less scholarly take on the earlier original research of Howard sociology professor E. Franklin Frazier, who a decade earlier wrote *Black Bourgeoise: The Rise of a New Middle-Class in the United States*, (New York: Collier Books, 1962).

Chapter 2—The Black Power Architect-Planner 1960s

1. See in its entirety Ted Gioia, *The History of Jazz* (New York: Oxford University Press, 1997), but particularly the first chapter "The Prehistory of Jazz; The Africanization of American Music," 4–27, that I believe supports my contention that the rhythmic aspects of Modern Architecture are derivative of the complex rhythmic structures of African and African-American music.

2. Locke, *The New Negro*.

3. A careful reading of many of the numerous works on twentieth-century black arts and culture will usually fail to yield the word *architecture* or a discussion of its relationship to the arts. A highly representative example of this genre is Richard J. Powell, *Black Art and Culture in the Twentieth-Century* (New York: Thames & Hudson, 1997), a small compact and scholarly book by Powell, an African-American who is a Duke University professor and chair of the Art and Art History Department. However, in Patton, *African-American Art*, Patton opens her book with a lengthy discussion on the African inspired or constructed archi-

tecture of the plantation slavery era. Patton mentions in her introduction that her intent to discuss black involvement in architecture beyond slavery gave way to editorial considerations. A minor exception to the avoidance of allusion to architectural discourse is Maulana Karenga, *Introduction To Black Studies*, (Los Angeles: University of Sankore Press, 1991), Chapter VII, "Black Creative Production," 296–299.

4. John Michael Vlach, *The Afro-American Tradition in Decorative Arts* (Brown Thrasher Books: The University of Georgia Press, 1990), 122–138.

5. This term was coined and popularized by city planner Paul Davidoff in the mid-1960s. The term signified the case of planning and design professionals, who normally represent the interests of local government units, instead representing the counter-interests of usually low-income community groups.

6. See Ruth Helen Cheney, "Advocacy Planning; What It Is, and How It Works," *Progressive Architecture*, September 1968, 102–115.

7. See Stokely Carmichael and Charles V. Hamilton, *Black Power: The Politics of Liberation* (New York: Vintage Books, 1992), 34–97.

8. In the 1960s Carl Anthony was a Berkeley trained architect who went on to establish a West Coast Bay Area wing of the advocacy movement.

9. See Melvin L. Mitchell, Harry J. Quintana, and Robert F. Jayson, "The Case For Environmental Planning Education At Black Universities," *Journal of the American Institute of Planners*, May 1970.

Chapter 3—"The Fire Next Time"—April 4, 1968

1. Four Howard University architecture school classmates and graduates Melvin Mitchell, Casey Mann, Robert Jayson, and Harry Quintana, who established the advocate planning group known as 2MJQ—the first initial of each man's last name.

2. Fifteen years later, Mayor Marion Barry would cut the ribbons to what is one of the most prominent and enduring monuments to

his legacy. After his 1979 inauguration he ordered the already designed $40 million Municipal Center plans scrapped and redesigned for the 14th and You Street site.

3. Vincent Scully, *American Architecture and Urbanism: New Revised Edition* (New York: Henry Holt and Company, 1988), 246–252.

4. From the time I arrived in Washington in 1960, "The Plan" has been a deeply held belief throughout all socio-economic strata of Black Washington. The litany was that: *White folks are secretly conspiring to retake "Chocolate City." They will do so through a "good government" strategy. Washington will be "gentrified." Along the way, whites will recapture political power by electing a white mayor and white city council majority. Then they will use zoning, urban renewal, historic preservation, and other municipal planning tools to push all low and moderate to middle-income blacks out to Prince George's County.* The problem with this theory is that while "The Plan" may yet happen to a large degree, it will not be because of a local white conspiracy. Inexorable urbanization-globalization forces will bring about "The Plan." Another major contributing factor will be the continued preference of the black middle class for detached mini-estates in the open spaces of the surrounding suburban counties. Most "nouveau" black middle class members eschew the inner city brownstone rehabilitations that are popular with many whites who have grown weary of suburban life and long commutes.

5. Etheridge, *Black Architects*, 122.

Chapter 4—The Marion Barry Era: The Rise (and Fall?)

1. The late Robert Kennard was younger than Williams and unlike Williams, actually did graduate from the highly regarded University of Southern California School of Architecture in the mid-1950s while I was in high school in Los Angeles. Kennard established an impressive—though primarily public sector—practice that survived him through a daughter and several younger black architect-partners he had groomed. Kennard's

lawyer-son was a Clinton appointed chairman of the Securities and Exchange Commission and was one of the most powerful public servants in America while on the SEC. Young Kennard has been indirectly responsible for implementing policies in the telecommunications industry that are facilitating the creation of serious black private wealth.

2. Henderson, *Two Case Studies*, 88 and 281.

3. Henderson, *Two Case Studies*, 335–345.

4. Courtland Cox and Ivanhoe Donaldson, two of the most influential and intellectually astute members of the Deep South SNNC campaigns, became Barry's key men for parceling out contracts of every type to black businesses. Cox and Donaldson quickly and aggressively escalated the policies started by the previous administration of Walter Washington.

5. See Harry Jaffe and Tom Sherwood, *Dream City: Race, Planning, and the Decline of Urban Policy in Washington, DC*, (Baltimore: The Johns Hopkins University Press, 1995), for a view that takes the position that Black Power under the Barry administration was more shadow and symbol than actual substance and achievement.

6. For an unsympathetic summation of Barry's political career and style, see Jonetta Rose Barras, *The Last of the Black Emperors: The Hollow Comeback of Marion Barry in the New Age of Black Leadership* (Baltimore, MD: Bancroft Press, 1998). See also Fred Siegal, *The Future Once Happened Here: New York, DC, LA, and the Fate of America's Big Cities* (New York: The Free Press, 1997).

7. For a full delineation of this aspect of Washington, DC, see in its entirety Larry Van Dyne, "The Making of Washington—Men of Vision and Ambition Who Built a Great City and Made Fortunes," *Washingtonian Magazine*, September 1987, Volume 23, No. 2.

Chapter 5—Barry, Black Architects, Housing and Downtown
1. Ted Hagans was the ultimate success story of a black Washingtonian in the rough and tumble, mostly all-white game of real estate development. Hagans graduated from Howard's civil engineering program in the early 1950s.

Chapter 6—The 1990s—A New Black Vanguard
1. In contrast to Monts' 6 million dollar developers fee—nearly all of it being pretax profit, the architect fee is 4 percent of the 30 million dollar hard cost. In an orthodox practice, the architect's fee is actually 90 percent expenses that must be paid out to engineering consultants, office overhead, drafting labor, and marketing costs.
2. Sorg worked for the Devroaux firm during the early eighties prior to forming her own company.
3. For a concise but informative contextual discussion of the Washington, DC, that coincides with the 1930–1970 era of the School of Architecture at Howard University, see Howard Gillette Jr., *Between Justice and Beauty; Race, Planning, and the Failure of Urban Policy in Washington, DC,* (Baltimore: The Johns Hopkins University Press, 1995), 135–207.
4. *Washington Business Journal*—Annual additions of the "Book of Lists" from 1972–1999.
5. Bradford Grant and Dennis Allen Mann (Ed.), *Directory Black Architects: Second Edition,* (Cincinnati: Center For The Study Of Practice, 1995), 138–141.

PART III—MANIFESTOS FOR THE NEXT GENERATION

Chapter 1—Beaux Arts-Bauhaus Myths, Rituals, and Fetishes
1. Colin Rowe and Robert Slutzky, "Transparency: Literal and Phenomenal," *Perspecta,* No. 8, 1963, Yale School of Architecture Magazine. This article first surfaced in 1955 as a highly influen-

tial unpublished paper that was circulated amongst architecture East Coast school heads.

2. For a typical example see R.E. Somol, "Still Crazy After All These Years," *Assemblage: A Critical Journal of Architecture and Design Culture*, Issue 36, 84–92, published by the MIT Press. UCLA architecture professor Somol provides a retrospective on the impact of Rowe (and Venturi) on architectural education in the second half of the twentieth-century.

3. See Alexander Caragonne, *The Texas Rangers: Notes From an Architectural Underground* (Cambridge: MIT Press, 1995), in its entirety for a detailed discussion of the educational pedagogy created by this group of men and their subsequent impact on American architectural education.

4. See Francis D. K. Ching, *Architecture: Form, Space, and Order* (New York: Van Nostrand Rheinhold, 1988), along with an accompanying series of similar styled books authored by Ching.

5. Rappaport has amassed a large body of published research on his scholarly critical assessments of architects. He finds their claims about studio wanting. Rappaport's perspective is that of a behavioral scientist. His research is housing, culture, and the accomplishments of indigenous people in the creation of their physical shelter and environments. See Amos Rappaport, "On the Nature of Design," lecture given at the University of Wisconsin-Atout, February 20, 1992, and published in *Center for the Study of the Practice of Architecture*, spring 1995, Issues 3–4, 32–44. See Rapport, *House Form and Culture*, (Englewood Cliffs, N.J.: Prentice-Hall, 1969). See also Thomas Dutton, "Design and Studio Pedagogy," *Journal of Architectural Education*, fall 1987, 16–25.

6. See Andrezez Pistranski and Julia Williams Robinson, (Ed.), *The Discipline of Architecture* (Minneapolis: University of Minnesota Press, 2001). See particularly the chapter, "Interdisciplinary Visions of Architectural Education: The Perspectives of Faculty Women," 235–259.

7. See Somol, "Still Crazy After All These Years."

8. Richard Meier, *Building the Getty*, (Berkeley: University of California Press, 1999).

9. See Williamson, *The Mechanics of Fame*, for an informative historical review of the relationship of stars as mentors. Thus far, this has not yielded concrete similar results for black architects who have toiled in the offices of stars.

10. Porter, *The Architect's Eye*, 157.

11. Kenneth Frampton, *Studies in Tectonic Culture: The Poetics of Construction in Nineteenth and Twentieth-century Architecture* (Cambridge: The MIT Press, 1996), 378.

12. See in its entirety Edward Robbins, *Why Architects Draw* (Cambridge: The MIT Press, 1997).

13. Robbins, *Why Architects Draw*, 45.

14. McCullough, *Abstracting Craft*, shows the path to an Information Technology based craft that will be much more enticing to a larger number of prospective black students than the traditional manual craft based studio.

15. See Franco Purini, "Three Directions For Architecture," 35–39, *New Architecture 5 (Truth Radicality and Beyond in Contemporary Architecture)*, Number 5, July 2000, Andreas Papadakis, Publisher, London, for a fuller development of the view of Gehry, et. al as sculpturers.

16. John E. Harrigan and Paul Neel (Ed.), *The Executive Architect: Transforming Designers Into Leaders* (New York: John Wiley and Sons, Inc., 1996), is a thorough treatise on the subject of the architect and his or her effectiveness in the highest levels of corporate, institutional, governmental, and private sector life.

17. Robbins, *Why Architects Draw*, 47.

18. Robbins, *Why Architects Draw*. 48.

19. Abraham Flexner, *Medical Education in the United States and Canada: A Report to the Carnegie Foundation* (New York: The Carnegie Foundation for the Advancement of Teaching, 1910).

20. See Thomas R. Fisher, *In the Scheme of Things; Alternative Thinking on the Practice of Architecture* (Minneapolis: University of Minnesota Press, 2000), for perspectives on this subject. Fisher was formerly an editor for *Progressive Architecture (now Architecture) Magazine* and is also the dean of the College of Architecture and Landscape Architecture, University of Minnesota.

21. Ernest L. Boyer, and Lee D. Mitgang, *Building Community; A New Future for Architecture Education and Practice,* (Princeton: The Carnegie Foundations for the Advancement of Teaching, 1996).

Chapter 2—"New Urbanism" Versus "New (Black) Urbanism" and Film

1. Martha O'Mara, *Strategy and Place: Managing Corporate Real Estate and Facilities For Competitive Advantage* (New York: The Free Press, 1999), 303–304.

2. See Frampton, *Studies in Tectonic Culture,* 379.

3. Reginald F. Lewis and Blair S. Walker, *Why Should White Guys Have All The Fun?* (New York: John Wiley & Sons, 1995). This book is absolutely must reading for any young person thinking about any type of business.

4. By now it is generally common knowledge that Michael Milkens, inventor of the "junk bond" mania and head of Drexel Lambert Company, could raise unlimited capital for a client seeking to sell stock in his company merely by issuing a letter starting with the now famous words, "We are highly confident…"

5. Dingle, *Black Enterprise Titans,* 27–49.

6. Edward Kennedy Ellington, *Music is My Mistress* (New York: Da Capo Press, 1973), 337.

7. See Douglas S. Massey and Nancy A. Denton, *American Apartheid: Segregation and the Making of the Underclass* (Cambridge: Harvard University Press, 1993), 84–114.

8. Andress Duany, "Speak Out: Architects Are Neglecting the Bulk of Housing Consumers, Causing a Dearth of Good Design and a Rift in the Profession," *Architectural Record,* April 1999, 23.

9. Michael Lecese and Kathleen McCormic (Ed.), *Charter of the New Urbanism: Congress For The New Urbanism* (New York: McGraw-Hill, 2000). See also Peter Calthorpe, *The Next American Metropolis: Ecology, Community, and the American Dream* (New York: Princeton Architectural Press, 1993).

10. William J.R. Curtis, *Modern Architecture Since 1900* (London: Phaedon Press Limited, 1996), 254.

11. Curtis, *Modern Architecture Since 1900*.

12. Jane Jacobs, *The Death and Life of Great American Cities* (New York: Random House, 1961).

13. Duany, *Speak Out*, 23.

14. Venturi, *Complexity and Contradiction in Architecture*. See also Venturi, *Learning From Las Vegas: The Forgotten Symbolism of Architectural Form* (Cambridge: The MIT Press, 1997). Together, these works chart what might appear to be a major shift in positions by Venturi.

15. Gary Stevens, *The Favored Circle: The Social Foundations of Architectural Distinction* (Cambridge: The MIT Press, 1998), 2. Professor Stevens goes on to accomplish his objective in over 200 pages of tightly reasoned analysis through the use of the theories of French sociologist Pierre Bourdieu.

16. See Larry Platt, "Magic Johnson Builds An Empire," *The New York Times Magazine*, December 10, 2000, 118–121, for a revealing look at the accomplishments and thinking of this former super-athlete-turned real estate developer and entrepreneur. Johnson's observations about the nexus between culture, economic development, and capital in black urban communities are insightful.

17. Hughes, *American Visions*, 338.

18. Walter Mosely, Manthia Diawara, Clyde Taylor, and Regina Austin (Ed.), *Black Genius: Black Solutions to African-American Problems* (New York: W.W. Norton & Company, 1999), 27–32.

Chapter 3—The Crisis in the HBCU Schools
1. Earl Graves, *How to Succeed in Business Without Being White* (New York: Harper Business, 1997), is in the same category as Lewis, *Why Should White Guys Have All The Fun?* Both of these books are *must reads* for young would-be African-American architects.
2. See Brosterman, *Inventing Kindergarten*, in its entirety.
3. Martin Pawley, *Theory and Design in the Second Machine Age* (Cambridge, Mass.: Basil Blackwell Ltd., 1990) and Reyner Banham, *Theory and Design in the First Machine Age* (Cambridge, Mass.: MIT Press, 1980), are two indispensable works best read together in sequence by today's young architects and students.
4. Frank Bosworth, III, the dean of architecture at HBCU Southern University up until 1999, received US Department of Education funding for an innovative project aimed at finding more structurally definitive ways to incorporate licensure into the academic curriculum. His background research for the DOE grant revealed the extent that the traditionally laissez-faire approach to licensure for Southern University graduates was resulting in unacceptably low rates of graduates taking the exam or successfully passing all parts within a reasonable time frame. My sense is that the situation at Southern may not be untypical of the other HBCU programs.
5. Paglia is referring to the French post-structuralist philosophers Michel Foucault and Jacques Derrida whose writings were brought into the architectural academy by architect Peter Eisenman, and became the generator of the architectural movement known as *Deconstructivism*.
6. See Nicholas Lemann, *The Big Test: The Secret History of the American Meritocracy* (New York: Farrar Straus and Giroux, 1999), for an informative discussion of the history, premise, and role of testing as the basis for admission to elite academic institutions.
7. The National Architectural Accrediting Board (NAAB) maintains a clear set of guidelines for accreditation that I do not believe pose

a problem to the radical overhaul of program and curricula needed at the HBCU schools.

8. Dingle, *Black Enterprise Titans of the BE 100s.*

9. Twombley, *Power and Style,* 3

10. Venturi, *Complexity and Contradiction in Architecture* is generally credited with being the basic treatise of the post-modern movement in architecture.

11. See Robert Goodman, *After the Planners* (New York: Simon & Schuster, 1971).

12. Goodman, *After the Planners,* 126.

13. John K. Edwards (Ed.), *Guide to Architecture Schools: Sixth Edition,* (Wash., DC: Association of Collegiate Schools of Architecture, 1998).

14. Mark Jarzombek, "Molecules, Money and Design: The Question of Sustainability's Role in Architectural Academe," Thresholds 18, Department of Architecture, MIT, 1999.

15. McCullough, *Abstracting Craft.*

16. See O'Mara, *Strategy and Place,* in its entirety for a complete exposition on the thought paradigm of corporate altitudes about facilities acquisition.

Chapter 4—Evolution of the Morgan Architecture School in Baltimore, 1980–2002

1. Grant, *Directory of Black Architects,* 148–150.

2. Christopher Weeks, *Alexander Smith Cochran: Modernist Architect In Traditional Baltimore* (Baltimore: Maryland Historical Society, 1995).

3. See Patricia Sellars (Ed.), *RTKL: Selected and Current Works* (Australia: The Images Publishing Group Pty Ltd, 1996).

4. From the classroom lecture notes of Anthony N. Johns dated November 11, 1985.

5. See Jonathan Barnett and John Portman, *The Architect As Developer* (New York: McGraw-Hill, 1976), for an overstated but illuminating delineation of an architect who popularized the idea of an effective dual role as a real estate developer. Predictably,

Portman, despite his spectacular hotel and mixed-use projects, is not viewed as a "serious" architect in the elite academic aligned world.

Chapter 5—A New African American Architect(ure) Canon
1. Daryl W. Fields, Kevin L. Fuller, and Milton S. F. Curry (Ed.), *Appendix: Culture/Theory/Praxis*, (Cambridge: Appendix, Inc., 1994), 82–103.
2. See Daryl W. Fields, "Architecture and the Black Subject; An Ethno-Historic Reconstruction" (A Doctoral Dissertation: Harvard University, 1995).
3. For "historiography" see in its entirety Panayotis Tournikiotis, *The Historiography of Modern Architecture* (Cambridge: The MIT Press, 1999), for a well written treatment on the history of "history writing" and its relationship to the modernist architecture movement and culture.
4. Curtis, *Le Corbusier; Ideas and Form*, 7.
5. West, *The Cornel West Reader*, 458.
6. See De Soto, Hernando, *The Mystery of Capital: Why Capitalism Triumphs in the West and Fails Elsewhere* (New York: Basic Books, 2000), 6.
7. See Rem Koolhaas, *Delirious New York* (New York: Oxford University Press, 1978), and *S, M, L, XL* (New York: The Momacelli Press, 1995).
8. See Franz Schulze, *Philip Johnson: Life and Work* (New York: Alfred A. Knopf, 1994), 89–91, 105–143.
9. Michael Pyatok, FAIA, *DESIGNER/builder Magazine*, "On Architecture and Power," July 2000, 5–6.
10. See Martin Pawley, *Terminal Architecture* (London: Reaktion Press, 1998), for a pessimistic assessment of the possible fate of an architecture profession that fails to come to terms with the Information Revolution.
11. See Derek T. Dingle, *Black Enterprise Titans of the B.E. 100s: Black CEOs Who Redefined and Conquered American Business* (New York:

John Wiley & Sons, Inc., 1999), with particular focus on the chapter "H. J. Russell & Company, The Builder," 155–172.

12. In addition to the sporadic publication of the National Organization of Architects (NOMA) newsletter, *blacklines magazine* and *designation magazine* are the only current exceptions.

13. Grant, and Mann, *The Professional Status of African-American Architects*, shows that 55 percent of licensed black architects are functioning as partners or principals in independent black-owned firms.

14. bell hooks, *Art On My Mind* (New York: The New Press, 1995), 145–151.

15. See hooks, *Art On My Mind*.

16. See hooks, *Art On My Mind*.

17. See Hughs, *Afrocentric Architecture*. Hughs differs from Travis in the level of interest that Hughs has in transcontinental African architecture that historically spans from 3000 BC, Pharonic Egypt to the present. I maintain that the Hughs emphasis is more appropriately characterized as "Afrocentric" in comparison to the primary Travis interest in African-American culture and its West African influences.

18. Travis, *African-American Architects in Current Practice*, 6–7.

19. Nkosa Ato Diop, "Jack Travis; Cultural Vanguard," *blacklines*, 10.

20. Further reinforcement of affluent black (and white) tastes for black cultural objects and environments has been substantiated in an informative and richly illustrated book by Howard University and Hampton University graduates and interior designers Sharne Algotsson and Denys Davis, *The Spirit of African Design* (New York: Clarkson Potter Publishers, 1996).

21. See Russell, *Black Genius*, 355–372. My information on McAfee was taken from Russell's 497 page anthology on important black achievers.

22. See Roger K. Lewis, *Architect? A Candid Guide to the Profession* (Cambridge, MA: MIT Press, Revised 1998 Issue). 264–65

23. Wiseman, *Shaping a Nation*, 383.

24. See Nelson George, *Hip-Hop America* (New York: Viking, 1998) in its entirety for an informative treatment of the origins, background, and current impact of Hip-Hop culture on American culture.

25. See Eduardo Rudolfski, *Architecture Without Architects* (New York: Museum of Modern Art, 1964) for a revealing photo essay of creative and artistic building by non-architects throughout history, western and non-western, including Black Africa.

26. See Wilkens, "(W)rapped Space: The Architecture of Hip-Hop" for a thoughtful essay on this subject.

27. For an informative discussion of this, see Norman Kelley and Davarian Baldwin, "Rhythm Nation: The Political Economy of Black Music," *Black Renaissance/Renaissance Noire*, New York University, Volume 2, No. 2, Summer 1999. See also George, *Hip-Hop America*, for an extended and informative discussion of the underlying "means of production" dimension of Hip-Hop cultural history.

Chapter 6—The Diasporic Perspective and an Alternative Future

1. Algotsson, *The Spirit of African Design.*

2. See Sandra Fitzpatrick, and Maria R. Goodwin, *The Guide to Black Washington: Places and events of Historical and Cultural Significance in the Nation's Capital* (New York: Hypocrene Books, 1990) in its entirety but particularly the introduction by Adele Logan Alexander, 17–25, for a concise physical sense of Black Washington, DC.

3. Carole Marks and Diana Edkins, *The Power of Pride: Stylemakers and Rulebreakers of the Harlem Renaissance* (New York: Crown Publishers, 1999), 172–185.

4. See Dingle, *Black Enterprise Titans of the B.E. 100s;* in its entirety for a review of the wide ranging creative mindset of today's black entrepreneur.

5. Gutman, *Architectural Practice,* provides frank general clarity about the historical and now escalating weakness of the authority of the architectural profession in comparison to the medicine, law, and engineering professions.

6. See Davis, *The Culture of Building*, 73–83 for another example of informed perspective about the subject of architect's predilections about certain types of clients and building types over others. The balance of this book is highly recommended reading.

7. Andres Duany and Elizabeth Plater Zyberk's transformation of the Miami University School of Architecture curriculum into a *New Urban Tradition* concentration is evidence of the acceptability of such an approach by accreditation authorities.

8. See Richard J. Powell and Jock Reynolds, *To Conserve a Legacy: American Art From Historically Black Colleges and Universities* (New York: Addison Gallery of American Art, 1999), for a review of the rich heritage and continuing capacity of the arts on the HBCU campus.

9. George Fraser, *Race For Success: The Ten Best Business Opportunities for Blacks in America* (New York: William Morrow and Company, 1998).

10. Fraser, *Race For Success*, 176–191.

11. Fraser, *Race For Success*, 180

Bibliography of Cited Works

BLACK ARCHITECTS & ARCHITECTURE

Anderson, Genell, *The Call of the Ancestors*. Washington, DC: AMAR, 1991.

Bird, Betty and Schwartz, Nancy, *Thematic Study of Black Architects, Builders, and Developers in Washington, DC*. Washington, DC: United Planning Organization, 1993.

Bond, Max Jr, "Still Here; Three Afro-American Architects: Julian F. Abele, Hilyard Robinson, and Paul R. Williams." *Harvard Design Magazine*, summer 1997, Cambridge.

Cheney, Ruth Helen, "Advocacy Planning; What It Is, And How It Works." *Progressive Architecture*. September 1968

Dozier, Richard Kevin, "Tuskegee: Booker T. Washington's Contribution to the Education of Black Architects." A Doctoral Dissertation—University of Michigan, 1990.

Etheridge, Harrison, "Black Architects of Washington, DC: 1900 to the Present." A Doctoral Dissertation, The Catholic University, Washington, DC, 1979.

Elleh, Nnamdi, *African Architecture: Evolution and Transformation*. New York: McGraw-Hill, 1997.

Fields, Daryl W; Fuller, Kevin L; and Curry, Milton S.F. (Ed.), *APPEN-DIX (Issues 1,2, & 3) Culture, Theory, Praxis.* Cambridge, Mass: Appendix Inc., 1993, 1994, & 1996.

Fields, Daryl W, "Architecture and the Black Subject: An Ethno-Historic Reconstruction." A Doctoral Dissertation, Harvard Graduate School of Design, 1995.

Fry, E. Louis Sr., "Louis Edwin Fry, Sr: His Life and His Architecture." An Unpublished Autobiography, Wash., DC, 1986.

Gradison, Kenrick Ian, "From Plantation to Campus: Progress, Community, and the Lay of the Land in Shaping the Early Tuskegee Campus." *Landscape Journal*, Volume 15, Number 1, spring 1996.

Henderson, Wesley Howard, "Two Case Studies of African-American Architects' Careers in Los Angeles: 1890–1945, Paul R. Williams, FAIA and James Garrott, AIA." A Doctoral Dissertation, Univ. of Calif. at Los Angeles, 1992.

Hudson, Karen, *Paul R. Williams Architect: A Legacy of Style.* New York: Rizzoli, 1994.

Hughes, David, *Afrocentric Architecture: A Design Primer.* Columbus, OH: Greyden Press, 1994.

Robinson, Harry G, FAIA and Edwards, Ruth Hazel, Ph.D., *The Long Walk: Place Making At Howard University.* Washington, DC: Moorland-Spingarn Research Center, 1998.

Travis, Jack (Ed.), *African-American Architects in Current Practice.* New York: Princeton Architectural Press, 1991.

Vlach, John Michael, *Back of the Big House: The Architecture of Plantation Slavery*. Chapel Hill: University of North Carolina Press, 1993.

_____, *The Afro-American Tradition in Decorative Arts*. Athens, GA.: Brown Thrasher Books, 1990.

BLACK ART, MUSIC, & CULTURE

Algotsson, Sharne and Davis, Denys, *The Spirit of African Design*. New York: Clarkson Potter Publishers, 1996.

Appiah, Kwame Anthony, *In My Father's House: Africa In The Philosophy of Culture*. New York: Oxford University Press, 1992.

Appiah, Kwame Anthony and Gates, Henry Louis, *Africana: The Encyclopedia of the African and African-American Experience*. New York: Basic Civitas Books, 1999.

Bearden, Romare and Henderson, Harry, *A History of African-American Artists From 1792 to the Present*. New York: Pantheon Books, 1993.

Benjamin, Tritobia Hayes, *The Life and Art of Lois Mailou Jones*. San Francisco: Pomegranate Art books, 1994.

Berlin, Edward A., *King of Ragtime, Scott Joplin and His Era*. New York: Oxford University Press, 1994.

Bernal, Martin, *Black Athena: The Afroasiatic Roots of Classical Civilization, Vol. I & II*. New Brunswick: Rutgers University Press, 1987, 1991.

Crouch, Stanley, *Always in Pursuit. Fresh Perspectives*. New York, Vintage Books, 1998.

Ellington, Edward Kennedy, *Music Is My Mistress*. New York: Da Capo Press, 1973.

George, Nelson, *Hip-Hop America*. New York: Viking, 1998.

Gioia, Ted, *The History of Jazz*. New York: Oxford University Press, 1997.

Harris, Leonard, *The Critical Pragmatism of Alain Locke: A Reader in Value Theory, Aesthetics, Community, Culture, Race, and Education*. Lanham, MD: Rowman & Littlefield Publishers, Inc., 1999.

hooks, bell, *Art on My Mind: Visual Politics*. New York: The New Press, 1995.

Howe, Steven, *Afrocentrism: Mythical Pasts and Imagined Homes*. London: VERSO, 1998.

Karenga, Maulana, *Introduction To Black Studies*. Los Angeles: University of Sankore Press, 1991.

Kelley, Robin D.G., *Yo' Mama's DisfunKtional!: Fighting the Culture Wars in America*. Boston: Beacon Press, 1997.

Kelley, Norman and Baldwin, Davarian, "Rhythm Nation: The Political Economy of Black Music." *Black Renaissance/Renaissance Noire*. New York, Vol. 2, No. 2, summer 1999, 8–21.

Kirschke, Amy Helene, *Aaron Douglas: Art, Race, & The Harlem Renaissance*. Jackson, MS.: University Press of Mississippi, 1995.

Lefkowitz, Mary R. and Rogers, Guy MacLean, *Black Athena Revisited*. Chapel Hill: University of North Carolina Press, 1996.

Lerner, Michael and West, Cornel, *Jews & Blacks: Let the Healing Begin.* New York: G.P. Putnam's Sons, 1995.

Lewis, Samelia, *African-American Art and Artists.* Berkeley: University of California Press, 1990.

Locke, Alain (Ed.), *The New Negro: Voices of the Harlem Renaissance.* New York: Touchstone, 1997.

Lubiano, Wahneema (Ed.), *The House That Race Built: Original Essays By Toni Morrison, Angela Davis, Cornel West, and Others On Black Americans and Politics in America Today.* New York: Vintage Books, 1998.

Murray, Albert, *The Omni-Americans: Black Experience and American Culture.* New York: Da Capo Press, 1970.

O'Meally, Robert G. (Ed.), *The Jazz Cadence of American Culture.* New York: Columbia University Press, 1998.

Patton, Sharon, *African-American Art.* New York: Oxford University Press, 1998.

Peretti, Burton W., *Jazz in American Culture.* Chicago: Ivan R. Dee, 1997.

Powell, Richard J., *Black Art and Culture in the Twentieth-Century.* London: Thames and Hudson, 1997.

Sowell, Thomas, *Race and Culture: A World View.* New York: Basic Books, 1994.

West, Cornel, *The Cornel West Reader.* New York: Basic Civitas Books, 1999.

Willett, Frank, *African Art: An Introduction.* London: Thames and Hudson, 1986.

BLACK POLITICAL HISTORY & THEORY

Bennett, Lerone Jr, *The Shaping of Black America: The Struggles and Triumphs of Blacks, 1619 to the 1990s*. New York: Penguin Books, 1975.

Brownstein, Elizabeth Smith, *If This House Could Talk: Historic Homes, Extraordinary Americans*. New York: Simon & Shuster, 1999.

Cobb, William Jelani (Ed.), *The Essential Harold Cruse: A Reader*. New York: Palgrave, 2002

Cruse, Harold, *Crisis of the Negro Intellectual: A Historical Analysis of the Failure of Black Leadership*. New York: Quill, 1967.

Carmichael, Stokely and Hamilton, Charles V., *Black Power: The Politics of Liberation*. New York: Vintage Books, 1992.

Franklin, John Hope and Meier, August (Ed.), *Black Leaders of the Twentieth-Century*. Chicago: University of Illinois Press, 1982.

Harland, Lewis, *Booker T. Washington in Perspective*. Jackson, MS.: Univ. of Mississippi Press, 1988.

Logan, Rayford W., *The Betrayal of the Negro: From Rutherford B. Hayes to Woodrow Wilson*. New York: Da Capo Press, 1997.

Marable, Manning, *Black Leadership*. New York: Columbia University Press, 1998.

Meier, August, *Negro Thought In America 1880–1915: Racial Ideologies in the Age of Booker T. Washington*. Ann Arbor, MI: The University of Michigan Press, 1988.

Mosely, Walter (Ed.), *Black Genius: African-American Solutions to African-American Problems*. New York: W.W. Norton & Co., 1999.

Moses, Wilson Jeremiah, *Afrotopia: The Roots of African American Popular History*. Cambridge, UK: Cambridge University Press, 1998

Robinson, Randall, *The Debt: What America Owes Blacks*. New York: Dutton, 2000.

Rydell, Robert (Ed.), *The Reason Why The Colored American Is Not In The World Columbian Expedition*. Chicago: University of Illinois, 1999.

Steele, Shelby, *The Content of Our Character*. New York: Harper Collins, 1994.

Washington, Booker T., *Up From Slavery*. New York: Bantam, 1963.

Wilson, Amos N., *Blueprint for Black Power: A Moral, Political, and Economic Imperative for the Twenty-First Century*. New York: African World Info Systems, 1998.

BLACKS & BUSINESS

Bundles, A'Lelia, *On Her Own Ground: The Life and Times of Madam C.J. Walker*. New York: Scribner, 2001.

Dingle, Derek T., *Black Enterprise Titans of the B.E.100s: Black CEO's Who Redefined and Conquered American Business*. New York: John Wiley & Sons Inc., 1999.

Fraser, George C., *Race For Success: The Ten Best Business Opportunities For Blacks In America*. New York: William Morrow, 1998.

Graves, Earl G., *How to Succeed in Business Without Being White*. New York: Harper Collins Publishers, Inc., 1997.

Lewis, Reginald, *Why Should White Guys Have All the Fun?: How Reginald Lewis Created a Billion-Dollar Business Enterprise*. New York: John Wiley & Sons, 1995.

Russell, Dick, *Black Genius: The American Experience*. New York: Carroll & Graf Publishers Inc., 1998.

Walker, Juliet E.K., *The History of Black Business in America: Capitalism, Race, Entrepreneurship*. New York: McMillan Library Reference USA, 1998.

AMERICAN ARCHITECTURAL HISTORY, THEORY & POLITICS

Andrews, Wayne, *Architecture, Ambition and Americans: A Social History of American Architecture*. New York: The Free Press, 1964.

Bonta, Juan Pablo, *American Architects and Texts: A Computer-Aided Analysis of the Literature*. Cambridge, MA: The MIT Press, 1996.

Boyer, Ernest L. and Mitgang, Lee D., *Building Community: A New Future For Architecture Education and Practice*. Princeton, NJ: The Carnegie Foundation for the Advancement of Teaching, 1996.

Cramer, James (Ed.), *Almanac of Architecture & Design*. Norcross, GA: Greenway Group, 2000.

Cosbie, Michael, "A White Gentleman's Profession?" *Progressive Architecture*, November 1994.

Caragonne, Alexander, *The Texas Rangers: Notes From an Architectural Underground*. Cambridge, MA: The MIT Press, 1994.

DeSoto, Hernando, *The Mystery of Capital: Why Capitalism Triumphs in the West and Fails Elsewhere*. New York: Basic Books, 2000.

Ellis, Joseph J., *American Sphinx: The Character of Thomas Jefferson*. New York: Vintage Books, 1998.

Edwards, John (Ed.), *Guide to Architecture Schools: Sixth Edition*. Washington, DC: Association of Collegiate Schools of Architecture, 1998.

Eisenman, Peter; Graves, Michael; Gwathmey; Hejduk, John; and Meier, Richard. *Five Architects*. New York: Oxford University Press, 1975.

Frampton, Kenneth, *Studies In Tectonic Culture: The Poetics of Construction in Nineteenth & Twentieth-Century Architecture*. Cambridge, MA: MIT Press, 1996.

Gill, Brendan, *Many Masks; A Life of Frank Lloyd Wright*. New York: Da Capo Press, 1998.

Goodman, Robert, *After the Planners*. New York: Simon and Schuster, 1971.

Gordon-Reed, Annette, *Thomas Jefferson and Sally Hemings; An American Controversy*. Charlottesville, VA: The University of Virginia Press, 1997.

Gutman, Robert, *Architectural Practice; A Critical View*. Princeton, NJ: Princeton Architectural Press, 1988.

Herrnstein, Richard and Murray, Charles, *The Bell Curve: Intelligence and Class Structure in American Life*. New York: Simon & Schuster, 1994.

Hughes, Robert, *American Visions: The Epic History of Art in America*. New York: Alfred A. Knopf, 1999.

Lamster, Mark (Ed.) *Architecture and Film*. New York: Vinata-Ash Press, 2000.

Leccese, Michael and McCormick, Kathleen (Ed.), *Charter of the New Urbanism: Congress for the New Urbanism*. New York: McGraw-Hill, 2000.

Lemann, Nicholas, The *Big Test: The Secret of History of the American Meritocracy*. New York: Farrar, Straus, & Giroux, 1999.

Merriam, Alan P., *The Anthropology of Music*. Chicago: Northwestern University Press, 1964.

Noble, David F., *America By Design; Science, Technology, and The Rise of Corporate Capitalism*. New York: Oxford University Press, 1977.

Oliver, Richard (Ed.), *The Making of an Architect 1881–1981: Columbia University and the City of New York*. New York: Rizzoli, 1981.

Reich, Robert B., *The Work of Nations: Preparing Ourselves for Twenty-first Century Capitalism*. New York: Vintage Books, 1992.

Roth, Leland M., *A Concise History of American Architecture*. New York: Harper & Row, 1979.

Scully, Vincent, *American Architecture and Urbanism*. New York: Henry Holt and Company, 1988.

Secrest, Meryle, *Frank Lloyd Wright: A Biography.* New York: Harper Collins, 1992.

Stern, Robert A.M., *Pride of Place; Building the American Dream.* Boston: Houghton Mifflin Company, 1986.

Thernstrom, Stephan and Thernstrom, Abigail, *America In Black and White; One Nation, Indivisible.* New York: Touchstone-Simon& Shuster, 1997.

Twombley, Robert, *Power and Style: A Critique of Twentieth-Century American Architecture in the U.S.* New York: Hill and Wang, 1995.

Upton, Dell (Ed.), *America's Architectural Roots: Ethnic Groups That Built America.* Washington, DC: Preservation Press, 1986.

Upton, Dell, *Architecture in the United States.* New York: Oxford University

Williamson, Roxanne Kuter, *American Architects and the Mechanics of Fame.* Austin, TX.: University of Texas Press, 1991.

Wolfe, Tom, *From Bauhaus to Our House.* New York: Farrar Straus Giroux, 1981.

Wiseman, Carter, *Shaping a Nation: Twentieth-century American Architecture and its Makers.* New York: W.W. Norton & Company, 1998.

Wojtowicz, Robert, *Lewis Mumford & American Modernism: Eutopian Theories for Architecture and Urban Planning.* Cambridge, UK: Cambridge University Press, 1996.

GENERAL ARCHITECTURAL THOUGHT

Banham, Reyner, *Theory of Design in the First Machine Age*. Cambridge, MA: The MIT Press, 1980.

Blake, Peter, *The Master Builders: Le Corbusier, Mies van Der Rohe, and Frank Lloyd Wright*. New York: W.W. Norton & Company, 1976.

Blau, Eve and Troy, Nancy J. (Ed.), *Architecture and Cubism*. Cambridge, MA: The MIT Press, 1997.

Brolin, Brent, *The Failure of Modern Architecture*. London: Studio Vista, 1976.

Brosterman, Norman, *Inventing Kindergarten*. New York: Harry Abrams, Inc., 1997.

Chipp, Herschel B., *Theories of Modern Art: A Source Book By Artists and Critics*. Berkeley, CA: University of California Press, 1968.

Cuff, Dana, *Architecture: The Story of Practice*. Cambridge, MA: The MIT Press, 1996.

Curtis, William J.R., *Modern Architecture Since 1900*. London: Phaidon Press Limited, 3rd Ed., 1996.

_____, *Le Corbusier; Ideas and Forms*. London: Phaidon Press Limited, 1997, 4th Ed., 1997.

Davis, Howard, *The Culture of Building*. New York: Oxford University Press, 1999.

Ellin, Nan, *Postmodern Urbanism*. New York: Princeton Press, 1999.

Etlin, Richard A., *Frank Lloyd Wright & LeCorbusier: The Romantic Legacy.* New York: Manchester University Press, 1994.

Fisher, Thomas R., *In the Scheme of Things: Alternative Thinking on the Practice of Architecture.* Minneapolis: University of Minnesota Press, 2000.

Giedion, Sigfried, *Space, Time and Architecture: The Growth of a New Tradition.* Cambridge, MA: Harvard University Press, 1971.

Jencks, Charles, *Architecture of the Jumping Universe.* New York: Saint Martin's Press, 1995.

_____, *Ecstatic Architecture: The Surprising Link.* Great Britain: Academy Editions, John Wiley & Sons, 1999.

_____, *Le Corbusier: And the Continual Revolution in Architecture.* New York: Monacelli Press, 2000.

Jarzombek, Mark, "Molecules, Money and Design: The Question of Sustainability's Role in Architectural Academe." *Thresholds 14,* MIT Dept. of Architecture & Planning, spring 1997, 32–36.

Lewis, Roger K, *Architect? A Candid Guide to the Profession.* Cambridge, MA: The MIT Press.

Newhouse, Elizabeth (Ed.), *Builders: The Marvels of Engineering.* Washington, DC: The National Geographic Society, 1992.

Pelli, Cesar, *Observations For Young Architects.* New York: Monecelli Press, 1999.

Press, Joseph, "Soul-Searching: Reflections From the Ivory Tower." *Journal of Architectural Education.* May 1998, Volume 51, No. 4.

Rand, Ayn, *The Fountainhead*. New York: The Bobbs-Merrill Co., 1943.

Rappaport, Amos, *House Form and Culture*. Englewood Cliffs, NJ: Prentice-Hall, 1969.

Risebero, Bill, *Modern Architecture and Design: An Alternative History*. Cambridge, MA: The MIT Press, 1982.

Rowe, Colin (Edited by Alexander Caragonne), *As I Was Saying: Recollections and Miscellaneous Essays*. Cambridge, MA: The MIT Press, 1996.

Rowe, Colin and Slutzky, Robert, "Transparency: Literal and Phenomenal." *Perspecta No. 8, 1963, Yale School of Architecture Magazine.*

Rudofsky, Bernard, *Architecture Without Architects*. New York: Museum of Modern Art, 1964.

Stevens, Gary, *The Favored Circle: The Social Foundations of Architectural Distinction*. Cambridge, MA: The MIT Press, 1998.

Sutton, Ira, *Western Architecture: From Ancient Greece To the Present*. New York: Thames and Hudson, 1999.

Tournikiotis, Panayotis, *The Historiography of Modern Architecture*. Cambridge, MA: The MIT Press, 1999.

Vitruvius (Translated by M.H. Morgan), *The Ten Books of Architecture*. New York: Dover Publications, 1960.

Venturi, Robert, *Complexities and Contradictions In Architecture*. New York: The Museum of Modern Art, 1966.

THE FUTURE OF ARCHITECTURE; _MANAGEMENT & *"DRAWING"*

Barnett, Jonathan and Portman, John, *The Architect As Developer.* New York: McGraw Hill, 1976.

Burden, Ernest, *Design Simulation: Use of Photographic and Electronic Media in Design Presentation.* New York: Whitney Library of Design, 1985.

Ching, Francis D.K. and Juroszek, Steven P., *Design Drawing.* New York: Van Nostrand Reinhold, 1998.

Ching, Francis D.K, *Architecture: Form, Space, & Order.* New York: Van Nostrand Reinhold, 1976.

Evans, Robin, *Translations From Drawing To Building And Other Essays.* Cambridge: The MIT Press, 1986.

Fisher, Thomas R., *In the Scheme of Things: Alternative Thinking on the Practice of Architecture.* Minneapolis: University of Minnesota Press, 2000.

Futagawa, Yukio (Ed.), *Paul Rudolph.* New York: Architectural Book Publishing, Inc., 1972.

Haviland, David S., (Ed.), *The Architect's Handbook of Professional Practice: Student Edition.* Washington, DC: AIA Press, 1996.

Harrigan, John, Ph. D and Neel, Paul, FAIA, *The Executive Architect; Transforming Designers Into Leaders.* New York: John Wiley & Sons Inc., 1996.

Heim, Michael, *Virtual Realism*. New York: Oxford University Press, 1998.

Kurzweil, Ray, *The Age of Spiritual Machines: When Computers Exceed Human Intelligence*. New York: Penguin Group, 1999.

Lockard, William Kirby, *Design Drawing (Revised Edition)*. Menlo Park, CA: Crisp Publications, Inc., 1982.

Mitchell, William J., *The Reconfigured Eye: Visual Truth in the Post-Photographic Era*. Cambridge, MA: The MIT Press, 1993.

_____, *City of Bits: Space, Place, and the Infobahn*. Cambridge, MA: The MIT Press, 1994.

_____, *e-topia: "Urban Life, Jim—But Not As We Know It."* Cambridge, MA: The MIT Press, 1999.

McCullough, Malcolm, *Abstracting Craft: The Practiced Digital Hand*. Cambridge, MA: The MIT Press, 1996.

O'Mara, Martha, *Strategy and Place: Managing Corporate Real Estate and Facilities for Competitive Advantage*. New York: The Free Press, 1999.

Pawley, Martin, *Theory and Design in the Second Machine Age*. Cambridge, MA: Basil Blackwell Ltd, 1990.

_____, *Terminal Architecture*. London: Reaktion Press, 1998.

Porter, Tom, *The Architect's Eye: Visualization and Depiction of Space in Architecture*. London: E., and F.N. Spon, 1997.

WASHINGTON, DC

Barras, Jonetta Rose, *The Last of the Black Emperors: The Hollow Comeback of Marion Barry in the New Age of Black Leadership.* Baltimore: Bancroft Press, 1998.

Bushong, William; Robinson, Judith Helm, and Mueller, Julie, *A Centennial History of the Washington, DC, Chapter: The American Institute of Architects—1887–1987.* Washington, DC: The Washington Architectural Foundation Press, 1978.

Jaffe, Harry and Sherwood, Tom, *Dream City: Race, Power, and the Decline of Washington DC.* New York: Simon & Schuster, 1994.

Gillette, Howard Jr., *Between Justice and Beauty; Race, Planning, And the Failure of Urban Policy in Washington, DC.* Baltimore: The Johns Hopkins University Press, 1995.

Siegal, Fred, *The Future Once Happened Here: New York, DC, LA, and the Fate of America's Big Cities.* New York: The Free Press, 1997.

Tennenbaum, Robert, *Creating a New City: Columbia, Maryland.* Columbia, MD: Partners in Community Building and Perry Publishing, 1990.

Van Dyne, Larry, "The Making of Washington—Men of Vision and Ambition Who Built a Great City and Made Great Fortunes." *Washingtonian Magazine,* September 1997, Volume 23, No. 2.

BALTIMORE, MD.

Dorsey, John and Dilts, James D., *A Guide to Baltimore Architecture: Third Edition.* Centerville, MD: Tidewater Publishers, 1997.

Fee, Elizabeth; Shopes, Linda; and Zeidman, Linda (Ed.), *The Baltimore Book: New Views of Local History*. Philadelphia: Temple University Press, 1991.

Hayward, Mary Ellen and Belfoure, Charles, *The Baltimore Row House*. New York: Princeton Architectural Press, 1999.

Olson, Sherry, *Baltimore: The Building of an American City*. Baltimore: The John Hopkins University Press, 1980.

Rusk, David, *Baltimore Unbound: A Strategy for Regional Renewal*. Baltimore: The Abel Foundation, 1996.

Sellar, Patricia (Ed.), *RTKL: Selected and Current Works*. Australia: The Images Publishing Group Pty Ltd, 1996.

Smith, C. Fraser, *William Donald Schaefer: A Political Biography*. Baltimore: The Johns Hopkins University Press, 1999.

Weeks, Christopher, *Alexander Smith Cochran: Modernist Architect in Traditionalist Baltimore*. Baltimore: Maryland Historical Society, 1995.

Index

N

Regency Street, 277
Reich, Robert, 368
Renaissance, 10-11, 19, 22, 51-53, 55-61, 63-64, 75, 109-110, 189, 193, 204, 207, 224, 227, 264, 270-271, 281-282, 296, 314-315, 325-326, 335-337, 357, 362-363
Rensselear Polytechnic Institute, 128
Reparations Settlement, 78
Republic Development Corporation, 167
Republican Party, 163, 319
Request For Proposals, 143, 176
residential shelter, 305
RFP, 143-145, 154, 159, 171, 176
Rhodes Scholar, 55
Richardson, Earl S., 250, 253
Richardson, Henry Hobson, 26, 64
Richmond, Virginia, 46, 166
RLA, 121-123, 145-149, 153-154, 156, 165, 168-170
Robbins, Edward, 195, 199, 350
Roberts, Don, 181
Robie House, 313-314
Robinson Hall, 116
Robinson, Harry G., 360
Robinson, Hilyard, 10, 43-46, 48, 50, 56, 58, 100, 106, 122, 125, 172, 179, 314, 316-318, 334, 359
Rock Creek Park, 101
Rockefeller Center, 52, 154
Rockefeller, John D., 154
Rockefeller, Rodman, 154
Rodgers, Theo, 255
Rogers, Archibald, 248
Rollins, Jerry, 293
Roman Baths of Caracalla, 172
Romanesque, 64, 312
Ronchamp, 263, 294
Ross, John, 119
Rotterdam, 47
Rouse, James, 103, 256
Rowe, Colin, 372
Roxbury, 190
rpm, 4
RTKL, 174, 233, 248, 354, 376
Rudolph, Paul, 105, 373
Russell, Dick, 366
Russell, Herman, 271

S

Sabouni, Inklas, 228, 309
Safdie, Moshe, 82, 300
Saint Albans School For Boys, 116
San Francisco, 8, 94, 335, 361

Sanders, James, 218
SAT, 116, 140, 168, 250
Saunders, Harold Lloyd, 135, 181
Schlessinger, Frank, 248
Schuyler, George S, 57
Scott, Emmett, 13, 36, 40
Scully, Vincent, 368
second black renaissance, 11
Segal, Raj, 230
Seriki, Olusola, 256
Sert, Jose Luis, 114
sex, 57
Shaping a Nation, 289, 322, 356, 369
Shaw Junior High School, 318
Shaw Urban Renewal Area, 120, 122
Sherwood, Tom, 375
shotgun house, 75
shotgun marriage, 151
Silcott, James, 99
Silicon Graphics class workstation, 187
Silvers, Arthur, 46, 343
Simmons, Harry, Jr., 90, 107, 174, 282, 344
Skidmore, Owings, and Merrill, 150, 325
Sklarek, Norma, 86
Skyles, Benjiman, 181
Smith, Duryea, 158
Smoot Company, 171
SMSA, 223, 246
Snipes, Wesley, 218
SNNC, 108, 135, 137, 347
socialization, 18, 42, 153, 186, 189, 191, 198, 202, 206, 236, 238, 244, 258, 270, 272, 276, 281, 283, 285, 291-292, 298-299, 306, 332
SOM, 150-153, 155, 157, 325
SOM Washington, 150
SOM-Childs, 151-152
Sorg, Suman, 144, 173
South Central Los Angeles, 4-5, 102, 134, 172, 343
Southern University, 41, 162, 223, 228, 309, 353
Southwest Urban Renewal Area, 122
Sowell, Thomas, 363
Spelman College, 85
Spriggs, Austin, 135, 181
Stanley Love-Stanley, 90, 94
Stanley, William J., 90
star architect, 85-86, 189, 275, 280, 295
Starobin, Sam, 162
Steele, Shelby, 365
Stevens, Gary, 372
Strategy and Place, 207, 351, 354, 374
Student　　　Non-Violent　　　Coordinating Committee, 111, 115, 125, 135

voodoo, 4
Vosbeck, Randy, 162
Vosbeck-D&P-Coles, 162
VVKR, 162

W

Walker, Henderson, 131, 181
Walker, Madam C. J., 59, 313, 336, 365
Wall Street, 209, 211
War Department, 47-48
Ward Eight, 164
Warren, Otis, 256
Washington Bullets, 168
Washington National Airport, 284
Washington Post, 154, 165
Washington Technical Institute, 129
Washington, Booker T., 39, 330, 365
Washington, Portia, 39
Washington, Roberta, 86
Washington, Walter, 119, 127, 135-136, 141, 148-149, 156, 162, 171, 317-318, 347
Washington-Baltimore, 223, 247
WASP, 9, 14, 83, 102-103, 130, 138-139, 324
WASP-Jewish, 147, 191
WASP-Jewish parlor game, 191
Watergate, 108
Watkins, Ted, 132
Watts Community Labor Action Committee, 133
Watts Riots, 129, 317
Watts, Daniel, 7
Welch, John, 49
Welton Becket, 318
West Africa, 11, 34, 63, 292, 337, 339
West African masks and sculpture, 52
West Baltimore, 249, 265
West, Cornel, 363
West, Frank G., 180-181
Western Development Corporation, 145, 154
Wheaton Plaza, 154
White Anglo-Saxon Protestant, 58, 79
White City, 31, 162, 312, 346
white cultural nationalism, 205
White Flint, 154
White Gentleman's Profession, 23, 92, 366
Whitley, James and John, 90
Whitley, Joyce, 90
Wichita, Kansas, 285
Wicker, Tom, 113
Wiehe Associates, 257
Wilkens, Roy, 113
Williams, Harry, 131, 181
Williams, Larry, 145

Williams, Paul R., 20, 80, 125, 314, 328, 334, 340-341, 359-360
Willis, Michael, 94
Williston, David, 43, 313
Wilmot, David, 154
Wilson, Dreck, 334
Wilson, John Louis, 59
Wilson, Yettikoff, 131
Wing, Cleveland, 46
Wiseman, Carter, 369
Worthy, George, 119
WPA, 59
Wright and Ellington, 71
Wright, Frank Lloyd, 5, 13, 26, 30, 52, 61, 64, 67-68, 71-72, 80, 105, 185-186, 196, 198, 271, 300, 312-313, 326, 338, 367, 369-371
Wright, Le Corbusier, and Mies, 64
Wright, Richard, 54
Wright, Rodner, 229, 308
Wright, Sullivan, and Richardson, 236

X

Xavier University, 3

Y

Yale, 105, 108, 111, 114, 150, 252, 348, 372
YMCA Building, 39
Yo' Mama's Disfunktional, 72, 362
Young, Coleman, 133

Z

Zimbabwe, 75
Zion, 16, 292

0-595-24326-6

Printed in the United States
53650LVS00003B/67-90

9 780595 243266